Today's over-consumption and environmental crisis requires human behaviour change at many levels, from the city to the household to the individual. But behaviour change has many dimensions and driving forces, ranging from media, to social innovation, technological and design advances for the transformation of our systems of consumption. This book explores the inter-connectivity of these dimensions in 22 thematically organised chapters, providing valuable insight into how to overcome the challenges of implementing positive behavioural change.

—Professor Steffen Lehmann, Professor of Sustainable
Architecture, University of Portsmouth, UK

Kristina Niedderer, Stephen Clune and Geke Ludden have skilfully brought together deeper issues of social impact as guidance for designers, managers of design, and other change practitioners. It is a collection of fresh, detailed accounts of the important and challenging aspects involved. I'm really pleased to enthusiastically recommend this book to; Designers and design managers . . . through a variety of real world case examples and design tools, this book provides an essential stimulus to pro actively engage with numerous impacts of design to bring about ethical, long term, social development. Strategies are presented which allow designed objects to be seen more clearly in terms of their future impact. Valuable and exciting possibilities for designers' experiential professional knowledge and development are also provided. And to; Design researchers. . . . through cross-disciplinary approaches, this book adds new and interesting critical detail to investigations of the design process, including individual user adaptation to existing design products and systems. This international network of influential scholars, have developed essential theories and new debates on the long-term social influence of design.

—Bob Jerrard, Emeritus Professor of Design Studies,
Birmingham City University, UK

Design for Behaviour Change

Design impacts every part of our lives. The design of products and services influences the way we go about our daily activities and it is hard to imagine any activity in our daily lives that is not dependent on design in some capacity. Clothing, mobile phones, computers, cars, tools and kitchenware all enable and hold in place everyday practices. Despite design's omnipresence, the understanding of how design may facilitate desirable behaviours is still fragmented, with limited frameworks and examples of how design can effect change in professional and public contexts.

This text presents an overview of current approaches dedicated to understanding how design may be used intentionally to make changes to improve a range of problematic social and environmental issues. It offers a cross-disciplinary and cross-sectoral overview of different academic theories adopted and applied to design for behaviour change.

The aim of the volume is twofold: first, to provide an overview of existing design models that integrate theories of change from differing scientific backgrounds; second, to offer an overview of application of key design for behaviour change approaches as used across case studies in different sectors, such as design for health and wellbeing, sustainability, safety, design against crime and social design. *Design for Behaviour Change* will appeal to designers, design students and practitioners of behavioural change.

Kristina Niedderer is Professor of Design and Craft at the University of Wolverhampton. Niedderer's research focuses on the role of mindfulness and emotions as a means to engender mindful interaction and behaviour change through design.

Stephen Clune is Senior Lecturer in Sustainable Design at Imagination Lancaster, Lancaster University. Stephen is a sustainable designer, researcher and educator; his core research interest focuses on how design (and design thinking) can assist in the move towards a sustainable society.

Geke Ludden is Associate Professor at the Department of Design, Production and Management at the University of Twente, The Netherlands. She studies how the design of products and services can support healthy behaviour or otherwise contribute to people's wellbeing.

Design for Social Responsibility
Series Editor: Rachel Cooper

Social responsibility, in various disguises, has been a recurring theme in design for many years. Since the 1960s several more or less commercial approaches have evolved. In the 1970s designers were encouraged to abandon 'design for profit' in favour of a more compassionate approach inspired by Papanek. In the 1980s and 1990s profit and ethical issues were no longer considered mutually exclusive and more market-oriented concepts emerged, such as the 'green consumer' and ethical investment. The purchase of socially responsible, 'ethical' products and services has been stimulated by the dissemination of research into sustainability issues in consumer publications. Accessibility and inclusivity have also attracted a great deal of design interest and recently designers have turned to solving social and crime-related problems. Organizations supporting and funding such projects have recently included the NHS (research into design for patient safety); the Home Office (design against crime); Engineering and Physical Sciences Research Council (design decision-making for urban sustainability).

Businesses are encouraged (and increasingly forced by legislation) to set their own socially responsible agendas that depend on design to be realized. Design decisions all have environmental, social and ethical impacts, so there is a pressing need to provide guidelines for designers and design students within an overarching framework that takes a holistic approach to socially responsible design. This edited series of guides is aimed at students of design, product development, architecture and marketing, and design and management professionals working in the sectors covered by each title. Each volume includes: The background and history of the topic, its significance in social and commercial contexts and trends in the field. Exemplar design case studies. Guidelines for the designer and advice on tools, techniques and resources available.

8 **Design Against Crime**
   Caroline L Davey, Andrew B Wootton

9 **Design for Healthcare**
   Edited by Emmanuel Tsekleves and Rachel Cooper

10 **Design for Personalisation**
   Edited by Iryna Kuksa and Tom Fisher

11 **Design for Behaviour Change**
   Edited by Kristina Niedderer, Stephen Clune and Geke Ludden

Design for Behaviour Change

Theories and practices of designing
for change

**Edited by
Kristina Niedderer, Stephen Clune
and Geke Ludden**

LONDON AND NEW YORK

First published 2018
by Routledge

2 Park Square, Milton Park, Abingdon, Oxfordshire OX14 4RN
52 Vanderbilt Avenue, New York, NY 10017

Routledge is an imprint of the Taylor & Francis Group, an informa business

First issued in paperback 2020

British Library Cataloguing-in-Publication Data
A catalogue record for this book is available from the British Library

Library of Congress Cataloging-in-Publication Data
Names: Niedderer, Kristina, editor. | Clune, Stephen, editor. | Ludden, Geke, 1978– editor.
Title: Design for behaviour change : theories and practices of designing for change / [edited by] Kristina Niedderer, Stephen Clune and Geke Ludden.
Description: 1 Edition. | New York : Routledge, 2018. | Series: Design for social responsibility ; 11 | Includes bibliographical references and index.
Identifiers: LCCN 2017012603 (print) | LCCN 2017031052 (ebook) | ISBN 9781315576602 (eBook) | ISBN 9781472471987 (hardback : alk. paper)
Subjects: LCSH: New products. | Product design. | Consumer behavior.
Classification: LCC HF5415.153 (ebook) | LCC HF5415.153 D467 2017 (print) | DDC 658.8/3—dc23
LC record available at https://lccn.loc.gov/2017012603

ISBN: 978-1-4724-7198-7 (hbk)
ISBN: 978-0-367-66987-4 (pbk)

Typeset in Bembo
by Apex CoVantage, LLC

Contents

List of figures   x
List of tables   xii
List of contributors   xiii
Preface   xvii
Acknowledgements   xix

PART 1
Design for behaviour change: its background and significance   1

1 **Introduction: designing for behavioural change**   3
   KRISTINA NIEDDERER, STEPHEN CLUNE AND GEKE LUDDEN

2 **Design's intrinsic relationship with change and its challenges
   for the 21st century**   9
   KRISTINA NIEDDERER, STEPHEN CLUNE AND GEKE LUDDEN

PART 2
Models, methods and tools for design for behaviour change   17

3 **Introducing models, methods and tools for design for
   behaviour change**   19
   KRISTINA NIEDDERER, STEPHEN CLUNE AND GEKE LUDDEN

4 **The Product Impact Tool: the case of the Dutch public
   transport chip card**   26
   STEVEN DORRESTIJN

5 **Design interventions for sustainable behaviour**   40
   DEBRA LILLEY, GARRATH WILSON, TRACY BHAMRA, MARCUS HANRATTY AND
   TANG TANG

6 **Design, behaviour change and the *Design with Intent* toolkit**   58
   DAN LOCKTON

7 **Tweaking interaction through understanding the user**   74
   JOHANNES DAAE AND CASPER BOKS

8 **Design for healthy behaviour**   93
   GEKE LUDDEN

9 **Facilitating behaviour change through mindful design**   104
   KRISTINA NIEDDERER

10 **Practices-oriented design**   116
   LENNEKE KUIJER

11 **Futuring and ontological designing**   128
   STEPHEN CLUNE

12 **The hidden influence of design**   138
   NYNKE TROMP AND PAUL HEKKERT

13 **Summary of design for behavioural change approaches**   150
   KRISTINA NIEDDERER, STEPHEN CLUNE AND GEKE LUDDEN

PART 3
Applying design for behaviour change   159

14 **Design for behaviour change: introducing five areas of
   application and related case studies**   161
   KRISTINA NIEDDERER, STEPHEN CLUNE AND GEKE LUDDEN

15 **Design for behavioural change and sustainability**   166
   STEPHEN CLUNE AND DAN LOCKTON

16 **Design for behaviour change for health and wellbeing**   184
   GEKE LUDDEN, REBECCA CAIN, JAMES MACKRILL AND FRANCES ALLEN

17 **Designing for behavioural safety**   200
   ANDREW MORRIS AND GRAHAM HANCOX

18 **Is 'Nudge' as good as 'We Think' in designing against crime?
   Contrasting paternalistic and fraternalistic approaches to design
   for behaviour change**   216
   LORRAINE GAMMAN AND ADAM THORPE

19 **Design for social behaviour change**   235
   EDWARD GARDINER AND KRISTINA NIEDDERER

20 **Reflecting on current applications of design for behaviour change**   250
KRISTINA NIEDDERER, STEPHEN CLUNE AND GEKE LUDDEN

PART 4
The current state and future of design for behaviour change   261

21 **Conclusion**   263
KRISTINA NIEDDERER, STEPHEN CLUNE AND GEKE LUDDEN

22 **Future prospects**   267
KRISTINA NIEDDERER, STEPHEN CLUNE AND GEKE LUDDEN

Index   273

Figures

4.1	Modes of interaction in the Product Impact Model	28
4.2	Product Impact Model with modes of interaction and effects	29
4.3	Changing trains between different companies requires a check-out and check-in	33
5.1	Overview of Design for Sustainable Behaviour research at Loughborough University	41
5.2	An augmented Theory of Interpersonal Behaviour (TIB) Model	43
5.3	Axis of influence	45
5.4	The radiator lights (feedback) attached to the radiator and window	46
5.5	Temperature setting and acclimatizer screen flow	48
5.6	Boost screen flows with *Heat Me* prompts	48
5.7	Illustration of the BISA showing motivational and behavioural aspects of heating practices	50
6.1	*Design com Intento*, a Brazilian–Portuguese translation of the toolkit by Luis Oliveira. A Czech translation by Jan Laky is also available	64
6.2	Alexander Ambridge's Twist kettle – requiring the user to set the desired water temperature by rotating the base	66
6.3	Alexander Ambridge's sketchbook showing how the *Design with Intent* cards were used directly to inspire concepts	67
7.1	Dimensions of behaviour change card 'Control'	80
7.2	Dimensions of behaviour change card 'Control' (back)	80
7.3	Dimensions of behaviour change card 'Obtrusiveness'	81
7.4	Dimensions of behaviour change card 'Encouragement'	82
7.5	Dimensions of behaviour change card 'Meaning'	83
7.6	Dimensions of behaviour change card 'Direction'	84
7.7	Dimensions of behaviour change card 'Empathy'	85
7.8	Dimensions of behaviour change card 'Importance'	86
7.9	Dimensions of behaviour change card 'Timing'	87
7.10	Dimensions of behaviour change card 'Exposure'	88
7.11	Dimensions of behaviour change card and how to use them	89
8.1	The 'design for healthy behaviour framework' connecting processes and stages of change to design strategies	98
8.2	Snacking 'tower'	99
10.1	A practices-oriented approach to reducing domestic energy demand	121
10.2	The MANGO concept and a variety of ways to use the pillow	123
10.3	A visualization of the Home Wear concept	124

11.1   Timeline of packaging innovations in Australia   131
12.1   An exploration of the user experience of influence in terms of being
        aware of the influence (salience of influence) and the experience of
        freedom in behaving (force)   142
12.2   The experience of autonomy represented as the function of force and
        salience   143
12.3   Mirror design to support doctors and nurses preparing their scrubs for
        surgery   145
12.4   Tomorrow's Menu, a platform to subscribe to a farm type and related
        meat production processes in order to decrease consumption of meat
        from intensive farming   146
12.5   Worktag, a service to apply for a job while hanging out on the streets   147
13.1   Scatter diagram positioning the nine design approaches by affinity to
        the individual-context continuum, and according to theoretical level   153
13.2   Design for behaviour change theories and approaches by
        agency continuum   154
15.1   Householder's annotation of her gas metre as 'difficult to use', because
        of its position in an exterior cupboard   177
15.2   Two examples from 'Drawing Energy', created by members of the public   178
15.3   How the Powerchord system works   179
15.4   Powerchord prototype being tested in a kitchen environment,
        monitoring a microwave oven and an electric kettle   179
16.1   Hospital courtyard produced by design agency Boex   188
16.2   Products designed for sequential use during different stages of change:
        cooling sleeve, mobile application and water bottle   191
16.3   Use of book design to hide cupboard doors and prevent confusion in
        dementia unit   193
16.4   The use of the Theory of Reasoned Action to understand acceptance
        of disability living aids   193
16.5a and 16.5b   Two demonstrator cases that apply strategies from
        persuasive technology to the case of stimulating taking regular
        breaks at work   195
17.1   Interior driver environment of Lotus 7   202
17.2   Interior driver environment of modern vehicle design   203
17.3   Pedestrian crossing facility   211
17.4   Traffic calming   212
17.5   Shared space road design   212
18.1   Locking practices for Sheffield stands versus the prototype bicycle
        parking stands as a single group   221
18.2   CaMden stand   222
18.3   Graph by Rose Ades from presentation 'Putting the Brakes on Bike
        Theft', London Bicycle Film Festival, Barbican, 2008   224
18.4   ATM Art Mat   226
20.1   Design for behavioural change case examples across the cognition–
        context and product–process continuum   254

Tables

5.1	Seven sub-goals	44
6.1	The *Design with Intent* toolkit lenses and patterns	65
7.1	Variation of the distribution of control described in the literature	76
7.2	Categorization of the empirical data: from 55 dimensions to 9 main dimension categories	78
15.1	Design strategies to reduce the intensity of consumption	169
15.2	Examples of design for behavioural change applied to energy, food and transport	170
15.3	Cycling policy indicators with strong policy relevance	174
17.1	Summary of different theories, concepts and applications of behaviour change	201
18.1	Twenty-five situational crime prevention techniques	218
18.2	Four tenets central to design for behaviour change	219
18.3	'EAST' principles	229
18.4	Problem solving and appreciative inquiry	230
20.1	Overview table of design for behavioural change examples and application	251

Contributors

Frances Allen is Postgraduate Researcher at WMG, University of Warwick. Fran is a Physiotherapist specializing in the prevention of health crises in the community. She has a special interest in the use of the home as a healthcare environment and the uptake of evidence-based design for dementia in the home.

Tracy Bhamra is Professor of Sustainable Design and Pro Vice-Chancellor (Enterprise) at Loughborough University. Professor Tracy Bhamra has a BSc and MSc in Manufacturing Systems Engineering and completed a PhD in Design for Disassembly and Recycling at Manchester Metropolitan University in 1995. In 2003 she established the Sustainable Design Research Group at Loughborough. Tracy is a Fellow of the Institution of Engineering & Technology (FIET), the Design Research Society (DRS) and the Royal Society for the Encouragement of Arts, Manufactures & Commerce (RSA).

Casper Boks is Professor in Sustainable Product Design at the Norwegian University of Science and Technology (NTNU) in Trondheim, Norway. Casper holds a Master's degree in applied econometrics and a PhD in sustainable design. His research interests currently focus on design for sustainable behaviour, and organizational, managerial and stakeholder conditions for successful implementation of sustainable product innovation.

Rebecca Cain is Associate Professor and Lead of the Experiential Engineering group in WMG at the University of Warwick. Rebecca is the lead convenor of the Design Research Society's Special Interest Group for Health, Wellbeing and Happiness. Her expertise is in methods to involve users in co-design processes for future products, environments and services, to create positive outcomes for people.

Stephen Clune is Senior Lecturer in Sustainable Design at Imagination Lancaster, Lancaster University. Stephen is a sustainable designer, researcher and educator; his core research interest focuses on how design (and design thinking) can assist in the move towards a sustainable society, with a particular interest in design as a facilitator of change. His work draws on a diverse range of tools from social practice theory, behavioural change and Life Cycle Analysis.

Johannes Daae is EcoDesigner at Bergfald Environmental Consultants in Oslo, Norway. Johannes holds a PhD in EcoDesign from the Norwegian University of Science and Technology (NTNU) and a Master of Design for Interaction from Delft University of Technology, the Netherlands. His research and work interests include sustainable product and service design in general, and particularly how products and systems can be designed to make people interact with them in the most sustainable way.

Steven Dorrestijn is Senior Researcher in the Ethics and Technology group at Saxion University of Applied Sciences, the Netherlands. In 2012 Dorrestijn completed his PhD thesis (*The design of our own lives: Technical mediation and subjectivation after Foucault*) at the University of Twente, the Netherlands. Previously he studied Philosophy in Paris and Philosophy and Mechanical Engineering at Twente.

Lorraine Gamman is Professor of Design at Central Saint Martins, at the University of the Arts, London, where in 1999 she founded the Design Against Crime Research Centre, which she continues to direct. She is also co-director of the Socially Responsive Design and Innovation Hub located there.

Edward Gardiner is Behavioural Design Lead at Warwick Business School, where he works on applying insights and methods from behavioural science to support the design of products and services with a social purpose. He previously worked for the advertising agency, RKCR/Y&R, and holds an MA in Natural Sciences from the University of Cambridge and an MSc in Cognitive and Decision Sciences from University College London.

Graham Hancox is Research Associate, Loughborough University. Graham holds qualifications in Ergonomics/Human Factors at both an undergraduate and PhD level from Loughborough University. He is working on a number of diverse research areas and projects. Examples include working on a range of projects in the Transport Safety research area using Human Factors to help prevent road accidents, injuries and fatalities. He is currently working in the area of National Security research, investigating Human Factors issues in the event of a Chemical, Biological, Radiological or Nuclear (CBRNe) incident.

Marcus Hanratty is Lecturer in Interaction and Product Design in the National College of Art and Design, Dublin. Dr Marcus Hanratty research focuses on the role design and technology play in shaping people's behaviours, with a particular interest in Design for Sustainable Behaviour and the role of emotion in behaviour change. His research activities are inherently interdisciplinary, but are led by a belief in the power of design practice and the designed artefact as agents of change and learning.

Paul Hekkert is Full Professor of Form Theory at Delft University of Technology. Paul conducts research on the ways products impact human experience and behaviour. With Matthijs van Dijk he published *Vision in Design* (2011), a book that describes their method to design for effect.

Lenneke Kuijer is Assistant Professor in the Department of Industrial Design, University of Eindhoven, The Netherlands. Lenneke Kuijer explored the implications of practice theory for sustainable design as a PhD candidate at Delft University of Technology and worked at the University of Sheffield as part of the DEMAND Centre.

Debra Lilley is Senior Lecturer in Design and is part of the Sustainable Design Research Group at Loughborough Design School, UK. Dr Debra Lilley has extensive knowledge and experience of applying user-centred sustainable design methods and tools to generate behavioural insights to drive design development of less-resource intensive products. Her current research focuses on design for sustainable behaviour, product lifespan extension, attitudinal response to ageing materials and design for circularity.

Dan Lockton is Assistant Professor, School of Design, Carnegie Mellon University. He is interested in how people's understanding of the world affects their actions, and how design affects, and is affected by this. Dan previously worked at the Royal College of Art, University of Warwick and Brunel University, on projects around energy, sustainability and participatory design. His PhD (2007–13) involved the development of *Design with Intent*, a pattern library for environmental and social behaviour change.

Geke Ludden is Associate Professor at the Department of Design, Production and Management at the University of Twente, The Netherlands. Geke is also a visiting fellow at University of Technology Sydney. Her current research centres on how the design of products and services influences people's behaviour and motivation and focuses on products and services that support healthy behaviour or that otherwise contribute to people's wellbeing.

James Mackrill is Lecturer in Design Engineering at the Dyson School of Design Engineering, Imperial College London. Jamie is also visiting tutor on Innovation Design Engineering and Global Innovation Design programmes at the Royal College of Art. Jamie's research interests concern how people experience and interact with their surroundings, and how this understanding can be used to improve human performance and experience.

Andrew Morris is Professor of Human Factors in Transport Safety and leads the Behavioural Safety Research and Injury Prevention Research Group at Loughborough University. Andrew graduated from York University in 1988 and holds postgraduate qualifications from the University of Birmingham including a Master's degree in Ergonomics and a PhD degree in Mechanical Engineering. Andrew also holds a position as a Visiting Professor at Hasselt University in Belgium and was awarded the US Government Special Award of Appreciation in recognition of outstanding leadership and special contributions in the field of motor vehicle safety.

Kristina Niedderer is Professor of Design and Craft at the University of Wolverhampton. Niedderer's research focuses on the role of mindfulness and emotions as a means to engender mindful interaction and behaviour change through design. Niedderer is founding editor of the journal *Craft Research*, Council Member and Secretary for Special Interest Groups of the Design Research Society and she leads the European project 'Designing for People with Dementia', Marie Skłodowska-Curie grant agreement No 691001 (2016-2020).

Tang Tang is Lecturer in Sustainable Design in the Faculty of Performance, Visual Arts & Communications at University of Leeds. Dr Tang Tang is a Lecturer in Sustainable Design and is part of the Experience Design Research Group in the School of Design at the University of Leeds, UK. She specializes in User-centred design for Sustainable Behaviour. Her current research interests include design for healthy behaviour and participatory and co-design for social sustainability.

Adam Thorpe is Professor of Socially Responsive Design at Central Saint Martins College, University of the Arts London (UAL). He is co-director of the Design Against Crime Research Centre and Director of the Socially Responsive Design Hub as well as Coordinator of the UAL DESIS Lab (Design for Social Innovation and Sustainability).

Nynke Tromp is Assistant Professor Social Design & Behaviour Change at the department of Industrial Design, Delft University of Technology. After her PhD and working as a social designer in practice at Reframing Studio, she now continues her study of the value of design in changing behaviour and counteracting social problems.

Garrath Wilson is Lecturer in Industrial Design and is part of the Sustainable Design Research Group at Loughborough Design School, UK. Dr. Garrath Wilson's primary research interests include Design for Sustainable Behaviour and the psychology of energy consumption and, more recently, resilient energy futures and product-service systems. Drawing upon an industrial design consultancy background, design has always been central to Garrath's research approach, generating concepts and prototypes as speculative agents and probes.

Preface

This book is one in a series, looking at the role of the design and the designer in a socially responsible context. Being concerned for society is not a new phenomenon amongst designers; indeed Ruskin and Morris at the turn of the 20th century actively pursued design and production in the material world in a manner consistent with moral and ethical values for the benefit of the wider society. However, during the 20th century, we saw not only a growth in the design professions but also a period in which the economies of the West, consumption and the use of the world's resources continued to grow at an alarming rate, contributing to the ongoing fragility of society and planet earth.

By the 1960s, designers began to actively consider the wider implications of design for society. Several approaches emerged, including green design and consumerism, responsible design and ethical consuming, ecodesign and sustainability and feminist design. In the 1970s, Papanek (1974), amongst others, encouraged designers to abandon 'design for profit' in favour of a more compassionate approach. In the 1980s and 1990s, profit and ethical issues were no longer considered mutually exclusive, more market-oriented approaches emerged, such as the 'green consumer' and ethical investment. The purchase of socially responsible, 'ethical' products and services was facilitated by the dissemination of research into sustainability in consumer publications. Accessibility and inclusivity also saw a great deal of design interest and activity and more recently designers have turned to resolving issues related to crime, health and education.

At the same time governments, businesses and individuals have become increasingly aware of what we are doing, not only to the world, but also to each other. Human rights, sustainability and ethics are all issues of concern, whilst the relationship between national economies and poverty struggles to be resolved. Global businesses have recognized the changing environment and are setting their own corporate social responsibility agendas. However, if businesses and organizations are to turn these ideas into reality, 'design' is an essential ingredient.

Designers make daily decisions with regard to the use of resources, to the lifestyle and use of products, places and communications. In order to achieve the needs of businesses, the desires of the consumer and the improvement of the world, the designer in making decisions must embrace dimensions of social responsibility. However, there is now a need to shift from focussing on a single issue towards taking a more holistic approach to socially responsible design.

This book takes us into a new domain that in recent years has been gaining particular attention, i.e. the role of design and designers in influencing behaviour, through the products, places and services they have a key role in creating. The book brings together leading authors and researchers to delve into the idea and process of design for behaviour change.

It illustrates the multiple perspectives, theories and tools that have been brought into play to influence and change behaviours. It provides a lens through which to consider the relationship between the individual and the designed 'thing', the degree to which each is influenced and the role of design in the process. For the first time it illustrates the multiple dimensions of the subject and offers cases studies as examples of approaches to behaviour change. It goes without saying that such a topic has its own concerns with being socially responsible, in terms of the ethics behind both tacit and explicit design aimed at changing behaviour and offers examples of societal and environmental challenges to which such design approaches can and probably should be taken. This book provides a comprehensive introduction to the topic; it offers insights on the practice and tools for application. It is an essential resource for future designers and design decision-makers to understand their role as change-makers.

Professor Rachel Cooper
Lancaster University, UK

Reference

Papanek, V. (1974). *Design for the real world*. St Albans, UK: Paladin.

Acknowledgements

We would like to thank several individuals and institutions that have enabled us to complete this book for their support. First of all, we would like to thank the Arts and Humanities Research Council, UK, for funding the initial research into 'Creating Sustainable Innovation through Design for Behaviour Change' (Grant number: AH/L013525/1) in 2014, out of which this book has arisen. The complete findings have been published in the full project report, which can be downloaded here: http://hdl.handle.net/2436/336632. All project information and further developments can be accessed through the project website: www.behaviourchange.eu. Second, we would like to acknowledge the role of the Special Interest Groups for Design for Behaviour Change of the Design Research Society, which has offered an important forum for discussion of our ideas. Third, we would like to thank series editor Rachel Cooper for her continuous support during the production of the book.

We would also like to thank all our contributors for their splendid input and hard work, and for putting up with our repetitive requests to align chapters to the format of the book and to finalize every small detail as well as our colleagues who have offered invaluable advice along the way. Last but not least, we would like to thank our families for bearing with us during the many hours of work on the volume.

Part 1

Design for behaviour change

Its background and significance

1 Introduction

Designing for behavioural change

Kristina Niedderer, Stephen Clune and Geke Ludden

Design impacts every part of our lives. The design of products and services we encounter in all areas and walks of life influences the way we go about our daily activities. It is hard to imagine any activity of our daily lives that is not dependent on a designed artefact in some capacity. Our clothing, mobile phones, computers, cars, tools and kitchenware all enable and hold in place our everyday practices. Design impacts our built and natural environment through urban planning and architecture, and it impacts our health and safety by promoting or restricting activities that may or may not be healthy, or cause harm. Cooper et al. (2011) explain that in the past 100 years, 'we have designed systems of transport, work, and entertainment that mean we are less active' (p. 135) and which can be counter productive to our health where they lead to a lack of exercise. Simultaneously designers have improved the diagnostic and treatment devices for the non-communicable diseases affected by this lack of exercise (Cooper et al., 2011). Design can furthermore shape our views and expectations of how we should behave in our world through its implicit values. For instance, designs of the mobile phone and web 2.0 platforms have changed the way we interact and plan for work and leisure, as well as shifting the expectations for when and where we are available.

The influence of design has been far reaching, with consequences not only intended, but also frequently unintended and often undesirable with regard to its effects on the environment or on our health and wellbeing. One example is the interior design of supermarkets, product offerings, food packets and related advertising material, which have all been designed (separately or together) to increase sales. However, the accumulative effect on diets may be found to have a much wider (although hopefully unintended) consequence of contributing to the rise in obesity and diabetes in Western society. While the unintended consequences of obesity are clearly undesirable, the intentional aim by industry to make a profit clearly holds a different perspective, which is demonstrated by continued attempts from lobby groups to water down regulations on sugar (Novak & Brownell, 2011), for example.

There is an increasing call on designers in the widest sense to draw attention towards, and respond to negative social and environmental issues. There is also a recent body of work focussing on how design's influence may be used to intentionally steer changes to improve a range of problematic social and environmental issues. However, despite design's clear influence on human behaviour and an emerging body of work on design and behavioural change, the understanding of how to intentionally use design to create change is fragmented, with limited frameworks for its effective implementation in professional and public contexts (Niedderer et al., 2014; Niedderer et al., 2016).

This edited volume on design for behavioural change therefore takes as its focus this body of work that deals with the influence of design: to review and contextualize existing approaches, and to explore the various perspectives and avenues available for positive change. This book thus aims to offer a thorough discussion about the understanding and responsible application of design in general, and design for behaviour change in particular, to contribute to and expand on current understandings of how we can (and should) design for behaviour change. In the remainder of this chapter, we elaborate and define the terminology and key themes that are used throughout the book and provide an overview of its approach, structure and individual chapters.

Defining design and design for behaviour change

'Design' is a much used, and not seldom misunderstood or even misused term. Hence, some clarification on terminology will be helpful to our readers to clarify our position and what we mean by design and behaviour change in this book.

From a linguistic point of view, the term 'design' can be used either as a noun or verb. As a noun, it generally denotes the outcome of a design process – a product in the widest sense, whether a physical thing, service or idea. As a verb, 'design' or 'designing' denotes a process that is used to change an existing situation into one that is preferred (Simon, 1969: 129). This process commonly includes different phases (creative ideation, development with or without stakeholders etc.).

The traditional notion of design is often associated narrowly with a physical 'product', e.g. graphic design creates graphics, product design products, furniture design furniture, interior design interiors etc. However, the physical 'product' as an output from design is becoming less dominant with the emergence of service design; co-design, and the shift to a more virtual world. Both are contributing increasingly to blurring the nature of the outcomes of design. Thus design 'products' may encompass any output from craft, fashion, product, urban, games, service or policy design, etc. We therefore use the term 'design' to refer to more than just physical objects, and associate the term broadly across the spectrum of design professions, including product and industrial design, packaging, interior and fashion design, interaction, game, service and service systems design, urban planning and others.

In terms of design as a process, we adhere to Simon's notion that designers in the process of designing are engaged generally not in describing existing situations, but in transforming existing situations into preferred ones (Simon, 1969: 129). Design as a process then is a way of thinking

> characterized by the capacity to use intuition and creativity for generating insights and solutions, rationality to analyze the necessary information and fit solutions in relation to a particular context, and empathy to understand the complexity of a problem from multiple perspectives. Design seesaws between subjective and objective knowledge and draws from a conscious inclusion of subjective perceptions and hunches and relates them to analysis and factual knowledge.
>
> (Clune et al., 2014: 6)

The notion of behaviour change in relation to design also requires some consideration. One of the key aspects of design is that it is related closely to both behaviour and change. Design is related to behaviour in that any artefact created affords an action by the user because of its function, whether physical, symbolic or social. (Ligo, 1984) and through its affordances, design can enable or stifle particular behaviours (Norman, 1988) creating change. Following a combination of behavioural economic and functional emotional approaches (Minton & Khale, 2014, Keltner & Gross, 1999, Keltner & Haidt, 1999, Roseman et al., 1994), we understand behaviour in the context of this book generally as people's actions in response to other people, things, environments and contexts, and as informed or affected by emotions as well as social and cultural preconceptions, with the purpose of negotiating external factors and internal goals.

As a distinct term, 'design for behaviour(al) change' is perceived as contentious in some areas, particularly when it has a focus overtly placed on the individual, and where it might be perceived as manipulation of the individual. Some people therefore have a preference for talking simply about 'designing for change'. However, we believe that the acknowledgement of human action in the design decision-making process as well as in its outcomes is important, and that the terms behaviour(al) change and design for behaviour change, are both terms widely understood and express this emphasis. Hence, we retain this terminology with the explicit acknowledgement of taking a broader view that encompasses both the individual and the environment as important factors for creating change. Accordingly, in this book, we seek to explore the full gamut of possibilities on how design may influence behaviours and environments to create change.

What the book sets out to do

Design for Behaviour Change can be a useful tool to address the multiple societal and environmental challenges that we face today that require action. However, as previous research has shown, design for behaviour change at present is neither fully recognized nor understood (Niedderer et al., 2014; Niedderer et al., 2016). This book therefore aims to offer a thorough discussion of both the theoretical and practical approaches to design for behaviour change to help improve its understanding and extend its application and responsible use.

To address this aim, the book takes two approaches: first, it provides an overview of current and emerging theories, approaches and tools of design for behaviour change with an explanation of the different scientific backgrounds and theories from the social and behavioural sciences they draw on. Second, it offers a discussion of their application in five different key contexts to demonstrate the relevance and effectiveness of design for behaviour change in these areas, including sustainability, health, safety, crime prevention and social issues. This book takes a broad sweep across these five key areas that are normally treated individually to bring them together and allow for both their comparison and a broad overview of the field. Through this dual approach, the book seeks to offer both theoretical understanding and practical guidance for researchers, design professionals, managers, design students and others interested in instigating positive change. It offers an overview of and new perspectives on the range of tools and techniques that have been developed for and used in the different sectors within the field.

The book proceeds in four parts. Part 1 (Chapters 1 and 2) offers an introduction to design for behaviour change in general, including a brief history, a discussion of design and its relationship to change, and the challenges faced in the 21st century. The aim of this part is to set the scene and context for the following parts of the book.

Because of design's close link with people and their behaviour, design draws regularly on behaviour change models from the behavioural and social sciences. In line with some of these theories, which we explore further throughout this book, Part 2 (Chapters 3–13) provides an overview of current and emerging design for behaviour change theories, models and tools including an explanation of the different scientific backgrounds and their adoption within design. Chapter 3 offers an introductory overview and a framework for mapping the different approaches presented throughout Part 2. The following four chapters introduce more general models and tools for how design for behaviour change theories can influence issues of sustainability. Chapter 4 introduces the Product Impact Tool, a tool that offers four perspectives on how theories of behaviour can be adopted within design practice and helps to address social and ethical questions concerning innovations. Chapter 5 presents a framework for designing interventions for sustainable behaviour from a user experience point of view. Chapter 6 presents the *Design with Intent* toolkit, a design pattern collection which aims to facilitate exploration of problem-solution spaces in behaviour change contexts, including sustainability but also other contexts. Chapter 7 again focuses specifically on sustainability presenting the Dimensions of Behaviour Change tool, which offers a 'crash course' for designers in how the mind of the user works.

Part 2 goes on to introduce two chapters that present theories on design for behaviour change that are related to health and wellbeing. In Chapter 8, support in changing health-related behaviour is then coupled to the notion of 'Stages of Change', introducing the Design for Healthy Behaviour framework. Chapter 9 again takes a more general approach to behaviour change and introduces mindfulness theory into design, focussing on how mindful design can promote responsible behaviour change. The following three chapters draw upon theories from sociology and psychology and provide insight into how these might be used in design for behaviour change with regard to broader considerations of user practices. In Chapter 10, social practice theory is introduced to explain how designers can study and draw upon user practices to change behaviour. Chapter 11 is underpinned by the philosophy of ontological designing looking at the potential role of futuring (forecasting, future scenarios and back casting) as a strategy to enable or disable future behaviours and practices of users from taking place. Finally, in Chapter 12, the experience of being influenced is discussed. The chapter focuses in detail on the perspective of the user and discusses the hidden influence of design. Chapter 13 concludes Part 2 with a review of the tools and case studies presented. It provides an analysis of how the different theories, models and tools compare and relate and offers a visual overview to map the field, its progress and gaps.

Part 3 (Chapters 14–20) focuses on the contexts in which these tools may be applied, illustrating the application of theories, approaches and tools to a variety of case studies. Chapter 14 provides the introduction to Part 3. It introduces the five application domains, including Sustainability, Health and Wellbeing, Safety, Design against Crime and Social Design, and discusses the broad challenges that these five domains face.

In Chapter 15, the challenges related to the domain of sustainability are presented with respect to reducing carbon dioxide emissions, by applying design for behavioural change strategies within the themes of energy, food, transport and consumption. Two case studies are discussed in depth in relation to encouraging cycling patronage in cities, and understanding end users' conceptualization of energy. Chapter 16 discusses how design for behaviour change will be of growing importance in the broad domain of health and wellbeing. Three case studies are provided with respect to reducing sugary drink intake, dementia care and wellbeing in the workplace. These are used to discuss how a variety of design for behaviour change approaches might be used in this domain. Chapter 17 introduces design for safety approaches and offers case studies of how theory has been applied by either designing away safety risks (e.g. via the fitment of guards, safety rails etc.) or utilizing design for behavioural change strategies to create a culture of safety. Chapter 18 and 19 go on to offer more social perspectives on design for behaviour change. Chapter 18 introduces multiple perspectives to design against crime, via an introduction to situated crime prevention, proposing more participatory and collaborative design-led approaches to behaviour change. Chapter 19 discusses the impact of design on social situations, exploring behaviour change in relation to doing 'social good' as well as its influence on 'social interaction'. The chapter presents six case studies that address design activism, innovation in communities, bottom-up participatory design processes, pedestrian-friendly streets and social media, with two case studies focussing on the intent, process and outcomes of the interventions respectively. Finally, in Chapter 20, we offer an overview of how the range of design for behavioural change approaches have been applied in the different domains to create desirable change. The chapter highlights the importance of a holistic approach to creating change that applies a combination of cognitive and context-based strategies.

Part 4 provides the conclusion to the book in two chapters. Chapter 21 provides an overview and reflection of the outcomes and findings of the discussion, as well as considerations of limitations of the book, gaps and future work in the area of design for behaviour change. Chapter 22 finally draws some broader reflections of the challenges and opportunities of design for behaviour change with regard to its future uses and benefits.

Through its four parts, this volume presents a wide overview of approaches and viewpoints of design for behaviour change as well as considerations of its benefits and limits. The book has arisen from the work on an Arts and Humanities Design in Innovation Research Grant (AH/L013525/1) in 2014, which brought together a number of colleagues from the UK and the Netherlands. The aim of the grant was to provide an overview of design for behaviour change, and the resulting work revealed the need to provide an overview of design for behaviour change across domain areas and to look at and develop better evidence of the application of the emerging approaches and tools.

Subsequently, members of the Arts and Humanities Research Council (AHRC) project team have worked together with a number of further invited authors, which were identified through the project research, to bring together an overview of current views, approaches and applications. The book has aimed to be as inclusive as possible within the parameters of its scope, aims and structure, while of course it can by no means be comprehensive.

The area of design for behaviour change at present is a fast-emerging field, and at present evidence of the effective application of design for the various design for behaviour change approaches is far from conclusive. Much further research will be required in this regard, but we hope that through the presentation of and reflection on the variety of views, theories and tools in this volume, it can serve as a source of inspiration and offer guidance in selecting and applying appropriate approaches that enable designers to design for behaviour change. Finally, we hope that the book will also offer a starting point for designers, producers and policy makers to consider their responsibility to use design for behaviour change to facilitate positive sustainable change for the environment and society.

References

Clune, S., Roggema, R., Horne, R., Hunter, S., Jones, R., Martin, J., & Werner, J. (2014). *Design-led decision support for regional climate adaptation* (p. 6). Melbourne, VCCCAR.

Cooper, R., Boyko, C. T., & Cooper, C. (2011). Design for health: The relationship between design and noncommunicable diseases. *Journal of Health Communication, 16*(2), 134–157.

Keltner, D., & Gross, J. J. (1999). Functional accounts of emotions. *Cognition and Emotion, 13*(5), 467–480.

Keltner, D., & Haidt, J. (1999). Social functions of emotions at four levels of analysis. *Cognition and Emotion, 13*(5), 505–521.

Ligo, L. L. (1984). *The concept of function in 20th century architectural criticism.* Ann Arbor, MI: UMI Research Press.

Minton, E. A., & Khale, L. R. (2014). *Belief systems, religion, and behavioral economics.* New York: Business Expert Press LLC.

Niedderer, K., Mackrill, J., Clune, S., Lockton, D., Ludden, G., Morris, A., Cain, R., Gardiner, E., Gutteridge, R., Evans, M., & Hekkert, P. (2014). *Creating sustainable innovation through design for behaviour change: Full report.* Wolverhampton: University of Wolverhampton, Project Partners & AHRC.

Niedderer, K., Mackrill, J., Clune, S., Lockton, D., Ludden, G., Morris, A., Cain, R., Gardiner, E., Gutteridge, R., & Hekkert, P. (2016). Design for behaviour change as a driver for sustainable innovation: Implementation in the private and public sectors. *International Journal of Design, 10*(2), 67–85.

Norman, D. A. (1988). *The psychology of everyday things.* New York: Basic Books.

Novak, N. L., & Brownell, K. D. (2011). Taxation as prevention and as a treatment for obesity: The case of sugar-sweetened beverages. *Current Pharmaceutical Design, 17*(12), 1218–1222.

Roseman, I. J., Wiest, C., & Swartz, T. S. (1994). Phenomenology, behaviours and goals differentiate discrete emotions. *Journal of Personality and Social Psychology, 67*(2), 206–221.

Simon, H. (1969). *The science of the artefact.* Cambridge, MA: MIT Press.

2 Design's intrinsic relationship with change and its challenges for the 21st century

Kristina Niedderer, Stephen Clune and Geke Ludden

Design's intrinsic relationship with change

Design has an intrinsic and powerful relationship with change. At the broadest level, design's relationship to change is so strong that we label parts of our history by the names of materials, artefacts, and technological developments characteristic of a time period, E.g. the stone age, bronze age, iron age, the industrial revolution, the computer age, and the internet age. Throughout history, the influence of inventions and technological developments, and associated designed goods, has radically transformed societies. For example, the early use of tools and simple agricultural machinery enabled a shift away from the hunter–gatherer and allowed new types of societies to develop. The industrial revolution, powered by steam, enabled mass production at an unprecedented scale, slowly improving living standards and allowing the middle class to emerge. The Model T Ford, the poster child for mass production via the assembly line, radically transformed the shape of our cities by offering affordable individual transport, shifting the mobilities of entire societies to the extent that many of us have become reliant on the use of cars.

Material artefacts, their virtual dimensions as well as the services that surround us enable us not only to complete our daily practices, but also influence the way we act.

Considering any room we might be in, we find ourselves surrounded by designed 'stuff' that enables us to do the work we do, and it seems hard to identify any activity we complete that is not dependent on a designed good in some capacity. These daily tasks are most likely dynamic, they will have changed and evolved over time through continual shifts in the social practices and technical developments, such as the move from cash to physical cheques to contactless payments. These changes have a deep impact on our lives, social practices and environments. As Latour states 'artifacts can be deliberately designed to both replace human action and constrain and shape the actions of other humans' (Latour, 1992: 225).

The change in production capabilities, promoted by design in form of products made desirable through advertising, promoted profound changes in worldview. Western and Western-influenced societies went from a culture of mending and reusing things to a throw-away culture, in part perhaps due to the emergence of non-recyclable plastics, but, more importantly, born out by the rise of consumerism. The roots of the consumer society can be seen to emerge from the development of the social structures of the 17th century onwards, and an early critique of it can be found at the end of the 19th century in Veblen's voice ([1899] 1994). In the 20th century, early industrial designers in the USA of the 1930s played a key role in the modern manifestation of consumerism. They presented futuristic design scenarios matched with an explicit desire to socially engineer society in their streamlining movement (Andrews, 2009). Against the background of the great depression, the underlying plan was for society to use design to consume its way out of the great depression and promote growth. This is a practice and worldview which persists and which design remains strongly associated with. For example, George W Bush's call post 9/11 – following the attack on the twin towers in New York – to start shopping can be seen to have arisen from a not dissimilar train of thought, and European policy, for example, still stresses growth at its heart – whether we look at the controversial CETA (Comprehensive Economic and Trade Agreement) deal signed in 2016 between Europe and Canada, or policy documentation concerning industry and innovation (e.g. European Commission, 2013).

This consumerist approach connects design intrinsically to economic growth with enormous implications on all parts of human life including health and environmental sustainability. The resulting impact of design can have both intended and unintended, desirable and undesirable effects. For example, while cars can be beneficial in terms of an individual's mobility, they have had consequential knock-on effects resulting in many negative effects such as increased CO_2 emissions, air pollution, pedestrian-unfriendly infrastructures, traffic congestion, and much more. Other examples already mentioned include the impact of computers and mobile phones on social interaction and on notions of connectedness, or the change of financial transactions from cash to physical cheques, to online banking, to contactless payment via card or phone.

While it is easy to look back through history to see the impact of major technological developments and design on change, we can also see that these have not always been planned or predicted. For example, the Sony Walkman was predicted to be a flop while indeed it proved a success and changed the way we consume music, but also had an influence on social interaction in public (Bull, 2006). With regard to sustainability, the issue of pollution through steam and later fuel engines was not understood for a long time, and we will have to deal with these consequences for years if not centuries to come. Thus, design may be seen to have an uneasy relationship with change and can be perceived as a double-edged sword. On the one hand, designers are concerned with addressing the consequences of a consumer society. On the other hand, they have been responsible for inflating it, making change a 'challenging subject for designers to come to grips with' (Moggridge, 2007: 656).

These changes are inevitably linked to behavioural changes on individual as well as societal levels, influencing and influenced by consumption behaviour as well as changes in our social behaviours, expectations and worldviews, which can often be at odds with each other. For example, individuals who desire to smoke may be initially fuelled by peer pressure, but when the societal values change, as with the proposal of the smoking laws in the UK in 2004 (BBC 16 November 2004), and their subsequent implementation, then suddenly the individual finds him/herself at odds with the social norm that he/she has conformed to previously.

In response to the challenges of design causing change in general, and behavioural changes in particular, design for behaviour change has emerged in recent years as an explicit field of design study. It specifically examines the relationship between design, behaviour, and change, and seeks to understand how we can intentionally change a given situation for a desirable environmental or social outcome, and what those changes should possibly be.

The emergence of design for behaviour change

Since the late 19th century and throughout the 20th century, there has been a number of designers and theoreticians who have written about the role and influence of design. William Morris prominently spoke out about the ethics of production (Szmigin & Carrigan, 2005). In *Ornament and Crime*, Adolf Loos (1908) discussed the relationship and ethics of visual appearance in design. During the period of the Bauhaus, Gropius and others followed on these two approaches to promote the famous dictum 'form follows function' in an attempt to develop a holistic approach to design by integrating craft and industrial productions, which albeit created much debate about the success of its results (Michl, 1995).

The capacity of designers to create change was subsequently most explicitly discussed by Simon in 1969, identifying that designers are engaged generally not in describing existing situations, but in *transforming* existing situations into preferred ones (Simon, 1969: 129). While explicit about the notion of change, the notion of ethos and consequence remains implicit since it is not elicited what is meant by 'preferred'. Papanek (1974) took up the baton in examining the consequences of production on the environment and society, followed by others in more recent years along different paths and domains of design.

As an area of study, design for behaviour change can be seen to emerge through the evolution of a variety of these design approaches, from an initial focus on functionality and aesthetics, to user-centred design, ergonomics, and user experiences, to a more nuanced understanding of the psychology of products and people's responses to them through persuasive technology, affective design, and emotion design amongst others. In the following, we discuss some of these approaches briefly to explain the development of design for behaviour change better and to position it in the field.

While the early efforts of design approaches often focused on enabling the broadest number of people in the population to effortlessly use a product intuitively, without the need for instruction, more recent approaches tend to consider the specifics of a situation as well as the conscious decision-making in the design and use of things made. Norman's 'psychology of everyday things' (1988) introduced to designers' key concepts from ecological psychology and human factors research, such as affordances, constraints, feedback and mapping, which have provided guiding principles to design for the intuitive use of artefacts. This work, conducted under the mantel of design psychology or behavioural design has been influential in leading to the development of design for behavioural change, despite not engaging in the specific language of behavioural change. Its later republication as the 'design of everyday things' (Norman, 2002) has been indicative of the emergence of design as a recognized field. In parallel, social scientists were developing a body of work explaining that design may be playing a more significant role in human actions than previously thought. For example Akrich (1992) identified the concept that design may be 'scripting' individual actions. A further shift in the focus of design started when researchers in the fields of design, computer science and marketing started to use theories from the social sciences to explain the effects of their design (e.g. Pine & Gilmore, 1999; Jordan, 2000). Triggered by these developments, design researchers started to build theories and strategies that go beyond primarily explaining the experience of products, to enabling designers to design for specific 'user experiences'.

Over time, design models and theories have progressed to be more explicit in their attempt to understand and explain the influence of design on behaviour, and detail how design may guide behaviour. In computer science, persuasive technology (Fogg, 2003) has become a leading approach, which focuses on how the design of interfaces etc. can support and or lead the user to navigate and experience a given interface, guided by intuitive ('persuasive') features. In the field of product design, Desmet and Hekkert (2002) introduced the framework of product experience, known also as affective design or emotion design. Another development regarding changing user behaviour is the serious games movement, which aims at improving learning through integrating multiple learning styles and games processes with entertainment. This movement has expanded rapidly to encompass 'a broad spectrum of application areas, e.g. military, government, educational, corporate, healthcare' (Susi et al., 2007: 1, Bellotti et al., 2013).

Most recently, a number of theories have developed that explicitly address design for behaviour change, such as the 'Loughborough model' (e.g. Lilley, 2009), *Design with Intent* (Lockton et al., 2010), or Mindful Design approaches (Niedderer, 2014), among others. These newer design for behaviour change approaches draw on different theories that stem from the behavioural and social sciences, integrating and developing them to provide new starting points and theories for considering change more explicitly in design. Their focus and remit has broadened in scope from a focus on the psychological effect of products, services, and designed environments to the effect they can have on people's actions and behaviour. In Part 2 of this volume, we bring together some of these newer and emerging design approaches to introduce, discuss, and compare them to demonstrate their conceptual approach and practical value.

Design challenges for the 21st century

As with any emerging field, standard processes, methods and associated value frameworks have not yet been firmly established. Concerning processes and methods, there is general agreement on the need for development. Boks (2012) identified that a lack of common terminology, formalized research protocols, and target behaviour selection are still key issues that generally have not been addressed and that hinder the coherent development and comparison of successful designs and their implementation.

With regard to the development of value frameworks, issues are more contentious. While it can be argued that designers have always attempted to utilize design to lead to 'preferable outcomes', in response to current recognitions of the important role of design, Jelsma (2006) calls for designers to take moral responsibility for the actions which take place as a result of humans interactions with artefacts. He posits that, whether intentional or not, 'artefacts have a co-responsibility for the way action develops and for what results. If we waste energy or produce waste in routine actions such as in the household practices, that has to do with the way artefacts guide us' (Jelsma, 2006: 222).

Whether we support Jelsma's position depends on the views we take: we can assume the designer to be in control of what and how he/she designs; we can assume the manufacturers to be in control through the investment and design briefs they provide; or politicians through setting policies; or we can assume end-users to be in control through buying or not buying, or the way they use any design. Most likely, we will find that all four groups (and maybe others, too) have some share in promoting or hindering change. Such issues have led to the emergence of an ongoing and much more explicit discussion about the deliberate influence of design; of the areas in which it is, could be, or should be applied; whether its influence should be implicit or explicit, voluntary or prescriptive; of the ethical consequences of one or the other in various contexts; who makes the decisions about what to change; who has the responsibility to change or facilitate change; and also of the approaches that are available and emerging to offer guidance and support. This debate about ethics, ownership, and responsibility is one of the key issues of design for behaviour change yet to be addressed. These questions are complicated by the complexity of assessing the impact of any design in the real world, in that the consequences may not always be foreseen. Despite the ethical dilemmas that design for behaviour change poses, we argue that there are a broad range of complex issues that will benefit from attention and change and, with Jelsma, we advocate design for behaviour change as an ethical stance to support sustainable development and change.

Besides these methodological and ethical questions, the discussion of design for behaviour change has to tackle also another issue: that of focus. Being a young field of study, which still lacks a shared terminology, research protocols and focus, knowledge is often tied to a specific research area or thematic. For example, design for behavioural change is often aligned to specific social or environmental problems that researchers are explicitly attempting to address. However, equally often there might be similar work in adjacent areas that is not recognized because of the lack of cohesion in the field. Problems in these areas are also often interlinked, which is another reason why they should not be looked at as problems of individual domains, but must be considered in a holistic way that acknowledges their complexity. This book therefore takes a broad sweep across five of the key areas that are normally treated individually to bring them together and allow for their comparison and a broad overview of the field. These five areas include

- Environmental sustainability, in improving the state of the planet
- Health and wellbeing, in addressing the numerous health crisis
- Safety of population, in the prevention of risk and harm
- Social design and
- Reduction in crime.

Finally, no doubt the greatest challenge is to actually achieve change at a scope and time scale required for the various problems associated with each of the five areas. Each of these five areas offers huge issues in themselves and it is easy to paint a grim picture of the economic and social costs related to each of them. The global cost of obesity has risen to $2 trillion annually (Dobbs et al., 2014), 1.25 million people die each year as a result of road traffic crashes (WHO 2016), with a further 800,000 estimate death related to particulate matter from transport and energy, which also contribute significant carbon dioxide emissions accelerating climate change. The reduction in carbon dioxide equivalent emissions suggested to overt catastrophic climate change is in the order of 90%. These examples show that each of the issues and problems in these five areas are intrinsically complex and also often interlinked.

While we are not naïve enough to suggest that all of the above would disappear through shifting behaviour, we believe that design can be employed to make a significant contribution in addressing the problems and challenges which we encounter in these five areas at both an environmental and an individual level. Clune (2010) suggests that it may not always be the lack of potential solutions to redress each of these major challenges, often it is the lack of adoption of an existing desirable 'behaviour' or 'solution'. Rather than trying to design a new artefact to address a specified challenge, the solution may be in designing to encourage the adoption of pre-existing solutions (walking, cycling, air-drying clothes, eating healthier etc.). Clearly, the decision process about change starts with the planning, conception, and production of any design, e.g. whether it is enough to change user behaviour to make less use of cars, to be more responsible in their use, to buy more sustainable cars, or whether it is necessary to change the stance of companies to build fewer cars, or to build to more sustainable standards, bringing the discussion back to both ethical and strategic issues of the debate.

In response to these challenges, with this volume, we seek to provide an overview and discussion of current and key issues and positions to develop the understanding of design for behaviour change, as well as its foundations and application. For this purpose, in the following parts, we introduce and review current approaches and look at their application through relevant examples as well as ethical implications across the five areas to allow for cross-comparison and cross-fertilization.

References

Akrich, M. (1992). The de-sription of technical object. In W. Bijker & J. Law (eds.), *Shaping Technology* (pp. 205–224). Cambridge, MA: MIT Press.

Andrews, T. (2009). Design and consume to Utopia: Where industrial design went wrong. *Design Philosophy Papers*, 7(2), 71–86.

BBC. (2004, 16 November). Smoking ban proposed for England. *BBC News*. Retrieved October 25, 2016, from http://news.bbc.co.uk/2/hi/health/4014597.stm

Bellotti, F., Kapralos, B., Lee, K., Moreno-Ger, P., & Berta, R. (2013, January). *Assessment in and of serious games: An overview.* Advances in human-computer interaction – special issue on user assessment in serious games and technology-enhanced learning archive. ACM, Article No. 1.

Boks, C. (2012). Design for sustainable behaviour research challenges. In M. Matsumoto, Y. Umeda, K. Maui, & S. Fukushige (Eds.), *Design for innovative value towards a sustainable society* (pp. 328–333). Dordrecht, NL: Springer.

Bull, M. (2006). Investigating the culture of mobile listening: From Walkman to Ipod. In K. O'Hara & B. Brown (Eds.), *Consuming music together: Social and collaborative aspects of music consumption technologies* (Volume 35 of the series Computer Supported Cooperative Work) (pp. 131–149). New York: Springer.

Clune, S. (2010). Design for behavioural change. *Journal of Design Strategies*, 4(1 Spring), 68–75.

Desmet, P. M. A., & Hekkert, P. (2002). The basis of product emotions. In W. Green & P. Jordan (Eds.), *Pleasure with products: Beyond usability* (pp. 60–68). London: Taylor & Francis.

Dobbs, R., Sawers, C., Thompson, F., Manyika, J., Woetzel, J., Child, P., McKenna, S., & Spatharou, A. (2014). *Overcoming obesity: An initial economic analysis.* London: McKinsey Global Institute.

European Commission. (2013). *Implementing an action plan for design-driven innovation* [Commission Staff Working Document]. Brussels: European Commission.

Fogg, B. J. (2003). *Persuasive technology: Using computers to change what we think and do.* San Francisco: Morgan Kaufman.

Jelsma, J. (2006). Designing 'Moralized' products. In P. P. Verbeek & A. Slob (Eds.), *User behavior and technology development: Shaping sustainable relations between consumers and technologies* (pp. 221–223). Berlin: Springer.

Jordan, P. W. (2000). *Designing pleasurable products: An introduction to the new human factors.* London: Taylor & Francis.

Latour, B. (1992). Where are the missing masses? The sociology of a few Mundane artifacts. In W. Bijker & J. Law (Eds.), *Shaping technology/building society: Studies in sociotechnical change* (pp. 225–258). Cambridge, MA: MIT Press.

Lilley, D. (2009). Design for sustainable behaviour: Strategies and perceptions. *Design Studies*, 30, 704–720.

Lockton, D., Harrison, D., & Stanton, N. A. (2010). The design with intent method: A design tool for influencing user behaviour. *Applied Ergonomics*, 41(3), 382–392.

Loos, A. (1908). *Ornament and crime.* Innsbruck, reprint Vienna, 1930.

Michl, J. (1995, Winter). Form follows what. *1:50 – Magazine of the Faculty of Architecture & Town Planning* [Technion, Israel Institute of Technology, Haifa, Israel], 10, 31–20.

Moggridge, B. (2007). *Designing interactions.* Cambridge, MA: MIT Press.

Niedderer, K. (2014). Mediating mindful social interactions through design. In A. Ie, C. T. Ngnoumen, & E. Langer (Eds.), *The Wiley Blackwell handbook of mindfulness* (Volume 1, pp. 345–366). Chichester, UK: Wiley.

Norman, D. A. (1988). *The psychology of everyday things*. New York: Basic Books.

Norman, D. A. (2002). *The design of everyday things*. New York: Basic Books.

Papanek, V. (1974). *Design for the real world*. St Albans, UK: Paladin.

Pine, J., & Gilmore, J. (1999). *The experience economy*. Boston: Harvard Business School Press.

Simon, H. (1969). *The science of the arteficial*. Cambridge: MIT Press.

Susi, T., Johannesson, M., & Backlund, P. (2007). *Serious games – An overview*. Technical Report HS-IKI -TR-07–001. Sweden: School of Humanities and Informatics, University of Skövde. Retrieved 30 October 2016, from www.diva-portal.org/smash/record.jsf?pid=diva2%3A2416&dswid=2979

Szmigin, I., & Carrigan, M. (2005). Exploring the dimensions of ethical consumption. In K. M. Ekstrom & H. Brembeck (Eds.), *E – European advances in consumer research* (Vol. 7, pp. 608–613). Goteborg, Sweden: Association for Consumer Research.

Veblen, T. ([1899] 1994). *The theory of the leisure class: An economic study of institutions*, Mineola, NY: Dover Publications.

WHO (2016). *Road traffic injuries*. Retrieved August 5, 2016, from www.who.int/mediacentre/factsheets/fs358/en/

.

Part 2

Models, methods and tools for design for behaviour change

3 Introducing models, methods and tools for design for behaviour change

Kristina Niedderer, Stephen Clune and Geke Ludden

One of the core aims in compiling this book was to offer support or guidance to designers, design researchers and others with influence in the area of design who have an interest in creating change, in selecting the appropriate approaches in order to design for behavioural change. Part 2 (Chapters 3–13) presents a selection of currently available approaches across the plethora of often-competing epistemologies (worldviews), disciplines, theories and models that inform how change may come about via design. While each chapter makes an important contribution in its own right, we believe that the real value of *Design for Behavioural Change* is in reading and understanding the chapters in relation to each other. Chapters 3 and 13 therefore offer an introduction and conclusion with the purpose of framing the individual discussions in Chapters 4–12. Chapter 3 provides an overview of the different perspectives that can be brought to bear on the approaches presented in the following chapters to assist in navigating them. These include their background in the behavioural and social sciences and their integration into design, the issue of application in relation to the agency divide, and their use and contributions to designing for behaviour change. Chapter 13 offers a reflection on the similarities, connections and differences of the various approaches presented, which is summarized in form of a visual map.

Building on the behavioural and social sciences

The scope of how design can be applied to change behaviour is very broad and multidisciplinary. The interest and investigation into behavioural change has originated from, and has been a foremost prerogative of, the behavioural and social sciences. This broad area, through both research and practice, has generated and contributed to a large number of insights and frameworks which seek to explain human behaviour in different ways and through different models. However, one approach will rarely be universal to all problems, and one discipline rarely holds all the answers. Design therefore draws regularly on a variety of models from the behavioural sciences, as is evident in the following chapters.

Just as there are many different models of behaviour change in the behavioural sciences, so there are many different approaches to behaviour change in design. Thus there is no accepted unified model of human behaviour in design. Also, generally there are no 'look-up tables' for designing for behaviour change, although a number of practical guides have been developed in different domains, e.g. Grout (2007) in medical design; Crow (2000) in architectural design against crime; Nodder (2013), Wendel (2013) and Anderson (2011) in user experience design and recent attempts have been made at practical cross-disciplinary syntheses (Daae & Boks, 2014; Lidman & Renström 2011; Dolan et al., 2012; Lockton et al., 2010; Pfarr & Gregory, 2010).

In order to navigate the diverse terrain and to select successfully those models and methods that will assist in delivering the desired outcome, it is important to know and understand the variety of behavioural and related design (research) models and methods, their individual purpose and relationships and which lens each offers to look at a problem. For example, three key reference texts of design identify 177 methods that could be applied to produce insight into any one given problem (IDEO 2002; Stickdorn & Schneider, 2010; Martin & Hanington, 2012). In order to achieve a holistic view of the often complex behavioural design problems, designers and design researchers need to draw on their capacity to synthesize multiple and often conflicting perspectives into a final solution (Dorst, 2006).

It is this *application and integration* of behavioural and other models which is of practical relevance in design – how those models can be translated, applied and tested in practice through use in the real world, rather than in laboratory studies. Box and Draper's view (1987: 424) that "essentially, all models are wrong, but some are useful" can be helpful in considering which approach(es) to apply. In the discussion of the selected models and related methods, we are therefore looking for the 'useful' parts and specifically how these might be applied in a setting beyond the academic world to drive innovation and lasting behaviour change.

Applying design for behaviour change and the context–cognition continuum

Considering the 'usefulness' or purpose, behavioural methods in design can be broadly grouped into two distinct but interrelated schools of thought using the agency structure divide, which includes the cognition-based individualistic rational choice theories and the context-related social structuralist theories. The individualistic rational choice theories of behavioural change (which have arguably been dominant) place agency with an individual to act. Models following these theories are founded on three broad principles: choice is rational, the individual is the appropriate choice of analysis and behaviours are self-interested (Jackson, 2005). The social structuralist theorists suggest that the person is not the appropriate level for analysis. Instead, behaviours in many instances can be viewed as consequences of societal norms and expectations that are held in place by the systems of provision and social structures that the individual lives within.

This divide builds on Clark's identification that change falls into approaches that primarily address the individual and those that address the context (Clark, 2010). This divide in behaviour change theory can be seen to date back to Lewin's (1935) early understanding of behaviour, that a person's behaviour (B) is a function of his or her own personality, or other 'internal' factors (P) and the physical and social environment (E) $B = f(P, E)$. On this basis, Clark (2010) has proposed the division of approaches into those that primarily address the *cognition* of the individual and those which address the *context* outside the individual. This divide can be further illustrated through Simon's metaphor of a pair of scissors (1990). Both 'blades' shape behaviour, but a model or technique will often concentrate on either individual cognition (mind, individualistic rational choice models) that may draw more on psychological approaches or on context (environment, social structuralism theories) that may draw more on a sociological approach and understanding of change. Chapters 4–12 introduce approaches across the agency spectrum that variously address the cognitive, the contextual or, to varying degrees, both.

The 'agency structure' divide in behavioural change theory is relevant for design because design has the potential to operate across this spectrum. At the individual level, design has a direct connection to the individual via the hybrid human–machine interactions, or readiness-to-hand (e.g. Heidegger's hammer [Heidegger, 1962]) of artefacts that physically constrain or enable actions. At a social structuralist level, design can be seen to reinforce the broader systemic structures and norms that provision society and within which individuals act (e.g. Latour, 2000). In this way "social practices and technological artefacts shape and are shaped by one another" (Smith & Stirling, 2007: 351).

We refer to this divide as the 'context-cognition continuum' in the discussion of design for behavioural change approaches, to categorize them in relation to how they may be attempting to influence change. For example, there are approaches that focus strongly on assisting individuals to navigate their way through a world that is scripting them to operate in a way that is problematic from an environmental perspective. These approaches tend to be situated at the cognition-based end of the spectrum, which traditionally has drawn on psychological models dealing with the individual. By contrast, sociology-based approaches tend to focus on trying to shift the broader structural and social environment so that the default actions are the most desirable, by primarily focusing on the environmental context. In some scholarly circles these may be seen as opposing worldviews. This may also be interpreted as looking at designing for change from differing scales, the micro focus of human-product interaction, compared to a macro focus on the environment and social interactions. We do not see this as an either/or approach since design operates, and is influential across a multitude of levels. Rather, we argue for the benefit of integrating them and seeing design problems from multiple perspectives to address them holistically.

Different uses and contributions of designing for behaviour change approaches

Within an holistic perspective, and in order to identify suitable approach(es), it is important for designers and anyone else concerned with behaviour change to identify where he or she would like to intervene, and from which perspective or worldview he or she will approach the design problem and the direction of change. Further, it is important to provide approaches for ideation and conceptual development of design ideas as well as processes by which designers may translate and realize them. Different models or methods may be appropriate depending on what the problem, and the problem-context, is, or where the designer is at within the design process. We identified three categories that are useful to help practitioners with the selection and application of appropriate theories and methods. These strategies attempt to do the following: (1) provide new insights into a situation to be changed, (2) approaches to assist in ideation and conceptual development or (3) provide a more holistic process for designers to design by.

These three categories are useful to help with the selection and application of appropriate theories and methods, and we offer them as yet another set of perspectives for reading the following chapters and we discuss them in Chapter 13.

As always, creating categories is artificial, and many of the approaches and methods discussed will fit two or even all three of these categories while they may only be discussed in one. Nevertheless we believe that the groups are useful in highlighting some of the most relevant issues, and hopefully the readers may extend that discussion in their minds to all those parts that we have not been able to cover in this book.

1. New insights into a situation to be changed

Generating new insights into how we see the world is a core concept in several of the following chapters, aiming to gain a better understanding of the activity or situation that is to be shifted, and in understanding design's role in it. Tromp and Hekkert (Chapter 12), Kuijer (Chapter 10), Clune (Chapter 11) and Dorrestijn (Chapter 4) offer a strong critique of contemporary society, and how design and technology may be influencing our everyday behaviours. For example, Tromp and Hekkert observe that contemporary researchers have "illuminated how mundane objects like doors and light switches prescribe specific actions, how the television and the microwave have co-construed family life, and how Tupperware or Barbie shapes our culture and sub-cultures" (p. 138). By acknowledging and understanding the hidden influence of design, we may be better positioned to design more appropriate intervention strategies in places that we may not first have considered as relevant.

Dorrestijn's product impact tool is a useful tool in providing a framework to interrogate existing design solutions in the world to assess both their influence and how they are impacting the individual. Kuijer's chapter on social practice theory and Clune's chapter on ontological design suggest that understanding historical trajectories over a significant period of time is one mechanism to gain a better understanding of how our contemporary present may have come about. This long-term approach assists in seeing the influence of design over time. As Dorrestijn (2012) states: "If one looks at history, then the bigger the timespan becomes, the smaller the influence of individual people seems to matter . . . Technical determinism concerns the determination of history by material and technical circumstances" (p. 1). These approaches therefore relate to our understanding of design's influence on the wider environmental context, rather than to understanding people's individual actions and behaviours.

Other chapters in this part are aimed at providing a greater insight and understanding into the individual's way of seeing and being in the world. They focus on a better understanding of an individual's cognitive decision-making processes, motivations and aspirations, and on how design might influence these, such as Lilley et al.'s use of goal framing and the theory of interpersonal behaviour (Chapter 5), and Ludden's use of the transtheoretical model of behaviour change (Chapter 8).

Many of the chapters implicitly suggest how we may create new designs to *assist* in creating change. An alternate concept of attentiveness through mindfulness is proposed by Niedderer in Chapter 9, creating awareness by disruption 'relating to the pragmatic or symbolic function. This must relate to the feature of the object or situation to be reflected on' (p. 110). This insight is significant as designers have a long history of creating change via the introduction of new designs and technology, but there is less of a history of actively *disrupting* existing ones. Although history is littered with disruptive technologies, usually these have been developed for the purposes of technical advance rather than to make a specific and responsible behavioural intervention, explicitly considering what may need to be disrupted to achieve change is relatively novel in design practice.

2. Processes to design by

If we acknowledge the central role of people within behaviour change, we must understand design as a social process at the heart of which are people. In order to integrate the human perspective within the design process, design for behaviour change has been look-ing to the social sciences and psychology. Adoption and integration of these approaches into the design process can happen in different ways. Several chapters offer an integrated approach in the form of a standalone guide or process that may potentially replace (part of the) traditional design process, while others offer a 'tandem approach' that may work alongside established design processes.

An example of the first is the approach by the Loughborough team (Lilley et al., Chap-ter 5) who propose a process of: "1. Understanding of the user's actions in context; 2. Selecting a behavioural target (where to intervene); 3. Selecting (or applying) a behav-ioural intervention strategy and 4. Evaluating the behavioural interventions" (p. 40) to enable the targeted interventions to be developed. In a similar fashion, Niedderer inte-grates mindfulness and a traditional design process approach in: (1) Identifying the design problem, (2) Identifying mindful solutions and (3) Implementing mindful solutions in design. These processes can be seen to follow a traditional, generic, problem-solving pro-cess but with integrated stages to take account of the human side.

Several of the chapters utilize the 'tandem' approach, attempting to provide guidance on how to match or select intervention strategies that are appropriate for the context of the situation. The Transtheoretical model of Behaviour Change offers insight into the stages that an individual has to go through in order to make a change. These stages are as follows: (1) Precontemplation, (2) Contemplation, (3) Preparation, (4) Action, (5) Maintenance and (6) Termination (Ludden, Chapter 8). In her chapter, Ludden posits that for each new intervention, specific design strategies are required for the different stages.

Also focussing on matching intervention strategies to problem situations, Daae and Boks's toolkit is concerned with the distribution of control in designing behavioural change interventions that stretches from where the user is in control to make a conscious decision, to where the product is in control (Chapter 7), and which shows parallels with the axis of influence drawn on in the Loughborough model (Lilley, 2007). Daae and Boks offer a useful synthesis table of Design for Behavioural Change (DfBC) strategies across what is termed the distribution of control (Chapter 7: p. 76), which we draw on in the conclusion to this Part to provide an overview map of the different approaches covered in this book and to illustrate their relationships.

3. Approaches to ideation and conceptual development

The final way that we see the chapters contributing to design for change is how they could be viewed as offering inspirational approaches that may assist in providing new insights and prompts for the conceptual generation phase of the design process. The toolkits from Lockton (Chapter 6) and Daee and Boks (Chapter 7) may be used in a similar capacity to Osborne's checklist during brainstorming (Osborne, 1963) or De Bono's thinking caps (De Bono, 1985). The toolkits enable designers to systematically think through a range of conceptual solutions by looking at the problem with differing lenses. This results in an increased number of conceptual solutions that may contribute to the situation you are seeking to change.

Such experimental play during conceptual development also provides new insight into the problem to be changed if following Wertheimer's (1959) approach of productive thinking. Wertheimer (1959) saw problem solving as grasping the structural relationships of a situation and reorganizing them until possible solutions are perceived. He maintained that this mental reorganization of the situation is achieved by applying various mental tools, which still persist today in creativity tools. These mental tools include trying to re-describe the problem in another way and the use of analogy as a way of shifting the mental paradigm. By reformulating the problem, new solutions become available. Conceptualizing new solutions may also encourage us to view the problem differently. Hence having multiple approaches to designing for change assists in unlocking possible solutions and insights into the problem.

Conclusion

We hope that the discussion of the background and possible perspectives of analysis and application for design for behaviour change approaches will be useful to the reader in reading and understanding the following chapters. Due to the complexity of issues inherent in each approach, we have grouped the following nine chapters roughly by area of application. The first four chapters of Part 2 provide a broad overview of general models and tools for how design for behaviour change theories can influence issues of sustainability; this is followed by two chapters that present theories on design for behaviour change related to health and wellbeing; which is then followed by three chapters that draw heavily upon theories from sociology and psychology, as well as the experience of being influenced. Throughout the following chapters, the reader will variously find surfacing the three issues discussed earlier: how the content of the chapters assists in generating new insights, provides processes to design by and assists in ideation and conceptual development for design for behavioural change. These ideas are discussed further and summarized in the conclusion to Chapter 13.

References

Anderson, S. P. (2011). *Seductive interaction design: Creating playful, fun and effective user experiences*. Berkeley, CA: New Riders.

Box, G. E. P., & Draper, N. R. (1987) *Empirical model-building and response surfaces*. New York: John Wiley & Sons.

Clark, G. L. (2010). Human nature, the environment, and behaviour: Explaining the scope and geographical scale of financial decision-making. *Geografiska Annaler: Series B, Human Geography, 92*(2), 159–173.

Crow, T. D. (2000). *Crime prevention through environmental design: Applications of architectural*. Woburn, MA: Butterworth-Heinemann.

Daae, J. Z., & Boks, C. (2014). Dimensions of behaviour change. *Journal of Design Research, 12*(3), 145–172. doi: 10.1504/jdr.2014.064229

De Bono, E. (1985). *Six thinking hats: An essential approach to business management*. London: Little, Brown & Company.

Dolan, P., Hallsworth, M., Halpern, D., King, D., Metcalfe, R., & Vlaevf, I. (2012). Influencing behaviour the MINDSPACE way. *Journal of Economic Psychology, 33*(1), 264–277.

Dorrestijn, S. (2012). *Product impact tool - technical determinism*. Retrieved May 16, 2017, from http://stevendorrestijn.nl/tool/english.html#/technisch-determinisme

Dorst, K. (2006). *Understanding design: 175 reflections on being a designer*. Amsterdam: BIS Publishing.

Grout, J. (2007). *Mistake-proofing the design of health care processes*. Rockville: Agency for Healthcare Research and Quality.

Heidegger, M. (1962). *Being and time*. New York: Harper & Row Publishers.

IDEO. (2002). *IDEO method cards*. San Francisco: William Stout Architectural Books.

Jackson, T. (2005). *'Motivating Sustainable Consumption': A review of evidence on consumer behaviour and behavioural change a report to the Sustainable Development Research Network*. Surrey: University of Surrey, Centre for Environmental Strategy.

Latour, B. (2000). When things strike back: a possible contribution of 'science studies' to the social sciences. *The British Journal of Sociology, 51*(1), 107–123. doi: 10.1111/j.1468-4446.2000.00107

Lewin, K. (1935). *A dynamic theory of personality – selected papers.* New York and London: McGraw-Hill Book Company, Inc.

Lidman, K., & Renström, S. (2011). *How to design for sustainable behaviour? A review of design strategies and an empirical study of four product concepts* (Master Thesis). Chalmers University of Technology, Sweden.

Lilley, D. (2007). *Designing for behavioural change: Reducing the social impacts of product use through design* (PhD Thesis). Department of Design and Technology, Loughborough University, Loughborough, UK.

Lockton, D., Harrison, D., & Stanton, N. A. (2010). *Design with Intent toolkit: 101 patterns for influencing behaviour through design.* Retrieved October 8, 2012, from http://research.danlockton.co.uk/toolkit/designwithintent_cards_1.0_draft_300dpi.pdf

Martin, B., & Hanington, B. (2012). *Universal methods of design: 100 ways to research complex problems, develop innovative ideas, and design effective solutions.* Quayside: Rockport Publishers.

Nodder, C. (2013). *Evil by design: Interaction design to lead us into temptation.* Indianapolis, IN: Wiley.

Osborne, A. (1963). *Applied imagination.* New York: Scribner's.

Pfarr, N., & Gregory, J. (2010). Cognitive biases and design research: Using insights from behavioural economics and cognitive psychology to re-evaluate design research methods. *Proceedings of DRS2010 Conference.* Montreal, Canada.

Simon, H. A. (1990). Invariants of human behavior. *Annual Review of Psychology, 41*, 1–19.

Smith, A., & Stirling, A. (2007). Moving outside or inside? Objectification and reflexivity in the governance of socio-technical systems. *Journal of Environmental Policy & Planning, 9*(3–4), 351–373. doi: 10.1080/15239080701622873

Stickdorn, M., & Schneider, J. (2010). *This is service design thinking.* Innsbruck: BIS Publishers.

Wendel, S. (2013). *Designing for behavior change: Applying psychology and behavioral economics.* Newton, MA: O'Reilly Media.

Wertheimer, M. (1959). *Productive thinking.* New York: Harper and Brothers.

4 The Product Impact Tool

The case of the Dutch public transport chip card

Steven Dorrestijn

The Product Impact Tool: introduction

This chapter presents the Product Impact Tool and illustrates its use with the case of the "OV chip card" (Dutch public transport e-paying system). The core of the Product Impact Tool is a model that contains examples of the different ways in which technology can impact people's lives. In addition, it includes workshop session guidelines for applying the model (Dorrestijn, 2012a, ch. 8). On the web version of the Product Impact Tool, which is under continuous development, introductory texts and movie clips are available as well as the aforementioned guidelines and materials.[1]

The Product Impact Tool originated from a research project in which industrial designers, design researchers and researchers in the philosophy of technology worked together to develop methods to "design for usability" (see Kuijk, 2012). In this context, a subproject about the impact of products on users investigated the question whether knowledge about this impact could help to anticipate and avoid problems of usability and technology acceptance and to design products in a way that they deliberately guide and change user behaviour.

This focus originates from reflections on work by a number of philosophers, historians, and anthropologists. For example, philosopher Langdon Winner (1986) revealed how the overpasses to Long Island in New York were intentionally designed very low by city planner Robert Moses to prevent buses from entering this area. In this way, the overpasses acted as a vehicle for Moses's political intention to keep away poor, black people. Winner used this as an example to show that "artefacts have politics". Media philosopher Vilém Flusser expressed something similar when he said that designing is an act of throwing "obstacles in other people's way" (Flusser, 1999, 59). Anthropologist and philosopher Bruno Latour asserted that we cannot understand human action and morality if we do not acknowledge the moral significance of things and he therefore saw behaviour constraints by technical products as "delegated morality" (Latour, 1992).

While these reflections comment on the role of artefacts and products per se, in order to implement knowledge about product impact on user behaviour in design, there is a need for concepts and frameworks aimed towards application (see e.g. Verbeek, 2005). On the side of the design discourse, one pioneer in this respect was Donald Norman (1988), who introduced the concept of "affordance" (from ecological psychology) to analyze what behaviours a product affords into usability studies. More recently the approaches of "persuasive technology" by BJ Fogg (2003) and of "nudge" by Thaler and Sunstein (2008) have both met much acclaim and there is further recent research in the field of design for behaviour change (as this volume testifies). The Product Impact Tool aims to combine such design-oriented approaches with the philosophical perspective.

Both from the perspective of design and from a philosophical perspective, the issue of behaviour-influencing technology raises pressing questions of a broad social and ethical nature, which this chapter also seeks to address: How does technology mediate human existence? Is it the responsibility of the designer to determine how people live and use technical products? Is it morally acceptable to influence people by means of technology? The project's aim of integrating knowledge about the impact of products on users and methods to improve usability is therefore bracketed by the larger philosophical question of how the relation between humans and technology can be understood and improved.

The contribution of the Product Impact Tool to design for behaviour change is that it offers a broad interdisciplinary collection of relevant concepts and examples. An important characteristic of the tool is that it combines both reflective and applied approaches. The scope of application is equally broad, ranging from improving product usability and acceptance to addressing ethical issues and social responsibility.

The Product Impact Tool: model

The core of the Product Impact Tool is a model covering a repertoire of effects of technology ordered according to four different modes of interaction.

Modes of interaction

If technical products influence users, the question can be asked "from which side" technology affects them. In this way, four modes of interaction can be distinguished, which are represented by the four quadrants of the diagram: before-the-eye, to-the-hand, behind-the-back, and above-the-head (Figure 4.1). These terms correspond to the following terms more common to the fields of design and exact sciences: cognitive, physical, background, and abstract. A theoretical grounding of why these four modes of interactions were chosen follows in a later section.

Before-the-eye is the mode of interaction that applies when technologies address the user's *cognition*. In this case, technology functions as a carrier of meaning or information. Products offer signs that inform our decision-making faculty. Think of light and sound signals, texts, shapes that are recognized as buttons and handles. In the model, the eye is the symbol for this connection, but the other senses can act as information receivers too.

To-the-hand interaction takes place through *physical* contact or affect on the senses. These most obvious influences of technology on humans are direct effects and affects on the human body and behaviour. Fences and gates may be archetypal examples. The hand symbolizes this interaction mode.

Behind-the-back designates influences yielded by technology in the wider environment or *background* which work only indirectly, without direct user-product interaction before-the-eye or to-the-hand. In this quadrant one finds in particular historical, geographical, and sociological insights about technology.

The *above-the-head* quadrant comprises a summary of generalizing views on technology, *abstracting* from concrete examples. These grand philosophical and ethical ideas do not literally make contact with the body, but are positioned above-the-head in the model.

Repertoire of effects

The modes of interaction framework serve to visually frame a repertoire of effects of technology. The categorization of three types of effect in every quadrant of the model

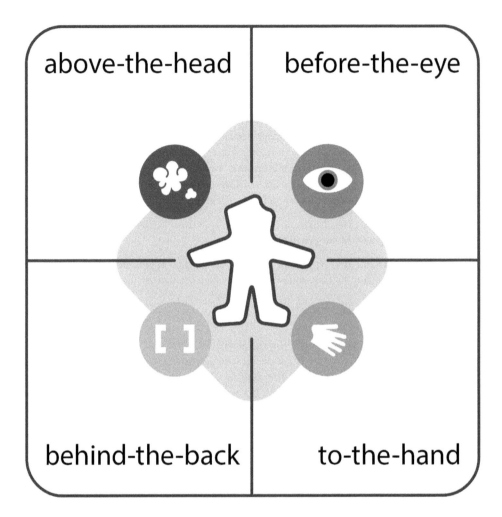

Figure 4.1 Modes of interaction in the Product Impact Model

Source: Steven Dorrestijn.

(twelve effects in total, see Figure 4.2) is the result of an attempt to balance comprehensiveness with clarity. Most of the terms used are common in thinking about technology and design, even in everyday language. References are given only in the case of literal adoption of examples or concepts. A discussion, including further references to examples and relevant concepts in the different theoretical disciplines can be found elsewhere (see Dorrestijn, 2012a, ch. 4; 2012b).

Before-the-eye: guidance, persuasion, and image

The first type of influence in this quadrant is *guidance* towards intended use. In design, this effect is addressed by aiming for self-evident forms and colours through product semantics

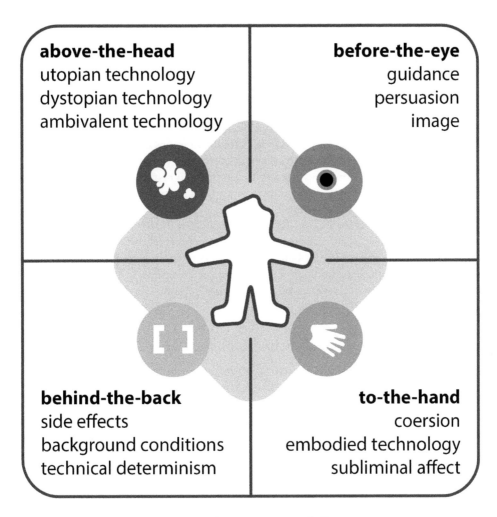

above-the-head
utopian technology
dystopian technology
ambivalent technology

before-the-eye
guidance
persuasion
image

behind-the-back
side effects
background conditions
technical determinism

to-the-hand
coersion
embodied technology
subliminal affect

Figure 4.2 Product Impact Model with modes of interaction and effects

Source: Steven Dorrestijn.

(e.g. Norman, 1988; Boess & Kanis, 2007), or by adding arrows and text, etc. The influence on human action can also be more intrusive: *persuasion* through design, termed after "persuasive technology" (Fogg, 2003). In this case technology not only guides towards proper use but is designed with the aim of interfering in people's behaviour, as in the case of pop-up banners on websites that, for example, persuade people to "buy today" or "click here". In either case, technology addresses the human decision-making process. A third type of effect is the expression of people's self-*image* or lifestyle by design. For example, products like clothing or cars (Miller, 2010: 104) allow people to shape and express their identity.

The mechanisms collected in this quadrant are drawn from the intersection of behavioural sciences and design. These insights have been gaining an increasingly widespread application in current practice in design. Think of design for usability, branding, and social design.

To-the-hand: coercion, embodied technology, and subliminal affect

The first type of influence in this quadrant is *coercion*. This is perhaps the most obvious of all impacts of technology. Examples are a fence to control people's access or a speed bump forcing car drivers to slow down (Latour, 1992).[2] A further category, *embodied technologies* (e.g. Ihde, 1990), concerns abilities such as writing with a pencil, riding a bike, or playing a musical instrument. Such activities are unthinkable without the associated artefacts, which typically must be handled with skill. Developing techniques of use (Tenner, 2003) involves much practice, but once accomplished the discipline of learning is soon forgotten. The objects involved come to be experienced as natural extensions of our body and smoothly integrated in our routine behaviours. *Subliminal affect* is the type of effect of being attracted or repelled by only half-conscious sensations, for example marketers advise supermarkets to introduce the smell of fresh bread and coffee to enhance people's experience of hospitality and influence their buying mood.

Influences by physical interaction are widely applied in the form of technical obstructions such as fences, locks, etc. Compared to product impacts that address the user's cognition, such physical interference in behaviours may seem more intrusive and remind one of an era of mechanical technology. Yet, the upsurge of interfaces based on touch and gestures shows that physical interaction remains fully important in the era of information and ambient intelligence.

Behind-the-back: side effects, background conditions, and technical determinism

Technologies or designs commonly have *side effects*. A product may perform its intended function well, but in the second instance the advantages with respect to the primary function may be undone by disadvantages on another level. Second, the successful functioning of a product is dependent on *background conditions*. A product may require an infrastructure for maintenance or provisioning, or the operation requires prescience and skills. *Technical determinism* means that technical developments, instead of responding to existing needs, may have a dynamic of their own and create or transform human values and needs.

Because this type of influence is indirect and because the environment extends endlessly, it is impossible to simply apply behind-the-back effects. But at least acknowledging the context can help to control risks. System engineering and designing product-service combinations are examples of actually approaching product and wider context together.

Above-the-head: utopian technology, dystopian technology, and ambivalent technology

What is, all these concrete impacts taken together, the meaning of technology as a whole? Does it liberate or control humanity? Is it desirable or dangerous to develop behaviour-influencing products? Claims on the meaning of technology in general are very diverse and often contradictory. *Utopian technology* denotes the very optimistic belief in progress by means of technology (the typical view in modernity). *Dystopian technology* refers to the opposite view, the fear of domination (prevailing in the twentieth century with the nuclear bomb and ecological crisis). The view of *ambivalent technology* is the prevailing view in contemporary philosophy of technology. While a profound hybridity of humans and technology is acknowledged, this is not evaluated with either euphoria or despair, but as always ambivalent.

The use of these generalizing ideas, abstracted from tangible and concrete examples, is not to materialize them in design. They do however inform thinking about technology, as in drawing future scenarios.[3] Moreover, these general views often figure in controversies about technology. That makes this quadrant in particular helpful for ethical reflection and discussion.

Theoretical backgrounds

The Product Impact Model has a background in research on "technical mediation". This term is used by scholars in the philosophy of technology and associated disciplines to denote that humans do not simply use technical products, but that technology has deeply transformed and marked human existence (McLuhan, 2003; Ihde, 1990; Feenberg, 2002; Kockelkoren, 2003; Verbeek, 2005). A book title by Peter-Paul Verbeek (2005) indicates that such research is about "*what things do*". Questioning the impact of products on users and society is a good starting point for translating technical mediation research to practical application and has led to the Product Impact Tool. This section discusses the theoretical position and background of this framework. What kind of model or theory about the impact of things is necessary and achievable?

The interaction and impacts between technical objects and people are, to an important degree, human and social phenomena which escape a fully objective description by some mechanistic theory. For, one can never altogether see through oneself. And by knowing about ourselves and acting upon that knowledge we also change ourselves. In terms inspired by the philosopher Michel Foucault (2000) a theory about *Product Impact* has a self-reflexive character: it concerns our attempt to understand and take care of our own condition of being regarding the impacts of technology. The categories of effects in the Product Impact Tool model should therefore be seen as expressions of *what we think things do to us*. This phrasing adopts Verbeek's notion of *what things do*, but adds an explicit reminder about the reflexive and performative character of product impact knowledge. As the tool aims to offer a repertoire of recognizable effects, rather than a complete explanatory theory, an advantage is that it allows us to use and compare examples and concepts from different times and across the disciplines.

The character of self-investigation is expressed in the Product Impact Tool Model by the question from which sides the impacts of technologies influence us. The approach and terms for discerning the four modes of interaction are inspired by phenomenological research in philosophy and media studies, in particular by Vilém Flusser and his posthumous book on "becoming human", *Vom Subjekt zum Projekt: Menschwerdung* (1994). Flusser reconstructs through historical-anthropological findings, etymological traces, and admirable philosophical imagination how humans first became humans by learning to use their hands and feet (*Vorderhand*). In a later stage, casting an eye (*Augenblick*) became more important for the human way of being in the world. This second more cognitive and analytical posture to the world eventually superseded the earlier physically immersed way of being.

The categorization also reflects different notions from Don Ihde's phenomenology of human-technology relations, and thereby the whole phenomenological history that Ihde synthesizes (Ihde, 1990, 72). To-the-hand reflects Ihde's "embodiment relation" (as well as Merleau-Ponty's "embodiment" and Heidegger's "readiness-to-hand"). The term *before-the-eye* is indebted to McLuhan's notion of "an eye for an ear" which is his abbreviation of his comparison of tactile-acoustic space and visual space (cf. McLuhan, 2003, 115). It equally reflects Ihde's "alterity" and "hermeneutic" relations and Heidegger's analysis of "presence-at-hand". The behind-the-back category resembles Ihde's "background" relation, and refers to McLuhan's notion of mediation by our technical environments. The "above-the-head" quadrant brings the non-empirical, generalizing philosophical conceptions of how technology influences us within the scope of the model of interaction modes. This reflects Hans Achterhuis's (2002) notion of a "utopia/dystopia syndrome" in philosophical debates about technology and his call for an "empirical turn" to complement abstract analysis.

The Product Impact Tool is not a theory in the sense of explaining human–technology interaction in some mechanistic way. Still it can help structure anyone's thinking about the effects of technology by summarizing a variety of conceptualizations and examples that researchers have thought of previously. That it allows comparing examples from different theoretical backgrounds and historical periods is a benefit of this model.

The case of the OV chip card

The public transport e-paying system in the Netherlands (OV chip card) serves as a good case to illustrate the use of the Product Impact Tool. The introduction saw a wide range of issues, from usability problems to important ethical concern about security, privacy, and freedom. I will show how the Product Impact Model helps to assess the OV chip card system as well as to imagine redesign options.

The OV chip card is a contactless card that employs radio-frequency identification technology (RFID). Travellers all need to have such a card and they need to check in and out every time they get on or off a train, bus or tramway. Buses and trams are equipped with a reader at the entrance and exits. In the case of the train and metro the readers are in the stations, either on the platforms close to the trains or at the entrance of the stations (Figure 4.3). Some stations are gated at the entrance, so that people have to check in before they go to the platforms. The OV chip card has been introduced nationwide in all the public transport companies' buses, trams, the subway systems, and trains.

The introduction has seen many problems, which have made the news headlines many times. In 2007, the Dutch Data Protection Agency (CBP) investigated the handling of data by the Amsterdam public transport company and concluded that too much data was collected and stored. Data was also insufficiently protected, for example against consumer profiling for personalized publicity (CPB 2007).

In 2008, computer security experts from Nijmegen University hacked into the RFID technology of the card (van den Broek, 2008). They were able to read and duplicate cards and to open gates. This prompted a lot of debate in society and parliament. The OV chip card was almost abandoned (see van't Hof, 2011).

Around 2009, when the public at large was introduced to the system, practical user problems came to the fore and attracted a lot of public attention. The main issue was the problem of *forgetting to check out* (a new and extra procedure compared to the old paper ticket system). In September 2010, it appeared that the public transport companies took half a billion Euros per month in deposit money due to "incomplete transactions" (Koot, 2010).

Meanwhile, the OV chip card has almost fully replaced the paper ticket. Moreover, the security debate has somewhat faded away. But forgetting to check out continues to be an issue. Research in 2014 showed that incomplete transactions led to 16 billion Euros cashed deposit money in a year (Schepers & Zwart, 2014).

Forgetting to check out: design for usability

OV chip card developers have greatly underestimated the practical obstacles of users having to learn the new travel procedures, and to adapt to the new behaviour required by

Figure 4.3 Changing trains between different companies requires a check-out and check-in

Source: Steven Dorrestijn.

the new system. The most critical issue appears to be that people forget to check out. The user-influencing effects in the before-the-eye and to-the-hand quadrants are helpful for conceiving concrete options for design improvements. Applying (cognitive) signs or (physical) constraints is always the most obvious way of introducing behaviour-guiding and changing elements. Alternating between the two options is a good strategy in brainstorming about redesign. So, how could assessing and redesigning cognitive and physical product impacts help?

To-the-hand

Smooth interaction, coming with a natural experience, is achieved when the chip card and other components of the system become embedded in routines of travellers (*embodied technology*). But even if the procedures and devices allow for a smooth interaction, especially during the initial period of habituation, users need extra help and other types of product impact can be helpful.

   An obvious strategy is physical *coercion*. The checkpoint gates applied in many subway stations and increasingly in train stations can be seen as belonging to this category. While the promise of coercion is that nothing can go wrong, it often happens that the problems people experience actually get worse if things still do go wrong.[4] Furthermore, coercion generally decreases user-friendliness and can be perceived as an infringement of personal freedom.

Before-the-eye

Besides physical coercion, the effects of *guidance* and *persuasion* are useful options. The advertising campaigns and intercom announcements on trains and buses that instruct travellers about the new procedures are examples of *guidance*. Another aid, which is better integrated in the design of the system itself is the pink colour that is part of the corporate style of the OV chip card. This does help to *guide* OV chip card users to the check in/out points. However, the system can and should be made to guide travellers much more strongly towards the right procedures. In the first years, shortage of checkpoints and sometimes illogical placement *misled* rather than *guided* people. The system made people *forget* rather than *remember* to check in and out.

   Another strategy could be to attempt to redesign elements of the OV chip card system in a way that they teach people a lesson, encourage, or seduce them (beyond merely providing guiding information). In the aforementioned workshops, participants considered how the card and gates could be made *persuasive* by making the interaction more challenging. Introducing a game element, "every tenth passenger travels for free", was one of the ideas. Turning the presentation of the card to the checkpoint into a more interesting procedure, by requiring a dance-like gesture with the card, was another (somewhat frivolous) proposal.

Freedom and privacy: societal and ethical issues

Whereas the right side of the Product Impact Tool model helps to assess and improve the concrete design and interface of products, the left side rather helps to bring up acceptance and ethical issues. The most important issues here have to do with privacy and freedom. An assessment in these dimensions may not yield concrete redesign options, but it can help to understand the context which needs to be taken into account when redesigning options for usability.

Behind-the-back

The electronic and radio frequency technology of the OV chip card is largely invisible and functioning *behind-the-back*. There are vast technical and organizational infrastructures that function as *background conditions* of the card and checkpoints. The usability issues of the card are to an important degree caused by the fact that the background infrastructure is far from perfect. The initial lack of checkpoints was already mentioned. Also, website procedures of subscription – to get the card working in the first place – were very complex (quite the opposite of the usability and flexibility that the system promised). Online skills and acquaintance with the registration procedures are therefore another background condition which can hinder for example elderly people and foreign travellers.

This brings us to *side effects* of the system. That elderly people and foreign travellers experience difficulties with access are unintended consequences. Undoubtedly, it was also unforeseen that, as a result of the system, travellers can now be seen queuing not only to get in but also to get out of buses, trams, and train stations. This interferes with the promise of fast and easy payment. While a chip card check-in replaces ticket stamping by the driver, travellers are focussed on the card reader, with the effect that many people pass the driver without greeting. Impairment of personal contact is a common social side effect of Information and Communications Technology, or Technologies (ICT's). *Let devices come along but not in between*, seems therefore a widely applicable design motto.

A further consideration of *behind-the-back* is whether the OV chip card responds to human needs and values, or whether this technology rather creates and changes those (*technical determinism*). Considering how the e-payment system transforms our needs and the values of privacy and freedom helps understanding acceptance issues, although it also precludes unambiguous moral evaluations. The OV chip card promises ease of use: fast and easy checking-in and checking-out, jumping on and off trains, switching between train and subway, etcetera, while payment proceeds automatically. This flexibility indeed fits a trend of our time, conditioned by all kinds of network technologies in our environment. We have permanent access to the Internet for the weather forecast, banking, e-mailing etcetera. As soon as people become used to the e-paying card, the activity structure of pre-planning a trip for the whole day, buying a ticket accordingly, and then sticking to the plan for the day, will very soon begin to feel outdated. Freedom is increasingly being associated with flexibility.

One can forecast that, in the age of flexibility, the ticket controls on the train will increasingly be experienced as outdated and paternalistic, referring to a 1950s style of discipline, a form of morality from the past. The old paper ticket was as much as the new chip card part of a regime that structures our behaviour, and that conditions particular experiences of freedom and privacy. Even the fact that the new system still requires people to go searching for a checkpoint belongs to the old structure of moral behaviour and does not appear congruent with the new trend of flexibility and ease. People will be prepared to connect their OV chip card to their bank account for automatic payment, but will be annoyed if instead of the promised flexibility and automatic payment they still get confronted with difficult and demanding procedures for checking in and out.

Above-the-head

The issues discussed from a historical and empirical perspective under technical determinism, can also be considered from a philosophical and ethical perspective. As already mentioned, there is a tension between the idea of eternal values for philosophical and ethical evaluation and determinism by concrete, temporal developments. Moreover, if some technology supports or rather threatens a certain value is often debated. In the case of the OV chip card, the ambiguity of the meaning of technology indeed comes to the fore or sometimes even divides a single person or group. Hackers of the card make allusions all the time to the fear of a "definitive demise of privacy" as well as the need for an "absolute secure chip". The latter idea, of a completely secure and controllable technology, is an example of the view of *utopian technology*. The counterpart, the view of *dystopian technology*, marks the claim that the chip card system would be the next step towards Big Brother.

Understanding the variety of these general ideas helps to understand debates about specific cases. Acknowledgment of how different people, for example the engineers and the users of a system have different stances is paramount for successful adoption of a technology. Ideas about the technology at an abstract level tend to dominate the debate about the public transport card. Such debates are all important but often also without a definitive conclusion. For that reason, the success or failure of the OV chip card will probably not so much depend on this debate about absolute security, but more on the user appropriation and solving of usability issues in practice. The recognition of both pros and cons to every technology and the importance of finding balance in practice is characteristic of the view of *ambivalent technology*.

Conclusions about the OV chip card case

The OV chip card is a good showcase for many of the effects of the Product Impact Tool, from the more practical effects on the right side of the model to the general views in the upper left quadrant. The debate surrounding the OV chip card has caused privacy and security issues to dominate the news. Security and privacy obviously deserve attention, but it is typical that this debate has taken precedence over attention to practical use problems. Difficulties in concrete interactions with the system are equally important. Although the new ticketing systems promise an increase of flexibility and comfort to travellers, there have been so many practical obstacles to this potentially great advantage that, during the introduction, the system was a usability nightmare. These more practical issues have been discussed and have been highlighted by zooming in with *to-the-hand* and *before-the-eye* quadrants of the model. The Product Impact Tool allows one zoom in and zoom out with the different dimensions of impacts and to understand usability problems in relation to acceptance issues and ethical debate.

At some point a spokesman for the Dutch Railways announced on TV that they wished to increase surveillance on trains, to make sure that 90 percent of people would be motivated to check in and out. This seems an impossible attempt to maintain a routine of ticket buying and showing the ticket on the train that was conditioned by the old system and transfer it to the new technical environment. If more control is needed, this shows that the system fails to live up to its promise of augmented flexibility and automatic payment. An analysis of the technical environment helps to understand this problem of usability, in the broad sense of successful adaptation in user routines. The same spokesman also said that a lot more checkpoints were to be placed and routings improved. That seems a much more obvious solution for improving the chip card system, and contrary to the first proposal, shows some acknowledgement of the impact of technology on behaviour.

The Product Impact Tool and responsible innovation

The Product Impact Tool contributes to understanding human-product interaction as well as to design for behaviour change. A distinctive characteristic of the Product Impact

Tool is its broad scope, from concrete human-product interaction to social and ethical issues. It can also help to address the question of how designers can mediate how we live. The perspective of product impact gives new impetus to the responsibility of designers.

Especially in the tradition of modernistic design theory and education, social engagement used to be an important aspect of design, often with utopian traits. With the advent of postmodernism, utopian grand narratives have become suspect and seemingly abandoned. But its social engagement, even utopian striving, has not disappeared or is coming back, as is shown from titles such as *Do good: How designers can change the world* (Berman, 2009) or *Expanding architecture: Design as activism* (Bell & Wakeford, 2008). However, in both of these books, the perspective of the impact of products (technical mediation) does not play an important or precise role. Berman for example makes an appeal to "not just do good design, but to do good". The focus here is on the intention of designers. How products themselves guide and change people is not explicitly addressed. These initiatives could benefit from integration with recent work on the empirically oriented philosophy of technical mediation.

In the field of design, Victor Margolin is a design critic who offers a good starting point for fruitful collaboration of design practitioners and design philosophers. He states that the focus of design should be broadened from "products" to "the way we organize possibilities for human action" (Margolin, 2002, 228). The complementary task is to show how society and designers can cope with product impact. Margolin estimates: "A greater awareness of how products contribute to personal experience will help everyone act more consciously and decisively within the product milieu as we seek to improve the quality of our lives" (55). Instead of ignoring the impact of the product milieu or trying to overcome it, the challenge is to employ it for the purpose of improving the quality of life.

What is required is to learn more about the social effects of technology. The impact of technology should not be ignored or rejected, but acknowledged as an important topic in design. However, it should be treated in a nuanced way. To avoid exaggerated and dangerous utopian programmes as well as dystopian fears, it would be necessary to employ and further develop a more precise and ambivalent understanding of technical mediation, such as proposed by the Product Impact Tool. The challenge is to employ technology moderately and wisely for the purpose of improving the quality of life.

Acknowledgements

Special thanks for collaboration on the Product Impact Tool to Tjebbe van Eemeren, Steffi Fleige, Jonne van Belle, Tjerk Timan, Wouter Eggink, Peter-Paul Verbeek, Martine Vonk, and for financial support to Saxion University of Applied Sciences, ClickNL, University of Twente.

Notes

1 Steven Dorrestijn, Product Impact Tool, www.stevendorrestijn.nl/tool
2 Tromp et al. (2011) term such an influence "decisive design" and employ "coercive design" for penalties other than by physical force. Thus they use the notion of decision (cognitive) to explain that products physically enforce. And the more physical term of coercion is used to explain the influencing of decisions. Similarly Thaler and Sunstein (2008) use the term "nudge" (physical) for influencing choice making (cognitive). The Product Impact Tool, instead of using the one to explain the other, aims to explicate the variety of interaction modes and impacts by mapping them next to each other.
3 Combining Product Impact and scenarios in design, both for improving product use (scenario-based design) and for future scenario planning is the topic of another publication (Dorrestijn et al., 2014).

4 Take the following anecdotes. An acquaintance had to wait in queue for a checkpoint so long that when she had finally checked in, the metro left. She then wanted to take a train heading in the same direction which just stopped on the adjoining platform. She had to check out of the metro and check in for the train. But checking out appeared to be impossible. The checkpoint just returned the message: you have already checked in. Frustrated she decided to jump in the train anyway. This got her trapped in the system and all the more frustrated, for at the station where she got of there were gates and not properly checked in her card did not open the gate.

Another anecdote concerns a professor of design and philosophy who hurried with a coffee in his hand to the train. Before him somebody passed a gate, the professor presented his card, heard friendly bleeps coming from everywhere in the station, and thought that the gate stayed open for him to enter. But the gate door closed, hit the coffee and spoiled the professor's shirt.

References

Achterhuis, H. (2002). Borgmann, technology and the good life? and the empirical turn for philosophy of technology. *Techné: Research in Philosophy and Technology, 6*(1), 64–75.

Bell, B., & Wakeford, K. (2008). *Expanding architecture: Design as activism.* New York: Metropolis Books.

Berman, D. B. (2009). *Do good: How designers can change the world.* Berkeley, CA: AIGA, New Riders.

Boess, S. U., & Kanis, H. (2007). Meaning in product use: A design perspective. In H. N. J. Schifferstein & P. Hekkert (Ed.), *Product experience* (pp. 305–332). San Diego: Elsevier.

CBP (2007). *OV-chipkaart: Verwerking van persoonsgegevens ten behoeve van de OV-chipkaart bij het GVB te Amsterdam.* Den Haag: College Bescherming Persoonsgegevens.

Dorrestijn, S. (2012a). *The design of our own lives: Technical mediation and subjectivation after Foucault* (PhD thesis). University of Twente, Enschede.

Dorrestijn, S. (2012b). Theories and figures of technical mediation. In J. Donovan & W. Gunn (Ed.), *Design and anthropology* (pp. 219–230). Surrey, UK and Burlington: Ashgate.

Dorrestijn, S., van der Voort, M., & Verbeek, P. P. (2014). Future user-product arrangements: Combining product impact and scenarios in design for multi age success. *Technological Forecasting and Social Change, 89*, 284–292.

Feenberg, A. (2002). *Transforming technology: A critical theory revised.* New York: Oxford University Press.

Flusser, V. (1994). *Vom Subjekt zum Projekt: Menschwerdung.* Bensheim: Bollmann.

Flusser, V. (1999). *The shape of things: A philosophy of design.* London: Reaktion Books.

Fogg, B. J. (2003). *Persuasive technology: Using computers to change what we think and do.* Amsterdam & Boston: Morgan Kaufmann Publishers.

Foucault, M. (2000). What is enlightenment? In P. Rabinow (Ed.), *Ethics. Subjectivity and truth: Essential works of Foucault 1954–1984* (Vol. I, pp. 281–302). London: Penguin.

Ihde, D. (1990). *Technology and the lifeworld: From garden to earth.* Bloomington: Indiana University Press.

Kockelkoren, P. (2003). *Technology: Art, fairground and theatre.* Rotterdam: NAI.

Koot, J. (2010, September 24). Reizigers-verliezen-iedere-maand-half-miljoen-euro-door-chipkaart. *Financieel Dagblad.* Retrieved September 29, 2012, from http://fd.nl/Archief/2010/09/24/reizigers-verliezen-iedere-maand-half-miljoen-euro-door-chipkaart

Latour, B. (1992). Where are the missing masses? The sociology of a few mundane artifacts. In W. E. Bijker & J. Law (Eds.), *Shaping technology/building society: Studies in sociotechnical change* (pp. 225–258). Cambridge, MA: MIT Press.

Margolin, V. (2002). *The politics of the artificial: Essays on design and design studies.* Chicago: University of Chicago Press.

McLuhan, M. (2003). *Understanding media: The extensions of man* (Critical edition by W. T Gordon). Corte Madera, CA: Gingko Press.

Miller, D. (2010). *Stuff.* London: Polity.

Norman, D. A. (1988). *The psychology of everyday things.* New York: Basic Books.

Schepers, B., & Zwart, G. H. K. (2014). *Onderzoek incomplete transacties: Eindrapport* (consultancy report). Zoetermeer: Panteia.

Tenner, E. (2003). *Our own devices: The past and future of body technology.* New York: Alfred A. Knopf.

Thaler, R. H., & Sunstein, C. R. (2008). *Nudge: Improving decisions about health, wealth, and happiness.* New Haven, CT: Yale University Press.

Tromp, N., Hekkert, P., & Verbeek, P. (2011). Design for socially responsible behaviour: A classification of influence based on intended user experience. *Design Issues, 27*(3), 3–19.

van den Broek, P., (2008). De schokgolf na de ontmanteling. *Vox, 8*(15), 14–18.

Van Kuijk, J. I. (Ed.). (2012). *Design for usability: Methods & tools – a practitioner's guide.* Delft: Design United/IOP-IPCR Design for Usability Research Project.

van't Hof, C. (2011). Gated station. In C. van 't Hof, R.V. Est, & F. Daemen (Ed.), *Check in-check out: The public space as an internet of things* (pp. 33–49). Rotterdam: NAI.

Verbeek, P.-P. (2005). *What things do: Philosophical reflections on technology, agency, and design.* Pennsylvania: Pennsylvania State University Press.

Winner, L. (1986). Do artefacts have politics? In Langdon Winner (Ed.), *The whale and the reactor: A search for limits in an age of high technology.* Chicago: University of Chicago Press.

5   Design interventions for sustainable behaviour

Debra Lilley, Garrath Wilson, Tracy Bhamra, Marcus Hanratty and Tang Tang

Introduction

Over recent years, significant research effort has explored ways to reduce environmental impacts of both the built environment and products. Most of this work has focussed on reducing the impact of the manufacture and disposal phases of the lifecycle leading to useful work in the fields of design for disassembly and recyclability, environmentally conscious materials and dematerialization (Wever et al., 2008). There has however been little attention paid to the impact of the use phase of the lifecycle and the environmental impacts that can occur there, particularly as a result of the way in which the user interacts with the product. This is starting to change as more and more research is suggesting that without considering the use phase, and particularly the user behaviour element of this, sustainable designs will not be able to reach their full potential (Wever et al., 2008; Boks, 2011). As a result the new research field of Design for Sustainable Behaviour (DfSB) has emerged and is concerned with the application of behavioural theory to understand users, and behaviour-changing strategies to design products, services and systems that encourage more sustainable use (Bhamra & Lilley, 2015).

   In this chapter, we bring together research from Loughborough University (UK) design scholars conducted over a 10-year period (Figure 5.1) to present a unified framework for designing interventions for sustainable behaviour. The phases of research, design and development of behaviour change interventions in the framework are as follows:

1.   Understanding the user's actions in context;
2.   Selecting a behavioural target (where to intervene);
3.   Selecting (or applying) a behavioural intervention strategy;
4.   Evaluating the behavioural interventions.

To illustrate the development of theory and application of practice, we draw on two large UK government–funded research projects; Carbon, Control and Comfort (CCC)[1] and Low Effort Energy Demand Reduction (LEEDR).[2] Within both projects, the design researchers at Loughborough University contributed to user research to identify behavioural determinants, as well as carrying out the designing and evaluation of behaviour change interventions. The chapter closes by reflecting on what we have learned and where we see further developments in the field emerging.

Understanding of the user's actions in context

Understanding user behaviour is regarded throughout the DfSB literature as a fundamental precursor to the application of behaviour-changing strategies (Tang & Bhamra,

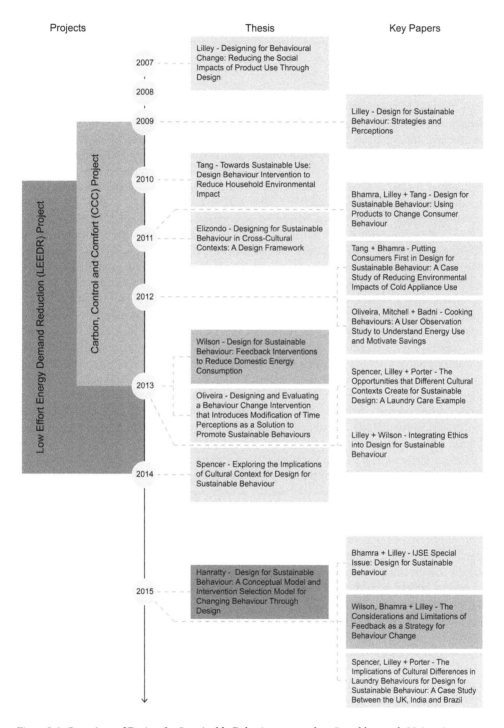

Projects   Thesis   Key Papers

2007 — Lilley - Designing for Behavioural Change: Reducing the Social Impacts of Product Use Through Design

2008

2009 — Lilley - Design for Sustainable Behaviour: Strategies and Perceptions

2010 — Tang - Towards Sustainable Use: Design Behaviour Intervention to Reduce Household Environmental Impact

Bhamra, Lilley + Tang - Design for Sustainable Behaviour: Using Products to Change Consumer Behaviour

2011 — Elizondo - Designing for Sustainable Behaviour in Cross-Cultural Contexts: A Design Framework

Tang + Bhamra - Putting Consumers First in Design for Sustainable Behaviour: A Case Study of Reducing Environmental Impacts of Cold Appliance Use

2012

Oliveira, Mitchell + Badni - Cooking Behaviours: A User Observation Study to Understand Energy Use and Motivate Savings

Wilson - Design for Sustainable Behaviour: Feedback Interventions to Reduce Domestic Energy Consumption

2013 — Oliveira - Designing and Evaluating a Behaviour Change Intervention that Introduces Modification of Time Perceptions as a Solution to Promote Sustainable Behaviours

Spencer, Lilley + Porter - The Opportunities that Different Cultural Contexts Create for Sustainable Design: A Laundry Care Example

Lilley + Wilson - Integrating Ethics into Design for Sustainable Behaviour

2014 — Spencer - Exploring the Implications of Cultural Context for Design for Sustainable Behaviour

Bhamra + Lilley - IJSE Special Issue: Design for Sustainable Behaviour

Hanratty - Design for Sustainable Behaviour: A Conceptual Model and Intervention Selection Model for Changing Behaviour Through Design

2015 — Wilson, Bhamra + Lilley - The Considerations and Limitations of Feedback as a Strategy for Behaviour Change

Spencer, Lilley + Porter - The Implications of Cultural Differences in Laundry Behaviours for Design for Sustainable Behaviour: A Case Study Between the UK, India and Brazil

Low Effort Energy Demand Reduction (LEEDR) Project

Carbon, Control and Comfort (CCC) Project

Figure 5.1 Overview of Design for Sustainable Behaviour research at Loughborough University

2008, 2012). Over a number of years, researchers at Loughborough University have integrated and assimilated different behavioural psychology models into DfSB to account for the extremely complex, and often quite individualistic, social and psychological structures (Chatterton, 2011) and multiple behavioural drivers which inform users' actions. The following section exemplifies two such endeavours using the Theory of Interpersonal Behaviour and Goal Framing.

To investigate thermal comfort in social housing to effect a reduction in CO_2 emissions from heating provision, Wilson (et al. 2010, 2013) used the Theory of Interpersonal Behaviour (TIB) (Darnton, 2008). TIB was explicitly selected due to its integrative nature (combining theory from other notable behavioural psychology models) and inclusion of habits, which intercede between intention and behaviour acting as a key determinant of the actual enactment of intention. Prior domestic energy consumption studies have highlighted habits as dominant, influencing factors (Steg & Vlek, 2009) and thus, their inclusion was considered essential.

TIB posits that the individual is central to a rational decision-making process, with behavioural action influenced by internal and external prompts that interact with the intentions (attitudes, social factors and emotions), habits and facilitating conditions unique to the individual and their context (Jackson, 2005; Chatterton, 2011). Within this model, intention is an antecedent to behaviour, with habits interceding as a key determinant to action. Habits form a routinized action where an achieved goal is satisfactory and repeatable, leading to a reduced perception of alternatives – a form of cognitive short cutting resulting in automaticity. Habits are, therefore, not just identified and assessed by repetition of action, but also by the cognitive processes that develop through frequency and association of the facilitating conditions and intentional factors (Polites, 2005; Lally et al., 2009; Steg & Vlek, 2009). Both intention and habit are in turn ruled by the facilitating or constraining conditions, the external factors that enable or constrain behaviour (Jackson, 2005; Chatterton, 2011). Thus the original TIB model was modified to include consideration of automaticity as well as frequency of habits (Figure 5.2).

From a psychological perspective, factors that lead to forming intentions are considered to have a direct and profound influence on behavioural action and domestic energy consumption, and may be mitigated by habitual actions, such as regularly opening windows in the pursuit of fresh air. Bluyssen (2009, 2010) and Nicol and Humphreys (2002) state that air quality and thermal comfort control is determined by several physical parameters in air pollution or temperature, which prompt change when manifested to levels of unacceptable discomfort, requiring corrective action. The intention to act is prompted, considered and acted upon; dependent upon the facilitating conditions. Can the window be opened or closed? Can the thermostat be turned up or down? An example of this is closing the window when feeling chilly. Wilson's (2013) thermal comfort research illustrated that habitual response is also present within the pursuit of fresh air, and, furthermore, is a powerful influence towards action. The propensity and vigour of the pursuit for fresh air within their study sample illustrated many of the prerequisite conditions for habitual action. Self-reported actions in both pre- and post-intervention studies illustrated that regardless of the indoor air quality and weather, windows were routinely opened, often without consideration for the heating system (Wilson, 2013). Can we still assume then that intentions are always considered and acted upon?

Frequency of past behaviour and high levels of automaticity was also evident within Wilson et al.'s (2013) study; actions were performed regardless of the external weather

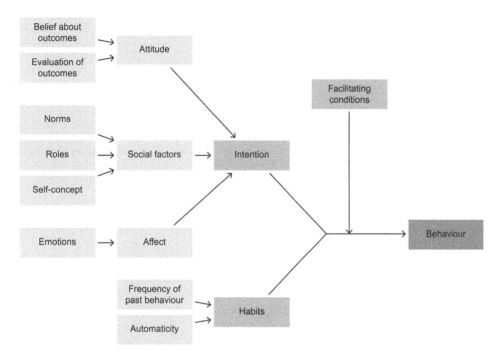

Figure 5.2 An augmented Theory of Interpersonal Behaviour (TIB) Model[3]

conditions and time of year when opening windows, although closing windows remained ruled by discomfort prompts rather than habitual behaviour (Wilson, 2013). Interestingly, this view of fresh air and airing out as being habitual has also been discussed by Hauge (2010), supporting a wider ritualized perspective of fresh air. In addition, an interesting comment from one of their participants encapsulated a notion of social and national identity, which has over time become automated: "*We've always been told us Welsh you've got to open your windows every morning. . . to air the house . . . my mother always used to do it. . . and my grandmother*" (Wilson et al., 2013). The wider ramifications for behavioural theory are that an intention to act may be prompted and acted upon, such as the social norm of being a Welsh mother or the weighting of values towards comfort, however, cognitive process over time becomes automated with actions performed without consideration of alternatives; dependent upon the facilitating conditions, such as time of day or knowledge of heating system control. Intentions may not always be considered and acted upon, but by understanding the behaviour and its antecedents, appropriate intervention strategies can be selected.

Goal framing

Goal Framing Theory (Lindenberg & Steg, 2007) identifies why people are doing what they are doing based on the prioritization of three goal frames: Gain, to guard and improve one's resources; Hedonic, to improve the way one feels right now; Normative, to act appropriately for the group. These high-level goals can be disaggregated into seven related

Table 5.1 Seven sub-goals

Goal Frame	Sub Goal	Motive
Gain	Value for money	To get value for money, pay a reasonable price, avoid wasting money
Gain	Quality	To get something of high quality and reliability, meeting one's highest expectations
Gain and Hedonic	Safety	To feel safe, calm and prepared for the unforeseen
Hedonic	Stimulation	To get something exciting, stimulating or unique, avoiding dullness
Hedonic	Convenience	To get something pleasant and comfortable, avoiding hassle and discomfort
Normative	Social Acceptance	To make a good impression, identifying with peers, conforming to expectations
Normative	Ethics	To act according to moral principles and obligations, avoiding guilt

Source: Barbopoulos (2012).

sub-goals (Barbopoulos, 2012). Hanratty (2015), applied Goal Framing Theory as the theoretical basis for understanding behavioural motivation behind showering.

The Enuf shower concept, developed as part of the LEEDR project, "is an automatic persuasive shower monitoring device" which uses feedback and behavioural prompts to encourage users to reduce showering times (Hanratty, 2015: 148).

To inform DfSB, intervention development qualitative data were gathered from 11 participating households, located within the East Midlands, on their showering routines using ethnographic video tours. Concurrently, quantitative data on water consumption was also captured via data logging. The frequency of showering was driven by 'normative goal frames' in relation to perceived social standards of hygiene, whereas 'hedonic goal framing' (e.g. comfort, pleasure and privacy) could be detected in relation to the duration of the shower. The final goal frame – 'gain' – was observed in participants who wished to minimize showering time to maximize productive time spent on other tasks.

Through comparing these theoretical approaches across the two case studies, it becomes clear that whilst the Theory of Interpersonal Behaviour enables a rich understanding of existing behaviour it is limited in its predictive capacity. Whilst Goal Framing Theory does not attempt to capture the origins or nature of the underlying knowledge, attitudes and beliefs of the individual, it does isolate potentially powerful active user goals frames which can be leveraged through behavioural interventions, thus offering a more practical framework to guide design practice.

Selecting a behavioural target

One of the earliest contributions to the DfSB field from Loughborough University was that of Lilley (2007) who unified three behavioural change strategies – feedback, steering and persuasion – into a coherent framework for Industrial Designers and originated the 'axis of influence'. The axis – a continuum that illustrates power in decision-making – places the user at one end and the product diametrically positioned at the other. The aforementioned strategies are then arranged along this spectrum denoting their relative behavioural 'control' (Lilley, 2007, 2009). Whilst the classification and categorization of

DfSB strategies has subsequently been expanded and refined over a number of years both within (e.g. Lilley, 2009; Tang, 2010; Tang & Bhamra, 2011) and outside of Loughborough University (e.g. Wever et al., 2008; Elias, 2011; Lidman et al., 2011; Lockton & Harrison, 2012; Daae & Boks, 2012) the axis remains a constant anchor.

For the purposes of explaining and exemplifying the behaviour change approaches which can be applied in (sustainable) product design, descriptions of each of the strategies in Figure 5.3 is presented in the following sub-sections, accompanied by an example drawn from the two aforementioned research projects.

Feedback

Feedback is an example of a consequence intervention; a performance indicator that focusses on the positive and negative costs of an enacted behaviour. Employed as a user-agentive tool, feedback can be used to link a specific interaction with a specific product to a specific cost, increasing the user's understanding of how the product works and increasing the user's consciousness of their own behaviour (Fischer, 2008; Darby, 2010). Information provided after an event can assist the user towards reflecting upon his/her behaviour and its cost – commonly conceptualized as a cognitive bridge between action and effect. Through this process of evaluation the antecedal structure underlying the decision-making process may be challenged, resulting in an influence of behaviour (Abrahamse et al., 2005; Burgess & Nye, 2008). The principles of feedback were operationalized within the design of a feedback intervention prototype as part of the CCC project. The aim of this device was to reduce domestic energy consumption whilst maintaining inhabitant-defined comfort levels.

Returning back to the example of fresh air pursuit, one of the concepts prototyped as part of the CCC project, the Radiator Light concept, focussed on illustrating the consequences of this conflicting use of heating and windows (Wilson et al., 2013). By framing contradictory actions (such as the window being open at the same time as the heating system being active), the intention was that the user would become more aware of the problem of 'waste' energy consumption created by his/her behaviour, whilst also increasing his/her knowledge of the products and environment over which he/she had control over, thereby challenging, through real-time feedback, his/her established routines. As the radiator surface temperature increased, a light affixed to the front of the radiator would glow white (25–43°C), changing to orange at an increased temperature (over 43°C) (Figure 5.4). If a window was opened at the same time as the heating system being

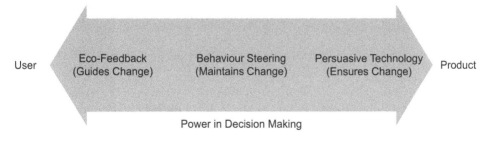

Figure 5.3 Axis of influence
Source: Lilley (2007).

Figure 5.4 The radiator lights (feedback) attached to the radiator and window

active, the light would change to red as a warning. When the light on the radiator changed between statuses, the prototype would also generate a clicking sound to alert the user of the change. If a window was opened without the heating system being active, no light would be provided as there would be no conflict on which to provide information. The user at all stages maintained control over his/her decision-making and actions.

Steering

In the centre of the axis is behaviour steering: an approach based on Jelsma and Knot's (2002) definition of scripts but expanded to include Norman's (1988) notion of affordance. Behaviour 'steers' or 'scripts', when embedded in the aesthetic or function of a product, can direct user behaviour in ways prescribed by the designer (Jelsma & Knot, 2002). Through the inscription of affordances and constraints, designers can encourage desirable behaviours whilst blocking undesirable ones (Jelsma & Knot, 2002). The EvokLamp, described below, offers a tangible example of how steering can be used within product design to target and influence behaviour.

The extent to which light has been used to create, and is synonymous with, comfortable environments is evident in the proliferation of electric fires in the UK that generate artificial light in the style of a pastiche coal fire (although the heating function of these appliances is rarely actually used) (Wilson, 2013). Coal fires visually bring to mind gratifying warmth and emotion-laden memories as the light is synonymous with the heat it produces. Developed as part of the Carbon Control and Comfort project mentioned previously, the EvokLamp is a rewarding side lamp that offsets a fluctuating ambient room temperature with inverse lighting. As the thermostat temperature is decreased by the occupant, the ideal state from an energy conservation perspective, the EvokLamp rewards the occupant with a warmer yellow/orange hued light. Conversely, if the occupant increases the room temperature via the thermostat, then the lamp responds by emitting a colder blue light; penalizing the user for his/her actions. As a safety feature, should the occupant drop the room temperature below a healthy level, the lamp glows a dim white to encourage the occupant to increase the temperature.

Persuasive technology

Persuasive technology augments and expands Fogg's (2003) theory of captology (a synthesis of computer products and persuasive techniques) to incorporate coercive strategies to ensure change, such as intelligent, context-aware technologies and ubiquitous computing which negate the user's decision-making processes (Lilley, 2007, 2009). The application of a persuasive technology approach can best be explained through the example of *Heat Me*.

Home heating is a complex behaviour which, when viewed in the context of rising UK CO_2 emissions, constitutes a significant sustainability challenge. Reducing the thermostat setting by one degree can save 310kg–360kg carbon dioxide emissions a year (Energy Saving Trust, 2015); motivating a reduction in temperature therefore represents an important target for behavioural intervention. UK households with multiple occupancy are on the rise, with an increasing trend towards multi-generational living: several generations of a family living under the same roof. What has traditionally been considered the 'user', an individual citizen or the consideration of a family as a single unit with homogeneous needs, values and actions, has been shown to no longer apply, especially within the context of home heating. Occupants have different heating needs and get used to a certain level of heat. Also, there are times when people just want more warmth and, as a result, thermostats often get turned up and left there. *Heat Me*, designed as part of the LEEDR project (Hanratty, 2015), is an interactive app which seeks to persuade occupants to turn the thermostat down to 18°C over a period of time. To avoid a sudden, jarring change in thermal comfort (often attributed to a relapse in temperature reduction) *Heat Me* features an 'Acclimatizer', which automates a gradual rate of reduction at less than 1°C a week (Figure 5.5).

Figure 5.5 Temperature setting and acclimatizer screen flow

Source: Hanratty (2015).

Figure 5.6 Boost screen flows with *Heat Me* prompts

Source: Hanratty (2015).

Increases to the baseline temperature are discouraged by in-built friction to the adjustment of the settings, however, *Heat Me* also acknowledges the desire for periodic 'heat boosts' and thus makes it relatively easy for users to raise the temperature (i.e. 21°C) for limited periods (Figure 5.6).

Selecting a behavioural intervention strategy

"One of the commonly agreed upon research challenge[s] in design for sustainable behaviour research is to overcome the lack of understanding of when to apply what type of behaviour-changing strategies" (Boks, 2012: 328). Through combining the research of Lilley, Wilson and Hanratty, key selection criteria have been established for guiding the designer.

Lilley (2009) suggests that interventions should be designed using multiple strategies ascending the axis of influence from 'informative' to 'persuasive' in a sequential manner, in response to three variables: the user's level of compliance, the gravity of the consequences of actions taken and the context in which the interaction takes place. The user's level of compliance is a function of his/her previous responses to behavioural intervention. For example, if an informative strategy, such as feedback, has been ignored, a behaviour-steering approach may be adopted, whereas the gravity of the consequences is calculated by evaluating and weighting predicted outcomes against socio-economic and environmental concerns (Lilley & Wilson, 2013). Hanratty (2015) points to a relationship between the context of the interaction, the relative level of reflectiveness or situationality of user's thoughts and actions and the impact of the resulting behaviour in the Behaviour Intervention Selection Axis (BISA) tool.

When dealing with highly situational behaviours, which are driven by context with little cognitive thought, designers are directed to employ determining strategies with a high level of obtrusiveness to disrupt and intervene in routinized thought processes and direct behaviour. Conversely, highly reflective behaviours require only low levels of obtrusiveness and an informative strategy (such as feedback) would suffice. Through aligning the concepts of situationality and reflectiveness to the strategies represented on the axis of influence (Figure 5.3), designers can select the required level of obtrusiveness.

Using *Heat Me* as an example, it is possible to see how the BISA could be applied in practice to inform strategy selection. The ethnographic research conducted within the family homes within the UK as part of the aforementioned LEEDR project to investigate domestic heating behaviours revealed the activation of all three goal frames: Hedonic Goal Framing in relation to comfort, Gain referring to cost and Normative in relation to the health of the children within the household. Interestingly, the latter goal frame dominated the other two in some cases where parents had prioritized their children's health. To respond to these goal frames in relation to the most prominent home heating behaviours, Hanratty (Hanratty, 2015) placed them on the axis of influence corresponding to different levels of intervention (Figure 5.7).

As seen in Figure 5.7, setting the heating programmer is a highly reflective behaviour requiring information, whereas to influence users who turn the thermostat up when cold, a behaviour with a greater level of situationality, an intervention on the determining end of the spectrum (such as Persuasive Technology) would be advisable.

A further dimension, or approach, which could be taken into account when selecting a DfSB strategy, is the more macro-level consideration of culture (Elizondo,

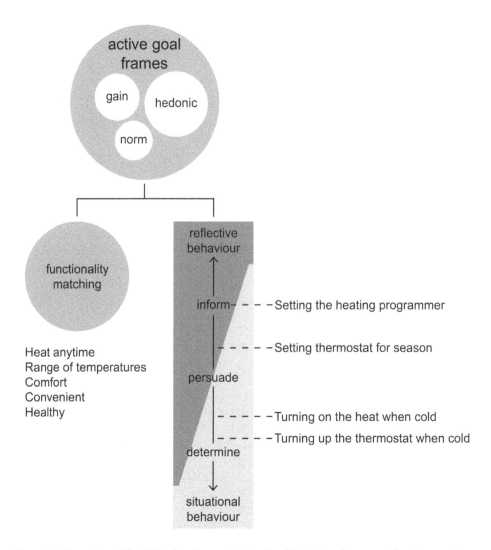

Figure 5.7 Illustration of the BISA showing motivational and behavioural aspects of heating practices

2011; Spencer, 2014). Through his exploration of laundry practices in three different contexts – Brazil, India and the UK – Spencer identified a range of culturally significant and culturally independent factors. The former being influencing factors which were common amongst the samples in their respective regions such as the external environment, other people, consumption, tools and inputs. The latter referring to factors which were different between individuals such as perceptions, aspirations, senses, views and income (Spencer, 2014; Spencer et al., 2013, 2015). Through a better understanding of behavioural influences at different levels, individual and collective, designers can build empathy with users in different contexts and better target interventions to reach wider constituent users.

Evaluating the behavioural interventions

Given the speed and momentum with which the field of design for behavioural change is growing, it is surprising how little attention has been given to the evaluation of behaviour-changing interventions. Both the lack of any serious longitudinal studies combined with the fractured nature of research (particularly across European academic institutions such as Delft University of Technology, the Norwegian University of Science and Technology and Chalmers University of Technology), has diverted attention almost exclusively towards the selection of strategies rather than towards the development of a unified framework for evaluation. Loughborough University, and in particular research conducted as part of the CCC project has made steps towards the development of evaluation criteria suitable for cross-study comparisons, disaggregating the evaluation of a behaviour-changing intervention into three components (Wilson et al., 2013; Wilson, 2013). These three components, framed in terms of a sustainability challenge, are the following: (1) *'Does the behaviour change intervention function for the context?'* (questions change depending on the behaviour change strategy employed); (2) *'Is the change in behaviour sustainable against the three pillars of sustainability, namely economic prosperity, environmental quality, and social equality?'* (Bhamra & Lofthouse, 2007) (these questions are relevant to the intervention context); and (3) finally, an evaluation of the actual change in behaviour is sought by asking *'has the user's behaviour changed as a consequence of the behavioural intervention?'* (relevant to all behaviour-changing strategies, regardless of context or strategy) (Wilson et al., 2013; Wilson, 2013). Using the example of the Radiator Light concept, referred to earlier in the chapter, the application of these evaluative components to a designed intervention can be illustrated through analyzing the results of two in-home installations of the prototype device (Wilson et al., 2013).

Considering the first of these core components, *'does the behaviour change intervention function for the context?'* it is interesting to note that the evaluation criteria applicable changes depending upon the intervention strategy selected. To illustrate, if one was to consider the evaluation of a feedback intervention then one would have to evaluate whether the metric in which information was provided was appropriate and as intended by the designer (Wilson et al., 2015). Feedback interventions, reliant on the provision of information to the user, would need to be assessed based on this functionality. Likewise, a behaviour-steering intervention would be evaluated on functions related to interaction expectations, such as design semiotics and affordances; and forcing or persuasive strategies would be evaluated based, for example, on installation factors and the maintenance of the intervention technology. Although present in most interventions, these specific evaluative factors in relation to these strategies are considered the most relevant due to their primary influence in determining behavioural outcomes.

The evaluation of the Radiator Light concept illustrated that through the provision of rapid, accurate and frequent information, the participants could instantaneously see any effect that their actions had on the heating system, either intentionally or unintentionally; this encouraged a period of investigation and optimization. This demonstrates that the device *did* function as intended by the designer within the context use.

The second component, *'is the change in behaviour sustainable?'* is dependent upon the intervention context. Taking an example from the CCC project and applying it to the three pillars of sustainability, one could argue that the Radiator Light's goal was to reduce the amount of CO_2 generated through a reduction in domestic energy consumption (an environmental issue), whilst ensuring that tenant comfort was maintained or increased (a social issue), in addition to reducing financial burden on the household (an economic issue). Interventions with different behaviour change goals and use contexts would clearly have different criteria against which to evaluate their sustainable impact (Wilson et al., 2013; Wilson, 2013).

Under the heading of social equality, one could also consider the ethical implications of the design and implementation of behaviour-changing interventions, especially as there is no clear consensus on what is 'ethical'. Ethics has been defined as "*a rational, consistent system for determining right and wrong, usually in the context of specific actions or policies*" (Berdichevsky & Neuenschwander, 1999: 52). Literature reviewed refers to several approaches or systems of ethics. Following De Vries (2006) we advocate a *consequentialist* approach in which the designer "*looks to the future and considers how to act in order to reach a situation of the best consequences for our decisions*". The focus of this approach is to investigate the potential effects of our actions. The outcomes of these predictions are then assessed against certain values (De Vries, 2006).

Alongside the development of strategy selection methods, researchers at Loughborough University have been actively considering how designers may take account of ethical issues inherent in influencing behaviour within their practice. To this end, several tools have been developed to support novice designers (Lofthouse & Lilley, 2006; Lilley & Wilson, 2013). The following questions, for example, can be used to evaluate the ethics of the user's changed behaviour, as well as the ethics of the process through which the design intervention was created. By asking a series of questions that integrate stakeholder perspectives, rather than a generic moral framework (that simply does not exist), decisions can be made in reference to relevant moral frameworks.

- Was the designer's original intent[4] for designing a behaviour intervention ethical? What change was the designer trying to achieve?
- Was the designer's original motivation for designing a behaviour intervention ethical? Why was the designer trying to achieve this change?
- Are the intervention methods employed by the designer, in order to change the user's behaviour, ethical?
- Has the designer/user/purchaser taken moral responsibility for the design intervention?
- To what extent is the user in control of the design intervention?
- Is the level of user control over the design intervention acceptably weighted against the intent and motivation of the designer?
- Have the democratic decision-making rights of all stakeholders been accounted for in the design process?
- Have the values and morals of all stakeholders been accounted for in the design process?
- Have the values of the stakeholder been evaluated against a robust ethical framework?
- Are the intended outcomes of the design intervention ethical?
- Have unintended interactions between the user and the design intervention been predicted and are ethical?
- Have unintended use contexts involving the user and the design intervention been predicted and are ethical?

In light of the absence of quantitative energy consumption data, it was not possible to conclusively attribute a reduction in environmental impacts related to energy consumption. However, the qualitative responses indicated a heightened awareness of the relationship between window opening, heat loss and (dis)comfort. Thus, the impetus to conserve energy was activated. Additionally, social benefit was derived, in the form of increased well-being, from the reduction in need to 'test' the radiator temperature by touching the surface.

The third component is to understand whether there has actually been a change in the user's behaviour, in other words, '*has the user's behaviour changed as a consequence of the behavioural intervention?*' By extension, has there been a change in the antecedent structure and habitual strength of the behaviour that has been targeted for change, depending upon the conceptualization of human action used within the study itself as a rational, decision-making process from a psychological perspective (Jackson, 2005; Chatterton, 2011), or as a more dynamic conceptualization of human agency within a nexus of social activities and frameworks (Pettersen, 2013; Kuijer, 2014); a social practice theory perspective? Considering the augmented Theory of Interpersonal Behaviour, as presented in Figure 5.2, relevant questions would relate to the underpinning cognitive structure of the user, both the user's intentions and degree of cognitive automaticity and repetition and the facilitating conditions of the context of operation (Wilson et al., 2013; Wilson, 2013).

The findings of the in-home evaluation of the Radiator Light revealed a perceptible change in knowledge and awareness; however, the action-awareness gap was not successfully breached, as the value weighting of consumption and comfort had not fundamentally changed, such as in the desire for fresh air.

The evaluation of this prototype, and that designed by Hanratty (2015) (e.g. *Enuf*), suggests that in order to evaluate a behavioural intervention's impact and its efficacy, it is imperative that data on existing behaviour (the baseline) and post-intervention behaviour is recorded. By establishing a baseline, not only can the interventions impact be meaningfully quantified and measured against a pre-intervention state, but the impact of external influences, such as a change in weather, government policy or friendship groups, can be contextualized and understood. Such data may be recorded in a multitude of ways, using qualitative research techniques such as user observations (Tang & Bhamra, 2012) or through quantitative measurement, such as the recording of energy or time usage (Oliveira et al., 2012; Oliveira, 2013). Preferably, a combination of qualitative and quantitative research techniques should be employed, such as in Hanratty (2015), who combined in-home ethnographic studies with the monitoring of domestic water and energy consumption data. Whilst quantitative data may be useful to quantify a change in a behaviour or impact metric empirically (such as number of actions repeated or a reduction in energy consumed), it fails to provide answers to the more subtle questions of how and why did the behaviour change and to what extent. By breaking down the components of an evaluation, the more common but rather limited approach to measuring behaviour change solely as a quantitative change in user action and consequence (such as energy consumption reduced by x%) can be avoided, and we can take a more three-dimensional view of the interventions' impact, which is vital to an iterative design process.

Conclusions

As outlined in this chapter, the work at Loughborough University has focussed on bringing clarity to the intervention strategies that can lead to behaviour change. The interventions developed using the three behaviour change strategies (Feedback, Steering and Persuasive Technology) have demonstrated that applying these within the design process can lead to more sustainable actions in a range of different contexts. Key to achieving this is the application of the Axis of Influence as part of understanding the context in which behaviour change is required. The particular context will mean that, to be effective, some interventions require the user to have more control whilst others will be more effective if the product or system is in control.

Recent developments around the selection of the strategy to be deployed have brought further clarity to this work. The Behaviour Intervention Selection Tool (BISA) has demonstrated an approach to enable designers to more easily select an appropriate DfSB strategy when developing interventions that take into account situational behaviours within the particular context. This more detailed approach has the potential to overcome the limitations of existing DfSB approaches and result in interventions which are more successful in the long term.

It is clear however that, without the effective evaluation of interventions, their success cannot be judged fully. It is for this reason that a parallel research activity at Loughborough University has been to develop evaluation mechanisms for Design for Sustainable Behaviour interventions. The challenge for this research has been the time required to undertake rigorous longitudinal studies of intervention use in real-world situations. However, with recent UK government research funding, these studies have been undertaken allowing the development of evaluation criteria and the start of a unified framework for the evaluation of DfSB interventions.

Overall, DfSB has been shown through the research at Loughborough University, and beyond, to be effective in being able to develop interventions that begin to change user behaviour towards more sustainable actions. In addition, the clear guidance that now exists though the axis of influence and the BISA tool enables more designers to apply these approaches in their work and ensure that, in the future, Design for Sustainable Behaviour is part of a designer's tool kit.

Acknowledgements

The Carbon, Control and Comfort project (CCC) (grant number EP/G000395/1) was supported by the UK Engineering and Physical Sciences Research Council (EPSRC). The interdisciplinary Low Effort Energy Demand Reduction (LEEDR) project was jointly funded by the UK Research Councils' Digital Economy and Energy programmes (grant number EP/I000267/1). For further information about the project, collaborating research groups and industrial partners, please visit www.leedr-project.co.uk. The authors would like to thank all the households who have generously participated in all of this research.

Notes

1 The CCC project was an interdisciplinary project carried out within the UK social housing sector which aimed to reduce domestic energy use by 20% through the user-centred design of feedback interventions to change behaviour.
2 The LEEDR project took an interdisciplinary approach to investigate energy and digital media use within privately owned homes in the UK with the aim of developing ICT-based interventions to help householders reduce their energy demand.
3 The original model was modified by Wilson to include consideration of automaticity as well as frequency of habits.
4 For a more nuanced discussion of the difference between 'intent' and 'motivation', read Berdichevsky and Neuenschwander (1999).

References

Abrahamse, W., Steg, L., Vlek, C., & Rothengatter, T. (2005). A review of intervention studies aimed at household energy conservation. *Journal of Environmental Psychology, 25*, 273–291.

Barbopoulos, I. (2012). *The consumer motivation scale: Development of a multi-dimensional measure of economical, hedonic, and normative determinants of consumption* (Licenciate Thesis). University of Gothenburg, Sweden.

Berdichevsky, D., & Neuenschwander, E. (1999). Towards an ethics of persuasive technology. *Communications of the ACM, 42*(5), 51–58.

Bhamra, T. A., & Lilley, D. (2015). IJSE special issue: Design for sustainable behaviour. *International Journal of Sustainable Engineering, 8*, 146–147.

Bhamra, T. A., & Lofthouse, V. A. (2007). *Design for sustainability: A practical approach*. Aldershot, UK: Gower Publishing Limited.

Bluyssen, P. M. (2009). *The indoor environment handbook – how to make buildings healthy and comfortable*. London: Earthscan.

Bluyssen, P. M. (2010). Towards new methods and ways to create healthy and comfortable buildings. *Building and Environment, 45*, 808–818.

Boks, C. (2011). Design for sustainable behaviour research challenges. *Proceedings of EcoDesign 2011 International Symposium*, Kyoto, Japan.

Boks, C. (2012). Design for sustainable behaviour research challenges. In M. Matsumoto, Y. Umeda, K. Masui, & S. Fukushige (Eds.), *Design for innovative value towards a sustainable society, Proceedings of EcoDesign 2011, 7th International Symposium on Environmentally Conscious Design and Inverse Manufacturing* (pp. 328–333). Dordrecht: Springer Netherlands.

Burgess, J., & Nye, M. (2008). Re-materialising energy use through transparent monitoring systems. *Energy Policy, 36*, 4454–4459.

Chatterton, T. (2011). *An introduction to thinking about 'Energy Behaviour': A multi model approach*. London: Department for Energy and Climate Change.

Daae, J., & Boks, C. (2012). Exploring behavioural psychology to support design for sustainable behaviour. *Journal of Design Research, 10*, 50–66.

Darby, S. (2010). *Literature review for the energy demand research project*. London: Ofgem (Office of Gas and Electricity Markets).

Darnton, A. (2008). *GSR behaviour change knowledge review: An overview of behaviour change models and their uses*. London: Government Social Research Unit.

De Vries, M. J. (2006). Ethics and the complexity of technology: A design approach. *Philosophia Reformata, the International Scientific Journal of the Association for Reformational Philosophy, 71*(2), 118–131.

Elias, E. W. A. (2011). *User-efficient design: Reducing the environmental impact of user behaviour through the design of products* (Doctor of Philosophy). University of Bath, UK.

Elizondo, G. M. (2011). *Designing for sustainable behaviour in cross-cultural contexts: A design framework* (PhD thesis). Loughborough University, Loughborough, UK.

Energy Saving Trust. (2015). *Thermostats and controls*. Retrieved March 19, 2015, from www.energy savingtrust.org.uk/domestic/content/thermostats-and-controls

Fischer, C. (2008). Feedback on household electricity consumption: A tool for saving energy? *Energy Efficiency, 1*, 79–104.

Fogg, B. J. (2003). *Persuasive technology: Using computers to change what we think and do (Interactive Technologies)*. San Francisco, CA: Morgan Kaufmann.

Hanratty, M. (2015). *Design for sustainable behaviour: A conceptual model and intervention selection model for changing behaviour through design* (PhD thesis). Loughborough University, Loughborough, UK.

Hauge, B. (2010). Fresh air at home: A sensory experience and social ritual. *Daylight & Architecture, 13*, 26–39.

Jackson, T. (2005). *Motivating sustainable consumption: A review of evidence on consumer behaviour and behavioural change, a report to the sustainable development research network*. Centre for Environmental Strategy, University of Surrey, Surrey, UK.

Jelsma, J., & Knot, M. (2002). Designing environmentally efficient services: A "script" approach. *The Journal of Sustainable Product Design, 2,* 119–130.

Kuijer, L. (2014). *Implications of social practice theory for sustainable design* (Doctor of Philosophy). TU Delft.

Lally, P., Van Jaarsveld, C. H. M., Potts, H. W. W., & Wardle, J. (2009). How are habits formed: Modelling habit formation in the real world. *European Journal of Social Psychology, 40,* 998–1009.

Lidman, K. M. E., Renström, S. E., & Karlsson, I. C. M. (2011). I don't want to drown the frog! A comparison of four design strategies to reduce overdosing of detergents. *Proceedings from the Conference on Sustainable Innovation 2011,* Farnham, UK.

Lilley, D. (2007). *Designing for behavioural change: Reducing the social impacts of product use through design* (Doctoral Thesis). Loughborough University, Loughborough, UK.

Lilley, D. (2009). Design for sustainable behaviour: Strategies and perceptions. *Design Studies, 30,* 704–720.

Lilley, D., & Wilson, G. T. (2013). Integrating ethics into design for sustainable behaviour. *Journal of Design Research, 11,* 278–299.

Lindenberg, S., & Steg, L. (2007). Normative, gain and hedonic goal-frames guiding environmental behavior. *Journal of Social Issues, 65*(1), 117–137.

Lockton, D., & Harrison, D. (2012). Models of the user: Designers' perspectives on influencing sustainable behaviour. *Journal of Design Research, 10,* 7–27.

Lofthouse, V. A., & Lilley, D. (2006). *What they really, really want: User centered research methods for design.* International Design Conference – Design 2006. Dubrovnik, Croatia.

Nicol, J. F., & Humphreys, M. A. (2002). Adaptive thermal comfort and sustainable thermal standards for buildings. *Energy and Buildings, 34,* pp. 563–572.

Norman, D. (1988). *The psychology of everyday things.* New York: Basic Books.

Oliveira, L. C. R. (2013). *Designing and evaluating a behaviour change intervention that introduces modification of time perceptions as a solution to promote sustainable behaviours* (PhD thesis). Loughborough University, Loughborough, UK.

Oliveira, L. C. R., Mitchell, V., & Badni, K. (2012). Cooking behaviours: A user observation study to understand energy use and motivate savings. *Work: A Journal of Prevention, Assessment and Rehabilitation, 41*(supplement 1), 2122–2128.

Pettersen, I. N. (2013). *The role of design in supporting the sustainability of everyday life* (PhD thesis). Norwegian University of Science and Technology, Trondheim, Norway.

Polites, G. L. (2005). *Counterintentional habit as an inhibitor of technology acceptance.* Eighth Annual Conference of the Southern Association for Information Systems, Savannah, Georgia, February 25–26.

Spencer, J. (2014). *Exploring the implications of cultural context for design for sustainable behaviour* (Doctor of Philosophy). Loughborough University, Loughborough, UK.

Spencer, J., Lilley, D., & Porter, S. (2013). The opportunities that different cultural contexts create for sustainable design: A laundry care example. *Journal of Cleaner Production, 107,* 279–290.

Spencer, J., Lilley, D., & Porter, S. (2015). The implications of cultural differences in laundry behaviours for design for sustainable behaviour: A case study between the UK, India and Brazil. *International Journal of Sustainable Engineering, 8*(3), 196–205.

Steg, L., & Vlek, C. (2009). Encouraging pro-environmental behaviour: An integrative review and research agenda. *Journal of Environmental Psychology, 29,* 309–317.

Tang, T. (2010). *Towards sustainable use: Design behaviour intervention to reduce household environmental impact* (Doctoral Thesis). Loughborough University, Loughborough, UK.

Tang, T., & Bhamra, T. A. (2008). *Changing energy consumption behaviour through sustainable product design.* DESIGN 2008, 10th International Design Conference, Dubrovnik, Croatia, May 19–22, pp. 1359–1366.

Tang, T., & Bhamra, T. A. (2011). *Applying a design behaviour intervention model to design for sustainable behaviour.* The Tao of Sustainability: An International Conference on Sustainable Design in a Globalization Context, Beijing, China, October 27–29, 2011.

Tang, T., & Bhamra, T. A. (2012). Putting consumers first in design for sustainable behaviour: A case study of reducing environmental impacts of cold appliance use. *International Journal of Sustainable Engineering, 5,* 288–303.

Wever, R., Van Kuijk, J., & Boks, C. (2008). User-centred design for sustainable behaviour. *International Journal of Sustainable Engineering, 1,* 9–20.

Wilson, G. T. (2013). *Design for sustainable behaviour: Feedback interventions to reduce domestic energy consumption* (Doctor of Philosophy), Loughborough University, Loughborough, UK.

Wilson, G. T., Bhamra, T. A., & Lilley, D. (2010). Reducing domestic energy consumption: A user-centred design approach. In R. Wever, J. Quist, A. Tukker, J. Woudstra, F. Boons, & N. Beute (Eds.), *Proceedings of knowledge collaboration & learning for sustainable innovation ERSCP-EMSU conference,* 2010 Delft, The Netherlands, 25th–29th October 2010 (pp. 200–222).

Wilson, G. T., Bhamra, T., & Lilley, D. (2015). The considerations and limitations of feedback as a strategy for behaviour change. *International Journal of Sustainable Engineering, 8*(3), 186–195.

Wilson, G. T., Lilley, D., & Bhamra, T. A. (2013). Design feedback interventions for household energy consumption reduction. *Proceedings of ERSCP-EMSU 2013 Conference, Sustainable Development and Cleaner Production Center,* Boğaziçi University, Istanbul, Turkey, 4–7 June 2013.

6 Design, behaviour change and the *Design with Intent* toolkit

Dan Lockton

Introduction

What has become known as 'design for behaviour change' has grown significantly as a field of research in recent years (e.g. Lilley, 2009; Wever, 2012; Daae & Boks, 2014; Niederer et al., 2014; Strömberg et al., 2015). The field aims, generally, to propose and evaluate design, which affects the social or environmental impacts of products, services, and environments in use, through attempting to *understand* and *influence* user behaviour – perhaps as part of what Suchman (2011: 15) calls "the rise of professional design as a dominant figure of transformative change." The degree of intervention varies with the boundary of how the 'problem' is considered, whether it is at the level of individual interaction with products, or part of a more systemic societal transition (Irwin et al., 2015).

Design for behaviour change must inherently involve a multidisciplinary approach, drawing on knowledge and models from other fields relating to human action. These include social, cognitive, and ecological psychology; decision research; behavioural economics; human-computer interaction (HCI); ethnography, science, and technology studies; cognitive anthropology; ergonomics; cybernetics; ethics; and architecture, as well as intersecting areas of design which focus on human experience and action, such as social implication design (Tromp & Hekkert, 2014), persuasive technology (Fogg, 2009), social practice-oriented design (Kuijer et al., 2013; Scott et al., 2012; Pettersen, 2015), product experience (Desmet & Hekkert, 2007), and transformational products (Hassenzahl & Laschke, 2014). In this context, designed 'interventions' largely involve the redesign of products, services, and environments, changing the *affordances* and *constraints* available to users, or the design of interfaces (often digital) which give users *information* and *feedback* on the use or the impact of people's actions, for example energy use, waste generation, or transportation choices (Lockton et al., 2008).

Understanding how designers' decisions affect people's actions, and what – if anything – to do about them, is central to much of the recent discussions in fields such as architecture (e.g. Watson et al., 2015), service design (e.g. Bisset & Lockton, 2010; Mager, 2010), and interaction design (e.g. Blevis, 2007). This entry of designers into the 'behaviour business,' as Fabricant (2009) has called it, accords with Herbert Simon's assertion that "everyone designs who devises courses of action aimed at changing existing situations into preferred ones" (Simon, 1996: 111) and, as Fry (2015: 8) notes, "almost everything in the environment around us is designed" – and everything that is designed affects what people do.

Some relevant cross-disciplinary considerations

As noted, the scope of how design can be applied to change behaviour is broad and extremely multidisciplinary. Many fields, in both research and practice, both within and without, what are termed the 'behavioural sciences,' have insights or frameworks to contribute, and each works with particular *models* seeking to explain human behaviour in different ways – even if those models are sometimes mutually incompatible (Gintis, 2007). For example, Darnton (2008) outlines 60 social-psychological and economic models of behaviour, and discusses their policy implications, without considering any arising from design and human factors research or even from ecological psychology.

There are some useful cross-domain, cross-disciplinary concepts, which can help frame and structure the discussion. None is the single 'right' way to think about things, but each offers something in terms of understanding how to integrate insights from different fields.

Enabling, motivating, or constraining

At the level of individual behaviour, most approaches are either about trying to get people *to do* something, or trying to get people *not to do* something. Most possible ways to do that are either about changing how *easy* or *difficult* it is to do something, or about getting people to *want* to do (or not to do) something. This is a primitive classification, and probably not complete. But as a simple way of categorizing design strategies, considering *enabling, motivating,* and *constraining* approaches offers a quick way to assess (and question) any design brief and the relevant strategies. The overall approach within a project may, of course, be dictated by the client or other stakeholders rather than being the designer's decision, but understanding whether the brief is about

- **enabling:** making the 'target' behaviour easier for a user to do
- **motivating:** trying to get users to want to perform or not perform a particular behaviour, or
- **constraining:** making an undesired behaviour harder to do

can be a useful first step. *Central route persuasion* (Petty & Cacioppo, 1981) along with much work in persuasive technology is about *motivating* behaviour, with attitude change being either a precursor or a result, although Fogg's *reduction* and *tunnelling* (Fogg, 2003) are arguably also *enabling* particular behaviours by making them simpler. Strategies aimed at influencing health and safety behaviour often employ a *constraining* approach.

A designer could potentially consider tackling any target behaviour through each of the three approaches – making it easier to do it (enabling), motivating users to do it, or constraining users so they have to do it. It is also relatively easy to apply the enabling/motivating/constraining distinction in reverse, i.e. looking at an existing example of design and assessing what the approach might have been.

The distinction between affordances, information flows, and constraints (see 'Systems, affordances, constraints, and information flows' section) maps quite well onto the enabling, motivating, and constraining classifications, respectively. In this context, it is important to distinguish between the *means* (the design strategies themselves) and the intended *ends* (the intended effects of the design on behaviour), because people do not always act as designers intend them to. A further consideration concerns how well the simplistic enabling/motivating/constraining framework applies to more complex systemic issues which are not simply about influencing individual actions. It raises the question whether the framework can take account of the messiness of transactional or game-theoretic situations in which enabling one person's actions constrains those of others, or wicked problems (Rittel & Webber, 1973; Buchanan, 1992) in which focussing on a single target behaviour may simply transform the problem into something else. What may seem a simple division into enabling, motivating, and constraining is somewhat less satisfactory when applied to the realities of complex situations.

Decisions, attitudes, and practices

Much human behaviour can be seen as decision-making, conscious or otherwise, and so understanding and influencing those decision-making processes is often the focus in work on behaviour change. This is most evident at present in the dominance of models from behavioural economics in the work of policy bodies such as the Behavioural Insights Team (Haynes et al., 2012), who apply theories such as Kahneman and Tversky's (1979) *prospect theory* and have a general focus on correcting 'cognitive biases' (Tversky & Kahneman, 1974; Thaler and Sunstein, 2008). As Plous (1993: xv) notes, "more research has been published on failures in decision making than on successes." Decision-making research is often about deviations from what is assumed to be rational choices, whether these are framed as shortcomings in human reasoning, or as practically adaptive strategies (Todd et al., 2012) from which designers or policy makers can learn.

This current dominance of behavioural economics has – at least politically – partly supplanted a previous focus on *changing attitudes and beliefs* as a precursor to behaviour change, exemplified by models such as Ajzen's (1985) 'Theory of Planned Behaviour.' As Stern (2000) and Guagnano et al. (1995) showed in relation to recycling behaviour, contextual factors, often related to the built environment (such as the lack of presence of kerbside recycling bins) will often trump even deeply held 'pro-environment' attitudes in terms of influencing actual behaviour. This is certainly not to decry the value and potential of increasing thoughtfulness (Grist, 2010; John et al., 2011) through the design of products, services, and environments, but simply highlighting that *contextual factors* – something with which designers are already very familiar – play an important role in affecting decision-making and hence behaviour.

Even where spatial or other contextual factors are included, most common current models primarily focus on *individual* decision-making, lacking consideration of the *social* or supra-individual aspects of decisions, and the evolving social practices which affect how people interact with their environment (Kuijer & de Jong, 2011; Shove, 2010; Wilhite, 2013). Hazas et al. (2012), specifically talking about 'design for sustainable behaviour' feedback interventions in the home, criticize the dominant models of individuals making "constant and active choices" about their behaviour around energy and resource use without taking sufficient account of the contexts of everyday life, social and time commitments, and negotiating priorities within a family or household. A similar argument can be made about behaviours at work, and indeed in domains such as health, wellbeing, performance, and productivity.

Classification, context, and cognition

There are many cross-disciplinary ways in which insights on behaviour, and practically applicable strategies and tools for influencing it, can be categorized or classified, ranging from spectrums of *power* or *control* (e.g. Jelsma, 2006; Nuffield Council on Bioethics, 2007; Wever et al., 2008; Lilley, 2007; Zachrisson & Boks, 2012) to more nuanced multidimensional 'field' or 'wheel' approaches (e.g. Tromp et al., 2011; Michie et al., 2011; Chatterton & Wilson, 2013).

One broad distinction in terms of strategies and tools drawn from other disciplines is between those which address primarily *cognition*, and those which address the *context* itself (Clark, 2009) – a division which Simon (1990) illustrated through the metaphor of a pair of scissors. Both 'blades' shape behaviour, but often a model or technique will concentrate on either cognition (mind) or context (environment). For example, to attempt to influence staff to take more exercise at work, a 'cognition' approach might focus on campaigns to increase mindfulness around health, or persuading staff that exercise was a good thing to do, while a 'context' approach might look at changing the environment (built, corporate, and social) itself, through making exercise easier, building more walking into daily activities, and so on.

Simon's scissors recall 'Lewin's equation' (1935) – $B = f(P, E)$ – a person's behaviour (B) is a function of his or her own personality (or other 'internal' factors, P) and environment (physical and social, E). This may appear obvious, but it highlights one of the major divisions in psychological approaches to behaviour, between those which focus on the 'person' and those which focus on the 'environment' (however defined) or the situation (Ross & Nisbett, 1992).

Design strategies aiming to influence behaviour can be grouped or assessed according to whether they primarily address the person or the environment, although in practice, design approaches, particularly those drawing on human factors research (e.g. Stanton et al., 2013) or taking a sociotechnical systems-level perspective, often *combine* contextual and cognitive considerations.

Systems, affordances, constraints, and information flows

In common with many areas of interaction design, design for behaviour change may benefit from the application of a 'systems' perspective to understand better the potentially complex interplay between technology and human behaviour. One relevant systems perspective is Donella Meadows's concept of 'leverage points,' intended to be generally applicable to complex, non-linear systems. As presented in Meadows (1999: 2; 2009), these are a list of 'places to intervene in a system,' ranked in tentative increasing order of effectiveness. Humans are part of the system just as much as technology and political structures. Hence there is no single leverage point dealing with 'human behaviour.' Rather, human decisions, abilities, and reactions can be inherent to each of the leverage points, and designers (if they have the opportunity) can address any of the leverage points. However, it is apparent that many designed interventions which specifically aim to influence user behaviour are concentrated on Meadows's leverage points 6, 5, and 4:

- the structure of information flows
- the rules of the system
- the power to add, change, evolve, or self-organize system structure.

These are aspects which designers are especially well placed to tackle through changes to the design of everyday products, services and environments.

Information flows mainly comprise different kinds of feedback and presentations of antecedent information (*feedforward*: Djajadiningrat et al., 2002). The *rules of the system* can perhaps best be framed from a design perspective as being about designing in actual *affordances* and *constraints* (Gibson, 1979; Norman, 1988; Shingo, 1986) on behaviour (and perhaps also rules for 'reward' and 'punishment'). The power to add, change, evolve, or self-organize system structure could be seen as related to the design of *adaptive systems*, i.e. systems which can perhaps adapt the information flows and affordances or constraints present, based on users' behaviour and the performance or context of the system's use.

The practical 'design for behaviour change' use of these leverage points is often a combination of one or more of them. Therefore, these categories are not a mutually exclusive definition of possible strategies for intervention, but a way of framing some possible leverage points. For example, Lockton et al. (2009) have linked themes around classification of affordances in design with the concept of *choice architecture* in behavioural economics (Thaler & Sunstein, 2008), highlighting the parallels between fields as part of the development of a design pattern approach (see 'Patterns and toolkits' section).

Mental models: ignore, work with, or shift?

A key concept in design for behaviour change is the notion of *mental models* (Gentner & Stevens, 1983). There are different ways of defining and representing the term (Jones et al., 2011; Moray, 1996), but one definition commonly used in human-computer interaction is described broadly by Carroll et al. (1987: 6) as "knowledge of how the system works, what its components are, how they are related, what the internal processes are, and how they affect the components." Users' mental models thus allow them "not only to construct actions for novel tasks but also to explain why a particular action produces the results it does" (p. 6).

The idea is that understanding user behaviour in context, as part of a design process, can (or should) involve investigating users' own understanding and mental models of the systems with which they are interacting; as Krippendorff (2007: 1386) puts it, "designers who intend to design something that has the potential of being meaningful to others need to understand how others conceptualise their world." In the context of design for behaviour change, mental models could be important if a user's current model leads him or her to behave or interact with a system in a way which is undesirable, dangerous, inefficient, or otherwise deemed deserving of a design 'intervention.'

The aim of a designer seeking to change behaviour via mental models would usually be to *shift* the user's mental model (if incorrect) to a more accurate one, perhaps by making the 'system model' evident (an aim of *ecological interface design*: Burns & Hajdukiewicz, 2004), via a series of analogical steps bridging the two models (Clement, 1991), or by increasing the repertoire of models available to users – as Papert (1980: xix) put it: "[learning] anything is easy if you can assimilate it to your collection of models." Alternatively, an aim could be to redesign a system so that it appears to work, or actually does work, in the way that the user assumes, *working with* his or her existing model even if incorrect (and thus turning it into the 'correct' model). In both cases, the effectiveness of the approach could be examined by measuring behaviour changes that have occurred as a result of intervention.

Both approaches require investigating users' current mental models of the systems they use. Within design research and in human factors, methods such as interviews, verbal protocol analyses, structured tasks (e.g. Payne, 1991), eye-tracking, cultural probes (Gaver et al., 1999), ethnography, and shadowing can all help reveal aspects of people's understandings and internal representations of situations, via examining and mapping interaction behaviour, routines, shifts in focus or even the errors people make. For example, in a design for behaviour change context, Terzioğlu et al. (2015) used cultural probes to explore and understand factors involved in consumers' actions around repairing broken household objects as a precursor to designing interventions. However, even with an extensive palette of methods, the fundamental difficulty that mental models (and aspects of understanding more generally) are "not available for direct inspection or measurement" (Jones et al., 2011: 2) remains.

Finally, we might consider situations where outright *ignoring* users' mental models – while still trying to influence behaviour – is an appropriate design approach. The most obvious ones are related to safety, where the designer is interested in a particular 'safe' behavioural outcome regardless of whether users' understanding is 'correct' or not.

Patterns and toolkits

It is important to recognize when exploring this area from a pragmatic design perspective that there is no accepted unified model of human behaviour. There are no 'look-up tables' for behaviour change, although theory and practice on behaviour-influencing design have been developed enough in particular specialist domains to allow the production of 'how-to' guides (e.g. Grout, 2007, in medical design; Armstrong, 2010, in advertising; and Crowe, 2000, in architectural design against crime; or in-depth disciplinary treatments such as Michie et al., 2014, in health behaviour change). A whole range of guides have emerged around behaviour change online and in digital contexts (e.g. Wendel, 2013; Nodder, 2013; Eyal & Hoover, 2013).

However, negotiating the large field of possible design strategies from different disciplinary backgrounds and traditions – and their appropriateness for different situations – can be a challenge for designers briefed with 'changing behaviour' in a particular context. Quite apart from the implied determinism in any 'how to' process, the ability to question and reframe the assumptions inherent in a brief, as part of a problem-framing (Dorst, 2015) or even problem-worrying (Anderson, 1966) approach, potentially requires the designer to have a much greater awareness of the problem–solution space (Maher et al., 1996). This includes both deeper contextual enquiry, through researching the situation in the field, and a knowledge of the repertoire of design approaches which might be applicable (Lawson, 2004). A number of toolkits and guides have been developed (e.g. Selvefors et al., 2014; Daae & Boks, 2014) which aim to provide designers with a more structured process for exploring these questions.

The design pattern format

One approach, taken by the author with the *Design with Intent* toolkit (Lockton et al., 2010; Lockton et al., 2013), is to provide an 'inspiration' guide for brainstorming, exploring problem–solution spaces and classifying existing ideas, drawing on examples and insights from different disciplines, and using a *design pattern* format.

A variety of 'creative thinking' techniques are commonly used to generate novel ideas as part of problem-framing and -solving processes, often in group-workshops, but also individually. Card-form tools such as IDEO's *Method Cards* (2003) often address this phase of the design process, either through acting as 'ideation decks' (Golembewski, 2010) or by suggesting appropriate design research methods or approaches to help frame the problem better. A format widely used in human–computer interaction (HCI), primarily in interface and web design, is that of the design pattern, which describes a form of presenting a situation, and/or possible solutions, in a structured way. The form, via adoption in software engineering in the late 1980s, stems ultimately from architecture: Alexander et al.'s (1977) *A Pattern Language*, which covers the design and layout of buildings, towns, and communities. Patterns are essentially recurring problem–solution instances, described in a referenceable way which enables practitioners to recognize the situation. The pattern form can help a designer recognize that a 'new' problem situation is similar or analogous to one encountered previously elsewhere, even in a different context. This makes them a useful format for cross-disciplinary transfer.

Design with Intent

Using elements of the pattern form, *Design with Intent* (Figure 6.1) aims to help designers and other stakeholders explore the space of behaviourally relevant design concepts through presenting examples and insights from different disciplines. This could lead to idea generation through use as a 'suggestion tool' to help a form of directed brainstorming, or as an exploratory, reflective, or teaching tool. Fincher (1999: 331) notes that "the pattern form is singularly well adapted for the sharing of good practice between practitioners," and certainly in HCI, patterns have been used as a pedagogical tool (e.g. Borchers, 2002; Kotzé et al., 2006) for students or novices learning about the discipline. The toolkit was developed via an iterative, participatory process, running workshops with students and designers throughout its development to understand how it is being used and how to improve its structure and content. The patterns were extracted – and abstracted – from an ongoing literature review of treatments of human behaviour in a range of disciplines, together with suggestions from readers of the project's blog and workshop participants.

In the toolkit, 101 design patterns for influencing behaviour are described and illustrated, grouped into eight 'lenses' – categories which provide different disciplinary 'worldviews' on behaviour change, challenging designers to think outside the immediate frame of reference suggested by the brief (or the client), and helping with transposing ideas between domains. The lenses (described in Table 6.1) are not intended to be ontologically

Figure 6.1 Design com Intento, a Brazilian–Portuguese translation of the toolkit by Luis Oliveira. A Czech translation by Jan Laky is also available

Table 6.1 The Design with Intent toolkit lenses and patterns

Lenses	Patterns
Architectural The Architectural Lens draws on techniques used to influence user behaviour in architecture, urban planning and related disciplines such as traffic management and crime prevention through environmental design	Angles; Converging and diverging; Conveyor belts; Feature deletion; Hiding things; Material Properties; Mazes; Pave the cowpaths; Positioning; Roadblock; Segmentation and spacing; Simplicity
Errorproofing The Errorproofing Lens represents a worldview treating deviations from the target behaviour as 'errors' which design can help avoid, either by making it easier for users to work without making errors, or by making errors impossible in the first place.	Are you sure?; Choice editing; Conditional warnings; Defaults; Did you mean?; Interlock; matched affordances; Opt-outs; Portions; Task lock-in/out
Interaction All the patterns are really about interaction design in one form or another, but the Persuasive/Interaction Lens brings together some of the most common design elements of interfaces where users' interactions with the system affect how their behaviour is influenced, including from the growing field of Persuasive Technology (Fogg, 2003)	Feedback through form; Kairos; Partial completion; Peer feedback; Progress bar; Real-time feedback; Simulation and feedforward; Summary feedback; Tailoring; Tunnelling and wizards
Perceptual The Perception Lens combines ideas from product semantics, ecological psychology, and Gestalt psychology about how users perceive patterns and meanings as they interact with the systems around them	(A)symmetry; Colour associations; Contrast; Fake affordances; Implied sequences; Metaphors; Mimicry and mirroring; Mood; Nakedness; Perceived affordances; Possibility trees; Prominence; Proximity and grouping; Seductive atmospherics; Similarity; Transparency; Watermarking
Cognitive The Cognitive Lens draws on research in behavioural economics and cognitive psychology looking at how people make decisions, and how this is affected by 'heuristics' and 'biases.' If designers understand how users make interaction decisions, that knowledge can be used to influence interaction behaviour. Equally, where users often make poor decisions, design can help counter this.	Assuaging guilt; Commitment and consistency; Decoys; Desire for order; Do as you're told; Emotional engagement; Expert choice; Framing; Habits; Personality; Provoke empathy; Reciprocation; Rephrasing and renaming; Scarcity; Social proof
Security The Security Lens represents a 'security' worldview, i.e. that undesired user behaviour is something to deter and/or prevent though 'countermeasures' designed into products, systems and environments, both physically and online, with examples such as digital rights management.	Coercive atmospherics; Peerveillance; Sousveillance; Surveillance; Threat of injury; Threat to property; What you can do; What you have; What you know; What you've done; Where you are; Who or what you are
Ludic Games are great at engaging people for long periods of time, influencing people's behaviour through their very design. The Ludic Lens includes a number of 'gamification' techniques for influencing user behaviour that can be derived from games and other 'playful' interactions, ranging from basic social psychology mechanisms such as goal-setting, to common game elements such as scores and levels.	Challenges and targets; Collections; Leave gaps to fill; Levels; Make it a meme; Playfulness; Rewards; Role-playing; Scores; Storytelling; Unpredictable reinforcement
Machiavellian The Machiavellian Lens comprises design patterns which, while diverse, all embody an 'end justifies the means' approach. This may be unethical, but is nevertheless commonly used to control and influence consumers through advertising, pricing structures, planned obsolescence, lock-ins and so on.	Anchoring; Antifeatures and crippleware; Bundling; Degrading performance; First one free; Forced dichotomy; Format lock-in/out; Functional obsolescence; I cut, you choose; Poison pill; Serving suggestion; Slow/no response; Style obsolescence; worry resolution

rigorous, but primarily a way of triggering multiple viewpoints within an ideation session. Each lens also represents a particular balance of emphasis on *cognition* or *context* (see above), e.g. the Cognitive lens is primarily about cognition, while the Architectural lens is primarily about context.

Case study: Twist Kettle, Alexander Ambridge

A brief case study of the toolkit's application in an educational context can help demonstrate one way in which it can be used. Alexander Ambridge, a final year BSc Product Design student at Brunel University, used the *Design with Intent* toolkit to generate concepts for his major project, the *Twist Kettle*. This aims to reduce the energy used by electric kettles, not by influencing people to use only the right amount of water, but by encouraging users to set the required temperature (between 65° and 100° C) to suit different kinds of drinks before the water is heated:

> Although there are a number of variable temperature kettles already available, my design has focused on the temperature setting interface to encourage users to interact with the temperature setting feature. The 360° base becomes a dial, so twisting the kettle sets the temperature (Figure 6.2).
>
> Setting the temperature on existing variable temperature kettles is an optional part of the process. I wanted the action of setting the temperature to become an essential part of the process (like the 'Interlock' card [one of the *Design with Intent* patterns]) although I didn't want the users to feel constrained. The dial base interface requires the user to only slightly change the way they use the kettle. Setting the temperature will become an extension of an existing action within the process of using the kettle. Every time the user places the kettle back down on its base they then must consider the temperature that they wish the kettle to heat to.
>
> (Ambridge, personal communication.)

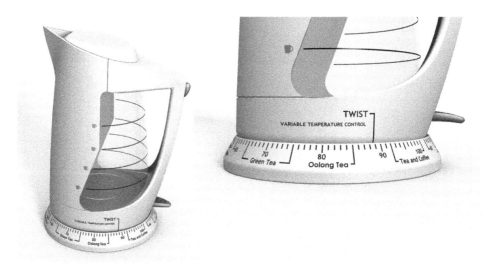

Figure 6.2 Alexander Ambridge's Twist kettle – requiring the user to set the desired water temperature by rotating the base

Figure 6.3 Alexander Ambridge's sketchbook showing how the *Design with Intent* cards were used directly to inspire concepts

Before arriving at the 'twist' concept, Ambridge used the toolkit cards for a comprehensive individual brainstorming process (Figure 6.3) in which he went through the cards on screen, first noting and sketching ideas on Post-It notes, and then elaborating on each as they were stuck (with printed versions of the cards) into his sketchbook. These earlier concepts drew on patterns including personality, emotional engagement, habits, commitment and consistency, feedback through form, nakedness, framing, and conditional warnings.

Discussion: models and assumptions

This chapter has opened up the complexity of the field of design for behaviour change through looking at some relevant cross-disciplinary considerations, and introducing the *Design with Intent* toolkit, which aims to bring together some of these insights from multiple disciplines. We have seen how it can be applied to a simple problem.

However, it is clear that we should question the perhaps deterministic assumptions embedded in much of the work that presumes one-to-one mappings between design features and resulting 'behaviours' (Broady, 1966; Lockton, 2012). People will not always behave how designers intend or expect them to (Kanis, 1998; Stanton & Baber, 2002; Redström, 2005), even as designers attempt to 'script' behaviour (Akrich, 1992; Jelsma & Knot, 2002). As Brand (1994: 178) puts it, in reference to the built environment, "All buildings are predictions. All predictions are wrong."

Assumptions about people – how they live, how they make decisions, and what affects their actions – are integral to the whole programme of design for behaviour change. Designers are engaged generally not in describing existing situations, but in *transforming* existing situations into preferred ones (Simon, 1981), in "act[ing] to change the actuality of the world" (Dilnot, 2015: 134). While these assumptions and issues surrounding them are not necessarily always explicit stances taken by designers or researchers, they embody tensions that arise when a new approach touches on areas that have previously been the preserve of other disciplines with different traditions, expectations, and aims.

We cannot avoid having models of people (Dubberly & Pangaro, 2007), but the question of how these models and assumptions are applied in design is of practical relevance – how those models can be translated, tested, questioned, and improved through use in the real world, rather than in laboratory studies. In this sense, it is wise to heed Box and Draper (1987): "essentially, all models are wrong, but some are useful" because from a design perspective, we are looking for the 'useful' parts. Designers' mental models of 'users,' or theories of action (Argyris & Schön, 1974) about how people behave (at least the simplified models which are implicit in the selection of particular features with the aim of influencing behaviour) are diverse, but necessarily reductive – and we should keep an awareness of this reductiveness in mind.

Looking at how designers themselves model 'their' intended users can be instructive in understanding how design for behaviour change techniques are applied in practice (Lockton et al., 2012). Considering which model(s) of users designers and other stakeholders in a project have can be useful for a more reflective design process, but also for understanding the different approaches to design for behaviour change that are taken in commercial or other practical applications. For example, some companies appear to model their customers as 'thoughtful' (and design accordingly), while others take a quite different approach. As Dunne (2005: 21–22) notes, "while electronic objects are being used, their use is constrained by the simple generalised model of a user these objects are designed around. . . we unwittingly adopt roles created by the human factors specialists of large corporations." Or, as Ranner et al. (2016: 1) put it, "in drafting a normal, everything else is treated as defective."

For example, in applications of design for behaviour change to reducing home energy use, Strengers (2011) considers it "alarming" that the model of individual householders as "micro-resource managers," and the language of "demand management," continue to dominate the design of feedback systems. Brynjarsdóttir et al. (2012: 950) describe persuasive design for sustainability as "a modernist enterprise," focussing both on individuals at the expense of broader social considerations, and on narrowing the broad scope of sustainability into "the more manageable problem of 'resource minimisation,'" drawing on Scott's (1999) conception of how states have attempted to make populations 'legible' through reducing their variety (of behaviour as of other characteristics). Fantini van Ditmar and Lockton (2016) explore the ways in which simplistic models of motivation underlie much of the quantified self behaviour change technology arising from Silicon Valley, while Whitson (2015) draws parallels between this gamified quantification and Foucauldian governance and normalization.

This criticism links well with approaches highlighting the potential value of considering social practices (Wilhite, 2013; Shove et al., 2012) in this area, rather than 'behaviour' – specifically because social practice theory's emphasis on shared activities and ways of meeting daily needs can "lift[. . .] understandings of resource consumption to [a] supra individual level" (Kuijer et al., 2013: 2). Scott et al. (2012: 280) call for "a more comprehensive understanding of 'users' as social creatures, and the role of consumption in everyday life, than has ever been undertaken through design." Nevertheless, adopting a practice-theory-based approach in a design process – treating practices as "a unit of design" (Kuijer et al., 2013: 1) – is not straightforward. Enabling the framing of problems to evolve and be expanded (Maher et al., 1996), while valuable in exploring the scope of sustainability or other social benefit considerations, can be difficult to translate directly into insights usable for designers.

There is potentially a need for a structured way of exploring the assumptions and implications inherent in design which seeks to influence behaviour, to enable a more reflective design approach. The next stage of the author's research aims to explore this in more detail.

References

Ajzen, I. (1985). From intentions to actions: A theory of planned behavior. In J. Kuhl & J. Beckman (Eds.), *Action-control: From cognition to behavior* (pp. 11–39). Heidelberg: Springer.

Akrich, M. (1992). The de-scription of technical objects. In W. E. Bijker & J. Law (Eds.), *Shaping technology/building society: Studies in sociotechnical change* (pp. 205–224). Cambridge, MA: MIT Press.

Alexander, C., Ishikawa, S., & Silverstein, M. (1977). *A pattern language: Towns, buildings, construction*. New York: Oxford University Press.

Anderson, S. (1966). *Problem-solving and problem-worrying*. Presentation to the Architectural Association, London, March. Retrieved from: http://web.mit.edu/soa/www/downloads/1963-69/TH_AALond-Lect_66.pdf

Argyris, C., & Schön, D. A. (1974). *Theory in practice: Increasing professional effectiveness*. San Francisco, CA: Jossey-Bass.

Armstrong, J. (2010). *Persuasive advertising: Evidence-based principles*. London: Palgrave Macmillan.

Bisset, F., & Lockton, D. (2010). Designing motivation or motivating design? Exploring service design, motivation and behavioural change. *Touchpoint: The Journal of Service Design, 2*(1), 14–27.

Blevis, E. (2007). Sustainable interaction design: Invention & disposal, renewal & reuse. In *Proceedings of CHI 2007* (pp. 503–512). New York: ACM.

Borchers, J. (2002). Teaching HCI design patterns: Experience from two university courses. In *Proceedings of CHI 2002: Workshop position papers*. New York: ACM.

Box, G. E. P., & Draper, N. R. (1987). *Empirical model-building and response surfaces*. New York: Wiley.

Brand, S. (1994). *How buildings learn: What happens after they're built*. London: Viking.

Broady, M. (1972 [1966]). Social theory in architectural design. In R. Gutman (Ed.), *People and buildings* (pp. 170–185). New York: Basic Books.

Brynjarsdóttir, H., Håkansson, M., Pierce, J., Baumer, E. P. S., DiSalvo, C., & Sengers, P. (2012). Sustainably unpersuaded: How persuasion narrows our vision of sustainability. In *Proceedings of CHI 2012*. New York: ACM.

Buchanan, R. (1992). Wicked problems in design thinking. *Design Issues, 8*(2), 5–21.

Burns, C. M., & Hajdukiewicz, J. R. (2004). *Ecological interface design*. Boca Raton, FL: CRC Press.

Carroll, J. M., Olson, J. R., & Anderson, N. S. (1987). *Mental models in human-computer interaction: Research issues about what the user of software knows*. Washington, DC: National Research Council.

Chatterton, T., & Wilson, C. (2013). The four dimensions of behaviour framework: A tool for characterising behaviours to help design better interventions. *Transportation Planning and Technology, 37*(1), 38–61.

Clark, G. L. (2009). Human nature, the environment, and behaviour: Explaining the scope and geographical scale of financial decision-making. *SPACES Online, 7*(2009–01), 3–22.

Clement, J. (1991). Non-formal reasoning in experts and in science students: The use of analogies, extreme cases, and physical intuition. In J. F. Voss, D. N. Perkins, & J. W. Segal (Eds.), *Informal reasoning and education* (pp. 345–362). London: Routledge.

Crowe, T. D. (2000). *Crime prevention through environmental design* (2nd ed.). Boston, MA: Butterworth-Heinemann.

Daae, J. Z., & Boks, C. (2014). Dimensions of behaviour change. *Journal of Design Research, 12*(3), 145–172.

Darnton, A. (2008, July). *Reference report: An overview of behaviour change models and their uses.* London, UK: Government Social Research.

Desmet, P. M. A., & Hekkert, P. (2007). Framework of product experience. *International Journal of Design, 1*(1), 57–66.

Dilnot, C. (2015). History, design, futures: Contending with what we have made. In T. Fry, C. Dilnot, & S. C. Stewart (Ed.), *Design and the question of history* (pp. 131–272). London: Bloomsbury.

Djajadiningrat, T., Overbeeke, K., & S. Wensveen. (2002). But how, Donald, tell us how? On the creation of meaning in interaction design through feedforward and inherent feedback. In *Proceedings of DIS'02: Designing interactive systems: Processes, practices, methods, & techniques* (pp. 285–291), London, UK, June 25–28, 2002.

Dorst, K. (2015). *Frame innovation.* Cambridge, MA: MIT Press.

Dubberly, H., & Pangaro, P. (2007). Cybernetics and service-craft: Language for behavior-focused design. *Kybernetes, 36*(9), 1301–1317.

Dunne, A. (2005). *Hertzian tales.* Cambridge, MA: MIT Press.

Eyal, N., & Hoover, R. (2013). *Hooked: How to build habit-forming products.* New York: Portfolio.

Fabricant, R. (2009, February 11). Behaving badly in Vancouver. *Design Mind.* San Francisco: Frog Design. Retrieved from http://designmind.frogdesign.com/blog/behaving-badly-in- vancouver.html

Fantini van Ditmar, D., & Lockton, D. (2016). Taking the code for a walk. *Interactions 23*(1), 68–71.

Fincher, S. (1999). Analysis of design: An exploration of patterns and pattern languages for pedagogy. *Journal of Computers in Mathematics and Science Teaching, 18*(3), 331–348.

Fogg, B. J. (2003). *Persuasive technology: Using computers to change what we think and do.* San Francisco, CA: Morgan Kaufmann.

Fogg, B. J. (2009). A behavior model for persuasive design. In Samir Chatterjee & Parvati Dev (Eds.), *Proceedings of the 4th international conference on persuasive technology* (Persuasive '09), Claremont, CA, April 26–29, 2009.

Fry, T. (2015). Whither design/whether history. In T. Fry, C. Dilnot & S. C. Stewart (Ed.), *Design and the question of history* (pp. 1–130). London: Bloomsbury.

Gaver, W., Dunne, A., & Pacenti, E. (1999). Cultural probes. *Interactions, 6*(1), 21–29.

Gentner, D., & Stevens, A. L. (Eds.). (1983). *Mental models.* Englewood Cliffs: Lawrence Erlbaum Associates.

Gibson, J. J. (1979). *The ecological approach to visual perception.* New York: Houghton-Mifflin.

Gintis, H. (2007). A framework for the unification of the behavioral sciences. *Behavioral and Brain Sciences, 30*(1), 1–16.

Golembewski, M. (2010). *Ideation decks: A card-based tool designed to help creative practitioners develop project ideas.* Horizon DTC report. University of Nottingham, UK.

Grist, M. (2010). *Steer: Mastering our behaviour through instinct, environment and reason.* London: RSA.

Grout, J. (2007). *Mistake-proofing the design of health care processes.* Rockville, MD: Agency for Healthcare Research and Quality.

Guagnano, G. A., Stern, P. C., & Dietz, T. (1995). Influences on attitude-behavior relationships. *Environment and Behavior, 27*(5), 699–718.

Hassenzahl, M., & Laschke, M. (2014). Pleasurable troublemakers. In S. Walz & S. Deterding (Eds.), *The gameful world* (pp. 167–195). Cambridge, MA: MIT Press.

Haynes, L., Service, O., Goldacre, B., & Torgersen, D. (2012). *Test, learn, adapt: Developing public policy with randomised controlled trials.* London: Cabinet Office.

Hazas, M., Bernheim Brush, A. J., & Scott, J. (2012). Sustainability does not begin with the individual. *Interactions, 19*(5), 14–17.

IDEO (2003). *IDEO method cards: 51 ways to inspire design.* Palo Alto, CA: IDEO.

Irwin, T., Kossoff, G., & Tonkinwise, C. (2015). Transition design provocation. *Design Philosophy Papers, 13*(1), 3–11.

Jelsma, J. (2006). Designing 'Moralized' products: Theory and practice. In P.-P. Verbeek & A. Slob (Eds.), *User behaviour and technology development* (pp. 221–231). Berlin: Springer.

Jelsma, J., & Knot, M. (2002). Designing environmentally efficient services: A "script" approach. *Journal of Sustainable Product Design, 2*(3–4), 119–130.

John, P., Cotterill, S., Richardson, L., Moseley, A., Stoker, G., Wales, C., & Smith, G. (2011). *Nudge, nudge, think, think: Experimenting with ways to change civic behaviour*. London: Bloomsbury.

Jones, N. A., Ross, H., Lynam, T., Perez, P., & Leitch, A. (2011). Mental models: An interdisciplinary synthesis of theory and methods. *Ecology and Society, 16*(1), article 46. www.ecologyandsociety.org/vol16/iss1/art46/

Kahneman, D., & Tversky, A. (1979). Prospect theory: An analysis of decision under risk. *Econometrica, 47*(2), 263–291.

Kanis, H. (1998). Usage centred research for everyday product design. *Applied Ergonomics, 29*(1), 75–82.

Kotzé, P., Renaud, K., Koukouletsos, K., Khazaei, B., & Dearden, A. (2006). Patterns, anti-patterns and guidelines – effective aids to teaching HCI principles? In E. T. Hvannberg, J. C. Read, L. Bannon, P. Kotzé & W. Wong (Eds.), *Proceedings of HCIEd2006–1: First joint BCS/IFIP WG 13.1/ICS/EU CONVIVIO HCI educators' workshop, Limerick, Ireland* (pp. 115–120). Limerick: University of Limerick.

Krippendorff, K. (2007). The cybernetics of design and the design of cybernetics. *Kybernetes, 36*(9/10), 1381–1392.

Kuijer, L., & de Jong, A. M. (2011). Practice theory and human-centered design: A sustainable bathing example. In *Proceedings of Nordes 2011* (pp. 221–27). Helsinki: Aalto University.

Kuijer, L., de Jong, A. M., & van Eijk, D. (2013). Practices as a unit of design: An exploration of theoretical guidelines in a study on bathing. *Transactions on Computer-Human Interaction, 20*(4), article 22.

Lawson, B. (2004). Schemata, gambits and precedent: Some factors in design expertise. *Design Studies, 25*, 443–457.

Lewin, K. (1935). *A dynamic theory of personality*. New York: McGraw-Hill.

Lilley, D. (2007). *Designing for behavioural change: Reducing the social impacts of product use through design* (PhD thesis). Loughborough University, Loughborough, UK.

Lilley, D. (2009). Design for sustainable behaviour: Strategies and perceptions. *Design Studies, 30*(6), 704–720.

Lockton, D. (2012). *POSIWID and determinism in design for behaviour change*. Working paper, Social Science Research Network. Retrieved from http://papers.ssrn.com/sol3/papers.cfm?abstract_id=2033231

Lockton, D., Harrison, D., & Stanton, N. A. (2008). Making the user more efficient: Design for sustainable behaviour. *International Journal of Sustainable Engineering, 1*(1), 3–8.

Lockton, D., Harrison, D., & Stanton, N. A. (2009). Choice architecture and design with intent. In W. Wong & N. A. Stanton (Eds.), *Doctoral Consortium Proceedings of NDM9—9th Bi-annual international conference on naturalistic decision making*, June 23–26, 2009, London, UK (pp. 1–7). Swindon: British Computer Society.

Lockton, D., Harrison, D., & Stanton, N. A. (2010). The design with intent method: A design tool for influencing user behaviour. *Applied Ergonomics, 41*(3), 382–392.

Lockton, D., Harrison, D., & Stanton, N. A. (2012). Models of the user: Designers' perspectives on influencing sustainable behaviour. *Journal of Design Research, 10*(1/2), 7–27.

Lockton, D., Harrison, D., & Stanton, N. A. (2013). Exploring design patterns for sustainable behaviour. *The Design Journal, 16*(4), 431–459.

Mager, B. (2010). Editorial: Isn't life always centred around influencing the behaviour of other people? *Touchpoint: The Journal of Service Design, 2*(1), 6–7.

Maher, M. L., Poon, J., & Boulanger, S. (1996). Formalising design exploration as co-evolution: A combined gene approach. In J. S. Gero & F. Sudweeks (Eds.), *Advances in formal design methods for CAD* (pp. 3–30). London: Chapman & Hall.

Meadows, D. (1999). *Leverage points: Places to intervene in a system*. Vermont: Sustainability Institute.

Meadows, D. (2009). *Thinking in systems: A primer*. London: Earthscan.

Michie, S., van Stralen, M. M., & West, R. (2011). The behaviour change wheel: A new method for characterising and designing behaviour change interventions. *Implementation Science, 6*, article 42.

Michie, S., West, R., Campbell, R., Brown, J., & Gainforth, H. (2014). *ABC of behaviour change theories*. London: Silverback Publishing.

Moray, N. (1996). Mental models in theory and practice. In D. Gopher & A. Koriat (Eds.), *Attention and performance XVII, cognitive regulation of performance: Interaction of theory and application* (pp. 223–258). Cambridge, MA: MIT Press

Niedderer, K., MacKrill, J., Clune, S., Evans, M., Lockton, D., Ludden, G., Morris, A., Gutteridge, R., Gardiner, E., Cain, R., & Hekkert, P. (2014). *Joining forces: Investigating the influence of design for behaviour change on sustainable innovation.* NordDesign 2014: 10th Biannual Conference on Design and Development, Aalto University, Espoo, Finland, August 27–29.

Nodder, C. (2013). *Evil by design.* New York: Wiley.

Norman, D. A. (1988). *The psychology of everyday things.* New York: Basic Books.

Nuffield Council on Bioethics. (2007). *Public health: Ethical issues.* Retrieved from www.nuffieldbioethics.org/sites/default/files/Public%20health%20-%20ethical%20issues.pdf

Papert, S. (1980). *Mindstorms: Children, computers, and powerful ideas.* New York: Basic Books.

Payne, S. J. (1991). A descriptive study of mental models. *Behaviour & Information Technology, 10*(1), 3–21.

Pettersen, I. N. (2015). Towards practice-oriented design for sustainability: The compatibility with selected design fields. *International Journal of Sustainable Engineering, 8*(3), 206–218.

Petty, R. E., & Cacioppo, J. T. (1981). *Attitudes and persuasion: Classic and contemporary approaches.* Dubuque, IA: William C. Brown.

Plous, S. (1993). *The psychology of judgment and decision making.* New York: McGraw-Hill.

Ranner, V., Lockton, D., Steenson, M. W., Galik, G., & Kerridge, T. (2016). *Plans and speculated actions.* In DRS 2016: Design, Research, Society: Future-Focused Thinking, 27–30 June 2016, Brighton, UK. Retrieved from http://drs2016.org/549

Redström, J. (2005). Towards user design? On the shift from object to user as the subject of design. *Design Studies, 27*, 123–139.

Rittel, H. W. J., & Webber, M. M. (1973). Dilemmas in a general theory of planning. *Policy Sciences, 4*, 155–169.

Ross, L., & Nisbett, R. E. (1992). *The person and the situation.* New York: McGraw-Hill.

Scott, J. C. (1999). *Seeing like a state: How certain schemes to improve the human condition have failed.* New Haven, CT: Yale University Press.

Scott, K., Bakker, C. A., & Quist, J. (2012). Designing change by living change. *Design Studies, 33*(3), 279–297.

Selvefors, A., Renström, S., & Strömberg, H. (2014). *Design for sustainable behaviour: A toolbox for targeting the use phase.* Eco-Design Tool Conference, Gothenburg, Sweden.

Shingo, S. (1986). *Zero quality control: Source inspection and the Poka-Yoke method.* Boca Raton: CRC Press.

Shove, E. (2010). Beyond the ABC: Climate change policy and theories of social change. *Environment and Planning A, 42*(6), 1273–1285.

Shove, E., Pantzar, M., & Watson, M. (2012). *The dynamics of social practice: Everyday life and how it changes.* London: Sage.

Simon, H. A. (1981). *The sciences of the artificial* (2nd ed.). Cambridge, MA: MIT Press.

Simon, H. A. (1990). Invariants of human behavior. *Annual Review of Psychology, 41*, 1–19.

Simon, H. A. (1996). *The sciences of the artificial* (3nd ed.). Cambridge, MA: MIT Press.

Stanton, N. A., & Baber, C. (2002). Error by design: Methods for predicting device usability. *Design Studies, 23*, 363–384.

Stanton, N. A., Salmon, P. M., Rafferty, L. A., Walker, G. H., Baber, C., & Jenkins, D. P. (2013). *Human factors methods: A practical guide for engineering and design* (2nd ed.). Farnham: Ashgate.

Stern, P. C. (2000). Toward a coherent theory of environmentally significant behavior. *Journal of Social Issues, 56*(3), 407–424.

Strengers, Y. A. (2011). Designing eco-feedback systems for everyday life. In *Proceedings of CHI 2011* (pp. 2135–2144). New York: ACM.

Strömberg, H., Selvefors, A., & Renström, S. (2015). Mapping out the design opportunities: Pathways of sustainable behaviour. *International Journal of Sustainable Engineering, 8*(3), 163–172.

Suchman, L. (2011). Anthropological relocations and the limits of design. *Annual Review of Anthropology, 40*, 1–18.

Terzioğlu, N., Brass, C., & Lockton, D. (2015). *Understanding user motivations and drawbacks related to product repair.* Sustainable Innovation 2015, 9–10 November 2015, Epsom, UK.

Thaler, R. H., & Sunstein, C. R. (2008). *Nudge: Improving decisions about health, wealth, and happiness.* New Haven, CT: Yale University Press.

Todd, P. M., Gigerenzer, G., & the ABC Research Group. (2012). *Ecological rationality: Intelligence in the world.* New York: Oxford University Press.

Tromp, N., & Hekkert, P. P. (2014). Social Implication Design (SID) – a design method to exploit the unique value of the artefact to counteract social problem. *Proceedings of the Design Research Society Conference 2014,* Umeå Design School, Umeå, Sweden.

Tromp, N., Hekkert, P., & Verbeek, P. (2011). Design for socially responsible behaviour: A classification of influence based on intended user experience. *Design Issues, 27*(3), 3–19.

Tversky, A., & Kahneman, D. (1974). Judgment under uncertainty: Heuristics and biases. *Science, 185*(4157), 1124–1131.

Watson, J., Clegg, C., Cowell, C., Davies, F., Hughes, C., McCarthy, N., & Westbury, P. (Eds.). (2015). *Built for living: Understanding behaviour and the built environment through engineering and design.* London: Royal Academy of Engineering.

Wendel, S. A. (2013). *Designing for behavior change.* Sebastopol, CA: O'Reilly.

Wever, R. (2012). Editorial: Design research for sustainable behaviour. *Journal of Design Research, 10*(1/2), 1–6.

Wever, R., van Kuijk, J., & Boks, C. (2008). User-centred design for sustainable behaviour. *International Journal of Sustainable Engineering, 1*(1), 9–20.

Whitson, J. R. (2015). Foucault's fitbit: Governance and gamification. In S. Walz & S. Deterding (Eds.), *The gameful world.* Cambridge, MA: MIT Press.

Wilhite, H. (2013). Energy consumption as cultural practice: Implications for the theory and policy of sustainable energy use. In S. Strauss, S. Rupp, & T. Love (Eds.), *Cultures of energy* (pp. 60–73). Walnut Creek: Left Coast Press.

Zachrisson, J., & Boks, C. (2012). Exploring behavioural psychology to support design for sustainable behaviour research. *Journal of Design Research, 10*(1/2), 50–66.

7 Tweaking interaction through understanding the user

Johannes Daae and Casper Boks

Introduction

Assuming that designers want to design for sustainable behaviour – what options do they have? What is their toolkit? Which control knobs can they slide when looking for ways to nudge users in the right direction, or away from the wrong direction? What is their room to play with? In the past 10 years, research has begun to address these questions, and gradually the field has realized that opportunities are many.

Jelsma's dimensions of 'script' (1997, 2006; Jelsma & Knot, 2002) was one of the first contributions to understanding how the design of products affects behaviour. He proposed that a script has a direction (how much the behaviour change is in line with the beliefs and values of the user), a force (how difficult the script makes it for the user to act differently to what is intended), a scale (whether the changes are made directly in the interaction between the user and the product, the function of the product or in the entire practice) and a distribution (how much control the user has over the behaviour). These dimensions are essentially an elaboration of the three notions derived from the concept of script proposed by Akrich: in-scription, prescription and de-scription (Akrich, 1992). Description is the purpose (e.g. do not forget to bring the hotel key back to the front desk), in-scription is the translation of the de-scription into the product (e.g. heavy weight on the key reminds guests to return the key) and prescription is what a devise allows or forbids the actor to do (e.g. forget to return the key to the front desk or not).

Around 2005, scripts were picked up by various researchers that today make up the Design for Sustainable Behaviour research community (see e.g. Boks et al., 2015). In 2005, Lilley et al. (2005) expanded on Jelsma's understanding by proposing a distinction between three types of design principles according to how strongly they affected the behaviour. In their structure, the concept of scripts covers the middle part of a spectrum together with what was called Behaviour Steering. On one side they added Eco-feedback, which aims at influencing the behaviour by providing information or feedback, and on the other 'Intelligent' Products and Systems, which take control of the behaviour away from the user and force desired behaviour or block inappropriate behaviour. This created a dimension, where – at one end – the users are in complete control and can choose to read and interpret the Eco-feedback, and further choose to alter their behaviour accordingly or not. At the other end, the users are forced to behave in the desired way by the 'intelligent' products or systems. Between these two extremes, users are guided towards the desired behaviour by the script, but without being forced. The identification of the categories between the two extremes makes it similar to Zaltman's (1974) classification of social change strategies, which includes re-educative Strategies (communication of fact, feedback), Facilitation (increase the ease), Persuasive strategies (involve bias in the structuring and presentation) and Power Strategies (involve the use and/or threat of force).

Elias et al. (2007) proposed a variation of this categorization of change strategies (although without a strong forceful intervention). He made a distinction between consumer education, feedback and user-centred eco-design. The former two are clearly at the end of the spectrum where the user is in control, whereas the latter is defined as "creating products where the most intuitive and comfortable way of using and interacting with a product or system is also the most environmentally friendly" (Elias et al., 2008), bringing it closer to the understanding of scripts.

Wever et al. (2008) proposed a similar categorization of change strategies to Lilley et al. (2005), with the inclusion of Behaviour Steering in the script category, and alternate phrasing of 'intelligent' Products and Systems as Forced Functionality, creating a clearer reference to the lack of control this type of principles allows the user to have. Bhamra et al. (2008) elaborated the distribution proposed by Lilley et al. by splitting it up into seven parts: Eco-information, Eco-choice, Eco-feedback, Eco-spur, Eco-steer, Eco-technology and Clever Design. The Eco-feedback strategies are similar to those of Lilley et al. apart from that simple information has been extracted and given the name Eco-information. The intelligent product and systems are similar to the Eco-technology and the strategies Lilley et al. call scripts and behaviour steering resemble Eco-choice and Eco-steering. In addition, Bhamra et al. have added Eco-spur and Clever Design, which are not included in the structure of Lilley et al. Eco-spur is meant to reward the intended behaviour, whereas Clever Design creates the desired end result without changing the user behaviour.

Based on the categorization of change strategies by Bhamra et al. (2008) and Wever et al. (2008), Lidman and Renström (2011) proposed a categorization, dividing the distribution of control into four categories; Enlighten (providing information or educating the user), Spur (encourage or tempt the user), Steer (guide the user) and Force (compel the user). In addition they proposed a category called Match, which does not aim to affect the behaviour of the user and thereby does not naturally have a position within the distribution of control. There are also two other categorizations, which have slightly different perspectives, but apply the same rationale. One is found in the introduction to the *Design with Intent* toolkit (Lockton et al., 2010b). Instead of describing how the product is affecting behaviour, Lockton et al. describe three different ways to perceive the user: Pinball (users do not think at all), Shortcuts (users take shortcuts and make choices based on how the options are presented) and Thoughtful (users take every opportunity to learn more about the world around them and their impact on it). These three categories describe the user perspective of the two extremes and the centre part of the distribution of control as described earlier. The other category was proposed by Tromp et al. (2011), and attempts to describe how products affect behaviour from how the user experiences it. They suggest a two-dimensional landscape, where the dimension of force is combined with a dimension of salience. The dimension of force is described with Persuasive or Seductive principles on one end and Decisive or Coercive principles on the other, creating a distribution similar to the one described earlier.

As the logic in these distributions is similar, the difference seems mainly to be a question of language in naming the scale from 'user in control' to 'product in control'. For example: the Distribution of Control or Force (Jelsma, 1997; Tromp et al., 2011); Axis of Influence (Lilley, 2007); or "Spectrum of Control" (Lockton, 2013) can all be considered as scales where the user has complete control on one end, and the product has complete control on the other end. Table 7.1 summarizes this distribution of change strategies in a single overview where at one end the user is in control. Design strategies at this end focus on providing the user with information or feedback. This information will in most cases have to be registered, interpreted, understood and reasoned upon before a behaviour change is possible. At the other end of the scale are design strategies that either force the user to behave in a certain way, or eliminate the users behaviour by acting automatically. As the user does not have any influence, these strategies may require limited or no attention from the user to change the behaviour. Between these two extremities are strategies with a varying degree of division of control. Solutions may range from simply enabling a certain type of behaviour, to guiding or steering the behaviour in the intended direction by making the desired behaviour easier, or the undesired behaviour more difficult.

Lockton (2010a) has done important research to open up the solution space further. A tool that has received much attention is the *Design with Intent* (DwI) toolkit, which consists of 101 patterns or principles for influencing behaviour. The patterns are structured into eight lenses according to the "worldviews" of how the designer approaches behaviour change (Lockton et al., 2010b). The eight lenses are as follows: Architectural, Errorproofing, Interaction, Ludic, Perceptual, Cognitive, Machiavellian and Security. Each pattern is presented on a separate card, and consists of a title, a question pointing out the function of the pattern, and an example of an application of the pattern with a short description and a picture (Lockton et al., 2010b). The patterns can be regarded as ways to achieve the desired level of control but also include a variety of cues that can be regarded as suggestions to play with other dimensions that may influence behaviour. The toolkit does not suggest which dimensions or pattern to employ – for this, one needs to research who the user is, what goes on in his or her mind and understand the surroundings that affect the behaviour to be changed. To this end, a tool called the Principles of Behaviour Change was developed at NTNU (Zachrisson et al., 2011; Boks & Daae, 2013), but this was still very much building on the distribution of control, combined with obtrusiveness, and did not consider other dimensions.

Table 7.1 Variation of the distribution of control described in the literature

User in control		Zaltman, 1974	Jelsma, 1997	Lilley et al., 2005b	Elias et al., 2007	Bhamra et al., 2008	Wever et al., 2008	Lockton et al., 2010	Lidman & Renström, 2011	Tromp et al., 2011
Informing	Information									
	Feedback	Reeducation		Eco-Feedback	Consumer education	Eco-information	Eco-feedback	Thoughtful	Enlighten	
	Enabling				Feedback	Eco-feedback				
		Facilitation				Eco-spur				
Persuading	Encouraging					Eco-choice			Spur	
	Guiding	Persuasion	Scripts	Scripts and Behaviour Steering	User Centred eco-design		Scripting	Shortcuts		Seductive/ Persuasive
	Steering					Eco-steer			Steer	
Determining	Forcing	Power		'Intelligent' Products and Systems		Eco-technical intervention	Forced-functionality	Pinballs		Decisive/ coercive
	Automatic								Force	

Product in control

Dimensions of behaviour change

To expand the work on the Principles of Behaviour Change tool, subsequently, other dimensions that designers could use were explored. The main idea was to explore the missing link between *understanding the user* and knowing *how design may affect behaviour*. The key question was this: would it be possible to know and develop guidelines for which type of design intervention would provide the best opportunity to affect user behaviour in the desired way?

Through creative workshops and interviews with both experts on design for sustainable behaviour and professional designers without experience in this field, empirical data was collected on how they thought designers may influence behaviour. As experts, we chose design practitioners, professionally employed at different design agencies and companies located in Oslo and Trondheim. Our empirical data was collected during five workshops at these companies, in workshop sessions that lasted for about two hours and had between two and six participants. All participants held at least a master's degree in industrial design and work with product and interface design on a daily basis (Daae & Boks, 2014).

After conducting the workshops, it was obvious that the dimensions suggested during the workshops operated on several different levels and were partly overlapping. Thus, the next step was to structure them in a clear and logic way. It was considered useful to try to structure them by finding opposing dimensions, along which designers could try to find the right level of employing the dimension depending on the understanding of the user and how he would react. Some of the dimensions suggested a continuous description along a scale, whereas others were found to be more suitable for a more discrete description, or even representing different logical concepts that are not necessarily opposing. However, the concept of dimensions along a scale between opposing mechanisms was maintained to explore its potential, partly in search of uniformity with 'control' and 'obtrusiveness', two dimensions which at that stage already had received some acceptance. Efforts were made to maintain the essence of all the dimensions and reduce loss of information as far as possible. Table 7.2 provides an overview of the dimensions that resulted from the workshops.

It was found that four of the dimensions – Control, Obtrusiveness, Direction and Empathy – were already known from literature. Whereas Meaning, Encouragement, Importance, Timing and Exposure were considered new dimensions in the context of the current design literature that contribute to the extension of the toolkit that designers can draw on when designing interactions.

Aiming towards such a toolkit, the dimensions needed to be translated into a format that would be usable for designers. After some consideration, it was decided to create a physical tool in the form of a series of relatively large A5 sized cards, as they would be relatively easy to understand, and with an inspiring and visual content that would facilitate discussion in a cooperative setting. Each card depicts a number of photos or illustrations that explain the dimension and how it may affect a user's behaviour. To help the designers understand the potential consequences of the different parts of the dimension, a number of likely advantages and disadvantages are briefly stated for each extreme, and in some cases also for the central part of the dimension. The reverse of each card contains some further elaborations on the dimension, providing additional support for designers.

Design for behaviour change tool

This section provides an overview of the dimensions and the related cards. Only the front side of each card is shown, with the exception of the Control card, for which both sides are shown. For the other cards, the explanations below the picture of the front side reflect what is written on the flip sides.

Table 7.2 Categorization of the empirical data: from 55 dimensions to 9 main dimension categories

Dimensions from the workshops	*Description of the dimensions*	*Proposed dimensions*
• Choice vs no choice • User in control vs product in control • Convince vs demand • Encourage vs impose • Information vs overruling • Force vs guide • Individual freedom vs greater good • Opt in vs opt out • On my way vs far away • Simple vs complicated • Information vs simplify • Forced usage vs punishment	*Shall the user or the product determine the behaviour?* Allow the user freedom of choice of action vs Forcing the user by giving product control	Control (known from literature; e. g. Jelsma, 1997; Lilley et al., 2005; Elias et al., 2007)
• Passive user vs active user • Obvious vs hidden • Open and inviting vs secretive and mysterious	*How much attention shall the design demand?* Demand attention or action from the user vs Use a subtle or obvious approach to reach a goal	Obtrusiveness (known from literature; Zachrisson and Boks, 2012; Tromp et al., 2011)
• Helpful vs annoying • Invite vs deter • Polite vs impolite • Stigmatizing vs elevating • Reduce usage vs increase usage • Reward vs don't reward • Good vs bad conscience • Much info/output vs little info/output	*Should the desired behaviour be promoted or the undesired discouraged?* The design leads the user towards the desired behaviour vs The design leads the user away from the undesired behaviour (Discrete scale)	Encouragement (novel)
• Fun vs meaningful • Emotional vs rational • Competition vs no competition • Wish vs should	*Does the design focus on rational or emotional purpose?* Motivate the user through fun (hedonic) vs Motivate the user through meaning (rational)	Meaning (novel)
• User agree vs don't agree • Meaningless vs meaningful • Primary function vs disconnected • Central function vs additional function • Trendy vs not trendy • Environmentally concerned vs not concerned	*Is the desired behaviour in line or opposing the wishes of the user?* The user is motivated to perform the behaviour vs The user is not motivated to perform the behaviour	Direction (known from literature; Jelsma, 1997)
• I know I do something vs the world knows it • Social norms vs individual norms • Consequences for me vs for others • Users responsibility vs others responsibility	*Is the user focussing on themselves or others and what others think?* Play on the user's concerns about himself or herself vs the user's concerns about others	Empathy (known from literature; mentioned by Tromp et al., 2011)
• Physical vs intellectual consequence • Fulfilment of dreams vs survival • Large consequence vs small consequence • Neutral sender vs non-neutral sender	*How important does the user consider the behaviour to be?* Make the user feels strong pressure vs Use weak pressure	Importance (novel)

Dimensions from the workshops	Description of the dimensions	Proposed dimensions
• Instructions vs feedback • long-term vs short-term consequences • Preventing vs reducing consequences	*Should the design target the user before, during or after the interaction?* The user experiences it now vs The user experiences it later	Timing (novel)
• Always vs particular situations • Rarely vs frequent usage • Dosage vs continuous	*How often will the user encounter the design?* The user is always affected vs The user is sometimes affected	Exposure (novel)
• Easy vs overkill • Perfect vs improved • One culture vs another • Opposing information • Engineering spec. vs usability spec. • New product vs adjust old product • Aesthetics vs usability	Not usable?	

Control (Figures 7.1, 7.2)

How much control the user has over the behaviour can vary from complete control to no control. If the user has much control, designers can only expect the user to behave the desired way if this is in line with their intentions. Having more control is often easier to accept for users, but will generally require more attention, and willingness to pay that amount of attention.

- By providing people with information of what to do, it is up to them if they choose to read it and follow up on it. Example: washing instructions on clothes.
- By making the desired behaviour the easiest or most intuitive, people are gently pushed while still being in control. Example: an ecobutton that easily puts the PC in minimum energy mode.
- By forcing people to behave in a particular way, the behaviour is guaranteed, but people might not accept it. Example: speed bumps forces drivers to proceed slowly.
- Providing people with feedback about their behaviour gives them the option to interpret it and change their behaviour accordingly if they desire to do so. Example: a water counter on the faucet.
- Making the desired behaviour obvious or enabling it may increase the likelihood that it occurs. Example: a dual flush button on a toilet.
- By making the desired behaviour happen automatically, it is guaranteed to happen. Example: opening a microwave door makes the microwave turn off automatically.

Obtrusiveness (Figure 7.3)

How obtrusive a design is will affect how likely it is that the user will become aware of it, but it will also affect how likely it is that the user accepts it. Sometimes the immediate attention of the user is required, whereas in other contexts the user must not be disturbed.

- By requiring extra actions, the attention of the user may be required and their attention is directed. Example: train carriages where the door only has a handle on the outside.

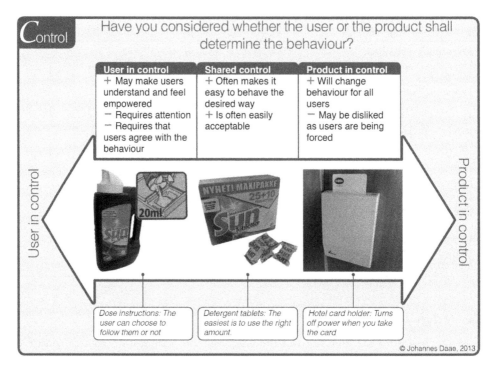

Figure 7.1 Dimensions of behaviour change card 'Control'

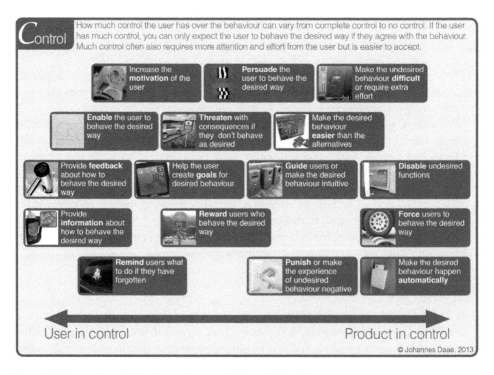

Figure 7.2 Dimensions of behaviour change card 'Control' (back)

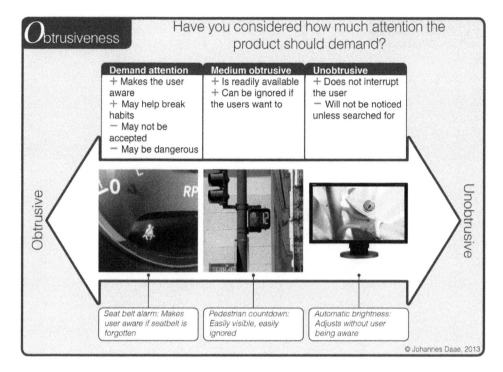

Figure 7.3 Dimensions of behaviour change card 'Obtrusiveness'

- If something is sufficiently easy, people may be aware of it without it requiring much attention. Example: using one dishwasher detergent tablet per washing.
- User instructions are often hidden and will only be seen if searched for. Example: instructions of how much dishwasher detergent people should use.
- If the information is presented there where the attention of the user is, it becomes more likely to be noticed. Example: presenting a message on the screen of the cell phone.
- Information may be presented in a way that is easy to see but does not require attention after it has been seen. Example: traffic signs.
- Sometimes it is important to avoid demanding the attention of people. Example: dash board information suggesting that it would be beneficial to change gear should not distract people from driving safely.

Encouragement (Figure 7.4)

When attempting to make people change their behaviour, designers can focus on which behaviour to avoid, on which way to behave or present alternative ways of behaving – all with various degrees of encouragement.

- Being presented with the positive consequences of their behaviour, people may be encouraged to behave that way. Example: showing how much money they may save by driving a hybrid car.

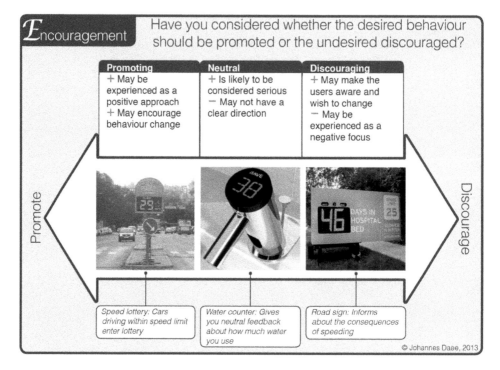

Figure 7.4 Dimensions of behaviour change card 'Encouragement'

- It is possible to present the consequences of behaviour without promoting or discouraging it. Example: presenting energy consumption and its cost.
- Being presented with how much worse certain behaviour is compared to that of others, users may feel bad and change their behaviour consequently. Example: presenting them with how much more energy they use compared to their neighbours.
- Being exposed to information about what other users do, users may want to behave in the same way. Example: stating how many other hotel guests reuse their towels.
- Instructions on how to behave can be presented without promoting or discouraging it in particular. Example: suggested traffic speeds.
- By making undesirable behaviour more difficult, it becomes less tempting to behave that way. Example: the Eco-kettle requires that people push a button for every cup they boil.

Meaning (Figure 7.5)

Sometimes people behave a certain way because they think it is the right way to behave, or because they are afraid of the consequences of behaving differently. Sometimes people might do something just because it is enjoyable or fun, or emotional in some other way.

- Everyday activities may become fun if they become competitions or games. Example: a bottle-bank-arcade makes recycling of bottles into a game.

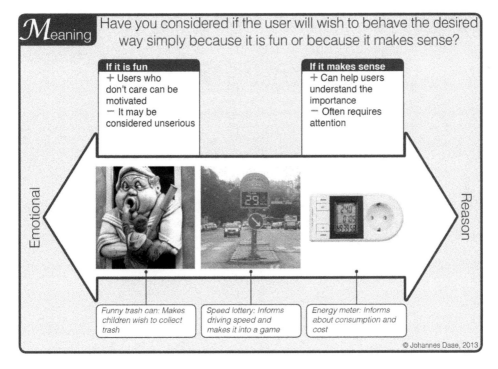

Figure 7.5 Dimensions of behaviour change card 'Meaning'

- Sometimes it can be enjoyable to behave in a rational way. Example: driving in a way that saves fuel and compete against yourself to see how low consumption you can manage.
- Explaining the consequences of an action may make people want to change it. Example: how much money people save on fuel by changing to a hybrid or electric car.
- Designers can use emotional triggers to influence people to behave in certain ways. Example: if the water level in a goldfish bowl reflects the water usage, people might use less water.

Direction (Figure 7.6)

The more the user will agree with the way the designer tries to make him or her behave, the more likely it is that he or she is willing to make an effort or even sacrifice to behave that way.

- If people want to achieve something, they are likely to be willing to make an effort to do so. Example: reading the washing instructions on new clothes before washing them.
- Even if people don't care if they do it or not, they might behave the desired way if it is sufficiently easy. Example: by making the opening of recycle bins indicative of their purpose.

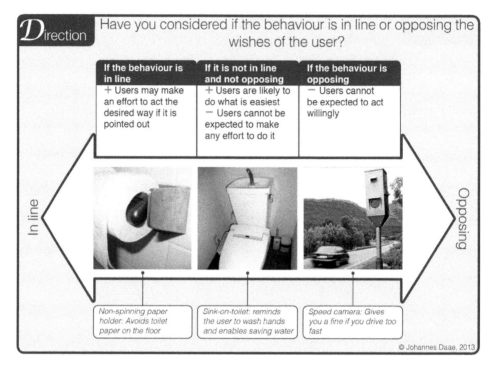

Figure 7.6 Dimensions of behaviour change card 'Direction'

- Sometimes people wish to do something that is undesirable. Products or interfaces can be designed to prevent this. Example: handles in the middle of benches to avoid loitering.
- People may accidentally do things they do not wish to do, and products can be designed to prevent it. Example: opening a microwave door makes the microwave turn off automatically.
- If people don't care about something, it might be possible to make them realize they care about other aspects. Example: making people aware about the costs connected to energy use, instead of the energy use itself.
- Sometimes people can be convinced to do something they would prefer not to do. Example: they may be convinced to ride a bike instead of driving a car in order to get fit or save money.

Empathy (Figure 7.7)

Whether people focus on themselves or on others and what others might think of them depends both on who they are, what they think is important and on the situation they are in.

- By making people set goals for their consumption and then help them monitor it, they can compete against themselves and be motivated to change their behaviour.
- Reminding people in private to do something that is desirable for the common good. Example: a sink basin on top of a toilet cistern reuses hand-washing water to flush the toilet, also adding a conservation message.

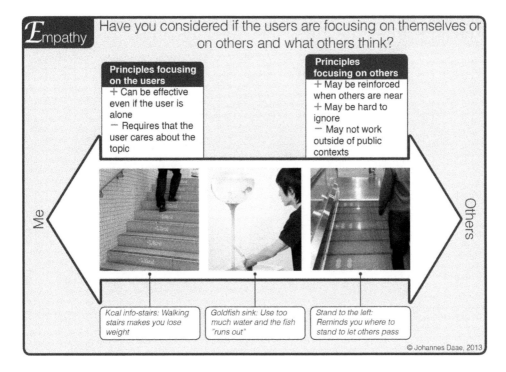

Figure 7.7 Dimensions of behaviour change card 'Empathy'

- By comparing people's behaviour with that of others, they can both understand how well they do and be motivated to change. This can also be used to create competitions.
- Informing people of the personal consequences of their consumption can motivate them to change their behaviour. Example: how much money the use of an appliance costs.
- Sometimes people can do something for personal gain, but if they succeed it is announced to others. Example: winning the bottle-refund lottery makes the machine play a melody.
- By making it obvious to others that people do something might motivate them to do it as they may experience recognition by others that way.

Importance (Figure 7.8)

How important someone considers certain behaviour, or the consequences thereof, to be will affect how much effort the user is willing to put into it. It will also affect to what extent people will accept design solutions that take away the possibility to control their own behaviour.

- Many people will gladly accept the interruption from the seat belt or front lights alarm in the car, because the consequences of forgetting to put the seat belt on or driving without front lights can be severe.
- By describing the consequences of a certain behaviour, more people might consider it to be more important. Example: how much water a hotel saves by not changing the sheets.

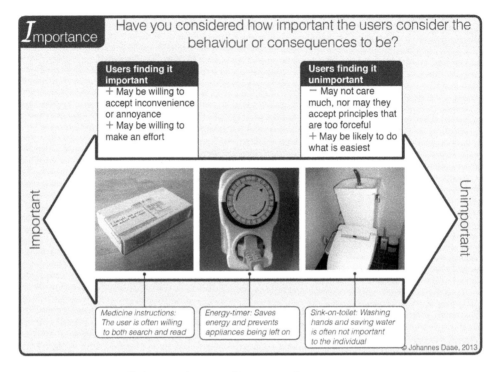

Figure 7.8 Dimensions of behaviour change card 'Importance'

- If people do not think something is important enough to affect their behaviour, it may be an idea to make the desired behaviour easier. Example: by shaping the opening of a recycle bin according to its purpose.
- If something is important, people may accept being forced into certain behaviour or functions being disabled. Example: opening a microwave door makes the microwave turn off automatically.
- To increase the likelihood of people doing something that they do not think is very important, make it easy or obvious for them to behave that way. Example: by informing people how long it will take until the next green traffic light.
- Sometimes it is necessary to punish those who are unwilling to behave the desired way. Example: speed bumps are really uncomfortable to cross with high speeds.

Timing (Figure 7.9)

Whether users encounter behaviour principles before, during or after the behaviour will affect how they are affected by them. Sometimes the context or the users disqualify some options because the users are unwilling to pay attention, or because the context does not allow them to be interrupted.

- Giving instructions of how to use a product, for instance how much dishwasher detergent to use, increases the ability to apply the right amount of detergent (if the instructions are read).

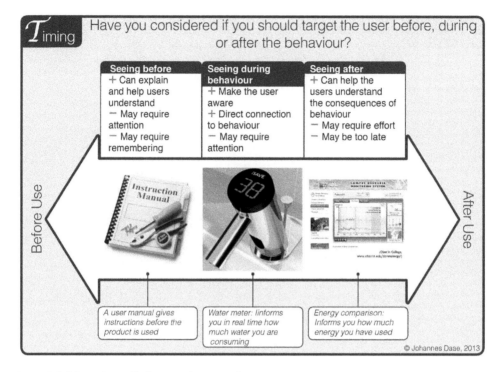

Figure 7.9 Dimensions of behaviour change card 'Timing'

- Presenting people with alternatives at the moment they are about to act may make them reconsider. Example: entering a red-cross lottery with the money from their bottle-refund.
- Car computers can inform people about how much fuel their cars have used on average. This can also be compared with their current driving.
- Explaining the consequences of particular behaviours can motivate people to change their behaviour in the future.
- People may act out of habit or be unaware of something. Reminding them at the moment of interaction can make them aware. Example: ATMs returning a bank card before giving out cash.
- Telling them what to do next may help people doing it. Example: sending a message saying that the phone is fully charged and that chargers should be unplugged to save energy.

Exposure (Figure 7.10)

Users have different needs, and exhibit different levels of acceptance, depending on how often they interact with a product. Something might work if the user encounters it rarely, but lose its effect or become annoying if the user encounters it every day.

- When people are about to do something they rarely do, they might need detailed instructions. They are more likely to read and follow it if the behaviour is important or less intuitive.

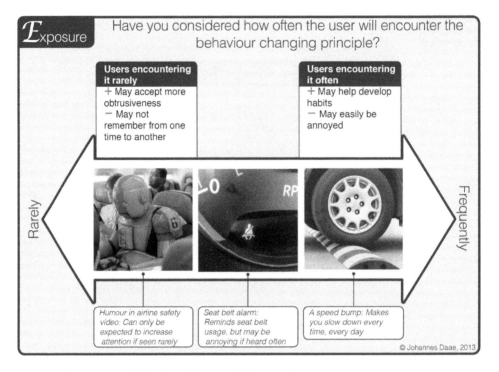

Figure 7.10 Dimensions of behaviour change card 'Exposure'

- Street light countdown displays provide people with information about expected waiting time every day. As they can easily be ignored, it is likely they will not annoy people.
- Very obtrusive designs, such as a heating element shaped as a light bulb that may raise awareness about energy consumption, but are not likely to be accepted if encountered daily.
- Having the main energy switch connected to a key card holder works well in a hotel room but might not be accepted in private homes where people would encounter it every day.
- Dishwasher detergent tablets are likely to make people use the right amount of detergent every time, as the desired behaviour also is the easiest.

The cards describing the dimensions were complemented by two cards explaining the tool. The first card explains how to use the dimensions of behavioural change cards, while the second introduces key principles in understanding the target group.

Reflection

The Dimensions of Behaviour Change (DBC) cards target similar design challenges in comparison with the *Design with Intent* (DwI) cards, and both decks aim to inform a design for sustainable behaviour process. However, the decks use a different approach to

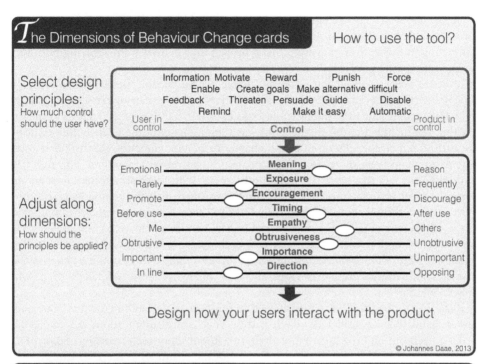

The Dimensions of Behaviour Change cards — How to use the tool?

Select design principles:
How much control should the user have?

Information   Motivate   Reward   Punish   Force
Enable   Create goals   Make alternative difficult
Feedback   Threaten   Persuade   Guide   Disable
Remind   Make it easy   Automatic

User in control ———————— Control ———————— Product in control

Adjust along dimensions:
How should the principles be applied?

Emotional — **Meaning** — Reason
Rarely — **Exposure** — Frequently
Promote — **Encouragement** — Discourage
Before use — **Timing** — After use
Me — **Empathy** — Others
Obtrusive — **Obtrusiveness** — Unobtrusive
Important — **Importance** — Unimportant
In line — **Direction** — Opposing

Design how your users interact with the product

© Johannes Daae, 2013

Understanding the target group

To find out how to change a target behaviour, it is necessary to understand why users behave the way they do. It is likely that the behaviour is caused by one or more of the following reasons. By identifying the most dominating of these reasons, it is possible to gain some understanding of how to change the behaviour.

The user tries to achieve a goal
Users may behave in a way they believe is the best or because they have a positive attitude towards this behaviour. Can they achieve their goal through the desired behaviour? Is it possible to convince them to change their goal? Can the alternative be presented in a way that makes them change their behaviour?

It is the easiest thing to do
Sometimes users behave in a particular way just because it is easy or it requires less effort than behaving in another way. Is it possible to change the behaviour by making the desired behaviour easier? Or by making the undesired more difficult?

Its how the user always do it
Sometimes users behave in a way just out of habit or because they are not even aware of their behaviour. A habit requires repetition in stable circumstances with positive reinforcement. By changing one of these conditions, for instance by changing the experience of using the product or removing the positive outcome, the habit might be broken and the behaviour changed.

Others expect it to be done that way
Sometimes users behave in certain ways because they believe it is the socially accepted thing to do or because they believe others expect it. It may not be feasible to change the social norms, but is it possible to make the user believe the desired behaviour is what is expected of him/her?

It is the morally right thing to do
Users may also behave according to their values or norms. It may be difficult to change these but perhaps it is possible to present the desired behaviour in a way that is in line with their values or norms.

© Johannes Daae, 2013

Figure 7.11 Dimensions of behaviour change card and how to use them

achieve this goal. DwI aims to help designers generate as many ideas as possible for changing behaviour through their design, whereas DBC aims to help designers make informed decisions about which strategies may be most suitable in relation to a certain design for sustainable behaviour challenge. This makes the two tools supplementary rather than competing. It is therefore suggested that a project may benefit from applying both tools for the appropriate purposes.

In 2015, a survey about the future of Design for Sustainable Behaviour research was undertaken, targeting expert researchers that had at least five years of experience with this field. The main results were published in Boks et al. (2015). One issue included in the survey (but not included in this publication) was a question about the relative importance of the various dimensions discussed in this chapter to provide direction for further research. The respondents were quite clear: Control and Obtrusiveness scored best. This may have to do with the fact that researchers are most familiar with these dimensions; they are in a sense the most obvious ones, but it is interesting to note that the respondents still think there is much further research potential related to these. Encouragement, Meaning, Timing and Frequency made up a middle group of dimensions that were considered as relatively interesting to research further. Direction, Importance and Empathy were considered dimensions that were least interesting for further research. One reason for this could be that these dimensions are less obvious, and it is somewhat more difficult to grasp what they entail.

Referring to the title 'Tweaking interaction through understanding the user', one question remains to be considered, which is this: what ethical implications are involved in making decisions on how users should behave without them even knowing? Some of the dimensions discussed in this chapter, and many of the examples in the DwI cards for that matter, may give rise to discussion, may be cause for concern or could be frowned upon: For example, is it okay for a designer to design a thermostat which intentionally indicates a room temperature that is two degrees higher than the actual room temperature, if that would lead to reduction of energy consumption? Berdichevsky and Neuenschwander (1999: 58) stated their golden rule of persuasion: "The creators of a persuasive technology should never seek to persuade a person or persons of something they themselves would not consent to be persuaded to do". They also were of the opinion that "the creators of a persuasive technology should disclose their motivations, methods, and intended outcomes, except when such disclosure would significantly undermine an otherwise ethical goal" (ibid.: 57). Within Design for Sustainable Behaviour, this last statement could be interpreted as a carte blanche for designers to manipulate users as they see fit, as long as the ethical goal of global sustainability is in sight. Discussion on this topic is ongoing, and has not resulted yet in a widely acknowledged code of ethics. As it was the intention of this chapter to explore ways that designers can influence behaviour, rather than discuss the ethical consequences of doing so, this issue is not explored further here. For a meaningful discussion on the ethical aspects of designers and industry influencing user behaviour, the reader is referred to Pettersen and Boks (2008) and Lilley and Wilson (2013).

Conclusion

The aim of this chapter has been to give an overview of the different 'dimensions', related to aspects of how the human mind works, that designers can draw on to design ways that users interact with products, interfaces and technology in general around them. Some of these are more obvious, such as how much control a designer can give a user, or how obvious or obtrusive a certain design feature is, and were therefore described early on in literature on this topic. Designers can also utilize a number of additional dimensions, such as considering importance and timing, or finding ways to appeal to meaning or how much empathy a user might have for others, or for himself or herself. The chapter also introduces a design tool, Dimensions of Behaviour Change, that designers may use to get inspired, or to get direction in finding the appropriate 'control knobs' and the degree to which these should be slid for creating an optimal design.

'What dimensions work best?' is a good question, but difficult to answer, other than with 'it depends'. Design for Sustainable Behaviour methodologies suggest that it is very important to understand both, what goes on in the mind of the user and what goes on around him or her. It is also important that the proper user research methods (such as ethnography, contextual enquiry and cultural probes) should be applied for achieving this, as interviews and surveys will generally not give sufficient insights into important aspects of behaviour such as habits and objective constraints of behaviour (Daae & Boks, 2015). What dimension works best will then depend first and foremost on the user. A woodstove study (Daae et al., 2016), where extensive applied ethnographic investigation was used to find out how a woodstove could be designed in a way that users would be more likely to exhibit recommended (and sustainable) ways to ignite and maintain a wood fire, revealed that simplicity (by for example using the dimensions Direction and Control) was attractive for many users. However, the ethnographic observations also suggested that some users would strongly resist such solutions, as they were convinced that burning wood is both an art and a science. Literature does not provide us with studies that have extensively tested different dimensions in a comparative and detailed way.

References

Akrich, M. (1992). The de-scription of technical objects. In W. Bijker & J. Law (Eds.), *Shaping technology, building society: Studies in sociotechnical change* (pp. 205–224). Cambridge, MA: MIT Press.

Berdichevsky, D., & Neuenschwander, E. (1999). Toward an ethics of persuasive technology. *Communications of the ACM, 42*(5), 51–58.

Bhamra, T., Lilley, D., & Tang, T. (2008). *Sustainable use: Changing consumer behaviour through product design.* Changing the Change: Design Visions, Proposals and Tools, Conference, Turin, Italy, July 10–12.

Boks, C., & Daae, J. (2013). Towards an increased user focus in life cycle engineering: Re-engineering manufacturing for sustainability. *Proceedings of the 20th CIRP International Conference on Life Cycle Engineering*, Singapore, April 17–19.

Boks, C., Lilley, D., & Pettersen, I. N. (2015). The future of design for sustainable behaviour, revisited. *Proceedings of the EcoDesign 2015: 9th International Symposium on Environmentally Conscious Design and Inverse Manufacturing*, Tokyo, Japan, December 2–4, 2015. To be published in a 2016 Springer book (forthcoming)

Daae, J., & Boks, C. (2014). Dimensions of behaviour change. *Journal of Design Research, 12*(3), 145–172.

Daae, J., & Boks, C. (2015, November 1). A classification of user research methods for design for sustainable behaviour. *Journal of Cleaner Production, 106*, 680–689.

Daae, J., Goile, F., Seljeskog, M., & Boks, C. (2016). Burning for sustainable behaviour. *Journal of Design Research, 14*(1), 42–65.

Elias, E., Dekoninck, E., & Culley, S. (2007). *The potential for domestic energy savings through assessing user behaviour and changes in design.* EcoDesign2007: 5th International Symposium on Environmentally Conscious Design and Inverse Manufacturing, Tokyo, Japan, December 10–13.

Elias, E., Dekoninck, E., & Culley, S. (2008). *Assessing user behaviour for changes in the design of energy using domestic products.* IEEE International Symposium on Electronics and the Environment, San Francisco, CA, May 19–21.

Jelsma, J. (1997). *Philosophy meets design*. Shortened version of a paper for presentation at the Annual Meeting of the Society for Social Studies of Science, Tucson, Arizona, October 23–26, pp. 1–14.

Jelsma, J. (2006). Designing "moralized" products. In P.-P. Verbeek and A. Slob (Eds.), *User behavior and technology development: Shaping sustainable relations between consumers and technologies* (pp. 221–231). Berlin: Springer.

Jelsma, J., & Knot, M. (2002). Designing environmentally efficient services; A "script" approach. *The Journal of Sustainable Product Design, 2*(3), 119–130.

Lidman, K., & Renström, S. (2011). *How to design for sustainable behaviour?* (Master thesis). Chalmers University of Technology, Gothenburg, Sweden.

Lilley, D. (2007). *Designing for behavioural change: Reducing the social impacts of product use through design* (PhD thesis). Loughborough University, Loughborough.

Lilley, D., Lofthouse, V., & Bhamra, T. (2005). *Towards instinctive sustainable product use*. 2nd International Conference: Sustainability Creating the Culture, Aberdeen Exhibition & Conference Centre, Aberdeen, November 2–4.

Lilley, D., & Wilson, G. T. (2013). Integrating ethics into design for sustainable behaviour. *Journal of Design Research, 11*(3), 278–299.

Lockton, D. (2013). *Design with intent: A design pattern toolkit for environmental & social behaviour change* (PhD thesis). Brunel University, London.

Lockton, D., Harrison, D., & Stanton, N. (2010a). The design with intent method: A design tool for influencing user behaviour. *Applied Ergonomics, 41*(3), 382–392.

Lockton, D., Harrison, D., & Stanton, N. (2010b). *Design with intent: 101 patterns for influencing behaviour through design v.1.0*. Windsor, UK: Equifine.

Pettersen, I. N., & Boks, C. (2008). The ethics in balancing control and freedom when engineering solutions for sustainable behaviour. *International Journal of Sustainable Engineering, 1*(4), 287–297.

Tromp, N., Hekkert, P., & Verbeek, P.-P. (2011). Design for socially responsible behavior: A classification of influence based on intended user experience. *Design Issues, 27*(3), 3–19.

Wever, R., van Kuijk, J., & Boks, C. (2008). User-centred design for sustainable behaviour. *International Journal of Sustainable Engineering, 1*(1), 9–20.

Zachrisson, J., & Boks, C. (2012). Exploring behavioural psychology to support design for sustainable behaviour research. *Journal of Design Research, 10*(1/2), 50–66.

Zachrisson, J., Storrø, G., & Boks, C. (2012). Using a guide to select design strategies for behaviour change: Theory vs. practice. *Proceedings of EcoDesign 2011, Design for Innovative Value Towards a Sustainable Society*, Kyoto, Japan, November 30–December 2, 2011, pp. 362–367.

Zaltman, G. (1974). Strategies for diffusing innovations. In J. N. Sheth & P. L. Wright (Eds.), *Marketing analysis for societal problems* (pp. 78–100). Urbana, IL: University of Illinois—Urbana-Champaign.

8 Design for healthy behaviour

Geke Ludden

Introduction: the growing need to think about healthy behaviour in a prospering society

Over the last decades, people in societies all over the world have moved from barely being able to survive to living in a state of abundance. While this development is of course very positive, it has also led to unhealthy lifestyles. Statistics on unhealthy eating habits in the UK and the USA (England, 2014; Stark Casagrande et al., 2007) tell us that only a small proportion of peoples diet meet the general dietary recommendations (consuming less saturated fat, added sugars and salt and eating enough fruit and vegetables). In addition, recent statistics on the degree to which peoples diet are active in these countries, as well as in others are low. In England, 66% of men and 56% of women claim to meet the recommendations of being active for at least 30 minutes five times a week (Centre, 2013). Similar results (including higher levels of self-reported activity and lower levels of measured activity) have been found for activity of USA residents (Tucker et al., 2011). Eventually, these unhealthy lifestyles will negatively affect the wellbeing of many people and lead to ever-increasing costs and demands in healthcare. Specifically, there is a dramatic increase in so-called lifestyle diseases such as obesity and diabetes (Lee et al., 2012). Although low levels of inactivity and unhealthy eating habits are not the only factors contributing to this trend, they do play a major role. Lifestyle changes could counter this trend and, consequently, multiple efforts have been made to raise people's awareness of the importance of living a healthier life. Traditionally, health interventions have taken the form of mass media campaigns aimed at raising awareness of health issues and of the benefits of living a healthy lifestyle. More recently, more innovative means of designing for healthy behaviour have been sought that include monitoring and coaching systems and the design of environments that encourage an active lifestyle. In this chapter, I will give an overview of the different means to design for healthy behaviour and I will introduce a design framework that is based on a dominant theory in the psychology of health behaviour change, the transtheoretical model of behaviour change developed by Prochaska and colleagues (TTM, Prochaska & Velicer, 1997). This design framework challenges designers to look at health behaviour change as a process and offers strategies to design products that guide people through a process of behaviour change until they have durably changed their behaviour.

Current strategies to encourage healthy behaviour

Current strategies to encourage healthy behaviour come in a variety of forms, some are aimed at the public at large and others at individuals or specific groups of people. I will discuss four types of strategies that are currently dominant: (1) traditional information campaigns, (2) monitoring and coaching systems, (3) the built (public) environment and (4) stand-alone objects. This section will discuss the benefits and limitations of these different strategies leading up to a discussion on how future strategies to encourage healthy behaviour might look.

Information campaigns

Campaigns raising awareness of the importance of eating fruit and vegetables and of being physically active are common in most Western countries (these include "2 Fruit 'n' 5 Veg Every Day" in Australia [see Dixon et al., 1998]; "5 a day for Better Health" in the USA [see Kramish Campbell et al., 1999] and "Fighting Fat, Fighting Fit" in the UK [see Miles at al, 2001]). Cavill and Bauman (2004) reviewed 15 campaigns with an explicit focus on physical activity and found that although campaigns do increase awareness of the issue of physical activity, most of them were not effective in actually changing people's behaviour. Other reviews on the effectiveness of campaigns and interventions aimed at increased fruit and vegetable intake suggest that although some types of interventions (e.g. involving smaller groups and risk populations) can be effective, in general, changes are often short lived (Ammerman et al., 2002; Stark Casagrande et al., 2007).

The preceding suggests that although mass media campaigns may lead to increased awareness of the importance of and the recommendations for leading a healthy lifestyle, they are not likely to be accompanied by durable lifestyle changes. Possibly, the messages transmitted in mass media campaigns are easily ignored or forgotten. At the same time, campaigns are competing with factors such as pervasive product marketing, powerful social norms, and behaviours driven by addiction or habit.

Monitoring and coaching systems

An alternative means of supporting people to change their behaviour can be found in the use of technology to support behaviour change. This category consists of interactive systems that try to persuade people to lead a more active life, to drink more water or to quit smoking. This type of intervention is promising because it is targeted at individuals and their individual needs but could at the same time reach a larger group of people than traditional, face-to-face interventions (e.g. seeking personal advice from a dietician or physiotherapist) can (Norman, 2007). Furthermore, people using these interventions could potentially use them at any place and at any point in time (Fogg & Hreha, 2010). Generally, such systems consist of some means to monitor behaviour. In web-based environments people can, for example, track their daily food intake by selecting food items from a list and adding it to a list. Other systems use dedicated devices with sensors or use sensors in devices that people already carry, such as smartphones, to track their behaviour. Subsequently, the data gathered by sensors is fed back to the user in some form. Often, these systems use a smaller device to provide direct feedback and combine this with an online or mobile application to provide more detailed feedback and overviews. The form that feedback takes also varies from a direct representation of measures taken to more symbolic representations that are perhaps more motivating. An example of a system that uses symbolic feedback is the UbiFit garden that was developed and evaluated in a user study by Consolvo et al. (2008). This system uses a smartphone for monitoring and feedback, and provides people with the metaphor of a flowering garden to indicate whether or not they have been sufficiently active.

Hermsen et al. (2016) reviewed the potential of digital solutions to support people through a change in habitual behaviour and concluded that these solutions can indeed disrupt unhealthy habits in the short term. However, these authors also found that their effectiveness to sustainably change habitual behaviour to healthier behaviour is so far undecided. The influence of several factors on sustained use need to be studied further. Among these are personal traits and social influence as well as several design-related factors. In previous work on adherence to web-based interventions, we have elaborated on how design factors may be of influence in reach and adherence of these systems (Ludden et al., 2015).

The built environment

The design of our environment can have a significant impact on our (healthy) behaviour. For example, changes to the design of staircases may be made that make them more attractive to use or easier to reach. The case of promoting to take the stairs instead of opting to use the elevator has been a rather popular one among researchers. Interventions have ranged from introducing point-of-choice prompts (mostly posters) (e.g. Eves et al., 2012) to increasing the attractiveness and accessibility of a stairwell (van Nieuw-Amerongen et al., 2009) to encouraging social behaviour as an incentive to take the stairs (Peeters et al., 2013). Although some of these studies have reported positive effects of environmental interventions on stair use, in a review of studies that used environmental interventions to increase health-enhancing physical activity, Foster and Melvyn (2004) found that most interventions had small positive effects on activity. For example, most studies that used posters and banners to promote stair use reported increases in stair use of less than 5%.

Another line of work in environmental interventions has been aimed at influencing people's food choices by changing the environment. Seymour and colleagues (2004) reviewed the impact of interventions that influenced the environment through food availability, access, pricing or information at the point-of-purchase. From this review, interventions on worksites and universities seemed to be most effective although in most studies, sustained behaviour was not measured. Many of the studies examined involved a strategy of information only and the authors argue that future research should focus on 'true environmental interventions' that involve strategies of access, availability and incentives because these seem more effective than providing information only. In their study on promoting fruit and salad purchases in cafeterias, Jefferey et al. (1994) incorporated an example of a 'true environmental intervention'. Their intervention consisted of doubling the number of fruit choices and increasing salad ingredient selection by three. In addition, they reduced the price of salad and fruit by 50%. The intervention had very positive results: both fruit and salad purchases increased markedly while the number of items purchased remained stable. People who were trying to control their weight and women were more likely to make the healthier food choices. When the intervention was removed, fruit and salad purchases dropped again to remain slightly above baseline.

Another approach in the design of healthy environments looks at how areas can be designed in a way that encourages 'active living'; being physically more active by walking or cycling, instead of using a motorized mode of transportation. Recently, the Design Council in London has started such an initiative called "Active by Design" (2014), bringing together examples of buildings and public spaces that encourage active living.

Similar to mass media campaigns, such interventions can potentially reach large groups of people, simply because many people can encounter them. In theories on behaviour change, approaches such as these have been described as "choice architecture" (Sunstein & Thaler, 2008; see also Chapter 4). Choice architecture describes the way in which decisions are influenced by how the choices are presented. Although this type of solution may trigger people to make the healthier choice at the spot, they are often single-event promotions of these healthier behaviours. As such, they are only relevant to people in the context that they encounter them in.

Stand-alone objects

As a final category, there is growing evidence that changing smaller elements and objects in our environment through design can also have positive effects on healthy behaviour. In contrast to the devices in the monitoring and coaching category, these objects are not part of an interactive system. For example, Wansink and colleagues have shown how many elements in the design of our environments, including the size of our plates (Wansink & van Ittersum, 2013) and the shapes of our glasses (Wansink & van Ittersum, 2007) influence food and drink intake in both adults and children. The following sections in this chapter will shed more light on how designers could capitalize on the effects that objects in our direct environment can have on leading a healthy life.

In the previous sections, I have sketched out a variety of ways in which design can contribute to supporting people in adopting healthier behaviour. Reviewing the effectiveness of these various means, it seems that whereas traditional mass media campaigns do succeed in raising awareness of health issues, they are often not successful in actually changing people's behaviour. Monitoring and coaching systems may seem effective for short-term behaviour changes but their effectiveness at the long term has not been established. Moreover, many of these systems seem to be aimed at people who are already willing and ready to change and they may not reach the people who need them most. As Herz (2014) argues in a recent article about these systems in *Wired* magazine, most of them are not particularly developed to support anyone other than healthy, young people, thereby ignoring the people who could most benefit from this technology (the old, the chronically ill, the poor).

On the other hand, while environmental interventions DO sometimes succeed in changing people's behaviour at the time and place where people encounter them they are not set out to help people to durably change their lifestyle. In the design of current health interventions, the motivational state of the user of the intervention is often not considered. In health psychology, stages of change models are used to define the different stages people go through from the moment they start thinking about changing their behaviour to the moment that they have durably changed it. The stages differ with respect to how ready and willing people are to change, i.e. their motivational state. A dominant model is the transtheoretical model of behaviour change (TTM) by Prochaska et al., (1992). Designing an intervention in such a way that it matches the typical behaviour of a person at a certain stage seems logical and it is, in fact, what many psychologists do when they develop traditional health interventions (e.g. Johnson et al., 2008). However, considering the stage of change that a person is in is generally not part of a designer's approach.

In work on designing for the stages of change, Ludden and Hekkert (2014) have made a categorization of how existing interventions correspond to the different stages of change in the TTM. From this categorization, a framework was developed that designers can use to design for the stages of change. Furthermore, my colleagues and I have started to explore how designers can deliberately design for the different stages of change implementing products and services that can be used sequentially (Ludden & de Ruijter, 2016).The next sections will introduce the TTM and the framework we developed to design for stages of change illustrated with examples.

Introducing the transtheoretical model of health behaviour change

Interventions can be designed to match the motivational states of people if designers adopt the Stages of Change model. If interventions are coherent with people's motivational states, they will be more likely to adopt them and use them, which is essential for moving through the stages of change. A closer look at the TTM and the design framework for the design of health interventions will explain some of the behaviour patterns within the stages of change.

In their work on health behaviour change, Prochaska and colleagues (Prochaska et al., 1992, and Prochaska & Velicer, 1997) identified five stages of change and 10 distinct processes of change from a comparative theoretical study. Prochaska et al. suggest that to make a durable health change, whether it is to quit smoking, to eat a healthier diet (e.g. less fat or sugar) or to increase physical activity, people pass through five stages:

- pre-contemplation
- contemplation
- preparation
- action
- maintenance.

In the first three stages, people built motivation to change and in the last two stages people act. People may move through these stages more or less quickly. For example, some people are stuck in the contemplation stage for long periods of time (chronic contemplation). Also, many people relapse from action or maintenance stages to an earlier stage, mostly to contemplate or prepare for another serious attempt at action. At the end of the five stages, durable behaviour change is reached. Figure 8.1 shows the stages of change and the process of moving through stages.

Next to the five stages of change, Prochaska et al. (1992) describe 10 processes of change that people who (self-)changed their behaviour reported to have used to progress through the stages. These processes are also depicted in Figure 8.1, below the stages of change in which people reported to have used them most. It has been argued that these processes of change should guide the development of intervention programmes, because people need to be able to use these processes to progress through the stages (Prochaska & Velicer, 1997). Psychologists have used the TTM to design their interventions so that they match the motivational state that people are in (e.g. Johnson et al., 2008). Research in the field with these 'traditional' interventions has shown dramatic improvements in retention and progress using stage-matched interventions (Prochaska & Velicer, 1997).

To further increase the effectiveness of health interventions, designers could adopt stages of change theory. This would enable them to design for the way people actually behave, and not for the way they want them to behave (Norman, 2007). This may seem contradictory, since the aim of these interventions IS to change people (or at least their behaviour). However, as Prochaska and Velicer (1997) put it: instead of expecting people to match the needs of the interventions, the interventions need to match the motivational states of people. Only if interventions are recognized as matching their motivational states, people will adopt them and use them, which is essential for moving through the stages of change.

The design for healthy behaviour framework

In the previous section, I have argued that interventions should match different stages of change. While interventions aimed at early stages of change should aim to raise awareness, interventions in later stages should be more focused on acting out and sustaining new behaviour. In the framework for the design of stage-matched interventions (Ludden & Hekkert, 2014; see Figure 8.1), processes of change, stages of change, design strategies and their relationships are represented. The processes of change are not strictly connected to each of the stages, because designers may use different processes to design interventions for different stages. Four types of design strategies have been defined that adhere to four different (design) aims: 'raising awareness', 'enabling', 'motivating' and 'fading out'. As can be seen from Figure 8.1, the design strategies spread over multiple stages.

Design strategies aimed at raising awareness

In the pre-contemplation and contemplation stage, people build motivation to change. Design strategies for 'raising awareness' can move people into a process of behaviour change, these are the strategies that help people evaluate the choices they have made so

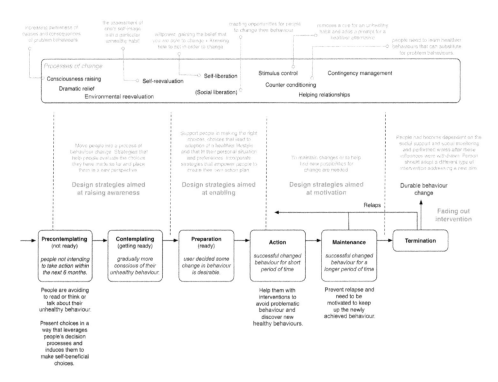

Figure 8.1 The 'design for healthy behaviour framework' connecting processes and stages of change to design strategies

far and place them in a new perspective. The result should be that they move into the preparation stage because they are ready (i.e. willing, feel capable) to change. Environmental interventions are particularly suitable for early stages of change because people can encounter them by chance. People in these stages will not yet be motivated to buy or even to start using a personal intervention. In order for a process of change to start, interventions in these stages should have an emphasis on raising awareness of the importance of and the benefits of changing. It is particularly difficult to design for these stages because needs and desires of people in these stages may be conflicting with the designer's intentions. A designer could address this challenge by connecting to other needs that people may have and introduce the intervention connected to those needs.

Design strategies aimed at enabling

The middle stages involve getting ready to change, deciding how to change and implementing the change. Here, design strategies that are aimed at 'enabling' are in order. We use the term 'enabling' to characterize interventions that support people in making the right choices; choices that lead to adoption of a healthier lifestyle and that fit their personal situation and preferences. In other words, interventions should incorporate strategies that empower people to create their own action plan. Environmental interventions for these stages could target avoiding problematic behaviour or discovering new healthy behaviours. Examples of these would be environments that facilitate healthy choices and in which information and opportunities can be found about how people can adjust their lifestyle to be healthier. As an alternative example, Figure 8.2 shows a jar for healthy snacks

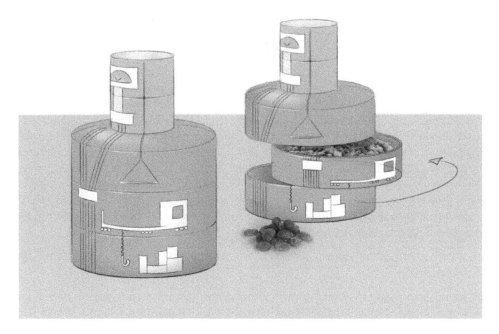

Figure 8.2 Snacking 'tower'

Source: Laura de Ruijter.

aimed at young children and their parents. The child is free to take snacks from the lower parts of the jar, but has to ask for the food that is in the upper parts of the jar. The change process that is addressed here is social liberation. Social liberation involves creating opportunities for people to change their behaviour. This 'snacking tower' offers children and their parents an easy and open procedure to deal with healthy snacking. (For a preliminary evaluation study around this concept, see Ludden & de Ruijter, 2016.)

Design strategies aimed at motivation

Well into the action and maintenance stages, motivating becomes the primary aim of interventions. In these stages, people have already adopted new behaviour and are working to prevent relapse. What people in this stage need most is support to keep up the newly acquired behaviour. Many personal interventions in the form of apps and devices (the category of monitoring and coaching systems that I have introduced on page 94.) seem to be designed for this stage particularly. Many of these systems feature some form of motivational feedback, often designed in the form of elements of gaming such as earning points or badges. Although environmental interventions may be less suitable for this stage at first glance (because people may need a more personal intervention), providing motivation that connects to the environment is certainly possible and may be experienced as a more 'real' and therefore more meaningful type of motivation than earning a badge. As an example, Dutch health insurance agency Menzis rewards its clients for a healthier lifestyle and gives them the opportunity to collect 'health points' that can be used for discounts on, for example, hiking routes. As another example, in some parks that are popular running areas, interval timers have been placed to motivate people to improve their running skills.

Design strategies aimed at fading out

In entering the termination stage, right before durable behaviour change is reached, interventions should incorporate a fading-out phase. Prochaska and Velicer (1997) found in their clinical trials a negative effect of stopping personal counselling. People had become dependent on the social support and social monitoring and performed worse after these influences were withdrawn. A similar effect could be expected for personal interventions and designers need to address this issue. A way to do this would be by offering users a way to assess whether or not they are ready (and willing) to stop using the intervention. Alternatively, in some cases, the influence or support an intervention offers could slowly diminish. The fading out of an intervention could take a variety of forms, depending on the mechanics of the intervention. For example, an intervention that would use reminders to motivate people (as the well-known running app Runkeeper does) could use less reminders if sustained behaviour is tracked, it might even switch from sending reminders to just sending acknowledgements.

Conclusion

In this chapter, I have showed the different strategies that are used to influence people's behaviour in order to support healthier lifestyles. I have also argued why and when these strategies might (not) be effective and how designers can use the stages of change framework to design products and services (in different categories) that truly support people in adopting and sustaining healthier behaviour. The strategies proposed in the design for healthy behaviour framework differ from other design for behaviour change strategies because they offer guidance specifically for designers that work in the domain of health and wellbeing. In order to create successful interventions here, a good understanding of people's motivational state is required, an aspect that is not part of most other strategies aimed at designing for behaviour change.

Making a change will, for most people, have to start right at the early stages of change (pre-contemplation) because when it comes to healthy lifestyles, many (most) people are in early stages of change (Kramish Campbell et al., 1999). Interventions in the environment that everyone can (and will) encounter are therefore essential to start a change process. Ludden and Offringa (2015) have discussed these previously as 'triggers' in the environment. Triggers in the environment can make people aware of the choices that they make and of the consequences of their choices. It is only after this first step that a process of change can start. In order to help people progress through the stages of change, it is essential that products and services are not separate entities that a user has to select according to the stage of change that he or she is in. Rather, designers should also focus on designing connections between the different products and services that are supportive in different stages of change. In this way, sequences of products or, in fact, more dynamic products and services could support people throughout a behaviour change.

We have to realize that any effort to support people in acquiring a healthier lifestyle operates in an environment that drastically needs systemic change. People constantly face an environment that persuades them towards unhealthy behaviour. Think, for example, of standing in line at a cash register and being confronted with unhealthy snacks. Or, think of the many cities in which it is almost impossible to use other forms of transportation than a bike. Nevertheless, the 'design for healthy behaviour framework' makes a contribution in providing a theoretical framework that explains how individuals can be encouraged to make change via design. So far the framework has not yet been widely applied and therefore its effectiveness has yet to be (fully) established. Our group is currently building a collection of evidence-based case studies that will build on and provide further support for using the framework.

References

Ammerman, A. S., Lindquist, C. H., Lohr, K. N., & Hersey, J. (2002). The efficacy of behavioral interventions to modify dietary fat and fruit and vegetable intake: A review of the evidence. *Preventive Medicine*, *35*(1), 25–41.

Cavill, N., & Bauman, A. (2004). Changing the way people think about health-enhancing physical activity: Do mass media campaigns have a role? *Journal of Sports Sciences*, *22*(8), 771–790.

Centre, H. A. S. C. I. (2013). *Is the adult population in England active enough?* Leeds: Health and Social Care Information Centre.

Consolvo, S., McDonald, D. W., Toscos, T., Chen, M. Y., Froehlich, J., Harrison, B., & Landay, J. A. (2008). Activity sensing in the wild: A field trial of UbiFit garden. *Chi 2008: 26th Annual Chi Conference on Human Factors in Computing Systems Vols 1 and 2, Conference Proceedings*, 1797–1806.

Dixon, H., Borland, R., DSegan, C., Stafford, H., & Sindall, C. (1998). Public reaction to Victoria's "2 Fruit 'n' 5 Veg Every Day" campaign and reported consumption of fruit and vegetables. *Preventive Medicine*, *27*, 572–582.

England, P. H. (2014). National diet and nutrition survey. In B. Bates, A. Lennox, A. Prentice, C. Bates, P. Page, S. Nicholson & G. Swan (Eds.), *National diet and nutrition survey. Results for year 1–4 (combined) of the rolling programme (2008/2009–2011/12)* (p. 201451). London: Public Health England.

Eves, F. F., Webb, O. J., & Mutrie, N. (2012). A workplace intervention to promote stair climbing: Greater effects in the overweight. *Obesity, 14*(12), 2210–2216.

Fogg, B. J., & Hreha, J. (2010). Behavior wizard: A method for matching target behaviors with solutions. *Lecture Notes in Computer Science, 6137*, 117–131.

Foster, C., & Melvyn, H. (2004). Changing the environment to promote health-enhancing physical activity. *Journal of Sports Sciences, 22*(8), 755–769.

Hermsen, S., Frost, J., Renes, R. J., & Kerkhof, P. (2016). Using feedback through digital technology to disrupt and change habitual behavior: A critical review of current literature. *Computers in Human Behavior, 57*, 61–74.

Herz, J. C. (2014). Wearables are totally failing the people who need them most. *Wired Gadgetlab.* Retrieved from www.wired.com/2014/11/where-fitness-trackers-fail/

Jefferey, R. W., French, S., Raether, C., & Baxter, J. E. (1994). An environmental intervention to increase fruit and salad purchases in a cafeteria. *Preventive Medicine, 23*, 788–792.

Johnson, S. S., Paiva, A. L., Cummins, C. O., Johnson, J. L., Dyment, S. J., & Sherman, K. (2008). Transtheoretical model-based multiple behavior intervention for weight management: Effectiveness on a population basis. *Preventive Medicine, 46*, 238–246.

Kramish Campbell, M., Reynolds, K. D., Havas, S., Curry, S., Bishop, D., Nicklas, T., . . . Heimendinger, J. (1999). Stages of change for increasing fruit and vegetable consumption among adults and young adults participating in the national 5-a-day for better health community studies. *Health Education Behavior, 26*(4), 513–534.

Lee, I. M., Shiroma, E. J., Lobelo, F., Puska, P., Blair, S. N., & Katzmarzyk, P. T. (2012). Effect of physical inactivity on major non-communicable diseases worldwide: An analysis of burden of disease and life expectancy. *The Lancet, 380*(9838), 219–229.

Ludden, G. D. S., & de Ruijter, L. (2016). Supporting healthy behaviour: A stages of change perspective on changing snacking habits of children. *DRS2016*, 27–30 June, Brighton, UK.

Ludden, G. D. S., & Offringa, M. (2015). *Triggers in the environment: Increasing reach of Behavior Change Support Systems by connecting to the offline world.* Paper presented at the Persuasive Technology, Chicago, US.

Ludden, G. D., van Rompay, T. J., Kelders, S. M., & van Gemert-Pijnen, J. E. (2015). How to increase reach and adherence of web-based interventions: A design research viewpoint. *Journal of Medical Internet Research, 17*(7): e172.

Ludden, G. D. S., & Hekkert, P. (2014). *Design for healthy behavior: Design interventions and stages of change.* Paper presented at The Ninth International Conference on Design and Emotion, Bogota, Colombia, October 6–9.

Miles, A., Rapoport, L., Wardle, J., Afuape, T., & Duman, M. (2001). Using the mass-media to target obesity: An analysis of the characteristics and reported behaviour change of participants in the BBC's 'Fighting Fat, Fighting Fit' campaign. *Health Education Research, 16*(3), 357–372.

Norman, D. A. (2007). *The design of future things.* New York: Basic Books.

Peeters M., Megens C., van den Hoven E., Hummels C., & Brombacher A. (2013). Social stairs: Taking the piano staircase towards long-term behavioral change. In S. Berkovsky, & J. Freyne (Eds.), *Persuasive Technology. PERSUASIVE 2013. Lecture Notes in Computer Science* (Vol. 7822). Berlin: Springer.

Prochaska, J. O., DiClemente, C. C., & Norcross, J. C. (1992). In search of the structure of change. In Y. Klar, J. D. Fisher, J. M. Chinsky & A. Nadler (Eds.), *Self change – Social psychological and clinical perspectives* (pp. 87–114). New York: Springer –Verlag.

Prochaska, J. O., & Velicer, W. F. (1997). The transtheoretical model of health behavior change. *American Journal of Health Promotion, 12*(1), 38–48.

Seymour, J. D., Lazarus Yaroch, A., Serdula, M., Michels Blanck, H., & Kettel Khan, L. (2004). Impact of nutrition environmental interventions on point-of-purchase behavior in adults: A review. *Preventive Medicine, 39*(2), 108–136.

Stark Casagrande, S., Wang, Y., Anderson, C., & Gary, T. L. (2007). Have Americans increased their fruit and vegetable intake? The trends between 1988 and 2002. *American Journal of Preventive Medicine, 32*(4), 257–263.

Sunstein, R. H., & Thaler, C. R. (2008). *Nudge: Improving decisions about health, wealth, and happiness*. New Haven, CT: Yale University Press.

The Design Council. (2014). *Active by design*. Retrieved April 10, 2014, from www.designcouncil.org.uk/projects/active-design

Tucker, J. A., Welk, G. J., & Beyler, N. K. (2011). Physical activity in U.S. adults: Compliance with the physical activity guidelines for Americans. *American Journal of Preventive Medicine, 40*(4), 454–461.

van Nieuw-Amerongen, M. E., Kremers, S. P. J., de Vries, N. K., & Kok, G. (2009, October 2). The use of prompts, increased accessibility, visibility, and aesthetics of the stairwell to promote stair use in a university building. *Environment and Behavior, 43*(1), 131–139.

Wansink, B., & van Ittersum, K. (2007). Do children really prefer large portions? Visual illusion bias their estimates and intake. *Journal of the American Dietetic Association, 107*(7), 1107–1110.

Wansink, B., & van Ittersum, K. (2013). Portion size me: Plate-size induced consumption norms and win-win solutions for reducing food intake and waste. *Journal of Experimental Psychology, 19*(4), 320–332.

9 Facilitating behaviour change through mindful design

Kristina Niedderer

Introduction: the need for mindful behaviour change

Behaviour change is increasingly recognized as an important means for building a sustainable future (Stern, 2006: xviii), not only concerning environmental sustainability but also with regard to social and economic issues (Chick, 2012). Design, in turn, can strongly influence behaviour change, because design surrounds us ubiquitously. Design is everywhere in the things we surround ourselves with at home, at work, during leisure activities, during travel. All subtly influencing our actions.

Dependent on the perspective taken, design can be seen as a problem or as a solution to many of the current social, economic or ecological issues. Indeed often design can have both at once desirable and undesirable consequences. For example, cars may be seen to provide solutions to social integration and mobility while at the same time causing environmental issues through pollution and resource depletion (Akerman et al., 2009: 2ff, Banister, 2008). Or, while traditional computer use has been shown to lead to sedentary behaviours associated with problems of obesity (Proper et al., 2011), its use for activity, online games, exergames, etc. can help increase sporting activities and counteract the first effect (Staiano & Calvert, 2011). Similarly, computer use can on the one hand increase our connectedness e.g. through e-mail and chat room/instant messaging, on the other it can increase symptoms of depression e.g. when increased time is spent on internet shopping, video games, etc. (Blaschke et al., 2009, Grieve et al., 2013, Morgan & Cotton, 2004).

Because of the versatility of design and the plethora of its often-unintended uses and serious consequences, it is essential that the behavioural scope of design is considered carefully by both designers and users alike to ensure responsible decision-making and actions by all involved. In order to encourage responsible decision-making, it is necessary to understand the complex interactions between people, objects and their environments as well as their motivations. Designers have developed different models to understand user behaviour, and to facilitate desired behaviours via design. Several of these models are discussed in the surrounding sections of this edited text. Key strategies for behaviour change put forward attempt to enable, motivate and or constrain behaviours (see Lockton et al., 2010, chapter 6), while design strategies may integrate principles of seduction, persuasion, coercion or prescription into objects (see Tromp et al., 2011).

However, the ability to design for appropriate behaviour remains challenging because of design's versatility and the unpredictability of users' actions (Tromp et al., 2011). While designers can imbue objects with affordances and strategies for behaviour change, they cannot predict the use made of them because of the user's ability for arbitrary action. The argument here is that it is important therefore not just to design the object's affordances in terms of enabling, motivating or constraining the user's actions, but to design for responsible decision-making of the user – as part of their motivation – with regard to their actions with the object. The use of mindfulness and its integration into design as 'mindful design' offers a way of promoting such responsible reflection.

The chapter first reflects on the nature of design and how it influences user behaviour, prior to introducing the concept of mindfulness. It discusses what mindfulness entails, why it is useful to achieve responsible decision-making and action, and how designers can embed mindfulness into design to create 'mindful design'. The chapter continues with a number of examples to demonstrate the application and effect of mindful design with regard to responsible behaviour.

Why mindfulness?

Historically, product design has arguably been associated with the desire to conceive and manufacture functional artefacts faster and cheaper, making them more affordable to the masses (Smith, 1776 [2010]: 29; Ligo, 1984). Functionality can be understood to include anything from practical function, such as being able to drink out of a glass or sit on a chair, to symbolic function, such as the purpose of items to convey style, or status or memory etc. (Ligo, 1984: 21ff; Niedderer, 2004: 61ff).

Although design has developed far from its humble beginnings, these two basic premises, mass production and functionality, remain, and have led to its ubiquity in our lives. This ubiquity means that design constantly surrounds and influences us, while its functionality directs our actions, leading inevitably to adapting our behaviours to it, causing behavioural changes at every level (Norman, 2002: x, 10ff, 40ff). For example, the use of a car will allow us to move more flexibly, perhaps to go to work further away from our home, visit friends, go shopping etc. Because of its convenience, we will often surrender to its use unthinkingly, while we could perhaps choose another means, such as public transport or cycling, that might be cheaper, more efficient to reach our destination or be more environmentally friendly, if we thought about it. Similarly, mobile phones connect us to people at the other end of the line, but often leave us oblivious to our surroundings and whether we interrupt conversations and interactions in our immediate surroundings, or even ignore traffic while walking or driving (Srivastava, 2005; Niedderer, 2014).

These examples as well as the ones mentioned earlier demonstrate that functionality is not neutral in that

> every act of [using] design involves choices that are deeply interested, in the sense that they necessarily serve someone's needs before (or to the exclusion of) those of other parties.
>
> (Greenfield, 2011)

This means that, while design has a desired direction, it is important to acknowledge the existence of often unintended or unexpected 'side effects' and consequences. Jelsma posits that designers should take moral responsibility for the actions that take place as a result of human interactions with artefacts, intentional or not, because

> Artefacts have a co-responsibility for the way action develops and for what results. If we waste energy or produce waste in routine actions such as in the household practices, that has to do with the way artefacts guide us.
>
> (Jelsma, 2006: 222)

If there is the need for designers to take responsibility and direct behaviour change, then the obvious question is how designers can do so. Dorrestijn (Chapter 4), with the *'Product Impact Tool'* offers guidance for designers via four aspects of conceptual, psychological, physical and technical guidance for the user. Dorrestijn's approach presumes the responsibility with the designer. By contrast, in this chapter, I want to investigate more closely the interplay between the responsibility of the designer – via a product's affordances – and the user's responsibility and freedom of decision-making. In order to do so, we need to look at the nature of design and how its functionality directs users' actions.

The functional approach, which underpins most design, is focussing the user on the intended action with an object (Niedderer, 2004: 61ff; Norman, 2002: 40). This function is intentionally created by the designer through the physical and semantic properties of the object. In addition, a semiotic message can be added which can be aligned or separate to the first two. For example, the physical shape of a mug affords holding liquid, the handle signifies an aid for lifting the mug to the mouth. A print on the mug might support this message, e.g. through printed lips and a hand at the rim and handle respectively indicating where to put your lips and hands, or through saying 'drink me' in an Alice-in Wonderland style fashion, thus supporting the intended practical function either through indexical or instructional signs. On the other hand, the mug may be embellished with a print that says 'poison' – adding some frisson and reflection about whether or not to drink the contents of the cup. In a third scenario, the user might not notice the print at all or ignore it and use the mug as a penholder, a dice shaker, a flowerpot or to put a treasure into it and bury it.

The mug example shows that while an object's semantic and semiotic messages can support its use or instil reflection on its use, the physical function affords many more options than ordinarily intended by the designer because of the ambiguity of the affordances that any one object owns (Norman, 2002; Niedderer, 2004: 61ff). It seems therefore that largely the designer cannot stop the user to make use of an object to his or her end. However, what the designer can do is to create awareness and reflection of the possible actions on the part of the user to encourage the user to take responsibility. This is to create mindfulness of the user's actions with the object and their consequences (Niedderer, 2007).

Mindfulness has been defined many times but for our purposes, following the Western psychological tradition of mindfulness (Langer, 1989; Langer & Moldoveanu, 2000a), it is understood as a process of creating awareness and attentiveness "to bring one's full resources to a cognitive task by using multiple perspectives and attending to context, which creates novel ways to consider the relevant information" (Luttrell et al., 2014: 258). For example, a person routinely commuting to work by car, when confronted with the need to take more exercise to improve his or her health, if mindful, might look at the bigger picture and decide to cycle to work in future thus not only increasing his or her exercise but at the same time reducing his or her CO_2 emissions. In this way, the health issues are not seen as something negative, but as an opportunity to improve one's lifestyle and responsible behaviour overall. By contrast, a mindless person might decide to go to the gym once a week, taking the car, thus adding an extra journey while getting exercise rather less frequently.

Applying mindfulness to design, we can define it as referring to the awareness and attentiveness of various persons (users) towards the object they are interacting with, towards their environment in the widest sense and towards the consequences of their actions with the object for themselves and others (Niedderer, 2007, 2014). It is useful to integrate mindfulness into design to facilitate behaviour change, because there are four key behavioural factors, which need to be addressed to facilitate behaviour change. According to Stern (2000: 416) these include:

1.   attitude,
2.   external context,
3.   personal capability and
4.   habit/routine.

Mindfulness comfortably addresses all four of these, because it draws attention to and induces reflection of one's pre-conceptions, one's own actions and the external context (Langer, 1989). It thus allows (re-)considering one's habits/routines and inherent attitudes in relation to the wider context, and in turn to re-assess one's personal capabilities for change.

Mindful design and how it works

Mindfulness has traditionally relied on meditation and education, because the state of mindfulness is elusive (Langer, 1989: 2, 9ff) and it is necessary to break through established patterns of experience and preconception to achieve mindfulness (Langer, 1989: 19–42). Meditation or education have been used as an external agent to disrupt these patterns and to open them to (re)inspection (Langer, 1989: 81–114; Udall, 1996: 107). Usually administered through a trainer or therapist to enable the state of mindfulness, this makes mindfulness reliant on external agents, which are not available generally.

By taking the role of 'external' agent, design can offer a valuable alternative or addition because it can be available in everyday contexts. Embedding mindfulness within design is useful because of design's ubiquitous role, which means mindfulness can be integrated directly into everyday life. For example, recent studies on computer-supported mindfulness found that appropriate design interventions can significantly surpass the effectivity of traditional mindfulness training (e.g. Chittaro & Vianella, 2013).

Besides its common application for therapeutic purposes, mindfulness – when embedded in design – can be applied to a broad variety of problems including health, sustainability, social issues, safety and crime prevention. Mindful design is based on two key principles: first, it requires raising attention through a 'disruption' of the object's function, i.e. of our expectation of how the object at hand works. Second, it needs to direct this attention to the content to be reflected on through some feature, which is called 'thematization' (Niedderer, 2007, 2014).

Function can be disrupted on either practical or symbolic level, or both. The disruption of the practical function is used regularly e.g. as part of safety features such as warning notices on computers (e.g. when saving a document) which briefly disrupt our consciousness, draw our attention to the desired content (thematization) and offer/require an additional action to complete the command (e.g. 'save/don't save/cancel') following reflection upon the thematization. Similarly, the symbolic function can be used to raise the user's attention: in a design experiment, a stripe or patch was painted in front of cash machines (or other counters) to denote a 'safe space' to deter thieves or intruders (Gamman & Thorpe, 2012; Chapter 18, this volume). Here, there is no physical barrier to deter anybody standing too close to the person using the cash machine. Instead, the design makes visible, symbolically, the social expectations of personal (safe) space and related behaviours of keeping distant. Any trespasser is seen to break these norms, enabling action to be taken to re-establish the norm.

Content, choice and complexity

The disruption within mindful design only works when it is accompanied by the 'thematization'. The thematization is the feature that directs the attention (which has been raised through the disruption) towards the desired content for reflection, and which must connect with the solution to the disruption. In the case of the computer safety feature, the thematization is provided with the sentence on screen ('Do you want to save the changes you made to. . . ?'), which explains why the process in question has been interrupted and offers different solutions in form of the clickable buttons (e.g. 'save/ don't save/cancel'). The availability of different solutions is important, because they offer choice. Choice makes us mindful because it requires conscious reflection on the different options available (Langer, 1989: 123), which in turn can lead to (Langer & Moldoveanu, 2000a: 2):

1. a greater sensitivity to one's environment,
2. more openness to new information,
3. the creation of new categories for structuring perception, and
4. enhanced awareness of multiple perspectives in problem solving.

As a point of caution, while adding more choices can increase reflection and thus mindfulness, too many options can make a design potentially confusing or annoying to use (Norman, 2002: xii). Therefore, it is important to maintain a balance between clarity of message and complexity of reflection.

In addition to content and choice, the proposed solutions can have different levels of meanings, adding complexity, helping to question established concepts. For example, in the case of the mobile phone, mindfulness might focus on the awareness of the different levels of interaction that are engendered through the phone: such as the interaction with the person at the other end of the line, that with the speaker's immediate social or environmental context which might be influenced by the first interaction, as well as the speaker's voice level.

The thematization thus has three 'mechanisms' or 'features' to guide attention, which comprise content, choice and complexity (Niedderer, 2014: 348–353). Of these the first two are essential features of the thematization, the third can offer an additional level for reflection.

Emotions and mindfulness

One important issue regarding mindful design is that mindless behaviour regularly tends to be driven by emotions (Niedderer, 2014: 354–357). Emotions, as a complex system linking actions, causes and consequences, have evolved as a protective mechanism to allow for quick reactions, guiding our judgement without requiring conscious decision-making (Keltner & Gross, 1999: 472–473). Through 'brief, rapid responses involving physiological, experiential, and behavioural activity [they help] humans respond to survival-related problems and opportunities' (Keltner & Ekman, 2000: 163).

Because emotions are quick and don't require deliberate decision-making, they are open to mindlessness because they promote a single perspective, e.g. an emotional response established in one situation may be unthinkingly transferred to a new situation where it might be entirely inappropriate. For example, answering one's mobile phone might be instilled by curiosity or by a feeling of duty: when on one's own and in a secluded space, taking the phone may be appropriate. The action of taking the phone is regarded as the *functional* emotional action, that enables relief of the original emotions (curiosity, worry). However, if for example, on a busy road or driving, in the quiet coach of a train or in conversation with others, answering one's phone would not be appropriate. In the first case, it might be a safety issue, in the second and third case it might be a lack of consideration and respect for fellow passengers or colleagues. Therefore, in these cases, attention to functional action only can lead to mindlessness. The challenge for design then is to take account of circumstances that surpass functional action.

While emotions can add to mindlessness, they can also be used as an incentive to support the function of mindful design (Niedderer, 2014: 356). This is because it is possible for opposing emotions to cancel each other out (Niedderer, 2014: 356). As indicated earlier, emotions generally are a response to a situation, and in turn lead to emotional actions to either maintain or change the situation. For example, if the phone rings, we take it to satisfy our curiosity or worry. If we cannot take it for any reason, we might react with frustration. In response to such situations, there are certain emotional actions that appear 'non-functional' in that they don't achieve the desired goal (taking the phone) but which offer a way of reducing emotional tension or negative emotion (frustration) within an individual. Although they do not change the situation, which has caused the negative emotions, they are able to generate positive emotions which can partially overlay or cancel out the original negative emotions (Cohn et al., 2009: 8).

This discussion has provided and overview of how mindfulness can be embedded within design in order for design to act as an external agent to instil mindfulness. Mindful design incorporates two mechanisms (disruption and thematization), which can work on different levels of content, choice and complexity. Furthermore, emotions play an important role in that on the one hand they may lead to mindlessness, and on the other hand they offer a way of promoting mindfulness and embedding it into design through utilizing both functional and non-functional emotional actions as an incentive. For example, in the 'safety feature', the fear of losing one's document, awareness of which is engendered through the disruption (banner), is ameliorated through the feeling of relief of the same feature and the safety options provided through it.

Mindful design – guidance for designers and examples

Having introduced the different aspects of mindfulness and how they can be embedded within design, this section is concerned with the creation and application of mindful design. Essentially, there are two ways in which the understanding of mindful design can be useful: first, to analyze existing designs to better understand them, and how and why they may work (or not) with regard to mindful behaviour change. Second, understanding mindful design can be used to identify and analyze relevant situations and to create designs to address them. Not all steps will be applicable to each case.

Mindful Design Guidance

The framework for mindful design has three stages: (1) Identifying the design problem, (2) Identifying mindful solutions and (3) Implementing mindful solutions in design. A revised and simplified version from Niedderer (2014: 357–360) is offered below.

1. Identifying the design problem

The design problem in mindful design is understood to be a situation or interaction where there is a lack of mindful action or intent, which can be improved with regard to the awareness and choices of the situation, rather than focussing solely on one determinate outcome.

Once a situation has been identified, there are several indicators that can be drawn on for its analysis:

1.1 The mode of interaction observed or to be addressed: human–object, human–human, and/or human–environment;
1.2 The emotions relating to the situation/interaction, including:

   1.2.1   Any emotional actions discernable: functional and non-functional;
   1.2.2   The nature of the emotions: positive, negative, appetitive, aversive, approach, avoidance and any tensions;
   1.2.3   The levels of emotions relating to the identified emotional actions: individual, social, cultural and any tensions between them;

1.3 From the (inter)actions and emotions, the underpinning premature cognitive commitments (prejudices) may be deduced.

On the basis of the analysis of these indicators, a judgement can be made as to the appropriateness of the (inter)actions in the context of the given situation, and thus with regard to the nature of the lack of mindful action.

2. Identifying mindful solutions

The second step focuses on identifying mindful criteria (content, choice, complexity) in response to the identified situation and its related indicators, as a basis for developing mindful design solutions that are able to create reflection. This includes identifying:

2.1 Different choices in relation to the predudice or (emotional) actions;
2.2 Different potential novel/ alternative perspectives related to the (emotional) actions;
2.3 Emotions that may serve as incentives or to cancel out inappropriate emotions.

3. Implementing mindful solutions in design

The third step is to implement the identified mindful solutions within and through design. It is likely to be easier to use and redesign relevant existing objects (or contexts) rather than introducing a new object into a situation, because of the likely greater acceptance. Identified mindful solutions are embedded into design objects or environments through the dual mechanism of disruption and thematization:

3.1 Create awareness by disruption relating to the pragmatic or symbolic function. This must relate to the feature of the object, action or situation to be reflected on.
3.2 Create reflection on the content through thematization using choice, complexity and emotions:

   3.2.1   Create choice by offering different options for responding to the function of the object. These may relate to both pragmatic and symbolic levels of function: individual functional or non-functional emotional action on the pragmatic level; social or societal emotions and their underlying norms or beliefs on a symbolic level.

3.2.2   Create multiple perspectives and offer multiple level interpretations that are new/different to that of the individual emotional action and related premature cognitive commitments by embedding different functional/non-functional emotional actions. These may be referring to basic emotions or to different social emotions and/or to cultural norms and beliefs.

3.2.3   Use positive emotions (e.g. positive, appetitive, approach-oriented emotions) as a motivation to encourage desired action(s). They can work as an incentive or deterrent, or to cancel out any emotions/emotional actions that are perceived as problematic either on the basis of empathy or by being perceived as a reward.

While previous research has focused on mindfulness in the social context, mindful design can also be applied in other contexts such as health, safety, sustainability and crime prevention. Mindful design can also work on several different levels of complexity forms from basic awareness on the (inter-)action with an object to awareness of multiple levels of social, cultural and environmental interaction. Several of the examples aforementioned have already been indicative of this. In the following, I provide three examples, drawn together from the above discussion, which demonstrate the broader application of mindful design at the three different levels at which it can operate, and with reference to the steps of the design guidance.

EXAMPLES

Mindful design – Level 1: addressing practical function and individual emotions   Returning to the safety feature of an everyday computer, as a simple example of safety design. In this example, the problem (1) is the danger of loss of information through inadequate human–object interaction (1.1), such as closing a document without having saved it, which is known to cause individual (1.2.1) negative (1.2.2) emotions such as e.g. fear, anger or frustration over losing information. In response to the problem, warning notices on computers (2) reminding us to save a document before closing it have become a common but powerful feature, which we heavily rely on and which offer us relief (2.3). Such features appear and briefly disrupt the requested function (3.1) if we do something that might cause us to lose information, as in trying to close a document without having saved it first. The computer raises our awareness by refusing the requested practical function temporarily (3.1) and brings up a banner that interrogates our action (3.2) that then requires an additional action to complete the command (3.2.1). The banner (3.2) alerts us to the content of the action and provides several choices (3.2.1 – e.g. 'save/don't save/cancel') for us to reflect on which action we really want to take. The choices are playing on our emotions in a rather simplistic but effective way, addressing our 'fear' and 'relief' of either losing important information or having secured it, and allowing us to take the appropriate emotional action (3.2.3). This is a very simple example, but it shows how powerful and pervasive mindful design can be.

Mindful design – Level 2: addressing practical function and social values   Focussing on the example of the mobile phone, they can often be perceived as being used mindlessly (1). Such mindlessness is engendered because they are solely designed to focus the user on the person at the other end (1.1), leaving the user oblivious to his or her surroundings (1.1), to whether he or she interrupt conversations and interactions in his or her immediate surroundings (1.1), or even ignore traffic while walking or driving (1.1), thus causing tension between different levels of human interaction (1.2.3).

One of the most common issues found is people 'shouting' into their phones, thus disrupting others around them (1). This phenomenon seems to arise from our imagination of talking to someone far away (1.3), which is intuitively transferred to the level of our voice to make it carry even though this is not at all necessary. Mindful design functions could easily be built in to cope with this phenomenon: for example, the phone could respond to 'shouting' by reducing the sound level of the speaker (3.1) until they reduce their voices, thus making them both aware of their actions and helping them to adjust to an appropriate level. This solution might of course be somewhat contentious because the temporary reduction in sound level (3.1), which might cause the speaker temporarily not to hear the person at the other end, is likely to cause negative emotions (3.2.3) until they have adjusted their own voice, and the voice level in the phone returns to normal as a 'reward' (3.2.3). It would therefore be better to find a way of designing a solution that would include (only) positive emotions, although that may not always be possible.

Another common issue is people taking phone calls (1) when involved in another action or social interaction (1.1; 1.2.1). Here, when the mobile is relaying a call, it could put up a humorous message querying whether it is appropriate for the user to take the call at this moment (3.1, 3.2), showing different symbols dependent on the environment (in social company, near street crossing, etc.) (2.1, 2.2) and offering different options, e.g. of declining, of diverting to the answerphone or to take the call (3.2.1). The humour of the message could offer an alternative emotion ('fun') to counter the ensuing emotions of frustration, anxiety etc. (2.3; 3.2.3) that might arise from not taking the call if the situation is not conducive.

The example of the mobile phone indicates that there can be tensions between the need of the individual and the collective (1.2.3): The mobile phone in a meeting or public space disrupts one conversation in favour of another, or disrupts the many in favour of the satisfaction of a single person (Srivastava, 2005: 123). As explained earlier, these points could well be addressed through a mindful design approach. Indeed, some conceptual designs of mobile phones have started to address such points, but have not yet been realized commercially (e.g. Hemmert et al., 2011) since many work through negative emotions which are not acceptable to phone companies for obvious reasons.

Mindful design – Level 3: addressing symbolic function and social values   The third example takes us back to safety design, but with a strong focus on social interaction. It is the example of a traffic junction in Drachten, The Netherlands (Webster, 2007). Similar examples exist by now in London and Coventry the UK. This junction had a very high incident rate (1), which was not improved by further signage. Following the shared space model, the traffic planners finally decided to take away all signs (3.1), which improved the traffic safety of the junction significantly.

Analyzing the design of the crossing from a mindful perspective, in this example it is not the actual physical function that is disrupted, but it is the symbolic rules which guide it (traffic lights, signage or road markings) that have been removed (3.1). This causes awareness because the expected guidance is missing (3.2.1), and requires traffic participants to take an alternative perspective (3.2.2), which includes actively thinking about how to navigate their environment and to take responsibility for managing the traffic to keep themselves and others safe (3.2.1).

This creates a radical change in behaviour forcing the users to proceed with much greater caution within a shared space intersection compared to a conventional intersection as the users are "mindfully" aware that all other road-users are in a similar 'uncontrolled' situation and have the same rights (2.2). It resulted in a clear improvement of the situation (Webster, 2007). The design works because it causes individuals to take note of their social context, and by doing so it requires them to take responsibility and thus it creates a safer traffic environment. Overall, it appears that many examples of social design respond to, or can be explained by, a mindful design pattern because they are reliant on social responsible action and reflection.

Conclusion

This chapter has introduced the concept of mindful design as an approach for designing for behaviour change. Mindfulness can be embodied in design through the design strategies of 'disruption' and 'thematization', which in turn draw on aspects of content, choice, complexity and emotions, to create awareness and reflection in the user. These strategies can be synthesized into a set of design guidelines in three stages: (1) Identifying the design problem, (2) Identifying mindful solutions and (3) Implementing mindful solutions in design.

The mindful design approach can help designers with the problem that they cannot predict and design for (or against) all the uses to which users may put any objects or products and users' behaviours with them, without resorting to coercive or prescriptive design solutions. Mindful design can thus help make the user aware of his or her actions with the object and his or her social or environmental context in order to stimulate conscious and responsible action on the part of the user. Like all behavioural design approaches, mindful design is not appropriate for all situations, such as where absolute safety is required. Nevertheless, the benefits of the use of mindful design – as exemplified by the shared space crossing – are increasingly recognized and employed in a wide variety of situations and settings.

Acknowledgement

The chapter draws on work conducted over the last 12 years, in particular work published between 2007 and 2014, and which is referenced and acknowledged where appropriate in the text.

References

Akerman, J., Banister, D., Dreborg, K., Nijkamp, P., Schleicher-Tappeser, R., Stead, D. and Steen, P. (2009). *European transport policy and sustainable mobility*. London & New York: Routledge.

Banister, D. (2008). The sustainable mobility paradigm. *Transport Policy*, *15*, 73–80. doi:10.1016/j.tranpol.2007.10.005

Blaschke, C. M., Freddolino, P. P., & Mullen, E. E. (2009). Ageing and technology: A review of the research literature. *British Journal of Social Work*, *39*(4), 641–656.

Chick, A. (2012). Design for social innovation. *Iridescent: Icograda Journal of Design Research*, *2*(1), 78–90.

Chittaro, L., & Vianella, A. (2013). Computer-supported mindfulness: Evaluation of a mobile thought distancing application of naive meditators. *International Journal of Human-Computer Studies*, *72*, 337–348.

Cohn, M. A., Fredrickson, B. L., Brown, S. L., Mikels, J. A., Conway, A. M. (2009). Happiness unpacked: Positive emotions increase life satisfaction by building resilience. *Emotion, 9*(3), 361–368 [preprint Retrieved April 29, 2012, from www.ncbi.nlm.nih.gov/pmc/articles/PMC3126102/pdf/nihms-222302.pdf]

Gamman, L., & Thorpe, A. (2012). From crime scripts to empathy suits – why role-playing and visualisation of user and abuser "scripts" regarding ATM crime can offer useful design tools to build empathy and catalyse design innovation. In *Proceedings of DRS 2012 Bangkok* (pp. 564–581). Bangkok, Thailand: Chulalongkorn University.

Greenfield, A. (2011, November 3). *Weeks 43–44: International garbageman.* New York: Urbanscale. Retrieved May 25, 2012, from http://urbanscale.org/news/2011/11/03/weeks-43-44-international-garbageman/

Grieve, R., Indian, M., Witteveen, K., Tolan, G. A., & Marrington, J. (2013). Face-to-face or Facebook: Can social connectedness be derived online? *Computers in Human Behavior, 29*(3), 604–609.

Hemmert, F., Gollner, U., Löwe, M., Wohlauf, A., & Joost, G. (2011). Intimate mobiles: Grasping, kissing and whispering as a means of telecommunication in mobile phones. *MobileHCI 2011*, Stockholm, Sweden, August 30–September 2.

Jelsma, J. (2006). Designing 'Moralized' products. In P. P. Verbeek & A. Slob (Eds.), *User behavior and technology development: Shaping sustainable relations between consumers and technologies* (pp. 221–223). Berlin: Springer.

Keltner, D., & Ekman, P. (2000). Emotion: An overview. In A. Kazdin (Ed.), *Encyclopedia of psychology* (pp. 162–167). London: Oxford University Press.

Keltner, D., & Gross, J. J. (1999). Functional accounts of emotions. *Cognition and Emotion, 13*(5), 467–480.

Langer, E. J. (1989) *Mindfulness.* Reading, MA: Addison Wesley Publishing Company.

Langer, E. J., & Moldoveanu, M. (2000a). The construct of mindfulness. *Journal of Social Issues, 56*(1), 1–9.

Ligo, L. L. 1984. *The concept of function in 20th century architectural criticism.* Ann Arbor, MI: UMI Research Press.

Lockton, D., Harrison, D., & Stanton, N. A. (2010). The design with intent method: A design tool for influencing user behaviour. *Applied Ergonomics, 41*(3), 382–392.

Luttrell, A., Briñol, P., & Petty, R. E. (2014). Mindful versus mindless thinking and persuasion. In A. Ie, C. T. Ngnoumen, & E. Langer (Eds.), *The Wiley Blackwell handbook of mindfulness* (Vol 1, pp. 258–278). Chichester: Wiley.

Morgan, M., & Cotton, S. R. (2004). The relationship between Internet activities and depressive symptoms in a sample of college freshmen. *CyberPsychology & Behavior, 6*(2), 133–142.

Niedderer, K. (2004). *Designing the performative object: A study in designing mindful interaction through artefacts* (PhD thesis). Plymouth University, Plymouth.

Niedderer, K. (2007). Designing mindful interaction: The category of the performative object. *Design Issues, 23*(1), 3–17.

Niedderer, K. (2014). Mediating mindful social interactions through design. In A. Ie, C. T. Ngnoumen, and E. Langer (Eds.), *The Wiley Blackwell handbook of mindfulness* (Vol 1, pp. 345–366). Chichester: Wiley.

Norman, D. A. (2002). *The design of everyday things.* New York: Basic Books.

Proper, K. I., Singh, A. S., van Mechelen, W., & Chinapaw, M. J. M. (2011). Sedentary behaviors and health outcomes among adults: A systematic review of prospective studies. *American Journal of Preventative Medicine, 40*(2), 174–182.

Smith, A. (1776 [2010]). Of the division of labour. In G. Lees-Maffei & R. Houze (Eds.), *The design history reader* (pp. 29–33). Oxford: Berg.

Srivastava, L. (2005). Mobile phones and the evolution of social behaviour. *Behaviour & Information Technology, 24*(2), 111–129.

Staiano, A. E., & Calvert, S. L. (2011). Exergames for physical education courses: Physical, social, and cognitive benefits. *Child Development Perspectives, 5*(2), 93–98. doi:10.1111/j.1750–8606.2011.00162.x

Stern, N. H. (2006). *The economics of climate change.* London: HM Treasury.

Stern, P. C. (2000). New environmental theories: Toward a coherent theory of environmentally significant behavior. *Journal of Social Issues, 56*(3), 407–424.

Tromp, N., Hekkert, P., & Verbeek, P. P. (2011). Design for socially responsible behaviour: A classification of influence based on intended user experience. *Design Issues, 27*(3), 3–19.

Udall, N. (1996). *An investigation into the heuristics of mindfulness in higher art and design education* (PhD thesis). University of Surrey, UK.

Webster, C. (2007). Property rights, public space and urban design. *The Town Planning Review, 78*(1), 81–101.

10 Practices-oriented design

Lenneke Kuijer

Introduction

Understanding the impact of design on human action and developing approaches to facilitate desirable behavioural change 'by design' are major challenges for the discipline of design. In efforts to address them, design draws on various other academic disciplines. The design approach presented in this chapter draws on practice theory, a form of social theory that takes practices – such as cooking, playing football, having a meeting or driving – as a unit of analysis. Following developments in other fields, such as Human-Computer Interaction (Kuutti & Bannon, 2014; Pierce et al., 2013), environmental policy (Doyle & Davies, 2012) and consumption studies (Warde, 2005), practice theory is increasingly drawn on by design researchers.

Like in other fields, these researchers argue that drawing on practice theory offers a valuable, novel way of approaching complex societal issues such as sustainability or health. Taking practices instead of products or interactions as a unit of analysis is argued to offer a systemic approach that can help grapple with rebound effects and user acceptance issues (Scott et al., 2009), as well as gaining a deeper understanding of the relations between artefacts and their users (Shove et al., 2007).

This chapter offers a concise introduction to practices-oriented design. Building on a design-tailored introduction of the theory in the next section, the third section provides a categorization of the various ways in which a practice approach has been interpreted in design research, after which the concluding section explains and illustrates a particular approach that was developed to tackle the challenge of reducing domestic energy demand.

A design-tailored introduction to practice theory

Practice theory forms a group of related theories that comprises a large and varied body of literature in the social sciences. In this section, only the part of this literature that has been repeatedly applied in design research is covered. These strands of practice theory have made their way from social theory into design theory mainly because they explicitly conceptualize the role of man-made artefacts in social stability and change. The main theorists in this section of practice theory are the following: Schatzki, a philosopher who considers human-made artefacts as part of material arrangements amid which practices are carried on and which they are altered by (Schatzki, 2010: 130); the cultural sociologist Reckwitz, who provides an overview of theoretical concepts of practice theory (2002b) and a discussion of the role of artefacts in the theory (2002a); and sociologist Shove and colleagues, who view materials as one of the elements of practices (e.g. Shove et al., 2012).

The following is a highly condensed, design-tailored interpretation of a number of concepts from practice theory.

Practices as the fundamental unit of analysis

In practice theory, society is viewed as a collection of practices and all human action as the performance of one or more practices. This collection of interrelated practices is considered the site of social stability and change. Reckwitz (2002b) explains this positioning as a middle ground between foregrounding either individuals or structures. Unlike some other theories, practice theory does not offer a model that explains human action according to a set of causal relations and factors (Kuijer & Bakker, 2015). Rather, it offers a conceptual framework to give a 'general and abstract account' (Schatzki, 2001) to gain understanding of a particular topic. One of these conceptual tools is the idea of practices as configurations of elements.

Practices as configurations of elements

Shove and Pantzar (2005) describe practices as configurations of elements. These elements are grouped into three types: materials, competences and meanings. In cooking, for example, materials include pots, cookers, knives, cutting boards, the food itself, a cooking book, the kitchen space and the human body. Competences are the skills and know-how applied when cooking, which are viewed as distributed between the person that does the cooking, for example skills of cutting vegetables and knowledge of baking techniques and skills embodied in the artefacts used, such as skills of cutting in a food processor, or knowledge contained in a written recipe. Meanings, finally, are rationales for engaging in the practice in its particular form, such as ideas about healthy eating or good parenting.

While this idea of a practice as a configuration of elements provides an analytical tool to understand relations between people and artefacts, it doesn't do much for understanding how such relations may change 'by design'. For conceptualizing change in practices, the notions of practice-as-entity and practice-as-performance are helpful.

Practices-as-entity and practices-as-performance

In practice theory, observable, situated behaviours of people are viewed and approached as *performances* of practices. More strongly put, all human behaviour can be viewed as the performance of one or more practices (Schatzki, 2001). These 'practices-as-performance' are considered to be loosely guided by the organizational dimension of practices, which Shove et al. (2012) refer to as the 'practice-as-entity'. What this notion of entity implies is that practices exist even though they are not performed at that moment, and that they can therefore travel as *entities* in space and time. Cooking, for example, has existed since the domestication of fire and cooking in Japan and cooking in the UK, although different in many respects are both recognized as forms of cooking.

Having established this distinction between entity and performance, it is important to note that they are recursively related; change in the practice-as-entity is both a consequence of and a catalyst for changes in their everyday performance. For example, the mainstream practice of personal washing in the Netherlands changed from weekly baths to daily showers when more people, in particular moments of performance, chose to take a shower instead of a bath. However, this could only happen because showering started to collectively be viewed as a pleasurable way of washing the body, and shower fixtures became common features of bathrooms.

Behavioural change as a reconfiguration of elements

In practice theory, behavioural change can be conceptualized as practice change. Shove et al. (2012) explain that 'practices change when new elements are introduced or when existing elements are combined in new ways' (p. 120). In other words, when aiming to change a practice, one way to do so is to introduce new elements into them. This is not a simple procedure. Integrating new elements into a practice requires a *reconfiguration* of elements and their links into a new configuration that works and makes sense. In practices of domestic heating for example, the introduction of natural gas infrastructure has rendered elements like coal sheds, coal scuttles, coal dust and skills of making and maintaining a coal fire obsolete, while piping, gas fires and new skills of setting thermostats and turning radiator valves became required to make the practice work. Importantly, reconfiguration of practices can only happen in performance. If a performance that integrates new elements in new ways is then repeated and spread, this new configuration becomes part of the entity. There are more ways to conceptualize change in practices, but discussing these would be beyond the scope of this chapter. The concluding section will elaborate on the idea of behavioural change as a reconfiguration of elements by presenting a particular practices-oriented approach.

Four interpretations of practices-oriented design

In this chapter, practices-oriented design is used as a term to emphasise that practice is about more than practice versus theory, practice versus research or practice as the realm of everyday life, because it includes the notion of practices as entities that organize and emerge from everyday performance. The origins of 'practices-oriented design' can be traced back to a collaborative research programme between social scientists and design researchers in 2005–2006. One of the outputs of the programme was a Practice Oriented Product Design Manifesto (Shove & Watson, 2006). Partly triggered by this pamphlet and a related publication in Design Issues (Ingram et al., 2007), practice theory has been picked up in design literature in a variety of ways. This chapter distinguishes four ways in which practice theory is applied in design research. The practices-oriented approach explained in the concluding section incorporates aspects of the first three types of practices-oriented design.

Analyzing situated practices

The first type uses practice theory as a conceptual framework for studying and analyzing situated performances of practices. This way of applying practice theory uses methods from user research such as workbooks, interviews, observations, surveys, context mapping and so on, but distinguishes itself by taking practices, instead of products, users or interactions as a unit of analysis. Examples of publications that propose and illustrate a situated analysis of practices to obtain design insights are Prendergast and Roberts (2009), who study the internet usage and modes of learning of elderly; Korkman (2006), who analyzes family cruise practices; Julier (2007), who studies iPod use in a community of teenagers and Hielscher et al. (2007), Scott et al. (2009) and Jégou et al. (2009) who study hair care, bathing and domestic heating practices respectively.

Tracing practices in space and time

A second type of practices-oriented analysis for design focuses more on the practice-as-entity by tracing and comparing practices over space and time. Munnecke (2007), in his 'deep-dive' approach proposes analyzing a practice's historic career in order to extrapolate its dynamics into 'an overview of future innovation opportunities'. Hielscher et al. (2008) perform a literature analysis of the history of hair care, and Scott et al. (2009) paint a culturally diverse overview of the histories of bathing. Other papers of this type focus on spatially removed alternative practices. For example Matsuhashi et al. (2009) compare bathing in India, Japan and the Netherlands; Pierce and Paulos (2011) focus on second-hand consumption practices; Wakkary et al. (2013) on do-it-yourself and repair and Clune (2010) on practices in developing societies. Again, the methods used aren't new, but the attention for history and non-mainstream practices derives from the conceptual link between performance and entity in practice theory.

Disrupting practices

A third type of application combines a focus on practices with a 'designerly' approach (Cross, 1982) to the problem at hand. Based on the idea that designers reframe problems and solutions in an iterative way, these approaches aim to gain understanding of the focal practice by disrupting it. Jégou et al. (2009) for example mention that their design process included propositions of different ways of organizing ones domestic environment in order to question domestic practices, to take a distance from them and 'enable the families to re-invent progressively their daily ways of living' (p. 33), and Scott et al. (2009) use 'practice oriented. . . triggers' to 'stir up creativity in practice' (p. 6) and eventually 'to help people reinvent ordinary practices' (p. 5). Kuijer et al. (2013) argue that this type of approach moves away from the analytic social science origins of practice theory by taking practices as a *unit of design*.

Reflecting on practices of design

While every proposed new design approach contains a critique on existing approaches, the fourth type of interpretation is different from the other three in the sense that it uses practice theory primarily to reflect on *practices of design*. Publications of this type include Kimbell (2011) on service design, Pettersen (2015) on sustainable design, DiSalvo and Redström (DiSalvo et al., 2013) on design research, Scott et al. (2012) on design education and Wakkary and Maestri (2008) on everyday design. This type of interpretation uses practice theory to reflect on the organizational and professional practices that design is a part of. Moreover, by viewing practices of design as integral to the ecologies of practices, which include those studied and intervened in by designers, highlights the mutually constitutive relations *between* practices.

To summarize, practice theory has been picked up in the design research community, where its implications for design have been interpreted in a variety of ways. Analysis of these varied interpretations revealed that while practice theory forms a useful framework for broadening situated analysis of products in use away from a focus on product-user interactions, the tracing of practices in space and time capitalizes on the conceptual framework by offering a structured way of 'thinking out of the box'. As the case study described in the concluding section will illustrate, such analysis forms a frame of reference to relativize the status quo of a selected problem space. Moreover, taking practices as a unit of design further helps designers to step away from tinkering with individual behaviour and to work with larger scales of change. The fourth interpretation does not feature explicitly in the case but forms an important playing field for further research.

Reconfiguring practices by design: a case of keeping warm at home

The approach presented below was developed in a research through design process, a form of applied research in which design projects and their outcomes are used as an integral part of the research process (Zimmerman et al., 2010). The design projects through which the approach described here was developed addressed issues of domestic energy demand, using cases on personal washing and keeping warm at home in the Netherlands. The resulting approach forms a recommended way of working based on practical experiences; it is however not a blueprint or a recipe for success. The approach is illustrated with material from the keeping warm case. This section is based on Kuijer and Jong (2012) and Kuijer (2014), which contain further details on the case.

Domestic heating takes up the largest single share of household resource consumption in most European countries (ENERDATA 2013). Common environmental policy and sustainable design responses to the question of how to save energy for heating homes either focus on improving the energy efficiency of heat provisioning, or on motivating people to turn down the thermostat (e.g. Lu et al., 2015; Chwieduk, 2003; Moll & Groot-Marcus, 2002). As this example aims to illustrate, a practices-oriented approach supports the identification and fleshing out of a different kind of response.

The approach, presented schematically in Figure 10.1, consists of two main parts. In the first part, practices are taken as a unit of analysis. This part works from a selected, resource intensive target practice – in this case keeping warm at home – to the identification of opportunities for desirable change. In the second part, practices are taken as units of design. Here, the opportunities identified in the first part are fleshed out into reconfigurations of the target practice that have potential to work.

Practices as a unit of analysis

A practices-oriented approach to reducing domestic energy demand implies considering energy as used for the accomplishment of everyday practices (Shove & Walker, 2014). To analyze domestic heating, the proposed approach therefore starts with the identification of a target practice, which in the domestic heating project became formulated as practices of keeping warm at home.

After selecting 'keeping warm' as target practice, the approach recommends the selection and quantification of consumption indicators. Purpose of this step is to set a target for the scale of change to aim for by looking beyond current day averages at spatial variety, and at historic change. With an idea of the range in levels of energy demand related to the practice, a challenging target to reduce towards can be set. This target is not set as something to achieve at all cost, but makes the scale of the potential for change explicit and opens the target up for discussion. In the keeping warm case, levels of energy consumption for domestic heating in Japan, and in Dutch households a century ago, formed the main points of reference. A reduction in the order of 60% – from 50 GJ to 20 GJ of energy

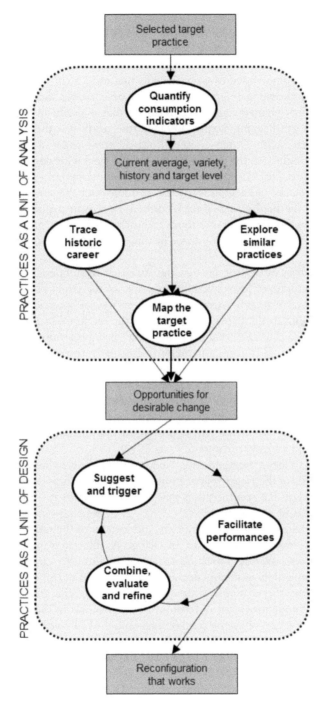

Figure 10.1 A practices-oriented approach to reducing domestic energy demand
Source: Kuijer (2014: 167).

use for heating per household per year – was set as a target (Kuijer & Jong, 2012). Not disregarding the fact that the target practice is in many ways different from these reference points, it highlights that keeping satisfactorily warm at home is possible with less than half of the energy required by the average Dutch household today.

The next step is to trace the practice's historic career. When tracing the target practice back in time it is recommended to go back centuries rather than years. Existing literature can be insightful for learning about the history of a practice, but sometimes lacks the type of everyday detail of elements and their relations that is useful in a practices-oriented design process. In the keeping warm case, literature study was therefore supplemented with two interviews with Dutch couples from different generations about their past. Besides offering insight into the details of how people lived with significantly lower levels of heating, it also provides a deeper understanding of contemporary practice. From analysis of the historic career of keeping warm for example, four shifts in practices of keeping warm at home in the Netherlands were identified. They were a shift from warm clothes to insulated homes, from heating one room to heating multiple rooms, from solid to liquid fuel and a shift of decisions about space heating from people to thermostats (Kuijer & Jong, 2012).

Next to an analysis of historic change, the approach recommends the analysis of spatially removed examples of low demanding variants of the target practice, i.e. alternative ways of keeping warm in other (sub)cultures. A variety of approaches for this form of analysis can be found in the papers referred to in the section 'Tracing practices in space and time'. The purpose of analyzing these 'desirable' examples is not to copy them, but to find inspiration from, and to form a frame of reference for the target practice. In the case of keeping warm, Japan emerged as an interesting case with its standards of living similar to the Netherlands combined with a significantly lower energy demand for domestic heating (Dril et al., 2012). Analysis of Japanese ways of staying warm at home – through literature study and a small-scale ethnographic study – revealed a lower level of space insulation and more locally oriented forms of heating such as the kotatsu – a low table with a heating element and a blanket (Kuijer & Jong, 2012).

While the steps so far are best performed iteratively and intertwined, it is recommended to postpone analysis of the target practice until analysis of historic career and spatial variety are well underway. Reason for this is that – as Hockey puts it – 'that which is closest may well be what is most difficult to see' (1993: 221). 'Stepping out' of what we take for granted everyday helps reveal the temporality and locality of the target practice, and thus makes it easier to identify opportunities for change. As illustrated in the section 'Analyzing situated practices', the target practice can be studied using a variety of 'user research' methods. When applied in an energy demand context, focus in this step is on unravelling the relation between the elements of the practice (images, skills and stuff) and levels of demand, and on the identification of tensions in the practice. In the keeping warm case, indoor temperature settings became central in making the link between practices of keeping warm at home and their levels of resource consumption. Tensions were found between uniform indoor temperatures and a high inter and intra personal diversity in situated comfort needs (Kuijer & Jong, 2012).

All these forms of analysis together provide a source of inspiration for the identification of opportunities for change. There is little guidance to offer on how exactly such opportunities can be identified, because they are highly project specific. In the example projects through which the approach was developed, opportunities combined tensions between elements in the target practice with aspects of desirable alternatives, either contemporary or historic. In the keeping warm case, the tension between increasingly uniform indoor climates and high diversity in situated needs for heat were combined with the identification of more person-oriented forms of heating and insulation that were found in Japan and Dutch history. The opportunity selected was to supplement space heating with more person-oriented alternatives (Kuijer & Jong, 2012), which was taken into the next phase.

Practices as a unit of design

As argued in Kuijer et al. (2013), taking practices as a unit of design implies disrupting existing practices and generating, through acting out, a variety of reconfigurations of the target practice that work. The second phase of the design process involves these elements and integrates them into an iterative, cyclic process in which acting out is central (see Figure 10.1). The process starts by shaping the opportunities identified in the previous phase into suggested 'proto-practices'. The proto-practice contains materials (prototypes and settings), competences (instructions) and meanings (suggestions) and steers towards a certain type of reconfiguration, but, especially in earlier cycles, remains open when it comes to the details of the performance. It is meant to trigger participants to creatively integrate these elements with others, available or imagined, into ways of doing that work for them.

The keeping warm at home project involved two main iterations, both integrated into student projects at Delft University of Technology. The first iteration entailed the development of person-oriented heat sources as part of the courses Interactive Technology Design and Sustainable Design, which resulted in a heated breakfast table, blanket, sweater and pillow. The second iteration involved a masters' graduation project that focused on a proto-practice around warm clothing. In the first design iteration, one of the proto-practices was the MANGO concept, which involved a heated pillow, new skills of hugging the pillow when feeling cold instead of turning up the thermostat and new meanings of enjoying the direct heat source instead of a distant radiator. The idea included a variety of uses as illustrated in Figure 10.2.

In the next step of facilitating performances, various triggers are used as the basis for acting out ways in which the proto-practice might work as a coherent reconfiguration of elements. These performances can take place in a lab (Kuijer et al., 2013), or in people's

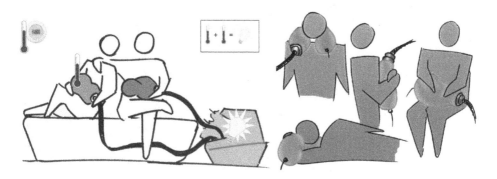

Figure 10.2 The MANGO concept and a variety of ways to use the pillow

Source: By Nina Boorsma, Barbara Denissen, Bas Lammers and Tom van de Water, Minor Sustainable Design, TU Delft.

own homes, and should aim to include a wide diversity of participants to generate a variety of reconfigurations. Forming a very small scale version of this step, the MANGO, together with its use instructions and suggestions was tried out in two different households for two days and three weeks respectively. It was held on the lap while sitting on the couch watching TV as well as when working at a computer sitting in a chair, and it was used in the neck while reading on the couch lying down.

In the third step of the cycle, documented performances are compared, dimensions of variety – e.g. the range of situations and ways in which person-oriented heating is performed – are distilled, levels of energy demand are assessed and, eventually, redesigns of the proto-practice are made. The redesign then forms the starting point for another round of performances. By repeating the process in subsequent iterations, the proto-practice is fleshed out and its configuration of elements becomes more 'high-fidelity'. Particularly in earlier stages, this redesign can be very different from the initial proto-practice.

The field studies with the MANGO and other personal heat sources revealed that in spite of their positioning as a partial replacement of space heating, they were used in addition to it, leading to increased rather than decreased energy demand. On top of this, there were indications that their relative immobility may invoke sedentary activity and therefore increase the need for heat. These findings, together with the initial analysis, formed the starting point for the second iteration, which changed direction away from person heating towards a focus on enlarging the role of warm clothing in practices of keeping warm. While putting on a sweater is a common sense, low-energy alternative to turning up the thermostat, it currently does not form a mainstream, acceptable way of keeping warm at home in the Netherlands. The proto-practice developed in this iteration embeds warm clothing in a coherent reconfiguration of practices of keeping warm (see Figure 10.3), including recommendations for the design and marketing of a range

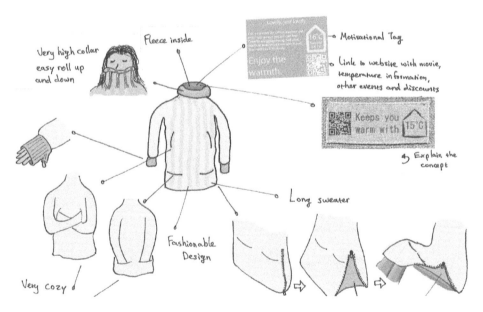

Figure 10.3 A visualization of the Home Wear concept

Source: TU Delft graduation project by Sjoerd Vonk for SusLabNWE.

of warm sweaters called Home Wear, a website and launch campaign including connections with an existing Dutch campaign initiative, and a thermostat interface. Importantly, this revised proto-practice explicitly integrates lower than average indoor temperatures (15–17°C). It therefore promotes a different idea of comfort that involves warm clothes and fresh air rather than warm spaces.

Conclusion

This chapter offers a brief introduction to practices-oriented design that aims to make its methods and underlying theories accessible to a wider audience. Inspired by similar developments in other fields, practices-oriented design has emerged in design research over the past decade. Its literature contains a variety of interpretations of the implications of taking practices as a unit of analysis and design. The practices-oriented design approach introduced in this chapter focuses on reconfiguring a target practice. The example shows that analyzing how practices change over time and vary across space reveals the relativity of the mundane everyday in practical terms. Within this contextualized awareness, a space opens up for design interventions that steer towards a future that is not only different in terms of technologies and behaviours, but also in terms of taken for granted needs, such as the need for heated spaces (of at least 18°C) to achieve indoor comfort. At the same time, a practice approach acknowledges that what people do has to work and make sense for them, which implies close engagement with everyday life contexts as integral to the design process. While the approach was developed in the context of domestic energy demand, these basic characteristics make it suitable for the identification and fleshing out of opportunities for tackling other types of societal challenges as well. A main challenge for design practice when taking practices instead of product-user interactions as the unit of analysis and design is managing the expanded problem and solution spaces. To incorporate this paradigm shift, further work is required to establish the implications (of this approach) for design practice and the webs of practices it is part of.

Acknowledgements

The PhD research underlying this paper was conducted at the Department of Industrial Design of Delft University of Technology. I would like to thank my PhD supervisors, all the students and participants that contributed to the design projects and my former colleagues at the DEMAND Centre and the University of Sheffield Geography department who helped me reflect on them.

References

Chwieduk, D. (2003). Towards sustainable-energy buildings. *Applied Energy*, 76(1), 211–217.

Clune, S. (2010). Inverting the solution into the problem: Design, practice theory and behavioural change for sustainability. In Yongqi Lou (Ed.), *Proceeding of cumulus*, ShangHai, China, 29 September–1 October 2010, pp. 25–31.

Cross, N. (1982). Designerly ways of knowing. *Design Studies*, 3(4), 221–227.

DiSalvo, C., Redström, J., & Watson, M. (2013). Commentaries on the special issue on practice-oriented approaches to sustainable HCI. *ACM Transactions on Computer-Human Interaction (TOCHI)*, 20(4), 26.

Doyle, R., & Davies, A. R. (2012). Towards sustainable household consumption: Exploring a practice oriented, participatory backcasting approach for sustainable home heating practices in Ireland. *Journal of Cleaner Production*, 48, 260–271.

Dril, T.V., Gerdes, J., Marbus, S., & Boelhouwer, M. (2012). *Energie trends 2012*. Retrieved from www.ecn. nl/publications/ECN-B--12-005.

ENERDATA (2013). Odyssee Energy Efficiency Indicators in Europe: Consumption per dwelling (at normal climate). *ENERDATA*. www.indicators.odyssee-mure.eu/online-indicators.html

Hielscher, S., Fisher, T., & Cooper, T. (2008). The return of the Beehives, Brylcreem and Botanical! An historical review of hair care practices with a view to opportunities for sustainable design. *Undisciplined! Design Research Society Conference 2008*, Sheffield Hallam University, Sheffield, UK. Retrieved from http://shura.shu.ac.uk/549/

Hielscher, S., Fisher, T., & Cooper, T. (2007). *How often do you wash your hair? Design as disordering: Everyday routines, human object theories, probes and sustainability*. 7th European Academy of Design Conference (EAD07): Dancing with disorder: Design, discourse and disorder, Izmir, Turkey.

Hockey, J. (1993). Research methods – researching peers and familiar settings. *Research Papers in Education*, *8*(2), 199–225.

Ingram, J., Shove, E., & Watson, M. (2007). Products and practices: Selected concepts from science and technology studies and from social theories of consumption and practice. *Design Issues*, *23*(2), 3–16.

Jégou, F., Liberman, J., & Wallenborn, G. (2009). *Collaborative design sessions of objects proposing energy-saving practices*. Energy Efficiency & Behaviour Conference, Maastricht, The Netherlands.

Julier, G. (2007). Design practice within a theory of practice. *Design Principles & Practices: An International Journal*, *1*(2), 43–50.

Kimbell, L. (2011). Rethinking design thinking: Part I. *Design and Culture*, *3*(3), 285–306.

Korkman, O. (2006). *Customer value formation in practice: A practice-theoretical approach* (PhD). Swedish School of Economics and Business Administration, Helsinki.

Kuijer, L. (2014). *Implications of social practice theory for sustainable design* (PhD thesis), TU Delft, Delft, NL.

Kuijer, L., & Bakker, C. (2015). Of chalk and cheese: Behaviour change and practice theory in sustainable design. *International Journal of Sustainable Engineering*, *8*(3), 219–230.

Kuijer, L., De Jong, A., & Van Eijk, D. (2013). Practices as a unit of design: An exploration of theoretical guidelines in a study on bathing. *Transactions on Computer-Human Interaction*, *20*(4), 22.

Kuijer, L., & De Jong, A. D. (2012). Identifying design opportunities for reduced household resource consumption: Exploring practices of thermal comfort. *Journal of Design Research*, *10*(1/2), 67–85.

Kuutti, K., & Bannon, L. J. (2014). The turn to practice in HCI: Towards a research agenda. *Proceedings of the 32nd Annual ACM Conference on Human Factors in Computing Systems*, Toronto, Ontario, Canada.

Lu, S., Ham, J., & Midden, C. (2015). Persuasive technology based on bodily comfort experiences: The effect of color temperature of room lighting on user motivation to change room temperature. *Persuasive Technology* (pp. 83–94). New York: Springer.

Matsuhashi, N., Kuijer, L., & Jong, A. D. (2009). *A culture-inspired approach to gaining insights for designing sustainable practices*. EcoDesign 2009: Sixth International Symposium on Environmentally Conscious Design and Inverse Manufacturing, Sapporo, Japan.

Moll, H., & Groot-Marcus, A. (2002). Households past and present, and opportunities for change. In M. Kok, W. Vermeulen, A. Faaij, & D. S. Jager (Eds.), *Global warming and social innovation; the challenge of a climate neutral society* (pp. 83–106). London: Earthscan Publications Ltd.

Munnecke, M. (2007). Future practices: Coshaping everyday life. *ICSID & IDSA CONNECTING '07 World Design Congress*, San Francisco, CA, October 17–20.

Pettersen, I. N. (2015). Towards practice-oriented design for sustainability: The compatibility with selected design fields. *International Journal of Sustainable Engineering*, *8*(3), 206–218.

Pierce, J., & Paulos, E. (2011). Second-hand interactions: Investigating reacquisition and dispossession practices around domestic objects. In *Proceedings of the 2011 Annual Conference on Human Factors in Computing Systems*, Vancouver, Canada.

Pierce, J., Strengers, Y., Sengers, P., & Bødker, S. (2013). Introduction to the special issue on practice-oriented approaches to sustainable HCI. *ACM Transactions on Computer-Human Interaction (TOCHI)*, *20*(4), 20.

Prendergast, D., & Roberts, S. (2009). Practice, systems and technology for elders. *Universal Access Information Society*, *8*, 59–61.

Reckwitz, A. (2002a). The status of the "material" in theories of culture: From "social structure" to "arte-facts". *Journal for the Theory of Social Behaviour, 32*(2), 195–217.

Reckwitz, A. (2002b). Toward a theory of social practices: A development in culturalist theorizing. *European Journal of Social Theory, 5*(2), 243–263.

Schatzki, T. (2001). Introduction: Practice theory. In T. R. Schatzki, K. K. Cetina & E. von Savigny (Eds.), *The practice turn in contemporary theory* (pp. 1–14). London: Routledge.

Schatzki, T. (2010). Materiality and social life. *Nature and Culture, 5*(2), 123–149.

Scott, K., Bean, J., & Kuijer, L. (2012). Teaching practice theory and sustainability in the design studio. *NCCR*, Göteborg, SE, 30 May–1 June.

Scott, K., Quist, J., & Bakker, C. (2009). *Co-design, social practices and sustainable innovation: Involving users in a living lab exploratory study on bathing.* Joint actions on climate change conference, Aalborg, Denmark.

Shove, E., & Pantzar, M. (2005). Consumers, producers and practices: Understanding the invention and reivention of Nordic walking. *Journal of Consumer Culture, 5*(1), 34–64.

Shove, E., Pantzar, M., & Watson, M. (2012). *The dynamics of social practice: Everyday life and how it changes.* London: Sage.

Shove, E., & Walker, G. (2014). What is energy for? Social practice and energy demand. *Theory, Culture & Society, 31*(5), 41–58.

Shove, E., & Watson, M. (2006). *Manifesto of practice oriented product design.* Retrieved from www.lancaster.ac.uk/fass/projects/dnc/papers.html

Shove, E., Watson, M., Hand, M., & Ingram, J. (2007). *The design of everyday life.* Oxford: Berg.

Wakkary, R., Desjardins, A., Hauser, S., & Maestri, L. (2013). A sustainable design fiction: Green practices. *ACM Transactions on Computer-Human Interaction (TOCHI), 20*(4), 23.

Wakkary, R., & Maestri, L. (2008). Aspects of everyday design: Resourcefulness, adaptation, and emergence. *International Journal of Human – Computer Interaction, 24*(5), 478–491.

Warde, A. (2005). Consumption and theories of practice. *Journal of Consumer Culture, 5*(2), 131–153.

Zimmerman, J., Stolterman, E., & Forlizzi, J. (2010). *An analysis and critique of research through design: Towards a formalization of a research approach.* Paper presented at the DIS2010, Aarhus Denmark.

11 Futuring and ontological designing

Stephen Clune

This chapter looks at the potential role of futuring (forecasting, future scenarios and back-casting) as a strategy to enable or disable future behaviours and practices from taking place. The chapter is underpinned by the philosophy of ontological designing in that 'things have the capacity to thing' (Willis, 2006).

The chapter starts from a different perspective to many cognition-based theories of behavioural change, in that the human agency is diminished in some ways. Ontological designing flips the notion of agency on its head, suggesting an equal, or greater agency is given to artefacts and environments. The chapter first introduces the concept of ontological designing, prior to outlining practical tools and methods that compliment the concept of ontological designing, and offers a contribution to design for behavioural change via futuring. These include the following:

Ways of seeing the problem you may be trying to change

- Timelines outlining the trajectory of practices and stuff
- Viewing stuff as actors. . . the game of ontological design.

Ways of visioning and acting for desired change

- Projecting forwards trajectories of practice
- Responding to trajectories via future scenarios.

Rather than ask the individual to act in a particular situation, these tools encourage the designer to take a step back, to look at the environment that the person is acting within, to see what the designed environment may be scripting. While not an explicit 'behavioural change' strategy, it examines deeply the role of the designed environment that influences our lives experience, and everyday practices and behaviours.[1]

What is ontological designing?

Heidegger's claim that we make our locations but we are also made by them (1971) illustrates the central argument of ontological design in that as we design, the things we design also design us: so design designs (*things have the capacity to thing*).

> The designs produced by designers come from their worlding as designers, the objects or systems that come from these designings in turn become parts of worlds and thus enter into worlding, this in ways in which as things they thing.
>
> (Willis, 2006: 91)

The concept of ontological design is based on the hermeneutic phenomenology of Heidegger (1962) and Gadamer (1976), with more explicit design interpretations presented by Winograd and Flores (1986), Willis (2006) as well as Fry (1994, 1999, 2009).

> Ontology means "of or belonging to the understanding of being." Put extremely simply, ontic refers to what is; ontology refers to enquiry of what is, while ontological refers to the condition or behaviour of what is.
>
> (Willis, 2006: 81)

Fry (2009: 23) explains ontological design via Bourdieu,[2] arguing that the structuring of habitus by design leaves us somewhat limited 'by the world we are born into, that we take to be the world itself' (2009: 23). Habitus, structures (designed things) and practices are intrinsically connected.

> As soon as we started to modify our environment and make a world for ourselves via the use of tools, we began to form practices that were to structure what we were to become. . . we are never just users but equally the used.
>
> (Fry, 2009: 24)

This circularity means that design is always more than what it currently names, for example, designed artefacts, the act of designing or the professional or academic discipline of design.

Winograd and Flores (1986) argued that the computer 'designs' rationalistic thinking into new human practices in a way that today we might say the iPhone 'designs' multitasking and connectivity into our lives. Design agency is therefore not solely in the hands of the designer, but rather in worlds that designers inhabit which are defined by certain concerns, practices and constellations of existing products. Industrial designer Harvey Molotoch, in his book *Where Stuff Comes From*, provides a similar insight into the relationship between practicing designers and social practices, although he does not explicitly articulate ontological design:

> Each innovation contributes not only to instituting a particular product, but also to the regime of interrelated objects and social practices within which the product is embedded. Designers use what is out there to yield new objects that themselves become part of the conditions under which designers do their next work.
>
> (Molotoch, 2003: 233)

The car is perhaps one of the most recognizable examples to explain 'things capacity to thing'. Henry Ford's 'car for the masses' did far more than enable people with the opportunity to drive. Individual mobility afforded by the car equally altered the 'planning of cities, suburbs, urban design, rural life, retail shopping, tourism, leisure and more' (Fry, 2009: 39). Once the car was viewed as a dominant transport mode, a range of services were designed that rely on the car. For example, many Australian supermarkets would not survive without the car. The dominance of the supermarkets may have led to the decline of local shops and alterations to the practice of shopping. On the extremes, car dependency could be seen as a contributing factor to an obesogenic urban environment, while the human-car hybrid facilitates increased emotions (changing our being) as drivers interact with other 'monsters in metal cocoon' human-car hybrids (Lupton, 1999: 57). The use of history illustrates the relational complexity of design unfolding ontologically. Rather than looking at design as a history of cultural artefacts or movements, it shows how design works ontologically as a process (Fry, 1999), with its compounding material and immaterial impacts on our world and thus on our being.

Why is ontological designing useful for design for behaviour change?

Ontological designing is useful for design for behavioural change as it greatly expands our understanding of the context that we hope to shift. At times behavioural change initiatives can appear to be like sending a child into a candy store to buy a piece of fruit, in that the suggested behaviour is counter to the entire designed world's expectations. Ontological designing draws attention to and provides a means to read design critically and relationally as it unfolds in the shaping of our worlds, and so on our being (and by default our practices and behaviours). It therefore gives the designed environments, systems and objects more weight in the shaping of social practice and behaviours than has hitherto been recognized.

Ontological designing has the capacity to be a practical theory that seeks to understand the production of materiality (images, objects, infrastructures) in relation to our being in the world. It brings to the fore the ever-present and dynamic process of human making. That 'the things designers make are always more than themselves, have implications beyond themselves and are disposed to behave in particular ways toward and away from humans, as they make their way in the world' (Lopes, 2005: 11). Ontological designing provides an antidote to the 'General lack of a sense of how design makes or breaks worlds' (Fry, 2009: 26). It can be understood as a particular type of design practice that seeks positive change. This is reliant on the capacity to 'see' and 'think' design ontologically.

Practical tools to see, act and create visions drawing on ontological designing

The practical tools to apply ontological designing are broken down into tools that assist in 'seeing' ontological designing through reflective praxis, and tools that assist in designing for the desired change. These four practical exercises are the following:

1. Timelines outlining the trajectory of practices and stuff
2. Viewing stuff as actors. . . the game of ontological design
3. Projecting forwards trajectories of practice
4. Responding via future scenarios.

The tools were developed as a practical means to assist designers grasp ontological design, by reframing their tacit knowledge as opposed to a reading of complex philosophy. This understanding may then inform a particular type of design that attempts to think forward and take responsibility for designs future designing. These tools have been tested in design education at Western Sydney, RMIT and Lancaster Universities, and utilized in industry workshops.

1. Timelines outlining the trajectory of practices and stuff

The first tool, a timeline outlining the trajectory of practices and stuff, asks participants to map out the trajectory of practice including significant social, technical, economic and political events. This task evolved from an initial question of 'why are we unsustainable, what was design's role in the unsustainability' (Lopes et al., 2007). The timeline assists participants to acknowledge the dynamic nature of practices and can then be re-read to identify the ability of 'things to thing'. As Shove, Watson et al. argue, this 'Retrospectively retelling of technological trajectories frequently reveals the critical role of prospective narratives within and as an integral' (2007: 97).

An example of its use was at the Australian Food and Grocery Commission (AFGC) Future of Packaging Forum, where participants were asked to create a 100-year timeline of significant innovations relating to packaging (Verghese et al., 2012; Figure 11.1). AFGC participants initially thought that supermarkets were introduced to Australia by a significant business leader who had imported the concept from the USA. However, the timeline tool enabled an ontological designing perspective, suggesting that packaging technology, refrigerators and the automobile were equal actors in the creation of the supermarket by enabling the replacement of the need for frequent shopping, or delivery services. This perspective assisted the packaging industry to see its contribution to daily life as far greater than simple innovation in new packaging materials. Packaging was a central actor in the creation of the supermarket. If one takes Jelsma's (2006) 'moralised design' perspective, packaging designers would be responsible for significant change associated in shopping and cooking practices. For example, we no longer order the exact quantity of food you require due to the fixed purchasing quantities of packaging. In a similar vein, one could argue that the restriction of preservative use in French bakeries maintains an entire industry and culture dependent on fresh produce. This would be vulnerable to change if preservatives and modified atmosphere packaging were introduced to significantly extend the shelf life of bread.

2. Viewing stuff as actors. . . the game of ontological design

Because design is pervasive and works upon us ontologically its agency is hard to see. The second tool, 'the game of ontological design', uses the metaphor of viewing stuff as actors to 'think' ontological design, and see design's agency. The game asks what did product X

Figure 11.1 Timeline of packaging innovations in Australia

Source: Verghese et al. (2012).

design, create, kill, proliferate, favour or alter. In an educational setting, this game of onto-logical design plays on Fry's claim that 'design designs' (1999: 6) by asking participants to visually map out answers to questions such as:

- What things did product X design?
- What things/products has the introduction of product X encourage/enable?
- What traditional skills and practices has product X affected?
- What products/activities are dependent on product X?
- What existing practices does product X deter?

The microwave and car make good examples to apply this line of thinking to (Ford's 'car for the masses' is discussed earlier), as they escalate design as having a far greater signifi-cance than first assumed. For example, the mapping of the microwave left one RMIT industrial design student stunned on how you could defrost food without the microwave. This is evidence of a lost practice or traditional skill. The proliferation of single serve microwave meals and associated 'microwave safe' packaging; a symbiotic relationship with the freezer and frozen meals; and the convenience to eat when you want shifting family eating arrangements are all frequently identified as being facilitated by the microwave. Design begetting design, creating and destroying practices.[3] Deeper analysis illustrates that the microwave may contribute to reframing one's way of seeing and thinking in the world. For example, it provides the expectation of eating on demand and immediate experi-ence, changing the requirement for planning and thinking ahead. It reduces our sense of dependence on family as we can eat in shifts independently. The associated innovative plastic packaging removes our dependency on fresh produce and what is locally seasonally available, removing us further from the production supply chain and direct engagement with that which sustains us. Plastics have been well covered as ontologically transforma-tive (i.e. Tonkinwise, 1998) suggesting that plastics changed our disposition to the material world by making disposability a new possibility.

The 'game of ontological design' tool illuminates the impact that design has had in shaping not only contemporary designs, but also our individual actions, and the future actions of designed artefacts and of designers. The process interrogates what is shaping one's own intuitions about design to help one 'think' ontological design from the past and present. Ontological designing puts forward the proposal that designed things change culture in incremental, though powerful ways (Lopes, 2005: 37).

3. Projecting forward trajectories of practice

The previous tools assist in seeing how design may be world shaping. The challenging next step is to project forward the historical trajectories of practice by expanding on the aforementioned tools to begin to consider what practices may become. This could be thought of as the knock-on effects of the present designs. What design may go on to design via the relational complexity of the material and immaterial, and its compound-ing impacts and consequences across time, can be closely associated with forecasting. For example, a new road may ease congestion, which may encourage more utilization of that road, and may facilitate the movement of people and facilities nearer to that road. This is referred to as 'road induced transport growth' (Zeibots, 2010), arguably one of the few areas where systems modelling tools are used to quantify the impact of design interven-tions (roads).

This type of forecasting is rarely attempted in mainstream design practice, yet thinking through evolutions of future practices (both positive and negative) is critical territory. We can no longer fall back on the argument that we simply did not know how the artefacts would play out in practice, as John Thakara states:

> The introduction of new mass technology – telegraph, railway, electrification, radio, telephone, televisions, automobiles, air travel – has always been accompanied by a spectacular package of promises. A certain Naïveté is excusable for the inventors of those early technologies. They had no way of knowing about the unforeseen consequences of their innovations. Today, we don't have that alibi. We know that new technologies have unexpected consequences.
>
> (2006: 3)

While the unexpected consequences cannot be foreseen in their entirety, the question can be asked: What may the proposed design 'design, create, kill, proliferate, favour, or alter?' to anticipate and design for the consequences of any new design. Conceptualizing what effects and impacts any future designs may have, and to make explicit what ontologies are chosen, is fundamental to progressive sustainability practice that aims to structure a sustainable future.[4]

However, it is acknowledged that forecasting futures is exceptionally challenging due to the relational complexity of our lived world. For example, the creativity brainstorming technique of morphological analysis (Zwicky, 1969) – while brilliant as an ideation tool – highlights the major challenge of forecasting, in that from only a limited set of ingredients thousands of possible combinations can be generated. How do you consider the infinite first-order, second-order or third-order impacts of your designs? One way of dealing with this complexity is the use of scenarios as 'thought experiments' within design practice to suggest propositional futures. This brings us to the fourth tool and the role of scenarios.

4. The role of scenarios

Anne-Marie Willis (2014) argues that 'Scenarios are not meant to be predictions of the future, they are a means to project likely future circumstances, in order to reflect on these and to inform action to be taken' (Willis, 2014: 2). Manzini and Jégou's argument for design-orientated scenarios are that they are probable hypotheses for discussion (Manzini & Jégou, 2003), and that if desirable, those with a vested interest may make them happen. Several key questions to make explicit when using scenarios are these:

- Where are you as a designer attempting to intervene?
- Are you accepting the projected future (forecast) and attempting to make this more habitable and sustainable? or
- Are you proposing a more desirable future that may require more radical intervention to bring about, and divert a business as usual forecast?

Scenarios (or interventions) may be viewed in terms of being proactive or reactive (Willis, 2014). Within climate change literature this may be more broadly referred to in terms of adaptation (reactive) or mitigation (proactive) to distinguish the design choices that you are given (Hamin & Gurran, 2009). Manzini and Jégou (2003) refers to this in terms of design treating the symptoms or treating the cause of the problem. Much of the individual design for behavioural change models may arguably attempt to adapt, or treat the symptoms rather than treating the root cause. Ontological design in practice opens up the scale of possible intervention points and encourages designers to make explicit where they may be intervening, and what their intervention may go on to design.

Robinson (1990) proposed the use of backcasting from promising future scenarios to the present as a useful tool to create a roadmap for how the desirable future may be realized. Within scenarios, the individual is often positioned within a future environment where desirable practices and behaviours would take place as defaults. For example, John Urry (2015) and the *Liveable Cities* project team generated future scenarios for a 'car free Birmingham'. These scenarios first conceptualized a city that does not require a car, prior to backcasting and identifying actions that would have to happen to materialize the scenario. This is very different to a behavioural approach that attempts to persuade an individual not to drive, or encourage him or her to use alternative transport. It is a highly context-driven approach that attempts to shape the environment so that the default actions are the most sustainable.

Streamlining in America: the grandest application of future scenarios

The use of future scenarios can often seem abstract; however, I would argue that they have a significant historical precedence in the streamlining design movement in the 1930s in the USA. At this time, future scenarios were exceptionally influential in communicating the promise of a better future (see Andrews [2007, 2009] for a theoretical account, and Bel Geddes's [1932] first-hand account of how designers used future scenarios to influence change). Designers at this time were arguably at their most influential, explicitly attempting total environmental reconstruction, with industry and consumers enrolled as a means to bring the promising visions (future scenarios) that would lead to economic recovery after the great depression to fruition. It is openly acknowledged that the consequences of this movement for sustainability are tragic (in promoting mass consumerism), however it is the communication methods the designers applied, and the influence of the visions and scenarios that is the focus, as opposed to the content.

A wide variety of techniques were used to leverage design agency, primarily by controlling 'what' the consumer saw and 'how' they saw it, both through future visions and within the products introduced. Future scenarios were central to their 'promise' (Geels & Smit, 2000) for a better society, marketing an ability to see beyond the present to envision and design future worlds. The grandest example of future scenarios is perhaps Norman Bel Geddes's *futurama* exhibition displayed at the 1939 New York World's fair, visited by an average 27,000 people a day (5 million in total) taking the audience on

> a 16 minute simulated low plane flight tour of America in the year 1960 – a 16,000 square feet [3,000 m^2] model made from one million trees, 50, 000 tear-drop shaped vehicles and half a million buildings. The landscape was viewed from the air as carefully planned cities and pastoral areas connected by a superhighway system.
>
> (Nye, 1994: 218)

Bel Geddes's 20-year future scenario illustrated the future of connected and car-dependent highways. Geels and Smit describe *futurama* as communicating the promise of technology in 'a smoothly functioning society, characterised by abundance and ease' (2000: 881–882).

This designer's promise was applied across numerous scales, evident by the catchphrase 'everything from a matchstick to a city; lipstick to locomotive' (Cheney & Cheney, 1992: 69). The industrial designers designed explicitly to locate us by defining the role for the consumer in their technocratic utopian visions. The future visions projected were embedded in the new products that proliferated, attempting to bring the utopian future to the present. They offered convenient labour-saving technologies produced from new materials (plastic), uniformly precise and dazzlingly modern. The arrival of a new modern designed age was evident and presented as a welcome reprieve from the chaos of the depression.[5] The movement reshaped expectations. Consumption of material goods was portrayed as morally correct as *worn out goods contribute nothing* to the economy. Product-based well-being was encouraged, new forms of leisure created and existing practices such as thrift and craft actively diminished. This change is most evident in the movement of the house from a site of production to a site of consumption (Andrews, 2007).

The implications on everyday practices and behaviours from the movement were enormous, shifting our notions of the home, hygiene, scientific management and the modern. Shove (2003) eloquently conveys the shifting dynamics of everyday practices in our comfort, cleanliness and convenience. We may attribute a rapid escalation and shift in practices directly to the 1930s design movement. A body of scholarship has been dedicated to demonstrating how radically society changed as designed artefacts proliferated with the advent of mass production and consumption, and the role of design in radically transforming human beings and becoming modern. The legacy of the movement is todays inherited 'normal', as Sheldon and Arens claim that '[the designer] has done more than redecorate or design things. . . . He has done something to our state of mind, he has made us a different people' (1932: 161 cited in Van Doren, 1940). Design has shifted our ontology via design.

This case study of the streamlining movement is included to illustrate the historical precedent of design using future scenarios, that ultimately influenced systemic change.

Conclusion: ontological designing and futurings relationship to behavioural change

One of the challenges of design for behaviour change identified in many of the chapters in this book is the lack of evaluation of the impact of design for behavioural change interventions. However, we have an entire history of design interventions that can be utilized to create insight into the potential impact of design. Ontological designing provides a philosophy that attempts to better understand the material and immaterial impacts of design on our world. This reading of the past is seen as essential if you are looking to intervene via design in future practice.

The proposed methods in this chapter may not target individual behaviours as the starting point, but look at the broader environment that the behaviours and practices take place with. If you are aiming to create large-scale change (required for sustainability), then ontological designing and the practical tools introduced in this chapter may assist in creating environments, products and practices that may 'mitigate' undesirable futures.

Acknowledgements

Stephen Clune is grateful to Tara Andrews and Abby Lopes who contributed to early drafts of this paper that have been subsequently developed.

Notes

1 The thinking was central to the EcoDesign Foundation in Sydney in the late 1990s, and is viewed as a central tenant to Tony Fry's work on design-led redirective practice (see Fry, 1994, 1999, 2009).
2 I draw upon Fry's (2009) reading of Bourdieu as opposed to the original source (Bourdieu, 1977). Artefacts are less pronounced by Bourdieu, described as the 'objectified state' of cultural capital (i.e. pictures, books and machines). The objectified state is one of three subtypes of cultural capital, which is one of four forms of capital (economic, social, symbolic and cultural) to which habitus depends.
3 The dialectic of sustainment may be introduced through the aforementioned tools as it becomes clear that creation is indivisible from destruction, making indivisible from unmaking, and futuring indivisible from defuturing (Fry, 2009). As new practices are introduced, existing practices may decline or die.
4 A body of work using qualitative methods forecasting social-technical change has also been developing outside the design discourse in the social-technical transition field (e.g. Elzen et al., 2002).
5 In contrast, the functionalism movement in Europe focused on simply made, 'functional,' low-cost furniture and goods for purchase by the work force.

References

Andrews, T. (2007). *The legacy of streamlining and un-sustainability in industrial design.* (Thesis: Master of Design by Research). University of Technology, Sydney.
Andrews, T. (2009). Design and consume to Utopia: Where industrial design went wrong. *Design Philosophy Papers, 7,* 71–86.
Bel Geddes, N. (1932). *Horizons.* Boston: Little, Brown, and Company.
Bourdieu, P. (1977). *Outline of a theory of practice.* Cambridge: Cambridge University Press.
Cheney, M. C., & Cheney, S. (1992). *Art and the machine: An account design in 20th-century America.* New York: Acanthus.
Elzen, B., Geels, F. W., & Hofman, P. S. (2002). *Development and evaluation of a new methodology to explore transitions towards a sustainable energy supply.* Report to NWO.
Fry, T. (1994). *Remakings: Ecology design philosophy.* Sydney: Envirobook.
Fry, T. (1999). *A new design philosophy: An introduction to defuturing.* Sydney: University of New South Wales.
Fry, T. (2009). *Design futuring: Sustainability, ethics and new practice.* Oxford: Berg Publishing.
Gadamer, H.-G. (1976). *Philosophical hermeneutics.* Translated and Edited by Linge. (Ed.), Berkeley: University of Californa Press.
Geels, F. W., & Smit, W. A. (2000). Failed technology futures: Pitfalls and lessons from a historical survey. *Futures, 32,* 867–885.
Hamin, E. M., & Gurran, N. (2009). Urban form and climate change: Balancing adaptation and mitigation in the U.S. and Australia. *Habitat International, 33,* 238–245.
Heidegger, M. (1962). *Being and time.* New York: Harper & Row, Publishers.
Heidegger, M. (1971). *Poetry, language, thought* (A. Hofstadter, trans.). New York: Harper Colophon Books.
Jelsma, J. (2006). Designing 'moralized' products. In P.-P. Verbeek & A. Slob (Eds.), *User behavior and technology development* (pp. 221–231). Dordrecht: Springer.
Lopes, A. M. (2005). *Ecology of the image* (Doctor of Philosophy). University of Sydney, Sydney.
Lopes, A. M., Clune, S., & Andrews, T. (2007). Future scenario planning as a tool for sustainable design education and innovation. *Connected 2007 International Conference on Design Education.* University of New South Wales, New South Wales.
Lupton, D. (1999). Monsters in Metal Cocoons: 'Road Rage' and Cyborg bodies. *Body & Society, 5,* 57–72.
Manzini, E., & Jégou, F. (2003). *Sustainable everyday, scenarios of urban life.* Milan: Edizioni Ambiente srl.
Molotoch, H. (2003). *Where stuff comes from.* New York: Routledge.
Nye, D. E. (1994). *The 1939 New York world's fair, American Technological sublime.* Cambridge, MA: MIT Press.
Robinson, J. B. (1990). Futures under glass: A recipe for people who hate to predict. *Futures, 22,* 820–842.
Shove, E. (2003). Converging conventions of comfort, cleanliness and convenience. *Journal of Consumer Policy, 26,* 395–418.

Shove, E., Watson, M., Hand, M., & Ingram, J. (2007). *The design of everyday life*. Oxford: Berg Publishers.

Thakara, J. (2006). *In the bubble*. Cambridge, MA: MIT Press.

Tonkinwise, C. (1998). *Everywhere and nowhere: An introduction to plastics information ecology newsletter*. Retrieved from http://changedesign.org/Resources/EDFPublications/Articles/Papers/Plastic1.htm

Urry, J. (2015). *Care free Birmingham*. Birmingham: Liveable Cities ERSPC event.

Van Doren, H. (1940). *Industrial design: A practical guide*. New York: McGraw-Hill.

Verghese, K., Clune, S., Lockrey, S., Lewis, H., & Crittenden, P. (2012). *Australian food and grocery council future of packaging white paper*. Melbourne: AFGC.

Willis, A.-M. (2006). Ontological designing. *Design Philosophy Papers*, 3.

Willis, A.-M. (2014). *Anne-Marie Willis*. Jordanian International Conference on Architecture and Design – JICAD Reality and Future Challenges, Amman, Jordan.

Winograd, T., & Flores, F. (1986). *Understanding computers and cognition: A new foundation for design*. Norwood: Ablex Publication Corporation.

Zeibots, M. E. (2010). *Induced traffic growth through the looking glass: A comparison of micro economic and systems-based explanations of travel behaviour and governance responses to urban motorway development*. 12th World Conference on Transport Research, Lisbon, Portugal.

Zwicky, F. (1969). *Discovery, invention, research – through the morphological approach*. Toronto: Palgrave Macmillan.

12 The hidden influence of design

Nynke Tromp and Paul Hekkert

Introduction

Design co-shapes our actions, our habits and routines, and thereby society at large. Now this observation is not new at all. Sociologists like Akrich (1992) and Latour (1992), philosophers like McLuhan (1964) and, more recently, Verbeek (2005, 2011), and historians like Clarke (2014) revealed the power of the artefact in social life. They illuminated how mundane objects like doors and light switches prescribe specific actions, how the television and the microwave have co-construed family life, and how Tupperware or Barbie shape our culture and sub-cultures. In the light of design for behaviour change, these examples are remarkable. It is only through reflection that we start to recognize this less immediate yet influential role of ordinary products. This indicates that design can seemingly bring about behaviour change as if it comes naturally to people. Although this may sound worrisome to some, we consider this a promising quality of design. After all, wouldn't it be great if the behaviours known to be beneficial to our wellbeing occur a bit more effortlessly? Wouldn't it be great if we did not have to struggle so much 'to do the right thing'?

Although the field of design for behaviour change is rapidly expanding, the substantial role design already plays in how behaviour comes about is not frequently addressed. The main reason for this is the hidden character of inherent product influence, and the difficulty this brings for 'grasping' it, as well as the ethical questions that arise when aiming to use this influence deliberately. To cope with this, the field of persuasive technology deliberately excluded hidden influence from their approach. In an attempt to avoid moral objections to the development of technology with the aim and power to change people's behaviour, Fogg (2003) explicitly states that persuasive designs should never be vague in their intent. In other words, for what purposes persuasive technology is used should always become clear through the design. A user of an ATM, a shopper at a web shop, or a sportsperson using a health-app should be aware and never be surprised that persuasive principles are applied in order to remind them to take their debit card after use, promote articles that match their desires, or support their training, respectively. In the proceedings of one of the first conferences on persuasive technology however, Redström (2006) already argues that any design has persuasive power, whether it was intended or not.

One clear exception to the dominant stance that influencing people secretly should be avoided is advocated by Thaler and Sunstein (2008). They propose the term 'nudge' to refer to the hidden pushes the environment gives us in how to behave, and call for a deliberate design of these to promote behaviours for a healthier, wealthier, and happier life. Although their position is contested for being paternalistic (Mitchell, 2005), we agree with their call to deliberately design this hidden influence and to direct it in support of our long-term and social interests. Nonetheless, we consider the behavioural economic view (that Thaler and Sunstein behold) too limited for designers to deal with the influence of products and services on human behaviour. Thaler and Sunstein, and with them many more scholars (e.g. Dijksterhuis & Smith, 2005; Kahneman, 2011), oppose the idea that human behaviour should be conceptualized as the consequence of deliberate and rational decisions. Much of human behaviour is driven by heuristics, and designers and policy makers should be aware of and even 'make use of' these heuristics. In our view, however, little guidance is provided in understanding what heuristics are dominant in a particular situation, and which other contextual factors may overrule them. On a different line of thinking, we consider the idea of "libertarian paternalism" as a conclusive stance to be free to design hidden influence deliberately. Little critical guidance exists in helping a designer to argue when and why it is morally acceptable to use the hidden power of design. In our view, taking a user viewpoint to the matter will therefore both increase the effectiveness of interventions, and their appropriateness in moral terms. Reflecting upon the hidden influence from a user experiential point of view can refine our considerations and support designers better in arguing for or against the use of it when promoting behaviours through design.

Experience of influence – five variables

Influence comes in many forms. Scholars in the field of communication and persuasion, traditionally a field marked by social psychologists, are all well aware of this and have spent decades in unravelling the principles of successful persuasion (e.g. Cialdini, 2003; Petty et al., 2005). For instance, the liking principle, "People say 'yes' to people they like", or, the principle of scarcity, "When something is scarce, people will value it more", have become commonplace in domains of sales and marketing. More recently, these principles have proven useful for designing the persuasive power of designs too, especially when the design embodies interactive technology and can really function as an agent. For instance, interventions like agents, avatars, and robots are currently developed that represent "real" characters that aim to persuade you to change your behaviour (e.g. Ham et al., 2015).

Although such principles are helpful in designing persuasion in interaction with technology, they are less helpful in explaining the inherent power of the artefact. It is difficult to explain the observation that families get together for dinner less frequently thanks to the microwave as the result of a persuasive principle embodied in its design. The complexity of the interaction between the microwave and the resulted behaviour change cannot be simplified to a cause-effect relationship. It is only by being cautious of the multiple factors that play a role, and their complex and looping interactions, that such influence of design is understood justifiably. This is one of the reasons that within the field of design for behaviour change, two diverging views seem to emerge: one relying on the (social) psychological principles as mentioned before, and one relying on sociological literature such as practice theory of Shove and others (2007), as was also discussed in Chapter 10 of this volume. In this theory for instance, the smallest unit of study is "a practice", which is built up of rules and norms, the physical environment including all the designs and the behaviours and actions that make up the practice. As such, they argue that the role of products in changing behaviours can never be understood or explained without cultural and contextual factors.

This means that gradually design researchers are developing opposing stances in how to understand the influence of design in shaping behaviour, similar to how psychologists and sociologists have built different and often incompatible worldviews. In our view, copying these opposing stances marginalizes design researchers as appliers of social theories rather than theory builders themselves. In contrast, design researchers should develop theory and methodology that improves design practice, and as such, strengthens the quality of a designer. One of the unique qualities of designer is their integrative thinking: the ability to integrate multiple and potentially opposing perspectives in one solution (Dorst, 2007). For design researchers this implies that, in order to strengthen this quality of the designer rather than to undermine it, *design* theories of behaviour change should be inclusive rather than exclusive to different social theories. There is no social issue today that can be understood – let alone be counteracted – through one single discipline. In developing products and services, designers often rely on a wide range of theories and explanations of the situation they design for. Although seemingly opposing, it is a designer skill to integrate these within their understanding of the situation and for proposing a solution. A laudable skill in the realm of social problems! Hence, theories from cognitive/social psychology, sociology, behavioural economics, systems thinking, anthropology, and evolutionary psychology all are of value to designers who aim to stimulate behavioural change through design. It is the role of the design researcher to provide theories that do justice to all perspectives and to develop new knowledge on how to integrate them. In other words, design theories and methodologies should support eclectic use of theories rather than to pinpoint the designer to a specific paradigm in behavioural science. In this chapter, we start to build this integrative lens for understanding and designing the influence of products and services: through an experiential viewpoint.

Many variables can play a role in how a person experiences influence. The same message to work less is experienced differently when it comes from your mother than when it comes from your boss. Not only do you have different relationships with both, you may additionally prefer the direct confrontation of your boss to the implicit hinting of your mother. On the other hand, the medium your boss is overthinking – a regulation that shuts off Wi-Fi after 5 pm – aims to change the overall working culture, while the course to balance work and private life that your mother advised, suggests you need to better deal with the situation. Who intervenes, why, through what medium, and how exactly clearly affects to a great deal how people experience the influence. It is our assumption that this experience shapes a person's inclination to change, and ultimately affects whether she will change behaviour. We argue that we should better understand influence as a complex interaction of multiple variables. In order to support further study of product influence from a user experiential point of view, we define the variables we consider relevant in the context of design below.

The origin of influence: Who is influencing and why? (Variable 1 [V1]: source of influence; V2: reasons for influence)

In a design context this question boils down to which organization or company is the initiator of the intervention, and what is the raison d'être of the design? It should be a deliberate design choice to communicate the initiator of the intervention or not. One can imagine that it can substantially affect how people perceive the design and their motivation to comply. Some people get the creeps when the government is trying to direct their actions, while others are suspicious to any initiative born out of commercial interests. On the contrary, well-established foundations may generate trust, which may act as a catalyst for change. And being ambivalent about the initiator of the intervention may also lead to suspicion.

Next to the source, the designer should deliberately decide whether to communicate the reasons for influencing or not. Sometimes people are unaware of the negative consequences of their actions. In that case, explaining this may have some effect. If people do not know that going on a ski holiday stimulates deterioration of forests, it may be helpful to explain this. Yet, in many cases it appears to have little effect (Rijnja et al., 2009). Only if people are expected to have strong affiliations with these reasons, or when the aim is to establish awareness more than actual behaviour change, it can support the effectiveness of the intervention.

The medium that exerts influence: What is influencing? (V3: medium, or type of design manifestation)

In reference to Simon (1969), any intervention to change an existing situation into a preferred one is considered a manifestation of design. In agreement with this definition, we consider laws, policies, education programmes, subsidies, and campaign manifestations of design. Nonetheless, the entrance of people educated in design (graphic, product, service, or interaction design) to the realm of behaviour change has led to a new range of instruments. One can imagine that a campaign along the road is experienced quite differently than a service. One of the benefits of designers in entering the field of behavioural change is that they have methodologies to develop products and services that provide value to people: that people desire, love to use, and are meaningful to people. Additionally, products and product-service combinations are literally action-able, in contrast to campaigns, laws, and regulations: they *afford* behaviours (Gibson, 1979; Norman, 1988).

The mechanism that explains the influence: How does it influence? (V4: strategy; V5: style)

When talking of influence, one talks about an interaction between an influential agent and an actor, in this case respectively the intervention and the user. In the light of this, the mechanism describes the (assumed or measured) relationship between the intervention and the behaviour: what characteristics of the design are related to what characteristics of the user, i.e. strategy, and how this is done, i.e. style. As an example we refer to the design project Reframing Studio in which an application was developed to stimulate people going through rough times to still spend time on maintaining their social network (Reframing Studio, 2016). By making the user aware of the time passed since the last moment of contact with a friend, the app intends to stimulate the user to initiate contact. By showing this information, the designers assumed the user would feel guilt or commitment to stay in touch and behave accordingly. As such, "depicting time passed" as a product function is related to "principles of guilt/commitment" and can be considered the strategy applied. Nonetheless, the design could still communicate this information in various ways, of which two were explored. In one version, the pictures of people in the user's network slowly faded away. In the second version, prompts were developed with messages saying "Hey, you haven't spoken to John for a while. Time to send a message?" These two variations illustrate the same strategy, but differ in their style of influencing. Both the strategy used and the way it is embodied in the design, define the mechanism.

When we argue that these fives variables define how influence is experienced, what do we exactly mean?

Experiencing autonomy while being influenced

Based on an analysis of a range of products – that were either designed to influence behaviour or appeared to have influenced behaviour – we stated that two different dimensions of influence define how it is experienced: force and salience – both refer to interaction qualities (Tromp et al., 2011). Influence can vary from weak to strong (force), and from implicit to more explicit (salience).

Salience The dimension of salience explains on the product-side that an intervention can be more or less explicit in its intention. On the user-side, salience explains that people can be more or less aware of the influence. But how can awareness be a dimension, since one is either aware or unaware of something? Here we need to understand salience in relationship to the five variables. The user may or may not be aware of the origin of the influence (V1 and V2), may or may not recognize the medium as influential (V3), and he may or may not be aware of the mechanism used by the designer and the effect this has on her behaviour (V4 and V5). Since awareness of influence plays at different levels, we can conceptualize salience as a dimension.

Force The dimension of force explains on the product-side that an intervention can be more or less forceful. On the user-side, force refers to the level of freedom people experience to behave otherwise. A limitation of freedom may have a large effect on the inclination of people to change their course of actions since it can cause reactance (Brehm, 1966). Brehm argues that freedom of behaviour is a pervasive and an important aspect of human life, and that a limitation of behavioural freedom by somebody else can cause psychological reactance. Reactance explains that by obstructing behaviours, these behaviours become more attractive. In that way, forceful interventions can even become counterproductive by actually encouraging undesired behaviour.

Knowing that the experience of influence is determined by force and salience, how can this help us understand the hidden influence of design? Or in other words, how can it help us understand better how design can change behaviour as if it comes naturally to people? To that end, we will elaborate on the dimensions and take a closer look at the gradual change of these and how that shapes user experience (see Figure 12.1).

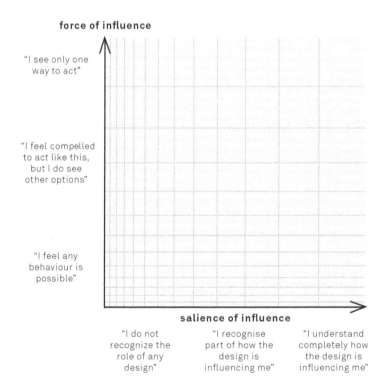

Figure 12.1 An exploration of the user experience of influence in terms of being aware of the influence (salience of influence) and the experience of freedom in behaving (force)

The y-axis refers to the experience of freedom to act. Maximal force means the user sees only one way to act. Moderate force would mean the user is driven to act in a specific manner but recognizes other options. Minimal force would mean the user feels any behaviour is possible. The x-axis refers to the awareness of the influence. As we saw earlier, awareness relates to the different variables. Maximal awareness means the user is aware of everything: she recognizes the intervention as influential (V3), she is aware of the source behind the intervention (V1) and the reasons for influencing (V2), and she recognizes both the strategy (V4) and style (V5) used to do so. Moderate awareness means the user is only aware of part of this. For instance, he/she recognizes the intervention as a deliberate attempt, but is not aware of the actual effect on his/her behaviour; or he/she does not recognize the intervention as a deliberate attempt, but is aware his/her behaviour has changed due to the intervention. Minimal awareness means the user is not aware of any of this.

If effective, this would mean that total unawareness of the influence (minimal salience) means that people feel as if they act autonomously (while we know their behaviour is affected). On the other hand, if the user feels as if any behaviour is possible (minimal force), this also means that any action as a consequence of interaction with the intervention is experienced as autonomously directed. This illuminates that the experience of autonomy can be represented as the diagonal dimension in the graph, going from experiencing autonomy to experiencing loss of autonomy[1] (see Figure 12.2).

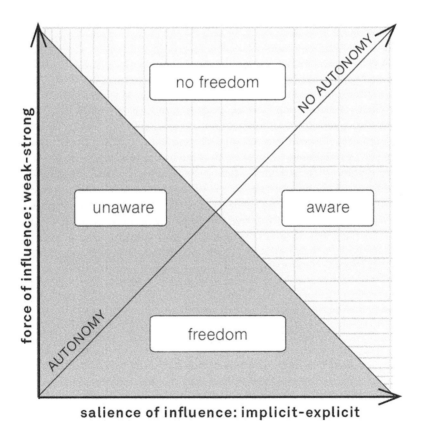

Figure 12.2 The experience of autonomy represented as the function of force and salience

With this advanced insight, we conceptualize the inherent and hidden influence of design as influence without loss of experienced autonomy. It also reveals that it is exactly this quality of products and services (to shape behaviour without users feeling like they lose autonomy) that is unique in comparison to traditional interventions like laws, fines, regulations, subsidies, and campaigns.

Designing the hidden influence

We will now highlight three strategies (of the eleven strategies presented in earlier work – Tromp et al., 2011) that we consider most supportive when designing hidden influence, and explain how they are used in a design project. Since "the strategy" is only one of the five variables that affect how influence is experienced, we will not only explain its application, but as well explain how it interacts with the other variables.

1. Activate physiological processes to induce behaviour

Panton is a design agency that delivers strategic and product designs for the medical sector. One of the areas of focus is to redesign the working environment to better support desired behaviour. In studying the use of different media to help staff to prepare for surgery, they came across many notes with do's and don'ts and additional warning signs. Some notes were used to make sure scrubs are worn correctly to ensure hygiene, e.g. that hair is completely covered. Panton wanted to support a more intuitive process to ensure people would install their garment correctly. Hence, they developed a life-size mirror that is showing only half of your body since the other half depicts how your scrubs should be organized (see Figure 12.3). By checking oneself in the mirror before entering the operation room, the user immediately *perceives* what has been forgotten or went wrong when sliding into their scrubs. As such, it avoids cognitive processing of elaborate checklists, but rather evokes direct action through perception.

Since the design is part of the hospital's environment, the origin of influence is known and accepted as a given. Users know why they are instructed and by whom, even though it is not communicated as part of the design. In its manifestation, the mirror is a blend between product and communication design. When implemented, the mirror would probably draw attention and would be recognized as deliberately placed to affect behaviour. Nevertheless, the perception-action that the design makes use of relies on unconscious processes and, as such, the design's mechanism is rather implicit. Overall, we consider this design moderately salient and moderately forceful, which means we expect people experience being influenced but still feel their actions as autonomously directed.

2. Trigger human tendencies for automatic, behavioural responses

In studying meat consumption, Anna Peeters, graduate student at our faculty, found out that people often have concerns for the environment, animal welfare, or public health, but seem to let these values be overruled when they are in the supermarket. In this context, people tend to go for the cheapest option and thereby unconsciously consume meat that is produced by intensive farming and forms a serious threat to exactly those values mentioned earlier. As a result, many interventions aim to convince people to change their consumption behaviour by obstructing this tendency to go for the cheapest option. Instead, Anna found a way to make use of it. She developed Tomorrow's Menu, a platform

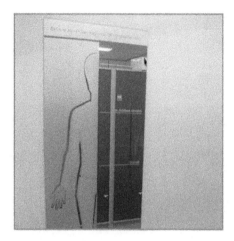

Figure 12.3 Mirror design to support doctors and nurses preparing their scrubs for surgery

Source: Design by Panton.

that allows users to subscribe to the category of farms that is most closely related to their personal values (see Figure 12.4). After subscribing and paying a monthly fee, meat that is produced by the type of farms you subscribed to becomes the cheapest option in the supermarket.

Tomorrow's Menu is developed as an independent platform that mediates between farms and supermarkets. Yet, since it is still at a conceptual stage, there is no "owner" yet. The credibility of the platform is an important factor in compliance with the system. The platform supports users to compare their values with objective descriptions of farm types and their effects on the environment, animal welfare, and public health. As such, the reasons for influencing are made explicit. But the user is invited to explore his values and is subsequently supported in acting accordingly. So even though the type of intervention would be recognized as persuasive, the way it redirects the automatic process at the supermarket will remain largely hidden. As such, we consider the design moderately salient and moderately forceful, which means we expect people are aware of the intentions behind the design, but not of its mechanism, and experience their actions as autonomously directed.

3. Create optimal conditions for specific behaviour

Many cities struggle with youngsters who don't have a degree, who are without a job, who are hanging out on the streets, and who commit an occasional crime. To prevent these youngsters from becoming serious criminals, many programmes are initiated to lead

Figure 12.4 Tomorrow's Menu, a platform to subscribe to a farm type and related meat production processes in order to decrease consumption of meat from intensive farming

Source: Design by Anna Peeters.

them to work. Nonetheless, a percentage of these youngsters are never reached. Sacha van Ginhoven, also a graduate student at our faculty, focused on these youngsters. Through research, she found out that these youngsters feel rejected by society. Programmes to lead them to work were experienced as ways to mould them to societal standards rather than to accept them as they are. As such, Sacha understood that to lead them to work, they should not be motivated to enter a job application process, but that the application procedure needed to be moved to the streets instead. She developed Worktags: stickers with QR-codes to be attached to locations of work, e.g. a bus stop for a bus driver vacancy, or near a construction area for a vacancy of a construction worker (see Figure 12.5). By scanning the QR code, youngsters could quickly record a video to express their interest instead of having to write a lengthy application letter. As such, the design created the optimal conditions for these youngsters to apply for a job.

We can only speculate about the source of influence, since this design too is still in a conceptual stage. We expect however, that the organization behind the service, as well as the reasons to stimulate youngsters to apply for the job, is not hidden but also not made very explicit. In fact, the service should be implemented as a regular job application procedure of which anyone could make use. Therefore, we consider the design minimally

Figure 12.5 Worktag, a service to apply for a job while hanging out on the streets

Source: Design by Sacha van Ginhoven.

salient in its influence and little forceful, which means we expect people experience their actions are autonomously directed.

These three designs reveal how designers can make use of the hidden power of design: to redirect it to promote pro-social behaviours rather than pro-self behaviours. In relation to Figure 12.2, the influence of these three designs are expected to fall into the covered triangle, and therefore people are expected to experience their behaviours as autonomously directed — even when they do feel an external force is attracting them (similar to how one may be attracted to jump into the water on a hot summer day).

Conclusion

Design has the power to change behaviour in a hidden way. This power can be philosophically understood in two ways. Either we understand human beings as "victims" of a deterministic design, or we see these changes in behaviours as the result of fundamental human needs and desires that people themselves may not be able to articulate, but which the design addresses successfully. In our view, the latter does more justice to the complexity of what makes us human. From an evolutionary perspective, we are wired with needs and desires, tendencies and motivations that we cannot undo, but have proven to lead to our survival. On top of this, we developed regulatory processes based on norms and knowledge that may overrule such tendencies or impulses. For instance, our "nature" screams "eat!" when we see a muffin, but our consciousness tells us it is bad for our health and activates our willpower to resist the temptation. In Kahneman's words, system 2 may overrule system 1 in directing our behaviour (Kahneman, 2011). Nonetheless, most of the time, the environment that is largely — if not completely — designed, appeals to our system 1 processes, i.e. the unconscious processes. It is simply impossible for people to make every action a conscious action, deliberately decided for: we would go crazy. So much of what we do is on automatic pilot, fed by nature and previous experiences. In our view, we should therefore design the environment so it helps us to do what increases our quality of life a bit more automatically. Many people do want to act more pro-socially, if it only would require a little less willpower.

Additionally, the power to restructure the environment and make socially responsible behaviours more natural and obvious is a unique power of design in comparison to conventional interventions like rules, regulations, subsidies, education, and campaigns. The latter type of interventions are often patches to a malfunctioning system. Design has the ability to fundamentally transform the system in which problematic behaviours rise. For instance, many scientists show that we have developed what is called an "obesogene environment". We have designed an environment in which physical activity is not needed, and in which greasy and sugary foods are available 24/7. As such, one wonders whether eating unhealthily and exercising too little is indeed abnormal behaviour in a normal environment, or whether it is actually normal behaviour in an abnormal environment. In our view, it is the latter. So instead of developing tools for people to fight the influence of the environment on their behaviour, we call for designers who dare to critically examine the environment and propose solutions that fundamentally change it. In fact, we argue that this is the only route to a truly social, sustainable future in the long run.

Note

1 Note that it remains a philosophical debate where agency is located.

References

Akrich, M. (1992). The de-scription of technical objects. In W. E. Bijker & J. Law (Eds.), *Shaping technology/building society: Studies in sociotechnical change* (pp. 205–224). Cambridge, MA: MIT Press.

Brehm, J. W. (1966). A theory of psychological reactance. In W. W. Burke, D. G. Lake, & J. W. Paine (Eds.), *Organization change – a comprehensive reader (2009)* (pp. 377–390). San Francisco: John Wiley & Sons, Inc.

Cialdini, R. B. (2003). Crafting normative messages to protect the environment. *American Psychological Society, 12*, 105–109.

Clarke, A. J. (2014). *Tupperware: The promise of plastic in 1950s America.* Washington, DC: Smithsonian Institution.

Dijksterhuis, A., & Smith, P. K. (2005). What do we do unconsciously? And how? *Journal of Consumer Psychology, 15*, 225–229.

Dorst, K. (2007). Design problems and design paradoxes. *Design Issues, 22*, 4–17.

Fogg, B. (2003). *Persuasive technology: Using computers to change what we think and do.* San Francisco: Morgan Kauffman Publishers.

Gibson, J. J. (1979). *The ecological approach to visual perception.* Mahwah, NJ: Lawrence Erlbaum Associates.

Ham, J., Cuijpers, R. H., & Cabibihan, J.-J. (2015). Combining robotic persuasive strategies: The persuasive power of a storytelling robot that uses gazing and gestures. *International Journal of Social Robotics, 7*, 479–487.

Kahneman, D. (2011). *Thinking, fast and slow.* New York: Farrar, Strays and Giroux.

Latour, B. (1992). Where are the missing masses? The sociology of a few mundane artifacts. In W. E. Bijker & J. Law (Eds.), *Shaping technology/building society: Studies in sociotechnical change* (pp. 225–258). Cambridge, MA: MIT Press.

McLuhan, M. (1964). *Understanding media: The extensions of man.* New York: McGraw-Hill.

Mitchell, G. (2005). Libertarian paternalism is an Oxymoron. *Northwestern University Law Review, 99*, 1–42.

Norman, D. A. (1988). *The psychology of everyday things.* New York: Basic Books.

Petty, R. E., Cacioppo, J. T., Srathman, A. J., & Priester, J. R. (2005). To think or not to think – exploring two routes to persuasion. In T. C. Brock & M. C. Green (Eds.), *Persuasion insights and perspectives* (2nd ed., pp. 81–116). Thousand Oaks, CA: Sage Publications.

Redström, J. (2006). Persuasive design: Fringes and foundations. In W. A. IJsselsteijn, Y. A. W. de Kort, C. Midden, J. H. Eggen & E. Van den Hoven (Eds.), *Persuasive technology: First international conference, persuasive 2006* (Vol. 3962, pp. 112–122). Berlin: Springer.

Reframing Studio. (2016). *Project network.* Retrieved July 7, 2016, from www.reframingstudio.com/projects/project-network

Rijnja, G., Seydel, E., & Zuure, J. (2009). Communicating from context: To higher effective governmental campaigns [Communiceren vanuit de Context: Naar Effectievere Overheidscampagnes]. In W. L. Tiemeijer, C. A. Thomas, & H. M. Prast (Eds.), *People making decisions: About the psychology behind choices and behaviour [De Menselijke Beslisser: Over De Psychologie van Keuze en Gedrag]* (pp. 185–204). Amsterdam: Amsterdam University Press.

Shove, E., Watson, M., Hand, M., & Ingram, J. (2007). *The design of everyday life.* Oxford: Berg.

Simon, H. A. (1969). *The sciences of the artificial* (First MIT Press Paperback Edition ed.). Cambridge, MA & London: MIT Press.

Thaler, R. H., & Sunstein, C. R. (2008). *Nudge: Improving decisions about health, wealth and happiness.* New Haven, CT & London: Yale University Press.

Tromp, N., Hekkert, P., & Verbeek, P.-P. (2011). Design for socially responsible behaviour: A classification of influence based on intended user experience. *Design Issues, 27*, 3–19.

Verbeek, P.-P. (2005). *What things do: Philosophical reflections on technology, agency, and design.* University Park, PA: The Pennsylvania State University Press.

Verbeek, P.-P. (2011). *Moralizing technology: Understanding and designing the morality of things.* Chicago: University of Chicago Press.

13 Summary of design for behavioural change approaches

Kristina Niedderer, Stephen Clune and Geke Ludden

The chapters in Part 2 have presented a diverse selection of design for behavioural change approaches. This summary chapter explores the approaches presented in relation to the psychological and sociological (and other) models that authors have drawn on. This is achieved by first presenting the spectrum of the chapters' contributions in relation to their psychological and sociological underpinnings, and by mapping the approaches against the agency–context continuum. In doing so, we aim to assist designers and others interested in behaviour change in identifying where and how the available approaches and strategies can be applied to create change. The chapter concludes with a discussion of how the concepts presented in Part 2 interrelate, and how they may be carried forward in designing for change.

Mapping psychological and sociological approaches to design for behaviour change

Psychological and sociological approaches and perspectives are drawn on by authors in Part 2 to better understand design's intrinsic relationship with human behaviour and action. In the next two sections, we discuss the origins of the different approaches, and how they have been utilized in Part 2 to create change.

Psychological approaches to change

The preceding chapters have drawn on a range of psychological theories and approaches from social, cognitive and ecological psychology, decision research and behavioural economics. At the most basic level, the focus of psychological approaches generally aims to provide a better understanding of individual cognition, what informs individual actions and understandings, so as to assist the individual in shifting these actions, although there are exceptions. More specifically, these concepts from psychology aim to better understand, and potentially influence attitudes, external contexts, personal capabilities, habits and routines (Stern, 2000; Langer, 1989), as well as symbolic functions and social values (Niedderer, Chapter 9). The following paragraphs summarize and group together three broad approaches that are aimed at understanding and influencing the individual.

Lilley et al. (Chapter 5), Lockton (Chapter 6), and Dorrestijn (Chapter 4) refer to Fogg's (2003) highly cited concept of persuasive technology, which focuses on *motivation, ability* and *triggers* (prompts) to encourage or discourage users to act in desired ways and draws heavily on cognitive psychology. For example, Fogg's *reduction* and *tunnelling* (Fogg, 2003) can be seen as triggers for *enabling* particular behaviours by making them simpler. Lilley et al. (Chapter 5) further utilize the Theory of Interpersonal Behaviour (TIB) and goal framing to inform intervention strategies. The theory of Interpersonal Behaviour (Darnton, 2008) is utilized in an amended way, and places the individual as a rational decision maker that can be influenced by internal and external prompts as he or she interact with attitudes, social factors and emotions (intentions). Understanding these intentions and associated behaviours provides an enhanced ability to select an appropriate intervention strategy. Goal framing was also used to gain a better understanding of the broad goals (outcomes) that motivate people do things, based on three values:

1. Gain, to guard and improve one's resources
2. Hedonic, to improve the way one feels right now
3. Normative, to act appropriately for the group.

The goals are disaggregated into a further seven related sub-goals (Barbopoulos, 2012) that could be translated into possible design intervention strategies.

The Transtheoretical Model of Health Behaviour Change, as applied by Ludden in Chapter 8, posits that there is a process to lifestyle change in form of a sequence of changes, or stages of change, which a person needs to follow to achieve sustainable lifestyle change. Understanding this process, and where the individual is in this process of change, will assist with designing more targeted intervention strategies that can help walk the user through the stages of change.

Niedderer's application of mindfulness (Langer, 1989, Chapter 9) suggests that mindfulness – as an attitude of awareness and attentiveness – can be embedded in design and as such can help users to make more responsible decisions.

Drawing on models from psychology, these three examples focus at least superficially on the individual. While the individual rational choice model of behavioural change has been heavily criticized (see for example Hallsworth & Sanders, 2016), it is important also to understand the value and differentiation afforded by this approach and that each of the three examples takes a very different view on the 'individual': Lilley et al.'s model works with established behaviours and aims to design in such a way as to utilize such behaviours to their benefit. Ludden's approach supports the user in achieving the changes he or she wishes to make, while Niedderer's model aims at raising the user's awareness to the choices he or she has available for action and change and the appropriateness of these choices in any given context. Thus, one could argue that all three of these approaches also incorporate some aspect of context, in that the context is designed to facilitate change or awareness leading to change.

A good example of the agency-traversing nature of psychological models is Norman's design-psychological approach on affordances. As one of the early entrepreneurs who applied psychological principals to design, he argued that if you did not know how to use a product it was due to an error in the product, not the person, and that better design could enhance the usability of products. The idea of affordances thus aligns closely to Akrich's (1992) and Jelsma's (2006) notion of scripts (in Daae and Boks, Chapter 7) that suggest that the design artefacts actually prompt and script the outcomes of human actions. If the human action is incorrect, then a portion of blame may be attributed to the product.

Sociological approaches to change

In contrast to the psychological based approaches that generally focus on the individual, a diverse range of principles and concepts from philosophy and the social sciences have been embodied in Part 2. For example Lockton draws on research from ethics, ethnography and cognitive anthropology (Chapter 6); Clune, hermeneutics (Chapter 11) and Kuijer, social practice theory (Chapter 10). These sociological approaches and concepts generally aim to understand the broader structural and societal issues that shape everyday life.

Dorrestijn's writing (Chapter 4) alone draws on a broad range of significant social scientists and philosophers. Dorrestijn utilizes Latour's (1992) work to explain the significance of material artefacts in creating the social world, and why things have a moral significance. He further draws on Verbeek's (2005), Ihde's (1990) and Heidegger's (1962) explorations of human-technology relations to assist designers in understanding design from multiple perspectives: physical, cognitive, environmental and abstract, in the aim to create a holistic understanding of behaviour-influencing technology for design practice.

Kuijer's (Chapter 10) describes mechanisms to analyze, trace and disrupt social practices via design, drawing on Schatzki's (2001) and Reckwitz's (2002) influential work on social practices, which posits the position of exploring everyday 'practices' as the fundamental unit of analysis. Two of the suppositions contained in this unit include that:

1. Most consumption occurs not for consumption's sake, but in the completion of everyday mundane practices in our everyday life and
2. Studying everyday practice provides a lens to circumnavigate the arguments within the agency cognition divides. Kuijer thus moves significantly away from a cognition-based perspective.

The philosophy of ontological designing is central to Clune's argument (Chapter 11), in that 'things have the capacity to thing' (Willis, 2006). Ontological designing flips the notion of agency on its head, suggesting an equal, or greater agency is given to artefacts and environments. The chapter thus moves still further away from the cognition-based perspective, discounting human agency to a large extent.

The use of sociological models can therefore be seen to assist designers in exploring the intrinsic connection between the technical and the social, through charting the influence of designed stuff on our lived social experiences, and the social influences on the creation of future stuff.

Mapping design for behaviour change according to the agency divide

Returning to Clark's (2009) concept of the agency divide, the earlier discussion has already indicated that there is not a rigid divide between approaches but rather that they offer a 'continuum' with *cognition* of the individual at one end and the environmental and sociological *context* at the other, on which we can position the strategies from the previous chapters dependent on their emphases.

Through close analysis, all approaches may be seen to incorporate aspects of both sides of the continuum to varying degrees, because design – as a contextual factor – takes a mediating role in human interaction with the environment. This can be either through adapting the context to the individual, through helping the individual to adapt to the context or through integrating the two. Thereby the first relates to the context-end of the continuum, and the second to the cognition-based end, with the last taking the middle ground where both meet to more or less equal parts.

We suggest therefore that it is important to pay attention to the direction of the mediation and influence, which any one design strategy aims to offer, and in which way this is achieved. For example, change can be mediated through explicit (knowingly) or implicit (un-noticed) influence, and/or it can be based on physical or psychological drivers that, combined, offer a number of different ways of designing for change including voluntary, seductive, persuasive, coercive or prescriptive mediation of change (see e.g. Chapters 6 and 12). Regarding framing the aspect of control, this has been described in the design literature for example as the 'distribution of control' (Daae & Boks, 2014) and 'axis of influence' (Lilley, 2007), which – according to Boks and Daae (Chapter 7) offer the same or very similar concepts albeit using a variety of slightly different language to articulate them.

Rotter's theory on internal and external locus control (1990) may be a further helpful lens here to analyze the relationship between the contextual and cognitive ends of the spectrum.

Rotter posits that moving towards an internal locus of control – where the individual perceives himself or herself to be in control – leads to a perception of empowerment, whereas where the external context determines human behaviour, e.g. through prescriptive design, the individual is more likely to have a feeling of disempowerment. Neither of course can truly work without the other, hence a balance between both internal and external factors is important to achieve change most effectively.

Following these considerations, we have grouped the concepts of the nine chapters of Part 2 into a scatter diagram (Figure 13.1) to provide a visual overview of the approximate position regarding their purpose of using the context to change the individual's habits, or helping the individual to adapt their attitude and actions (perhaps irrespective of context). In the diagram, we have added the Y-axis to indicate the type of help the chapters give to designers ranging from theoretical frameworks to toolkits.

To visualize the wider context in which these nine approaches are situated, we provide a second diagram (Figure 13.2) that includes also the theories that have been mentioned in passing (the dominant theories of each chapter are highlighted in grey), but for the detailed discussion of which there has not been space in this volume. The figure highlights that the majority of the chapters sit within the middle ground of the cognition–context continuum, with the exception of the outliers in Ludden's Design for healthy behaviour (Chapter 8) which is more context orientated, and Clune's Ontological design (Chapter 11) that deals more heavily in how the designed environment holds behaviours and practices in place. While most design approaches sit in the middle ground, one

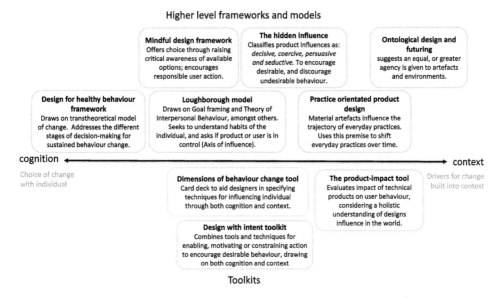

Figure 13.1 Scatter diagram positioning the nine design approaches by affinity to the individual-context continuum, and according to theoretical level

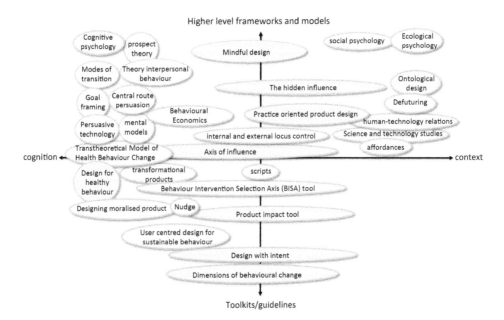

Figure 13.2 Design for behaviour change theories and approaches by agency continuum

can see that a higher number of underpinning theories are identified on the left-hand side of the figure that relate to individual cognition. This may be representative of the dominance that cognition-based psychology has historically had in relation to explaining behaviour. The position of the design approaches in the middle ground appears indicative of the integrative nature of design in drawing and acting upon both, the context and the individual.

The discussion and close analysis of the different design for behaviour change models and toolkits highlights the need to consider the relationship and disposition of both individual and context carefully to provide a holistic assessment that takes account of the different influencing factors and their direction and relationship to each other. This is because change occurs most likely and effectively when all aspects – the individual-cognition, the environmental and sociological context – are considered to understand the material opportunities, challenges and obstacles as well as the human element, including emotional and value premises that may drive motivation. The different approaches discussed in Part 2 each offer the designer a different angle, and we hope that the discussion and overview map will help designers and everyone else involved in designing for change to better recognize the issues at hand and locate an appropriate approach.

Contribution of design and behaviour change approaches introduced in Part 2

In the introduction to Part 2, three themes were introduced with respect to how the design for behavioural change approaches introduced may make a contribution and be mobilized by designers and practitioners, these were by providing:

- New insights into a situation that may be changed

- Approaches to ideation and conceptual development
- Processes that designers may design by.

For this conclusion of Part 2, we want to look at the relationship of these three themes, rather than the themes in isolation.

In order to gain new insights into any given situation to be changed, two basic inter-linked conditions have to be fulfilled: there has to be the recognition of the need for change, and there needs to be a view on what needs to change and why. Both generally emerge through observation of some kind, often in an iterative process. For example, a client sees that something in the company or in the public sphere is not working, too much litter on the streets, or new thermostats that do not lead to the expected energy savings. There can of course be multiple perspectives about the what (or who) and why, for example, is it the public who behaves badly by throwing away litter when they should not, or does this behaviour indicate some other issues, such as not enough bins? Observation and consultations with all user factions is therefore an important aspect of the design process to understand what the issue or issues are. Three explicit toolkits were presented in the Part 2 (Chapter 4, 6 and 7) offering advice towards how to observe such situations to determine the issue: Dorrestijn's Product Impact Tool offers four perspectives for inter-rogation and also closely describes the observation process. Lockton's Design with Intent and Boks and Daae's Cards both offer a broad range of starting points for both observation and designing, while Niedderer's mindful design approach uses emotional intelligence to identify issues for social design intervention.

Besides offering starting points for observation, several chapters also provide approaches to ideation and conceptual development. Both toolkits, by Lockton as well as by Boks and Daae, offer guidance of situations and human as well as product behaviour that can not only be used for the analysis of situations observed, but also for the conjecture and development of new scenarios and concepts. Similarly, Ludden as well as Niedderer offer guiding steps starting with observation of a situation through to identifying relevant sus-tainable health or mindful concepts. The chapters in Part 2 thus offer different kinds of processes – from observation through to ideation and conceptualization – that designers and others may use to develop new solutions to existing situations.

Most of the approaches are concerned, for obvious reasons, with the conceptual starting point of the design process rather than with the details of visual, aesthetic, formal or functional realization. This is because changing behaviour essentially requires a re-conceptualization of the problem setting. What becomes also apparent is that the design process in design for behaviour change is closely associated with the design research process, adding the com-ponent of critical investigation and reflection and an awareness of the wider conceptual context to be found in the research literature of design, psychology and the social sciences. Frameworks drawn on that have emerged strongly in design research include for example Desmet and Hekkert's general framework for product experience (2007) which attempts to break down the components that contribute to the experiential impacts of new products, in the experience of aesthetics, meaning and emotions via products.

This tradition and research process thinking is apparent in Tromp and Hekkert's chapter when considering the question whether the product or the user is in control where they draw on relevant behavioural literature to elaborate how our life would be constricted if we made conscious decisions for every action we completed. They thus gain insights into everyday human behaviour: many of our day-to-day actions and behaviours are habitual, in that we place little conscious and cognitive thought into their completion once mas-tered. They then systematically follow the argument through to ascertain what affect the detail of conscious and unconscious actions have on designing for behaviour change. Parallels to this can also be found in Niedderer's chapter.

Besides sociological, psychological and other traditional science approaches, core design approaches from user-centred design, ergonomics and architecture are drawn on by Lockton within Design with Intent, along with the relative new comer human-computer interaction (HCI). Equally, sound user-centred design research offers value and is identified as crucial in several chapters (e.g. Daae and Boks) as an important part of the process of designing for behaviour change. This indicates that there is a strong consciousness emerging among designers that design is not restricted to form, function, ergonomics and aesthetics, but that emotion, experience and many other factors are equally important to consider, especially where human behaviour is part of the design problem.

In conclusion, Part 2 has presented a diverse range of design for behavioural change approaches from a theoretical perspective that aims to inform a fuller understanding of the range of possibilities that could be drawn on in informing design for change. Part 3 presents design for behavioural change approaches as applied across a range of domains to illustrate more closely how design for behavioural change has been applied in practice.

References

Akrich, M. (1992). The de-scription of technical objects. In W. Bijker & J. Law (Eds.), *Shaping technology, building society: Studies in sociotechnical change* (pp. 205–224). Cambridge, MA: MIT Press.

Barbopoulos, I. (2012). *The consumer motivation scale: Development of a multi-dimensional measure of economical, hedonic, and normative determinants of consumption* (Licenciate Thesis). University of Gothenburg, Gothenburg.

Clark, G.L. (2009). Human nature, the environment, and behaviour: explaining the scope and geographical scale of financial decision-making. *SPACES Online, 7*(2009–10).

Daae, J. Z., & Boks, C. (2014). Dimensions of behaviour change. *Journal of Design Research, 12*(3), 145–172. doi: 10.1504/jdr.2014.064229

Darnton, A. (2008). *GSR behaviour change knowledge review: An overview of behaviour change models and their uses.* London, UK: Government Social Research Unit.

Desmet, P. M. A., & Hekkert, P. (2007). Framework of product experience. *International Journal of Design, 1*(1), 57–66.

Fogg, B. J. (2003). *Persuasive technology: Using computers to change what we think and do.* San Francisco, CA: Morgan Kaufman.

Hallsworth, M., & Sanders, M. (2016). Nudge: Recent developments in behavioural science and public policy. In F. S. Bristol (Ed.), *Beyond behaviour change: Key issues, interdisciplinary approaches and future directions* (pp. 113–132). Bristol: Policy Press.

Heidegger, M. (1962). *Being and time.* New York: Harper & Row Publishers.

Idhe, D. (1990). *Technology and the lifeworld: From garden to earth.* Bloomington, IN: Indiana University Press.

Jelsma, J. (2006). Designing 'moralized' products. In P.-P. Verbeek & A. Slob (Eds.), *User behavior and technology development* (pp. 221–231). The Netherlands: Springer.

Langer, E. J. (1989) *Mindfulness.* Reading, MA: Addison Wesley Publishing Company.

Latour, B. (1992). Where are the missing masses? The sociology of a few mundane artifacts. In W. Bijker & J. Law (Eds.), *Shaping technology/building society: Studies in sociotechnical change* (pp. 225–258). Cambridge: MIT Press.

Lilley, D. (2007). *Designing for behavioural change: Reducing the social impacts of product use through design* (PhD thesis). Loughborough University, Loughborough.

Reckwitz, A. (2002). Toward a theory of social practices: A development in culturalist theorizing. *European Journal of Social Theory, 5*(2), 243–263.

Rotter, J. B. (1990). Internal versus external control of reinforcement: Case history of a variable. *American Psychologist, 45*(4), 489–493.

Schatzki, T. (2001). Introduction: Practice theory. In T. R. Schatzki, K. K. Cetina and E. von Savigny (Eds.), *The practice turn in contemporary theory* (pp. 1–14). London: Routledge.

Stern, P. C. (2000). New environmental theories: Toward a coherent theory of environmentally significant behavior. *Journal of Social Issues, 56*(3): 407–424.

Verbeek, P.-P. (2005). *What things do: Philosophical reflections on technology, agency, and design.* Pennsylvania: Pennsylvania State University Press.

Willis, A. M. (2006). Ontological designing. *Design Philosophy Papers, 4*(2), 69–92.

Part 3

Applying design for behaviour change

14 Design for behaviour change

Introducing five areas of application and related case studies

Kristina Niedderer, Stephen Clune and Geke Ludden

Part 3 of this book explores the real-world application of design for behavioural change principles and tools within five thematic areas. These five areas are as follows:

- Sustainability
- Health and wellbeing
- Safety
- Design against crime
- Social design.

Each area will be reviewed through one of the following chapters. We have chosen these five areas for two reasons: First, they are areas essential for the development of a functional, safe and healthy society, and second, these areas have emerged as most prominent in the discussions about design for behaviour change and hence offer a good range of examples and case studies for review and comparison. Within the chapters, experts in these fields describe how design for behaviour change has been applied in each area by outlining the scope of its application in their respective sectors, by providing an overview of the approaches used, and by detailing promising case studies as well as future challenges and directions required for designers to lead and contribute to creating desirable change. In the following, we introduce each of the five areas to offer some framing considerations of the problems and challenges faced in each.

With respect to the sustainability of the planet '[w]e are using 50 per cent more resources than the Earth can provide, and unless we change course that number will grow very fast – by 2030, even two planets will not be enough' (WWF, 2012: 1). Climate change is one of the consequences of this rapid escalation in resource use, which requires equally bold reduction targets to lead us to sustainability. For example, the degree of change in CO_2 emissions required to re-orient the planet towards a more sustainable society is an enormous 90%. Such a scale in resource reduction can and will occur only through a combined socio-technical shift. Technology alone is not enough. It will require the alteration of the everyday life of a large segment of the population and its associated behaviours. For example, what we eat, how we move about, stay warm, and consume will all have to change to become more sustainable.

Chapter 15, which tackles the important and yet by some still contested issue of sustainability, engages with three key questions: (1) What is the sustainable change we are seeking? (2) Who are we asking to make those changes? and, (3) How can design aid in bringing about that change?

The chapter begins by addressing these questions and by presenting an overview of the inherent sustainability challenges faced by society in relation to areas of housing and energy, consumption, food, and transport. Clune and Lockton discuss design initiatives in response to these challenges from a theoretical and practical perspective, and then present two in-depth case studies. They first attempt to understand the large variation in cycling patronage between cities through a predominately context-based approach to design for behaviour change for sustainability. Second, they utilize a predominately cognition-based response in trying to better understand user conceptualizations of energy to enable meaningful feedback to users.

In the area of health and wellbeing, there are a large number of different issues that require attention and in which design could make a contribution. Key issues are the prevention of disease, managing long-term disease, as well as fostering wellbeing and happiness.

The impact of diseases such as 'cancer, mental illness, cardiovascular disease, respiratory disorders and diabetes, have major long-term impacts on individuals, their families and their communities' (Willcox, 2014: 2). A causal link has been established between some of these diseases behaviour and lifestyle. The World Health Organization (WHO, 2006) estimate that at least 80% of all heart disease, stroke and diabetes cases, and 40% of all cancers, are preventable. In the context of Australia alone, Willcox (2014) suggests that addressing six key behavioural risk factors, including smoking, high risk alcohol use, physical inactivity, intimate partner violence, obesity, and inadequate diet, may potentially save Australia 2.3 billion dollars annually. These behavioural risk factors are all areas where design for behavioural change has an opportunity to make a significant contribution.

Design may also assist with managing long-term diseases, such as diabetes and Chronic Obstructive Pulmonary Disease (COPD) that require life-long management and attention from care professionals. This care is increasingly being offered in the home in a decentralized manner. This is part of a paradigm shift in healthcare where the emphasis is placed on self-management for both health and disease. This means the 'patient's' home is increasingly being used as the main care environment thanks to the introduction of new technologies.

Fostering wellbeing and happiness is a third and relatively new area of study that focuses on the flourishing or optimal functioning of people, groups, and institutions (Gable & Haidt, 2005). Wellbeing and happiness offers of course a benefit in itself but it is also studied as a means of managing and preventing disease. For example, it has been suggested that a causality between emotional wellbeing and long-term physical illness exists (Lamers et al., 2012).

Chapter 16 on health and wellbeing provides a broad overview of design for behavioural change approaches used in this domain, followed by three detailed case studies that serve as examples of how design for behaviour change theories and tools have been applied in relation to the following:

1. Reducing sugary drink intake – drawing on the Design for Healthy Behaviour Framework.
2. Redesigning homes for care – illustrating how design has an important role to play in the acceptance of in-home care equipment required for dementia care, which in turn can lead to changes in behaviour which allow people to remain living at home for longer.
3. Encouraging breaks to be taken at work to avoid 'burnout' – drawing on principles of Persuasive Design.

Another area that is drawing on behaviour change is the area of safety design and management. With regard to road and transport safety, for example, 1.25 million people die each year as a result of road traffic accidents (WHO, 2016), with a further 800,000 estimated deaths related to particulate matter from transport and energy, suggesting transport and mobility is a key area for the application of design for behavioural change. In regards to workplace accidents, the transport, construction, fishery and forestry industries are the three industries with the highest causalities per capita, with 'up to 90 per cent of all accidents are triggered by unsafe behaviours which tend to interact with other negative features that are evident within a particular system' (Chapter 17: 206).

In the design for safer behaviour chapter (Chapter 17), Morris and Hancox introduce two broad approaches to safety: (1) The engineering perspective termed 'Safety Engineering', which involves the 'fitment of rails, guards and personal protective equipment to reduce the hazards prevalent in an industrial environment' (Chapter 17: 200). (2) The behavioural intervention approach, which focuses on policies, processes, training, and culture. These safety engineering and behavioural interventions are discussed across a variety of different sectors, including occupational safety (particularly in work and industrial environments), healthcare (e.g. hospital environments), transport, and perhaps most importantly the domestic environment. A range of theoretical approaches are introduced throughout the chapter including Safety Engineering, Theory of Planned Behaviour, Health Belief, Stages of Change, Motivational Interventions, Choice Architecture, Safe by Design, Design with Intent, and Mindful Design. The chapter illustrates how the use of multiple approaches is preferred to achieve long-term safe behaviours, as no approach in isolation offers a magic solution.

Turning to the area of crime and crime prevention, behaviour of course has a central role. Crimes can include a diverse range of offences from bike theft to card theft, from burglaries and robberies to cyber crime. According to the Design Council (2011) the costs of crime are incurred in three ways:

1. The cost incurred in anticipation of crime (the cost of security and prevention)
2. Costs incurred as a consequence of crime, and
3. The cost of responding to crime.

In addition, there is emotional and physical stress placed upon victims.

Heavy penalties have historically been used as a deterrent to crime, as has been a focus on early intervention programmes through education and schooling (Erol et al., 2000). More recent literature suggests that many crimes may be opportunist, and that shifts in the designed environment may assist in acting as a deterrent to prevent these types of crimes. This concept, called Situated Crime Prevention (SCP), is a body of theory that has explored how the designed environment may deter crime, and is a focus of Chapter 18. In this regard, Gammon and Thorpe state that Design Against Crime (DAC) 'seeks to find new ways to modify the environment in which routine "accidents" (or in this context "crimes") take place by anticipating and designing against actions before they happen, so that they are prevented. It aims to achieve this by attempting to inhibit, deter or thwart criminal behaviours or, alternatively, to generate new types of behavioural responses that exclude crime' (Chapter 18: 216).

The chapter on design against crime by Gammon and Thorpe begins by outlining traditional approaches to designing against crime in situational crime prevention (SCP) and related approaches to modifying behaviour. They then proceed to illustrate how socially responsive design against crime draws upon SCP as well as more participatory, and asset oriented design approaches to deliver interventions that reduce opportunities for crime. They describe their collaborative design-led approach to behaviour change developed in the context of design against crime. The chapter discusses the collaborative 'we think' way of working to that of the traditional 'nudge' design and argues that the participatory design-led approach delivers a 'fraternal' rather than 'paternal' strategy for behaviour change that is transformative in its means as well as its ends. Two case studies from the Design Against Crime Research Centre – Bikeoff and ATM Art Mat – are utilized to illustrate how participatory design approaches have been applied in conjunction with traditional SCP strategies. The chapter closes with a strong suggestion that 'bottom up' participatory strategies associated with socially responsive design may deliver more democratic social transformations, than individual targeted behaviour change 'nudges'.

The final thematic of this section looks at the emerging area of Social Design. Social design can be seen as the broad term that brackets the diverse practices and domains concerned with doing 'social good' as well as 'social interaction'. Gardiner and Niedderer argue that the impact of design on social behaviour change has remained largely ignored and under-researched because social aspects are often underpinning one of the four themes discussed in the other chapters and therefore often overlooked. The chapter on social design reviews the emerging interest in social behaviour change in relation to current approaches of design for behaviour change. It explores what is meant by design for social behaviour change, and analyzes the different levels of its application as intent, process, and output. These are discussed in relation to six case studies that demonstrate the role and benefits of social design.

The examples concerning design intent include design ingenuity driving activism to overcome local planning legislation that was perceived as unduly restrictive, and community innovation amongst refugees to take ownership of their lives by designing their own communications and information networks. The two examples demonstrate the need of communities for self-determination and ownership to facilitate healthy social relations, and that creative vision can help overcome obstacles and – at times literal – barriers. The discussion on design process continues the theme of self-determination by exploring the design processes involved in enabling participants to take the lead in developing their own solutions, such as in the case of the Field Guide to Human-Centred Design in 2015 (IDEO.org, 2015) or The Knee High Design Challenge that looked at reframing problems that existing approaches to public health had so far failed to address. The focus on design outcomes of social design looks at the shared space movement and social media as examples for shifting social interactions. Examples are the courteous and responsible interaction between cars and pedestrians through a mindful shared space design approach, or the use of social media which change how people socialize and interact with potentially both positive but also negative consequences where there is an absence of positive social norms.

Our aim in contrasting the application of design for behaviour change approaches in these five different areas of application is for the reader to better see the similarities and differences of their applications. Often, different language is used in different fields to discuss issues, obscuring the commonalities between them. By contrasting the applications in the different areas, we hope that the reader will be able to see beyond such specific language to identify similarities where different fields can learn from each other.

References

Design Council. (2011). *Designing out crime*. London: Design Coucnil Design and Technology Alliance Against Crime.

Erol, R., Cooper, R., Press, M., & Thomas, M. (2000). Co-designing against crime. In S. A. R. Scrivener, L. J. Ball, & A. Woodcock (Eds.), *Collaborative design* (pp. 173–182). London: Springer.

Gable, S. L., & Haidt, J. (2005). What (and why) is positive psychology? *Review of General Psychology, 9*(2), 103–110.

IDEO.org. (2015). *The field guide to human-centered design*. San Francisco: IDEO.

Lamers, S. M. A., Bolier, L., Westerhof, G. J., Smit, F., & Bohlmeijer, E. T. (2012). The impact of emotional well-being on long-term recovery and survival in physical illness: A meta-analysis. *Journal of Behavioral Medicine, 35*(5), 538–547.

WHO. (2006). *Constitution of the World Health Organization*. Retrieved August 5, 2016, from www.who.int/governance/eb/who_constitution_en.pdf

WHO. (2016). *Road traffic injuries*. Retrieved August 5, 2016, from www.who.int/mediacentre/factsheets/fs358/en/

Willcox, S. (2014). Chronic diseases in Australia: The case for changing course. *Australian Health Policy Collaboration Issues*, paper No. 2014–02. Melbourne, Australian Health Policy Collaboration.

WWF. (2012). *Living planet report: Summary*. Gland, Switzerland: World Wide Fund For Nature. Retrieved October 1, 2016, from www.wwf.se/source.php/1477203/Living-Planet-Report-2012_summary.pdf

15 Design for behavioural change and sustainability

Stephen Clune and Dan Lockton

Introduction

The possibility of irreversible change to our planet through the ecologically damaging and unsustainable use of resources has been the topic of many publications since the early 1960s (for example Carson, 1962; Meadows, 1972; World Commission on Environment and Development, 1987). According to a growing body of literature we are living beyond the ecological limits of our planet and a reduction in resource and CO_2e emission intensity of up to 95% is required by Western countries to avert irreparable damage (Vergragt, 2004; EU, 2013). It is also argued that there is a causal relationship between increased resource consumption in everyday life, and increased CO_2e emissions[1] (e.g. Lenzen, 1998). Such a large-scale reduction in resource use will involve making products from less resource-intensive materials and transitioning to an alternative energy system (crudely termed technical solutions which has been the focus of eco–design), as well as changes in the resource-intensive behaviours of people's everyday lives (crudely termed 'social solutions'). This chapter focuses on the latter, looking at how design may assist in changing resource-intensive behaviours for sustainability.[2] For designers, one of the most elementary sustainable design philosophies is to 'find solutions with a significantly reduced environmental impact, that are capable of working, and encourage their adoption' (Clune, 2010b: 2).

When discussing design for behavioural change for sustainability, three important questions can be asked: What are the sustainable changes we are seeking? What role can design play in promoting the required changes? And with who, and where are we seeking to intervene? This chapter attempts to provide insight into these questions. It begins by presenting an overview of the sustainability challenges involved with energy, food, transport and consumption. These are discussed in relation to the greenhouse gas emission intensity of the four areas (measured in carbon dioxide equivalent [CO_2e]). CO_2e emissions are arguably one of the most significant global environmental sustainability indicators, and are used in this chapter as a proxy environmental indicator.[3] Design initiatives that respond to these challenges from a theoretical and practical perspective are then discussed. The chapter closes by presenting two in-depth case studies that explore a predominately context-based approach to design for behavioural change in cycling, and a predominately cognition-based approach to design for behavioural change in understanding consumers perception of energy.

What sustainable changes are we seeking?

Design for Sustainability acknowledges that the scale of change required for a sustainable planet is enormous (as discussed earlier). To address such broad targets requires an understanding of the current embodied CO_2e emissions. These can broadly be broken up into four areas (Hertwich & Peters, 2009):

- Household energy use (on average 19% of an individual's CO_2e emissions globally)
- Food (on average 20% of an individual's CO_2e emissions globally)
- Transport (on average 17% of an individual's CO_2e emissions globally)
- Consumption of goods and services (on average 16% of an individual's CO_2e emissions globally).

Each of these themes can be broken down into key activities and practices where designers may be able to have influence in reducing CO_2e emissions. The key drivers of emissions that could form the basis of design for behavioural change interventions are outlined in the next sections.

Housing and energy

Energy use in the home accounts for approximately 19% of an individual's CO_2e emissions globally (Hertwich & Peters, 2009). Whilst many energy efficiency measures focus on technical solutions such as building, product and appliance design, household behaviour plays a significant role in household energy consumption and as homes become more energy efficient, the behaviours of their occupants become increasingly significant (Palmer & Cooper, 2013). Studies have suggested greenhouse emissions reductions of up to 29% from behavioural changes in household energy use alone (Ürge-Vorsatz et al., 2009, Lopes et al., 2012).

In the UK, the majority (78%) of domestic energy use is associated with space and water heating (DECC, 2012: 21), suggesting that reducing space and water heating is a priority area related to housing in the UK. Energy consumption in the home, particularly with respect to space heating has received a significant amount of scholarly attention in the design for behaviour change community. For example, practice-orientated product design has been applied to encourage personal heating (Kuijer, 2014: 223), and feedback mechanisms have been designed to communicate energy consumption and prompt alternate behaviour (see for example 27 feedback meters in Lilley, 2011). The second case study in this chapter provides a more in-depth look at some of the issues in this space.

Food

The consumption of food contributes to a significant proportion of a person's overall greenhouse gas emissions (Dey et al., 2007) and accounts for 20% of an individual's CO_2e footprint globally (Hertwich & Peters, 2009). While agricultural production is responsible for 19%–29% of global anthropogenic greenhouse gas emissions (Vermeulen et al., 2012), the everyday practices and behaviours of consumers are also crucial. It is estimated for example, that 30% of food purchased for home consumption is not eaten and wasted (FAO, 2013). While food is significant in terms of an individual's environmental impact, it also has significant implications for health, with the global economic cost of obesity estimated to be at *$2 trillion* annually (Dobbs et al., 2014). The WWF Livewell report suggests that these two elements are interrelated, with a healthy diet also being generally a more sustainable one (Macdiarmid et al., 2011).

Practices that may reduce an individual's food related CO_2e emissions and their estimated impacts include the following: eliminating meat consumption (35% reduction in

CO_2e emissions), avoiding domestic food waste (12% reduction), purchasing local (5% reduction) and avoiding packaging waste (3%) (Hoolohan et al., 2013: 1065). Applying design solutions to encourage the uptake of these practices is an emerging area of research and arguably the least explored amongst the four themes of food, energy, transport and consumption. Other approaches have sought to apply design at a more systemic level, for example preventing domestic food waste through better packaging design and portion control (Holdway, 2011; Wikström et al., 2014). The labelling of the health impacts of food is also becoming mainstream (less so environmental impacts); however, as Mckenzie-Mohr (2000) argues, providing information alone does not necessarily lead to behavioural change. In a supermarket context, choice architecture by proximity, where the purchase of healthy food increases when it is placed in near proximity has also been used (Bucher et al., 2016). However, it could also be argued that the food industry has a very sophisticated understanding of how to alter the designed environment to encourage the consumption of food and beverages (for example by product placement and buy one get one free promotions).

Transport

Transport-related emissions account for an estimated 17% of an individual CO_2e footprint globally (Hertwich & Peters, 2009), and approximately a quarter of all UK emissions (DECC, 2016). According to DECC, 'Road transport is the most significant source of emissions in this sector, in particular passenger cars' (DECC, 2016: 16). Encouraging a shift to low emission mobility would involve designing interventions that prioritize walking and cycling, a shift to public transport, along with reducing air travel.

Reducing transport use requires an understanding of the end practices that transport is utilized for. For example, reducing and replacing business travel with conference calls requires a different approach to replacing international holidays.

Consumption of goods and services

The consumption of goods and services contributes on average to 16% of an individual's CO_2e footprint globally (Hertwich & Peters, 2009). This can be viewed as the throughput of stuff in our everyday life. While elementary, the recycling hierarchy of avoid, reduce, re-use, recycle (and regenerate) is a useful starting point to identify strategies that guide desired practice. The most desirable approaches seek interventions in front-of-pipe solutions (i.e. the top of the hierarchy) that avoid consumption, rather than seeking to recycle better, or manage pollution or waste.

Numerous sustainable design strategies exist that address each element and that reduce the intensity of consumption (see Table 15.1), for example, emotionally durable design and product-service systems may reduce material intensity of products. More recently, the collaborating consumption and sharing economy movements offer the potential to move towards less materialistic or 'asset-light' lifestyles.

It is useful to identify targeted behaviours that would be desirable to change, however it is important to acknowledge that such behaviours are not completed in isolation from everyday life. That is, the behaviours are not completed for the behaviour's sake, but are part of an often complex and interrelated set of day-to-day practices. As Wilhite (2013) points out in relation to energy, people are not 'using energy': its use through 'behaviour' is a consequence of humanity, in all its diversity, dealing with

Table 15.1 Design strategies to reduce the intensity of consumption

Strategy	Design option
Avoid	Designed to dematerialize the product (e.g. from CDs to digital music)
	Designed to eliminate the product or practice
Reduce	Designed to minimizes the amount of physical material used in production
	Designed from materials with a lower ecological footprint
	Designed to reduce the throughput of materials over the product's life
	Designed for longer life (e.g. emotionally durable design)
Re-use	Designed from re-used materials
	Designed for more uses (e.g. multiple purpose products)
	Designed for more users (e.g. the collaborative economy, product-service systems)
Recycle	Designed from recycled materials
	Designed for ease of recycling
Regenerate	Designed to regenerate the natural environment
	Designed to encourage social interaction

the social practices and needs of everyday life – comfort, light, sustenance, sanitation, entertainment, social activity and so on, and the same applies to many other aspects of consumption. The approach of identifying target behaviours against each theme has some limitations, in that there are thousands of individual target behaviours that could potentially be changed. Wellbeing is emerging as a more holistic starting point that may encompass multiple behaviours, by asking people what it would be like to live in a healthy and happy society, and how design could help bring this about. To be healthy and happy by default may also engage a range of activities that often cross over as being pro-environmental. For example, health and happiness is the first design principle in the bioregional sustainable development guide: their master plan for Sonoma Mountain 'ensures no resident needs to walk for more than five minutes to reach local shops and amenities' (Desai & Searle, 2016: 1).

What role can design play in promoting the required changes?

The role design can play in promoting the required changes is enormous. A plethora of design for behaviour change strategies that reach across the cognition–context continuum have been introduced in the previous chapters of this edited text. For example, appealing to an individual's cognition to complete a range of pro-environmental behaviours (e.g. to set the thermostat lower or dress warmer) to redesigning the environment (context) so that those behaviours may be mitigated in the first instance (like designing a house that does not require heating and cooling). The themes of food, energy, transport and consumption provide a framework to seek out design examples across this cognition–context continuum, and encompass a range of design disciplines. A selection of design examples has been mapped out in Table 15.2 to illustrate the diversity of scope and possible intervention points in designing for change. One of the challenges within this space is evaluating what type of interventions may be most effective considering: the scale of change required, the complexity of quantifying impacts, and the lack of evidence-based case studies. However, there is a growing critique that relying solely on the individual to act sustainably is futile in an environment that may be scripting unsustainable behaviours as a default. It is like sending a child into a candy store to buy an apple.

Table 15.2 Examples of design for behavioural change applied to energy, food and transport

	Example	Approach and explanation	Design discipline	Target
Energy	Energy meters	Feedback and alerts of energy consumption to promote or trigger an alternate behaviour e.g. Watson and Onzo meters (Wanvik, 2014).	Product design	Individual
	Cool Biz	Alter social norms, Japanese Ministry of Environment encouraged a relaxed dress code so that three piece suits would not be worn in summer, and setting the thermostat to 28°C to save on cooling (MOE, 2005). Fashion designers supported the policy with a range of smart attire for 28°C.	Fashion design	Individual and structure
	Heuristics and Thermal comfort	Understand the heuristics and mental models of end-users to inform the design of thermostat interfaces and controls (Lockton et al., 2013).	Systems design	Individual and structure
	Person heating	Social Practice Theory and design used to redesign alternate heating practices that heat the person, rather than the room (Kuijer, 2014).	Product/furniture design	Individual and structure
	Air-con off	Error proofing, automatically turn off heating/air-conditioning when rooms are vacant making negative behaviour near impossible.	Product design	Structural
	Passive architectural design	Eliminate heating and cooling via passive building design that require no additional (or very minimal) heating or cooling (see for example Lovins, 2007).	Architecture	Structural
Food	Carbon labelling on packets	Awareness/information provision on food packaging of carbon footprints.	Packaging design	Individual
	Nutritional labelling on packets	Awareness/information provision on pack to communicate the nutritional value of food, and flag possible risks.	Packaging design	Individual
	Portion control packaging	Choice architecture by portion control. Packaging was redesigned so that smaller portions can be opened individually to assist in reducing food waste (Holdway, 2011).	Packaging design	Individual and structural
	Proximity to healthy food	Choice architecture by proximity. There is an increase in healthy food and water consumption when in near proximity. A decrease in unhealthy food consumption when food placed at a distance (Bucher et al., 2016).	Retail design	Structural

Transport	Car dashboard feedback	Feedback of fuel consumption, dashboard prompts/triggers to change gear etc.	Automotive design	Individual
	Walking school bus	Removal of barriers/provision of service to make the desired behaviour easier and safer.	Service design	Individual
	IDEO coasting bike	Ethnographic research identified cycling could be made more appealing by designing a back-to-basics bike (Moggridge, 2008).	Product design	Individual
	Paris Velib bike share	Removal of barriers/provision of service to make the desired behaviour convenient for short trips (see Clune, 2010b).	Product system service	Individual and structure
	Trondheim bike lift	Removal of barriers: cycle lift assists riders to climb the steepest hill in Trondheim making the desired behaviour easier (Wanvik, 2014).	City planners	Individual and structure
	Walkable cities	Removal of barriers: provision of safe, walkable streets and restriction or calming of car use. (see for example Gehl, 2010).	Urban design/city planning	Structural
	Curitiba Rapid Bus Transit	Systems approach to redesign the bus network to achieve light rail transit speeds via priority lanes and bus platforms.	City planning/ product design	Structure
	Car share schemes	Provision of service that provides an alternative to individual car ownership (e.g. Zip car).	Product system service design	Structure
	Lift share car pool schemes	Provision of services via online platform for institutions and festivals to co-ordinate carpooling (e.g. lifshare.com).	Service design	Structure

With whom and where are we seeking to intervene?

With who, and where are we seeking to intervene via design is a critical question to ask. For example, Farmar-Bower when discussing the obesity epidemic in Australia states that 'Such increases [in obesity] suggest a system failure rather than simply numerous individuals happening to put on weight' (2013: 4). At other times design interventions may need to be aimed at a target population in order to be effective. For example, with respect to transport, the top 10% of emitters are responsible for 43% of emissions and the bottom 10% for only 1% (Brand & Boardman, 2008). To add complexity, change also occurs through the development of new practices that will replace or shift existing ones. For example, the collaborative consumption movement, driven by web 2.0 platforms enables new practices of car sharing, couch surfing and Uber rides that arguably enable 'asset-light' lifestyles to occur. We argue this is not driven by direct change interventions or campaigns that ask individuals to share more, or own less.

The design strategies to create change may shift depending on the level of ambition in where to intervene, whether targeting individual behaviour, or creating systemic structural change. For targeted behaviours, design approaches typically use motivating behaviour or persuasion to increase the attraction for the individual user to do something (Niedderer, 2013, Lockton et al., 2010), or they use prescription or prevention measures by redesigning the environment to enable or decrease desirable or undesirable behaviour respectively (e.g. Lockton et al., 2010, Tromp et al., 2011). This offers four basic approaches:

- Making the 'target' behaviour easier for people to do
- Making an undesired behaviour harder for people to do
- Trying to get people to want to perform a particular behaviour
- Trying to decrease people's inclination to perform a particular behaviour.

For systemic structural change, a broader range of design tools, solutions and stakeholders may need to be engaged. It has also long been argued that for design to contribute to a sustainable society, the ambition of designers may need to progress from making product-level improvements, to more systemic innovation. Encouraging a person drive a car more efficiently via a prompt on the dashboard is good, yet limited when attempting to achieve the suggested 80–95% reduction in CO_2e emissions. Brezet (1997) proposed that for eco-design to achieve large-scale reductions in resource use, a move is needed from product improvement and redesign to systems innovation. A range of Design for Sustainability practitioners are engaging with design that resembles a systems or meta-design approach, e.g. Ryan's (2011) work in urban transformation via eco-acupuncture or transition design (e.g. Irwin, 2015) with the objective to create structural change. The emergent rise of design thinking, co-design, product-service systems and service design suggests that design's application beyond products is maturing rapidly.

Case studies of design for behavioural change

Two case studies are discussed in the following section that represent the extremes of the cognition–context continuum. The first case study examines some design initiatives that have successfully increased the percentage of cycling in European cities and is predominately context focused dealing with systemic change. The second case study explores approaches to deepening our understanding of people's mental models and understanding of energy use, to provide input to the design process, which is predominately cognition based.

Encouraging cycling by design – a review of best-practice case studies

This cycling case study was selected with the desire to try and understand why 36% of trips taken in the Netherlands occur via cycling, and only 3% in the United Kingdom (EC, 2014). Why is there such as enormous variation in cycling patronage between the countries, and what has been design's (in the broadest sense) contribution to this?

When exploring answers to the above question, it became clear that city and county governments with high cycling patronage in Europe have developed and sustained plans to support, construct and fund bicycling facilities since the 1970s. The provision of a designed environment that includes bike lanes (preferably separate), bridges, priority traffic signals, traffic calmed streets and secure parking were central strategies to increased levels of cycling in all case studies (Pucher & Buehler, 2007). The most important factor in making cycling safe, convenient and attractive in a sample study of six European cities was 'the provision of separate cycling facilities along heavily travelled roads and at intersections, combined with extensive traffic calming of residential neighbourhood'. Dales et al. agree in the key contribution from the designed environment stating that 'cities with the highest cycling levels, and those that have successfully grown cycling levels over relatively short periods, generally afford cycling good physical protection or effective spatial separation from motor traffic, unless traffic speeds and volumes are low' (2014: 8).

The quality of designed infrastructure appears to be a central design element facilitating cycling (Rietveld & Daniel, 2004; Pucher & Buehler, 2007; Pucher et al., 2010; Dales et al., 2014). A range of road and pavement designs that manage the safe separation of cyclists from cars are presented by Dales et al. (2014) from European and the UK cities. There is a significant difference in patronage and infrastructure levels between Amsterdam (high modal share) and London (low modal share), for example segregated cycle lanes have a density of 3.1 km/km^2 in Amsterdam and 0.35 km/km^2 in London (Pucher et al. 2010 cited in Sun Qi, 2014: 40). In high-income, car-dependent cities, the limited provision of safe cycle routes combined with an assumption that cyclist will ride on existing roads generally results in a low number of mostly male cyclists, with very low patronage from children, women and elderly people (Pucher & Buehler, 2008).

However, better roads and cycling rights of way (while critical) is only part of the story. In cities with a substantial modal share of cycling, a range of complementary interventions have been put in place (Pucher & Buehler, 2007: 64; Pucher et al., 2010) including the following:

*   *Additional infrastructure provision:* bike parking, showers, integration with public transport
*   *Supportive land use planning:* policies foster relatively compact, mixed-use developments that generate more bikeable shorter trips
*   *Pro-bicycle programmes:* comprehensive traffic education and training of both cyclists and motorists, and a wide range of promotional events intended to generate enthusiasm and wide public support for cycling
*   *Restrictions on car use:* making the alternative action more difficult. Car use is made expensive, less convenient and less necessary through a host of taxes and restrictions on car ownership, use and parking.

Table 15.3 Cycling policy indicators with strong policy relevance

Cycling Policy Initiatives	Description and measure
Directness	
1 detour factor	Distance per straight line distance
2 delay	Seconds paused per km while cycling
3 average speed	Average speed measured in km/h
Comfort (nuisance)	
4 stop frequency	Number of stops per km
5 slow cycling and walking	Percentage of the time the speed is below 10 km/h
6 traffic	Number of times in succession bikes are omitted or interact with other road users (% of trip length)
7 infrastructure nuisance	Number of times in succession bikes interact with infrastructure per kilometre (0.01 x trip length in m/km)
8 no priority rights	Number of intersections per km without give-way to cyclist rights
9 Turn	Number of turns per km
Comfort (pavement)	
10 vibrations	V-Ft: weighted sum of scores for vibration
Attraction	
11 noise	V-Fg: weighted sum of scores for sound level
Cyclists Satisfaction	
12 bicycle	Percentage dissatisfied from survey
13 bike comfort	Percentage dissatisfied from survey
14 road safety	Percentage dissatisfied from survey
15 social security	Percentage dissatisfied from survey
16 approach theft bikes	Percentage dissatisfied from survey
17 ambitions of municipal cycling policy	Percentage dissatisfied from survey
18 general opinion municipal bicycle policy	Traffic Policy indicators: strong policy relevance on a grade from 1–10
Traffic Policy indicators	
Competitiveness of bike cycle time compared to car travel time	
20 bike journeys faster	Percentage of movements when cycling is faster than car
21 cost per journey	Parking cents/hour
22 car ownership	Number of passenger cars per 1,000 residents (2000–2003)
23 offer Public transport: Metro	Presence of underground
24 offer OV: Train Stations	Number of train stations per square km built
Road safety	
25 security	Number of fatalities per 100 million km
26 number of road traffic accidents	Per 10,000 population/population ★10,000
Road infrastructure	
27 density roads	Path length municipal and water board roads per square km built

Source: Ververs and Ziegelaar (2006).

As with most design for behavioural change interventions, a distinct lack of quantitative data restricts the causal analysis between the trialled interventions and increase in modal share being made. Two studies that attempted such causal analysis were completed by Ververs and Ziegelaar (2006) and Rietveld and Daniel's (2004). Ververs and Ziegelaar's study (2006) was commissioned by the Bicycle Institute for Policy Research in the Netherlands. It identified 27 out of 72 cycling and transport policy initiatives that had a strong correlation to high cycling modal share. These are outlined in Table 15.3.

In addition, Rietveld and Daniel's (2004) cycling study in the Netherlands supports Ververs and Ziegelaar's findings (2006), suggesting two key ways of encouraging bicycle use: improving attractiveness by reducing generalized costs and making competing modes more expensive. Generalized costs include physical effort, influenced by design factors such as slopes and the frequency of stops as the 'provision of direct routes and a small number of stops clearly contribute to the attractiveness of the bicycle as a transport mode' (Rietveld & Daniel, 2004: 545). The examples presented thus far fall under the design domains of urban planners and landscape architects. At a product design level, attempts have been made to make the cycling more attractive, such as IDEO's costing platform. IDEO attempted to transform the cultural image of cycling in the USA, with Shimano's coasting product platform, which was a flagship project for IDEO's user-centred design process (Moggridge, 2008). Coasting was released as a new type of bike for the large demographic in the USA who no longer ride, yet still have fond memories of riding as a child. Component supplier Shimano developed the product platform to integrate into major bike brands in Trek, Giant and Raleigh. The 'coasting' bike simplified cycling, had automatic gears and a back pedal brake, and won numerous design accolades. Grey literature (Roth, 2010) suggests that the cultural context and service design of bike shops run by sport enthusiasts with limited interest in leisurely commuting was a weak point in the customer journey map of returning cyclists, and the coaster's success.

The principles identified above correspond to the broad principle of change in making the 'target' behaviour easier for people to do, and making an undesired behaviour harder for people to do. Time for change to occur is one additional element identified by Dales et al. (2014) and Wardlaw (2014).

> Cities with the largest cycling levels and most cycling-friendly street use cultures have achieved that status as a result of policy and associated action over the long term, with an incremental approach to improving provision. Continuity of commitment to cycling as a desirable and benign mode, one worthy of major investment, is essential.
>
> (Dales et al., 2014: 7)

The cycling case study can be viewed as an example of where systematic structural change (cycling patronage) has been achieved through longitudinal support for a desirable practice, facilitated heavily by design in the form of critical infrastructure.

Powerchord and Drawing Energy: exploring people's understanding of energy use

Energy use is one of the major issues on which design for sustainable behaviour has concentrated. This case study on energy use takes a very different approach to the previous case study on cycling in arguing that existing design for behavioural interventions with respect to prompting reductions in energy use have been misdirected with respect to understanding people's conceptualization of energy, and this case study will therefore present an alternative design-based research approach. The majority of work on influencing energy use through individual behaviour change focuses on numerical, visual feedback displays for electricity or gas use, with the assumption that feedback will prompt the user to adjust his or her behaviour. There are numerous studies and meta-analyses looking at the effectiveness of different kinds of feedback (real-time, summary, normative and so on) in this context, and the adoption of these kinds of displays. While some influence on behaviour, leading to changes in energy use has been found relating to feedback displays (e.g. Kobus et al., 2012), the situation is complex. Simple numerical feedback may not take account of the realities of household life (Brynjarsdóttir et al., 2012; van Dam et al., 2009; Hargreaves et al., 2013) or people's *understanding* of units and quantities (Strengers, 2011), nor link people to the wider comprehension of the energy system (Boucher et al., 2012). Most visual displays require the householder to look at the display – often a small LCD or a web dashboard – regularly in order to be able to act on it and for it to have any effect, thus assuming a model of individual householders as 'micro-resource managers' (Strengers, 2011). While there have been some more ambient coloured light-based feedback systems for displaying electricity use – such as Gustafsson & Gyllenswärd's (2005) *Power Aware Cord*, DIY Kyoto's *Wattson* and Ambient Devices' *Orb* and clever use of thermal imaging (Goodhew et al., 2015) – these are exceptional. Many approaches lump 'energy demand' together as a number, disconnected from everyday artefacts, the realities of household life and people's diverse understandings of the systems around them.

There is an opportunity for design-led research placing artefacts and the narratives of practices more centrally, because – on the most basic of levels – it is through both everyday appliances, and artefacts such as these in-home displays that people actually experience energy use. Within HCI and design research, Pierce and Paulos (2010) call for more work on *materializing* energy, while novel approaches such as those of Mazé & Redström (2008) and Boucher et al. (2012) bring an artefact-driven perspective to the field.

The disconnect between people's understanding and conceptualization of energy, and existing feedback mechanisms prompted empirical work to seek a better understanding of people's daily interactions and understandings of heating, lighting, appliances, energy monitors and energy. The SusLabNWE project (a large multidisciplinary collaborative European Living Lab) worked with and visited nine diverse households across London and the South-East to document people's stories. This was followed with a 'logbook' probe study that including activities exploring themes such as metaphors for energy, social influences on energy use, and narrating everyday energy-related routines and frustrations through annotation (Figure 15.1; Lockton, Renström et al., 2014).

Based around themes emerging from these interviews and logbooks, co-creation and maker workshops with householders and designers were held which created concepts for new kinds of interfaces or devices that participants felt would help them reduce their energy use. One of the main themes emerging was the general *invisibility* of energy in modern life, and the consequences of this for behaviour and everyday practices. Householders' mental models of energy itself, and energy-using systems such as heating (Revell & Stanton, 2014; Lockton et al., 2013), together with the relative importance of different energy-using systems in the home, were partly determined by what was most salient – such as lighting – rather than 'hidden' uses such as heating and cooling (this aligns with other research, e.g. Attari et al. [2010] and Kempton and Montgomery [1982]). By people's own admission, much of the energy 'wasted' at home through particular behaviours, such as leaving heating on when going out, or leaving lights on elsewhere in the house, was partly due to its invisibility from the perspective of where they were at the time. People questioned how they could change how they use energy when they can't easily see or feel it, or get a sense of the changing rate at which it is being used. We found confusion with the different characteristics of energy use by different appliances (e.g. the 'spike' of a kettle compared with the continuous power drawn by lighting), and units, for example between kilowatts as a measure of power and kilowatt-hours as a measure of energy.

The theme of energy's invisibility was explored through visualization beyond numbers (Bowden et al., 2015), and transitioning to another sense: *sound* (Lockton, Bowden et al., 2014). In terms of visualization, a research activity in probe study logbooks asked people

Figure 15.1 Householder's annotation of her gas meter as 'difficult to use', because of its position in an exterior cupboard

to visualize on paper (through media including pens, crayons, inks and pastels) their ideas, mental imagery (Galton, 1907), mental models, experiences and notions of what energy 'looks' like. The activity was completed with a variety of participants including visitors to design exhibitions at London Design Festival 2013 and 2014, and with teenagers as part of the UK Art Science Prize 2014. What emerged was a collection of nearly 200 drawings that present a diverse and multifaceted picture of this often intangible and amorphous subject, which suggested a broad and sometimes contrasting range of personal definitions and conceptualizations of energy (Figure 15.2), which, if better understood, may enable more targeted and meaningful feedback interventions.

The drawings illustrate participants' aesthetic perceptions and judgement of energy via metaphors, categorizations, characterizations and associations, leading to possible design implications for new forms of energy feedback or display (Bowden et al., 2015).

These perceptions were explored through *sonification* (Walker & Nees, 2011) of energy use. One householder suggested that being able to 'listen' to whether appliances were switched on or not, and what state they were in (e.g. listening to a washing machine will give a good idea as to where it is in its cycle), was potentially more useful for understanding how to reduce energy use than a visual display. Another householder suggested – in response to discussion of smart metering and demand-based pricing changes – that being able to 'hear' the load on the grid (for example, a pleasant background hum could become

Figure 15.2 Two examples from 'Drawing Energy', created by members of the public

discordant as the grid's frequency changes due to high demand, or the tick of a clock could become temporarily faster) would be less intrusive than, for example, a text message or a flashing light. There are echoes of early work in calm technology and ubiquitous computing, such as Natalie Jeremijenko's *Live Wire (Dangling String)* (Weiser & Brown, 1995), or Ernevi et al.'s (2007) *Erratic Radio*, in which the 'display' fits with the existing daily visual landscape and *soundscapes* (Schafer, 1977) of the environment. Sonification of energy use along these lines could enable ambient comprehension of energy use with multiple appliances, including pattern recognition and state changes (Serafin et al., 2011).

To explore near-real-time energy sonification the *Powerchord* (Figures 15.3 and 15.4) was developed, an Arduino-based system which reads data from individual appliances monitored in parallel, mapping these figures to ranges defined in code, which then trigger particular sounds, building on the idea from our co-creation work with householders around fitting into the existing daily soundscapes of the home – something more like the tick of a clock, or the sound of distant church bells, 'repurposing' them with extra energy information rather than being part of the 'increasing clutter of beeps and bleeps' (Serafin et al., 2011: 97) of feedback. This 'blended sonification' (Tünnermann et al., 2013) meant that recordings of these sounds, suitably modified could be used; power ranges were defined to match the typical ranges found in household appliances, from <10W for trickle charging, to >2kW for electric heaters. For each power range, for each appliance, Powerchord plays a particular audio track, looped until the power range changes. Any audio tracks can be used – including tones, sound effects or music – on a user-replaceable micro SD card. Powerchord can thus act as a platform for different kinds of ambient energy sonification research.

The prototypes primarily used *birdsong* (from http://xeno-canto.org) in blackbirds, house sparrows and herring gulls so that different intensities of song (number of birds, agitation level) map to power ranges. Connecting people better to the wider, complex systems around them, in which their behaviour plays a part. The Powerchord prototype was demonstrated at the Victoria & Albert Museum's 'Digital Design Weekend' 2014 to around 40 members of the public, switching on a fan heater at different power levels to hear the changes in birdsong. This activity enabled the completion of quick response sheets that suggested the kinds of sounds people believed would be useful for understanding the energy use characteristics of different appliances and activities. This has enabled us, working with sonic interaction designer Claire Matthews (http://claire-matthews.com), to create and explore the possibilities of a range of 'sound packages' for Powerchord,

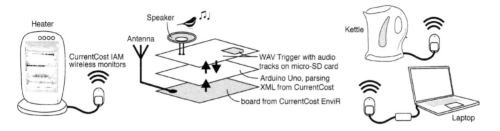

Figure 15.3 How the Powerchord system works

Figure 15.4 Powerchord prototype being tested in a kitchen environment, monitoring a microwave oven and an electric kettle

including ever-more-complex jazz and acoustic guitar schemes, a log fire progressing from crackling to roaring, the sound of increasing numbers of coins being dropped, other natural sounds such as rain intensity, different animal sounds from mice to elephants, and even dog whistles so that the family dog perhaps learns to howl at high energy use, becoming the 'household expert' on it.

For designers, the experience of the Powerchord (while a work in progress), has tested methods to broach questions on the public understanding of energy, novel forms of feedback, and the affordances and value of research through design methodologies. Using 'things' – prototypes, artefacts, drawings – in this way enables ways of knowing which are qualitatively different to those enacted in other disciplines addressing the same broad questions, in this case around design for sustainable behaviour and energy use. Artefacts enable the materiality of energy (Pierce & Paulos, 2010) to be manifested, discussed and explored practically. The results illustrate the capacity for design research in this space in attempting to understand and reconcile an individual's personal definitions, understanding and conceptualizations of energy, with feedback mechanisms that are meaningful and work with those understandings.

Conclusion

At the beginning of this chapter we posed three crucial questions in design for behavioural change for sustainability:

1. What are the sustainable changes we are seeking? The chapter provided an overview of some of the key sectors where targeted design for behavioural change may be applied in relation to sustainability. These four areas are housing/energy, food, transport and consumption. A key message is that the scale of change required for sustainability is incredibly large and the actions that design attempts to make must be strategic in order to make a difference.
2. What role can design play in promoting the required changes? The chapter illustrated the diverse roles that design can play across the cognition–context continuum, from intervening at the individual level, to broader structural and systems based interventions.
3. With who, and where are we seeking to intervene? The chapter suggests that to create change all levels of the cognition–context continuum should be engaged with. Different design for behavioural change tools and strategies are suited to intervening at different levels. The more complex the action or problem (like the wicked problems of obesity) the further away it moves from individual agency and cognition, and the more challenging it is to identify design-led product solutions.

Two contrasting case studies were presented in the chapter. The cycling case study reinforces the message that effective change occurs when a combination of approaches is used, i.e. the environmental context is addressed through the provision of safe and convenient cycle infrastructure, and the individual is addressed through pro-cycling programmes. The energy case study explored the value of designers attempting to better understand people's understanding of the energy systems they encounter and interact with. This enabled designers to work with an individual's conceptualization of the system in order to create meaningful feedback.

Notes

1 CO_2e stands for carbon dioxide equivalent, which is a measure of the warming potential of each greenhouse gas. It is used in this chapter as it is inclusive of all gases with warming potential, not only carbon dioxide. The EU reduction targets are between 80–95% from 1990 levels.
2 The surrounding chapters on social design and health in Part 3 are associated closely to social sustainability, therefore this chapter discusses issues related specifically to environmental sustainability.
3 We acknowledge that there are a broad range of important environmental indicators, including water quality, air quality, land use and biodiversity.

References

Attari, S. Z., DeKay, M. L., Davidson, C. I., & Bruine de Bruin, W. (2010). Public perceptions of energy consumption and savings. *Proceedings of the National Academy of Sciences, 107*(37), 16054–16059.

Boucher, A., Cameron, D., & Jarvis, N. (2012). Power to the people: Dynamic energy management through communal cooperation. *Proceedings of DIS 2012*, Newcastle, UK.

Bowden, F., Lockton, D., Gheerawo, R., & Brass, C. (2015). *Drawing energy: Exploring perceptions of the invisible*. London: Royal College of Art.

Brand, C., & Boardman, B. (2008). Taming of the few – the unequal distribution of greenhouse gas emissions from personal travel in the UK. *Energy Policy, 36*(1): 224–238.

Brezet, H. (1997, January/June). Dynamics in ecoDesign practice. *UNEP Industry and Environment, 20*, 21–24.

Brynjarsdóttir, H., Håkansson, M., Pierce, J., Baumer, E. P. S., DiSalvo, C., & Sengers, P. (2012). Sustainably unpersuaded: How persuasion narrows our vision of sustainability. *Proceedings of CHI 2012*, Austin, TX.

Bucher, T., Collins, C., Rollo, M. E., McCaffrey, T. A., Vlieger, N. D., Bend, D. V. D., Truby, H., & Perez-Cueto, F. J. A. (2016). Nudging consumers towards healthier choices: A systematic review of positional influences on food choice. *British Journal of Nutrition, 115*, 2252–2263.

Carson, R. (1962). *Silent spring*. Boston: Houghton Mifflin.

Clune, S. (2010a). Design for behavioural change. *Journal of Design Strategies, 4*(1), 68–75.

Clune, S. (2010b). *Inverting the solution into the problem: Design, practice theory and behavioural change for sustainability*. Young Creators for Better City and Better Life, College of Design and Innovation Tongji University, Shanghai.

Dales, J., Jones, P., Black, R., Hoe, N., Mayo, A., Parkin, J., & Strong, M. (2014). *International cycling infrastructure best practice study*. Report for Transport for London. London, UK: Urban Movement. Retrieved November 7, 2016, from http://content.tfl.gov.uk/international-cycling-infrastructure-best-practice-study.pdf

DECC (2012). *Energy efficiency statistical summary*. London, UK: Department of Energy and Climate Change.

DECC (2016). *2014 UK Greenhouse gas emissions, final figures*. London, UK: Department of Energy and Climate Change.

Desai, P., & Searle, G. (2016). *Sonoma Mountain Village*. Retrieved September 15, 2016, from www.bioregional.com/sonoma-mountain-village/

Dey, C., Berger, C., Foran, B., Foran, M., Joske, R., Lenzen, M., & Wood, R. (2007). Household environmental pressure from consumption: An Australian environmental atlas. In G. Birch (Ed.), *Water, wind, art and debate: How environmental concerns impact on disciplinary research*. Sydney: Sydney University Press.

Dobbs, R., Sawers, C., Thompson, F., Manyika, J., Woetzel, J., Child, P., McKenna, S., & Spatharou, A. (2014). *Overcoming obesity: An initial economic analysis*. London: McKinsey Global Institute.

EC (2014). *Special Eurobarometer 422a, quality of transport*. Brussels: European Commission, Directorate-General Communication "Strategy, Corporate Communication Actions and Eurobarometer" Unit.

Ernevi, A., Palm, S., & Redström, J. (2007). Erratic appliances and energy awareness. *Knowledge, Technology & Policy, 20*(1), 71–78.

EU (2013). *What is the EU doing about climate change? Climate action*. Retrieved October 2, 2013, from http://ec.europa.eu/clima/policies/brief/eu/index_en.htm

FAO (2013). *Food wastage footprint: Impacts on natural resources*. Summary Report. Rome: Food and Agriculture Organisation of the United Nations.

Farmar-Bowers, Q., Higgins, V., & Millar, J. (Eds.). (2013). *Food security in Australia challenges and prospects for the future*. New York: Springer.

Galton, F. (1907). *Inquiries into human faculty and its development*. London: Dent.

Gehl, J. (2010). *Cities for people*. Washington: Island Press.

Goodhew, J., Pahl, S., Auburn, T., & Goodhew, S. (2015). Making heat visible: Promoting energy conservation behaviours through thermal imaging. *Environment and Behaviour, 47*(10), 1059–1088.

Gustafsson, A., & Gyllenswärd, M. (2005). The power-aware cord: Energy awareness through ambient information display. *Poster Proceedings of CHI 2005*, ACM, New York.

Hargreaves, T., Nye, M., & Burgess, J. (2013). Keeping energy visible? Exploring how householders interact with feedback from smart energy monitors in the longer term. *Energy Policy, 52*, 126–134.

Hertwich, E. G., & Peters, G. P. (2009). Carbon footprint of nations: A global, trade-linked analysis. *Environment Science and Technology, 43*(16), 6414–6420.

Holdway, R. (2011). *Final report: Packaging design to reduce household meat waste*. Oxon, WRAP and Giraffe Innovation.

Hoolohan, C., Berners-Lee, M., McKinstry-West, J., & Hewitt, C. N. (2013). Mitigating the greenhouse gas emissions embodied in food through realistic consumer choices. *Energy Policy, 63*(0), 1065–1074.

Irwin, T. (2015). Transition design: A proposal for a new area of design practice, study, and research. *Design and Culture, 7*(2), 229–246.

Kempton, W., & Montgomery, L. (1982). Folk quantification of energy. *Energy Policy, 7*(10), 817–827.

Kobus, C. B. A., Mugge, R., & Schoormans, J. P. L. (2012). Washing when the sun is shining! How householders interact with a household energy management system. *Ergonomics, 56*(3), 451–462.

Kuijer, L. (2014). *Implications of social practice theory for sustainable design*. (PhD thesis). Department of Industrial Design. Delft University of Technology, Delft.

Lenzen, M. (1998). Primary energy and Greenhouse gases embodies in Australian final consumption; an input output analysis. *Energy Policy, 26*(6), 495–506.

Lilley, D. (2011). *Design for sustainable behaviours, how others have done it*. Retrieved July 30, 2016, from www.design-behaviour.co.uk

Lockton, D., Bowden, F., Brass, C., & Gheerawo, R. (2014). *Powerchord: Towards ambient appliance-level electricity use feedback through real-time sonification*. UCAmI 2014: 8th International Conference on Ubiquitous Computing & Ambient Intelligence, Belfast, December 2–5.

Lockton, D., Harrison, D. J., Cain, R., Stanton, N. A., & Jennings, P. (2013). Exploring problem-framing through behavioural heuristics. *International Journal of Design, 7*(1), 37–53.

Lockton, D., Harrison, D., & Stanton, N. (2010). The design with intent method: A design tool for influencing user behaviour. *Applied Ergonomics, 41*(3), 382–392.

Lockton, D., Renström, S., Bowden, F., Rahe, U., Brass, C., & Gheerawo, R. (2014). *Energy storytelling through annotating everyday life*. BEHAVE 2014: 3rd European Conference on Behaviour and Energy Efficiency, September 3–4, Oxford.

Lopes, M. A. R., Antunes, C. H., & Martins, N. (2012). Energy behaviours as promoters of energy efficiency: A 21st century review. *Renewable and Sustainable Energy Reviews, 16*(6), 4095–4104.

Lovins, A. (2007). *Rocky Mountain Institute visitor guide*. Snowmass: Rocky Mountain Institute.

Macdiarmid, J., Kyle, J., Horgan, G., Loe, J., Fyfe, C., Johnstone, A., & McNeill, G. (2011). *Livewell: A balance of healthy and sustainable food choices*. Commissioned by WWF-UK. Aberdeen, Rowett Institute of Nutrition and Health, University of Aberdeen.

Mazé, R., & Redström, J. (2008). Switch! Energy ecologies in everyday life. *International Journal of Design, 2*(3), 55–70.

McKenzie-Mohr, D. (2000). Promoting sustainable behaviour: An introduction to community based social marketing. *Journal of Social Issues, 56*(3), 12.

Meadows, D. H. (1972). *The limits to growth: A report for the Club of Rome's project on the predicament of mankind*. London: Potomac Associates.

MOE (2005). *Result of "Cool Biz" campaign*. Retrieved August 8, 2009, from www.env.go.jp/en/press/2005/1028a.html

Moggridge, B. (2008). *Innovation through design*. International Design Culture Conference, Korean Design Research Institute, Seoul National University, IDEO.

Niedderer, K. (2013). Mindful design as a driver for social behaviour change. In *Proceedings of the IASDR Conference 2013*, Tokyo, Japan.

Palmer, J., & Cooper, I. (2013). *United Kingdom housing energy fact file*. Retrieved October 31, 2016, from www.gov.uk/government/uploads/system/uploads/attachment_data/file/345141/uk_housing_fact_file_2013.pdf

Pierce, J., & Paulos, E. (2010). Materializing energy. In *Proceedings of DIS Conference on Designing Interactive Systems*. Arhus, Denmark. DIS '10. ACM Press, New York.

Pucher, J., & Buehler, R. (2007, December). At the frontiers of cycling: Policy innovations in the Netherlands, Denmark, and Germany. *World Transport Policy and Practice, 13*(3), 8–56.

Pucher, J., & Buehler, R. (2008). Making cycling irresistible: Lessons from The Netherlands, Denmark and Germany. *Transport Reviews, 28*(4), 495–528.

Pucher, J., Dill, J., & Handy, S. (2010). Infrastructure, programs, and policies to increase bicycling: An international review. *Preventive Medicine, 50* (Supplement), S106–S125.

Qi, S. (2014). *Barriers and facilitators to cycling in European cities: A comparative case study of cycling in London and Amsterdam* (MSc). Cardiff University, Cardiff.

Revell, K. M. A., & Stanton, N. A. (2014). Case studies of mental models in home heat control: Searching for feedback, valve, timer and switch theories. *Applied Ergonomics, 45*(3), 363–378.

Rietveld, P., & Daniel, V. (2004). Determinants of bicycle use: Do municipal policies matter? *Transportation Research Part A: Policy and Practice, 38*(7), 531–550.

Roth, Y. (2010). *What caused Shimano's coasting-program to fail?* Retrieved April 14, 2016, from https://yannigroth.com/2010/05/12/what-caused-shimanos-coasting-program-fail/

Ryan, C. (2011). *Eco-acupuncture: Designing future transitions for urban communities for a resilient low-carbon future.* State of Australian Cities Conference, Sydney.

Schafer, R. M. (1977). *The soundscape: Our sonic environment and the tuning of the world.* Rochester, VT: Destiny Books.

Serafin, S., Franinovic, K., Hermann, T., Lemaitre, G., Rinott, M., & Rocchesso, D. (2011). Sonic interaction design. In T. Hermann, A. Hunt, & J. G. Neuhoff (Eds.), *The Sonification handbook* (pp. 87–110). Berlin: Logos.

Strengers, Y. (2011). Designing eco-feedback systems for everyday life. *Proceedings of CHI 2011,* Vancouver, Canada.

Tromp, N., Hekkert, P., & Verbeek, P. (2011). Design for socially responsible behaviour: A classification of influence based on intended user experience. *Design Issues, 27*(3), 3–19.

Tünnermann, R., Hammerschmidt, J., & Hermann, T. (2013). Blended sonification: Sonification for casual information interaction. *Proceedings of the International Conference on Auditory Display (ICAD2013),* Łódź, Poland.

Ürge-Vorsatz, D., Novikova, A., Köppel, S., & Boza-Kiss, B. (2009). Bottom – up assessment of potentials and costs of CO2 emission mitigation in the buildings sector: Insights into the missing elements. *Energy Efficiency, 2*(4), 293–316.

van Dam, S., Bakker, C. A., & van Hal, J. D. M. (2009). The mediating role of home energy management systems. *Proceedings of First European Conference on Energy Efficiency and Behaviour,* Maastricht.

Vergragt, P. J. (2004). *Leap frogging to sustainable households.* 8th Greening of Industry Conference, Ways of knowing, University of North Carolina, Chapel Hill.

Vermeulen, S. J., Campbell, B. M., & Ingram, J. S. I. (2012). Climate change and food systems. *Annual Review of Environment and Resources, 37*(1), 195–222. doi: doi:10.1146/annurev-environ-020411-130608

Ververs, R., & Ziegelaar, A. (2006). *Explanatory model for bicycle use municipalities: A study commissioned by Fietsberaad* (translated). The Netherlands: Bicycle Institute for Policy Research.

Walker, B. N., & Nees, M. A. (2011). Theory of sonification. In T. Hermann, A. Hunt & J. G. Neuhoff (Eds.), *The Sonification handbook* (pp. 9–39). Berlin: Logos.

Wanvik, J. (2014). *Trampe CycloCable, reach the top with the bicycle lift!* Retrieved April 1, 2014, from http://trampe.no/en/home

Wardlaw, M. J. (2014). History, risk, infrastructure: Perspectives on bicycling in the Netherlands and the UK. *Journal of Transport & Health, 1*(4), 243–250.

Weiser, M., & Brown, J. S. (1995). *Designing calm technology.* Retrieved February 15, 2016, from www.ubiq.com/hypertext/weiser/calmtech/calmtech.htm

Wikström, F., Williams, H., Verghese, K., & Clune, S. (2014). The influence of packaging attributes on consumer behaviour in food-packaging LCA studies – a neglected topic. *Journal of Cleaner Production, 73,* 100–108.

Wilhite, H. (2013). Energy consumption as cultural practice: Implications for the theory and policy of sustainable energy use. In S. Strauss, S. Rupp, & T. Love (Eds.), *Cultures of energy: Power, practices, technologies.* Walnut Creek: Left Coast Press.

World Commission on Environment and Development. (1987). *Our common future.* Oxford: Oxford University Press.

16 Design for behaviour change for health and wellbeing

Geke Ludden, Rebecca Cain, James Mackrill and Frances Allen

Health and wellbeing

With an ageing population, increase in stress-related diseases and unhealthy lifestyles, to name but a few, there are a myriad of challenges for improving both health and wellbeing of people. These challenges might be addressed by design. Design within this domain can aim to elicit positive behaviour changes to address health and wellbeing issues. The field of health and wellbeing is broadly defined. The official WHO definition of health formulated in 1948 (WHO, 2006) describes health as "a state of complete physical, mental and social wellbeing and not merely the absence of disease or infirmity." This definition would "leave most of use unhealthy most of the time" and recently there has been some debate about this definition (Huber et al., 2011) suggesting a less stringent view on what being healthy really means. Broadening to the definition of wellbeing, Seligman (2011) proposes that wellbeing is a multi-componential concept comprising positive emotions, engagement, meaning, positive relationships and accomplishment (PERMA).

Several researchers have found that there is a bidirectional relationship between both health and wellbeing: health influences wellbeing and wellbeing itself influences health. Both physical and mental health influence wellbeing (Diener & Chan, 2011; Dolan et al., 2008) and there are a number of correlations between wellbeing and physical health outcomes, such as improved immune system response, higher pain tolerance, increased longevity, cardiovascular health, slower disease progression and reproductive health (Howell et al., 2007; Steptoe et al., 2005). A meta-analysis even showed that emotional wellbeing predicts long-term prognosis of physical illness (Lamers et al., 2012). These interactions play a role in influencing health and wellbeing and make clear that there are many opportunities for design for behaviour change to contribute to health and wellbeing.

Research in public health monitors the health of communities and populations at risk to identify health problems and priorities in an effort to encourage prevention rather than cure. It also aims to provide conditions in which people can be healthy by organized measures to prevent disease, promote health and prolong life among the population as a whole. In Chapter 8, Ludden has already discussed the rise of unhealthy lifestyles (i.e. smoking, poor diet and a lack of physical activity) leading to diseases like obesity, diabetes and COPD (Chronic Obstructive Pulmonary Disease). For a growing group of people, these diseases require life-long management of illness and attention from care professionals. Moreover, a substantial number of people suffer from mental illnesses such as depression and anxiety disorders. Depression is among the illnesses with the largest burden of disease, with a high impact on quality of life and yielding enormous economic costs (Cuijpers et al., 2007; Mathers & Loncar, 2006). Long-term prospects for those with mental health issues are not much better. People diagnosed with mental health illness face seriously heightened risks for other diseases such as diabetes, heart disease and hypertension (Leigh & Flatt, 2015). Adding to this, an aging population creates an increasing burden on health and social care services. These developments, combined with an increased attention for patient-centered care (see e.g. Anderson & Funnell, 2005) have led to a paradigm shift in healthcare where the emphasis is placed on self-management in both health and disease.

Toward the wellbeing end of the continuum, research in psychology has increasingly used the concept of positive psychology, 'the study of happiness' (see e.g. Lyubomirsky, 2008). Rather than studying mental illness, positive psychology focuses on studying the conditions and processes that contribute to the flourishing or optimal functioning of people, groups and institutions (Gable & Haidt, 2005). In design, theories of positive psychology have been used to study how design can contribute to the happiness of individuals (Desmet & Pohlmeyer, 2013). Pohlmeyer (2012) constructed a design wellbeing matrix that specifies how design can have an impact on the different elements in Seligman's Wellbeing Theory. The wellbeing matrix for example shows how the value that material objects bring (e.g. a phone providing the function to call a friend or relative) can contribute to wellbeing beyond its material presence.

To support Public Health, in prevention of diseases as well as in physical healthcare and in mental healthcare, the design of products, environments and services plays an increasingly important role. In this chapter, we first sketch two important areas where the design of products and services can positively contribute to health and wellbeing. Although supporting lifestyle changes is an important area in itself, we will not further elaborate on this area because it was already discussed in quite some detail in Chapter 9. This chapter will go on to provide a short overview of design for behaviour change approaches used in this domain illustrated by three case studies that will serve as examples of how theories and tools in design for behaviour change can be used to design for health and wellbeing.

Shifts in care – empowerment and care at home

The developments in our society with respect to health described in the introduction not only impose a large economic burden because people are often left unfit for work, they also pose a large burden on our healthcare system and have led to the paradigm shift in the organization of healthcare that we have seen in recent years. This paradigm shift entails that the patients' home is increasingly seen and used as the main care environment and that patients are increasingly in control of managing their care process and delivering care (self-care).

For example, to improve mental health at home, therapies have been developed in the form of web-based applications that patients can use in their own time and at their own pace. These therapies can either be stand-alone or they can be monitored by a care professional (in a form of blended care). Although this development vastly increases the amount of people that can be reached by mental healthcare, it also contributes to a growing number of people that do not follow their treatment as intended by the care professional. For example, analyses of current web-based interventions show that many systems are only used by a specific group of users (women, highly educated), and that even they often do not persist and drop out as the intervention unfolds (Dulmen et al., 2007). The design of these systems for some part determines their efficacy, as Ludden et al. (2015) have recently argued. By having an effect on how well and how frequent the web-based applications are being used, design has an indirect effect on the efficacy of the online therapy. Several design directions have been proposed to positively influence people's desire and motivation to use at home self-care programmes. Next to offering therapy for mental conditions, online programmes are currently available for a range of other conditions and are increasingly used by people to manage a chronic disease rather than as a cure. Furthermore, recent developments have led to increased use of mobile applications that people can use on their phone or on a tablet to allow monitoring of daily activities and performing exercises throughout the day at any place (see e.g. Blake, 2008).

At home treatments can also consist of a combination of a medical device (such as a blood-pressure meter) and a web-based application that allows people to send data to a carer and communicate with health professionals and peers. For example, pregnant women who need regular blood pressure monitoring do not have to visit the hospital any longer to do so; they can now take measurements at home and transmit these to their care professional through a private, online service center. In many cases, treating people at home is less expensive and it empowers patients to be in control of their own recovery process. Patient empowerment has been shown to increase treatment efficacy (Wong-Rieger & Rieger, 2013). With respect to the use of medical devices, the increased focus on at home use means that there is a need for devices that are not only understandable and easy to use but that people will also welcome into their homes and lives. Design, and design for behaviour change specifically, can capitalize on these needs. For example, a recent study focused on how the interactive and playful design of devices for Bright Light Therapy can better motivate people to adhere to their therapy (Siepel et al., 2015). Future developments in connected (medical) devices and sensor networks will lead to even wider opportunities for care at home that seamlessly integrates into people's daily lives and activities.

Health and the environment

The relationship between health and the environment has been subject to much focus in the academic research field. This relationship can be at the human response to the existing space around them, for example, natural environments enhancing subjective wellbeing (Kaplan, 1995), but also through design intervention to allow people to respond or use a particular environment in a new way. For example, design interventions promoting physical activity might include staircases that are more attractive and inclusive to use, such as the piano staircase in Stockholm. In this project, a staircase was painted to resemble the keys of a piano and tempted 66% of people away from using the escalator (Design Council, 2014). Other examples include the provision of bike lanes, bridges, priority traffic signals, traffic-calmed streets and secure parking to increase levels of cycling to benefit individual health (Pucher & Buehler, 2007). Indeed, the National Health Service (NHS) in the UK is acknowledging this with the project "NHS Forest." The project aims to improve the health and wellbeing of staff, patients and communities through increasing access to green space on or near to NHS land and encourage greater social cohesion between NHS sites and the local communities around them (NHS Forest, 2014).

Hospitals and other healthcare facilities provide examples of a specific context in which design for behaviour change exists and one where both personal and environmental factors can elicit change. It is expected that hospitals should promote healing through the creation of an overall inviting, calming and engaging environment (Douglas & Douglas, 2005). Indeed, Ulrich et al. (2004: 3) comment:

> A growing scientific literature is confirming that the conventional ways that hospitals are designed contributes to stress and danger, or more positively, that this level of risk and stress is unnecessary: improved physical settings can be an important tool in making hospitals safer, more healing, and better places to work.

Healthcare environments can have a variety of negative psychological, physiological and behavioural manifestations that work against wellness (Ulrich et al., 1991). These include stress and anxiety for both patients and staff, raised heart rate and cortisol levels evidenced in patients, and inefficiencies in team working by healthcare staff (Ulrich et al., 1991). Design interventions focusing on environmental change can counter these negative effects to produce more positive experiences, behaviour and interactions, at a personal level as well as on a group level. For example, the view of green space encourages enhanced restoration, relaxation and reduced pain medication caused by a moment 'away' from the cacophony of the hospital environment (Ulrich, 1984; Mackrill et al., 2013); healthcare team performance can be improved through periods such as quiet time, where activities are kept to a minimum to allow patient notes to be taken without disturbance and allowing rest periods for patients. As these examples show, design in the context of healthcare is far more than simply providing comfortable chairs or pleasant decoration; it is about the provision and delivery of care. The Design Council (UK) investigated strategies for reducing violence and aggression in the Emergency Department, and proposed onsite environmental signage and leaflets to ensure that a consistent level of information is provided to reduce anxiety. This links to the theory of locus of control (Folkman & Lazarus, 1988), that defines the cognitive control of emotion towards environmental stressors. If an external stressor in the environment (such as a noise) is moved from being perceived as external, where the person perceives he or she has no control over it, to internal where one can process the stressor more meaningfully and has a level of control, then the resultant emotion is more positive and the person can cope with the situation better. Folkman and Moskowitz (2000) state that such insight can help one believe that the stressor is not something to be feared and can even enable an individual to find positive meaning in an on-going stressful event. Therefore, design strategies which aim to improve wellbeing do not necessarily consist purely of a physical form, but can also include information to mediate individual response to environment and the stimuli that exists within it. An example of this might be better way finding within a healthcare environment what reduces anxiety of visitors through better information provision, thus implicitly altering their locus of control over the event.

An integrated approach to the design of healthcare spaces can cater for psychological, physiological and behavioural considerations. This is highlighted by the UK-based design company Boex who produced outside seating designed specifically for a space of quiet reflection within a Healthcare Centre in the UK. The oak timber surfaces feature hand carved letters depicting connections to the local area. The messages portray popular activities within the local surroundings in order to engage with the visitor (see Figure 16.1). Such spaces not only provide an area for personal contemplation but also offer family, visitors and patients the opportunity to congregate. Importantly, the space highlights natural elements, which have a positive effect on health and wellbeing and promote coping behaviour through social interactions whilst within the hospital environment.

Figure 16.1 Hospital courtyard produced by design agency Boex
Source: Boex (2016).

Design for behaviour change approaches for health and wellbeing

The work by Niedderer et al. (2014) is useful to frame the design for behaviour change strategies and methodologies used in the health and wellbeing domain. Little work in this domain has studied the efficacy (magnitude of change) and outcome (designed output) of different design for behaviour change approaches in the same context but several promising strategies have been explored. One specific strategy to design for healthy behaviour was elaborated on in Chapter 8, introducing the transtheoretical model of health behaviour change. Other specific strategies deployed with the health and wellbeing domain are discussed later, with exemplars given.

To improve the general level of wellbeing of people with dementia who live in a care facility, Visch et al. (2011) explored several design interventions that were aimed to stimulate people with dementia. The aim of the project was to investigate how designers can make use of elements of gaming to increase the motivation of users. The basic principles of persuasive technology are reflected in the design outcomes presented (triggers, motivation, ability). For example, they designed a device that would project a pattern of leaves on a table that invited inhabitants of the care facility to stroke through the leaves thereby changing the pattern. The patients with dementia were thus stimulated (physically as well as mentally) in a gentle way through engagement with the technology. This is an example of using the theory of planned behaviour in design. Lee et al. (2011) used strategies from behavioural economics to persuade people to make healthy choices. Through studying several interventions to promote healthy snacking in the workplace, Lee et al. (2011) created interventions aiming to present choices in a way that leverages people's decision processes and induces them to make self-beneficial choices. For example, one of the interventions they designed was a robot that would present two types of snacks, whereby it was made easier to pick a healthy snack (apple) than it was to pick a less healthy snack (cookie). By removing the cue for an unhealthy habit (eating cookies is made slightly more difficult) and adding a prompt for a healthier alternative (picking the apple as a snack is made slightly easier) the choice for the healthier option is pre-programmed. In essence, this can be seen as a form of choice architecture.

Another approach that is of value in the domain of health and wellbeing is that of mindful design. As introduced in previous chapters, mindfulness refers to a mindset of openness and alertness, which regards any information as novel, pays attention to the specific context and considers the information from different perspectives (Niedderer, 2013). Models of Mindful design accommodating contexts of environment, human-object interaction and social interaction and that are based upon principles of mindfulness that are present within the health context. Health professionals' comments reported in Niedderer et al. (2014) offered an example of behaviour change on an interpersonal level through patient empowerment, which draws on ideas of mindfulness. Their example explains that instead of healthcare professionals trying to provide all the answers to patient's problems, they begin by asking the patient what he or she has been doing recently to help his or her health. This changes the conversation direction from the start.

In summary, a variety of approaches can be used to elicit behaviour change within the domain of health and wellbeing and within the healthcare setting. As yet there is no clear pattern as to the type of behaviour change strategy that is most effective here. Partly, this can be explained by the broad definition of the domain and the different areas that it includes, for example, a focus on the individual or on the wider public. On the other hand, the domain could benefit from research that is more evidence based. In the following section, we will discuss three more substantial examples of how design for behaviour change approaches have been applied to the different areas within the domain of health and wellbeing.

Exemplary case studies

From the previous sections, we have seen the wide range of opportunities for design for behaviour change in the health and wellbeing domain. This section will introduce three case studies that each focus on one specific area of this domain. The first case study will introduce a design approach focused on the individual; it is aimed at prevention and proposes a sequential view on behaviour change. The second case study demonstrates how people make physical adaptations to their home to live with dementia. The adaptations encourage positive behaviour change which allows people with dementia to remain living at home for longer. The third case study introduces designing with nature to translate the restorative effects of nature to designed artefacts in situations where real contact with nature is not possible.

Supporting the individual towards a healthier lifestyle: sugar to water

This case study takes the Design for Healthy Behaviour Framework (see Chapter 8) as a starting point and focuses on lowering the daily intake of sugar-containing beverages. The development of and rationale behind the case have been described more elaborately in Ludden and Offringa (2015).

For many people, their daily intake of sugar is too high, which negatively effects their general health and wellbeing. Limiting the intake of sugar-containing beverages can be a solution to this problem. This case study introduces three different products that can sequentially be used in three different phases of behavioural change.

The first product was designed to match the motivational state of people in the early stages of behaviour change. For this stage, two important issues have to be addressed. First, people in this stage do not want to change, and, therefore, they will not be willing to buy a product that supports behavioural change. Second, the product should incorporate a design strategy aimed at raising awareness. During the idea-generating phase, several ways of distributing information at low cost were explored such as stickers and (foldable) leaflets. Eventually, it was decided to choose a product that would be seen as a more valuable item (and that would therefore less easily be discarded). The product that was designed for this phase was a cooling sleeve that displays the amount of sugar that different types of beverages contain (see Figure 16.2). The cooling sleeve would be available as a free gift that could be handed out to people on the street. The print on the sleeve contains a QR code that connects to a mobile application that was designed to support a second phase of behaviour change.

To develop the product that should support the next stage of change, that of preparation, the designer of the intervention incorporated a design strategy aimed at enabling. To move through this stage, people need to move from raised awareness to actually acting on a desired behaviour change. During this phase, people have to come to realize that they should and that they are able to change their behaviour. Therefore, it is important that an intervention can provide advice or possible actions that are relevant for a specific person to enable him or her to take action. In such a situation, an interactive application (also referred to in this context as a Behaviour Change Support System or BCSS) is a valuable solution because it allows organization of data and personalized feedback (cf. Oinas-Kukkonen & Harjumaa, 2009). To make the BCSS easily accessible, we chose to design a mobile application. The application supports people in tracking their daily intake of sugar-containing beverages and gives them personal advice on how they can best change their daily habits, thus enabling them to take the next step towards the desired behaviour change. After a week, the application creates personal advice and recommendations based on the provided data that support the user to take the step into an action phase. In this phase, people actually implement the behaviour change based on the recommendations of the application.

Finally, the system will recognize from the behaviour pattern that the user is ready to take yet another step in the behaviour change process: towards the stage of maintenance.

Figure 16.2 Products designed for sequential use during different stages of change: cooling sleeve, mobile
        application and water bottle

Source: Photo taken at exhibition 'Mind the Step' during Dutch Design Week 2014.

The system at this point recommends the product that links to the third phase. The product that was designed for this third and last phase incorporated a design strategy aimed at
motivation. The best alternative to drinking sugar-containing beverages is drinking water.
Therefore, a variety of alternatives were explored which motivate people to drink water,
including light indicators and timers. Eventually, to avoid irritation, the designer opted
for a less intrusive and demanding solution. The product designed for the third phase
was a water bottle that supports the achieved behaviour change by using an hourglass to
remind the user to drink water at least every hour. In a small trial, the link between the
first two phases was studied by presenting a group of 18 people with the first product
of the sequence, the cooling sleeve. Two weeks later, respondents were asked about their
general opinion on the cooling sleeve, whether or not it had raised their awareness of the
amount of sugar in drinks, and whether or not they had used the QR code to move to
the next phase (in the trial this was a movie rather than a website). Results were generally
positive, the cooling sleeve indeed raised awareness and 15 out of 18 participants had used
the link to the next phase. While it has yet to be determined whether following through
on this approach will actually durably change people's behaviour, this case study shows
that designing for stages of change is a promising approach.

Using design for behaviour change approaches to look at how people make physical adaptations to their home to live with dementia

In the UK, one in 14 people over 65 and one in six people over the age of 80 will be
diagnosed with dementia (Alzheimer's Society, 2014). Dementia is an umbrella term for
a range of symptoms caused by degeneration of areas of the brain causing diverse symptoms including cognitive impairment and loss of functional capacity. There is growing

evidence as to how symptoms of dementia can be ameliorated by the design of the physical environment, which can positively encourage some behaviour changes in people with dementia. These can enable them to remain living at home for longer.

For example: people with dementia display impaired colour and texture discrimination. Therefore, appropriate design uses contrasting colours and task lighting to assist in the location and appropriate use of furniture thus reducing wandering behaviour (Pollock & Fuggle, 2013). Conversely, painting doors in colours that blend in with the surrounding walls can prevent wandering and access to unsafe areas (Marquardt et al., 2014; see also Figure 16.3).

Although aspects of dementia-friendly design and their ability to help change behaviour in people with dementia are now becoming increasing popular with designers of acute and residential care environments, these design modifications are not necessarily readily made by people in their own homes. However, given the shift to care at home, it is important that dementia-friendly design is introduced in people's homes as well.

Work by Marquardt et al. (2011) used cross sectional data from home assessments and questionnaires to look at levels of self-directed home modifications for people with dementia. The modifications seen in the study were predominantly those to address safety and falls prevention such as grab rails, door locks and walk in showers. The most common reason for rejecting modification advice by carers was the feeling that it was not needed or not helpful. The study concluded that more research is needed on how to improve awareness for home adaptations in dementia and how to engage care givers to make environmental changes (Marquardt et al., 2011).

A report from the Australian Housing and Urban Research Institute (Gabriel et al., 2015) found that modifications to bathrooms were more common than those in other areas. Respondents indicated that bathroom modifications were made for two reasons: to enable independence or to promote safety. The carers interviewed highlighted that independent toileting was a priority, with several respondents describing both additive and behavioural modifications undertaken to assist with personal care tasks (Gabriel et al., 2015)

One explanation for the apparent dichotomy between the acceptance and rejection of different home adaptations comes from the Theory of Reasoned Action. This theory proposed by Ajzen and Fishbein (1980) states that behaviour is a product of intention which in turn is created by attitudes and beliefs (Figure 16.4).

Perceptions and reactions about objects can be positive or negative. Designed objects do not just provide a material or functional quality, their value also lies in the assistance of and towards personal goals (Desmet & Pohlmeyer, 2013). These feelings form salient beliefs that are immediate and go on to form our attitudes and response towards an object. The failure of people with dementia and their carers to accept some form of housing adaptation can be linked to negative salient beliefs towards these designed objects.

Findings by Heywood (2005) lend weight to this. In interviews with people who underwent a series of home adaptations for a variety of long-term conditions, they found that items such as commodes had negative connotations and this made them less desirable. Belief itself is created, in part, by subjective norms which is the influence of perceived opinions of others over the individual (Hagger et al., 2007). In the case of the commode as with other living aids, its presence is a visual indicator of the impairment of the user and a reminder of the abilities he or she has lost. The perceived stigma of this often proves intolerable for both people with dementia and family carers for instance when visitors come into their home environment, therefore the equipment is rejected.

Figure 16.3 Use of book design to hide cupboard doors and prevent confusion in dementia unit
Source: Boex (2016).

Belief	•Disabilty equipment looks like it belongs in a hospital
Attitude	•Equipment will make my home feel like a hospital
Intention	•I do not want disability equipment in my home
Behaviour	•Declines to have disability equipment

Figure 16.4 The use of the Theory of Reasoned Action to understand acceptance of disability living aids

This highlights that design has an important role to play in the acceptance of equipment and home adaptation in dementia care, which will in turn lead to changes in behavior which allow people to remain living at home for longer. It highlights a juxtaposition between 'Positive design' which enhances subjective wellbeing and functional design to assist physical health (Desmet & Pohlmeyer, 2013). Good design which takes into account the salient beliefs of people at home, can lead to increased uptake, which in turn leads to improved quality of life for people with dementia and decreased burden on those who care for them. Therefore, there needs to be further research into how negative beliefs affect the acceptance of living aids, coupled with efforts to produce more acceptable designs.

Using design to change's peoples' behaviour in the workplace: remembering to take a break

The two demonstrator cases in Figures 16.5 are examples of how design could influence people's behaviour at work. In the design process for both of these cases, the Persuasive Design Model by BJ Fogg (Fogg, 2003) was used by incorporating the three factors that according to the PSD model can support acquiring new behaviour (Trigger, Motivation and Ability).

In the introduction to this chapter, we have already highlighted a rise in mental illnesses. As a more concrete example, in 2011, 13% of the working population in the Netherlands had burnout-related symptoms (Driessen & Hooftman, 2011). Research on work behaviour has shown that people often find it difficult to get away from their working activities to replenish and relax (Breedveld & van den Broek, 2004). It is generally agreed that burnout is work related and that people at least feel completely drained of energy (Hoogduin et al., 2001). Taking this as a starting point, there were two student projects initiated at the University of Twente in the Netherlands targeted at using design to change the common habit of not regularly taking breaks from work.

The first project focused on inviting people to take a break by using a design that appealed to all the senses by drawing on inspiration from nature. The demonstrator product that was the result of this project (Figure 16.5b) is a relaxation corner. The designer started by gathering natural stimuli for all the senses and analyzed this collection to eventually define a desired experience for every modality. The final design of the relaxation corner consists of a set of benches with cushions and a centre piece in the shape of an egg. Inside the egg a humidifier is placed, it reminds people to take a break by releasing a scent, at the same time inviting people to come to the relaxation corner. In this corner, multiple elements have been used that can be re-configured at will but yet create a coherent whole when put together. The different elements offer unpredictable output; for example, a sound similar to the sound rain sticks produce can be heard when someone sits on a bench. Once seated, the elements offer opportunities to move and explore, the round shape of the egg for example invites people to push it over, after which it will return to its original upright position.

In this way, the relaxation corner aims to change people's behaviour at work by inviting and reminding people to take a break and facilitating exploration (as they could explore nature) offering a moment of (soft) fascination to cognitively restore.

The second demonstrator case (Figure 16.5b) was designed with the same aim to change people's habits of not regularly taking breaks from work. As an additional aim, this project was designed to stimulate social interaction by taking breaks together. The demonstrator

Figure 16.5a (above) and 16.5b (below) Two demonstrator cases that apply strategies from persuasive technology to the case of stimulating taking regular breaks at work

product that resulted from this project therefore consists of an individual part combined with a social part. The individual part of the concept is a small lighting device, a pebble, that sits on an individual's desk. When a break is due, the light will fade, triggering the user to stand up and walk over to the coffee table that functions as a charger for the lighting devices. When the lighting device is placed on the table, an ambient glow emerges. When more than one lighting device is placed on the table, lighting patterns appear, thus making it more inviting for people to (ask their colleagues to) take a break together. After about three minutes, the individual lighting device shows that it has been charged sufficiently, signaling that the owner of the lighting device can go back to work. Again, the combined setup reminds people to take regular breaks and offers a moment to cognitively restore.

For both restorative break setups prototypes were built that were evaluated against conventional break setups using two separate but similar experiments. For the second break setup, differences were indeed found. Notably, after taking a break from a cognitive (stressful) task, participants scored higher on positive affect (positive emotions) when they had used the break setup that made use of the interactive lighting table and pebble (Ludden & Meekhof, 2016). For the other break setup, no differences were found although participants did report that they enjoyed the interaction with the bench and the egg.

Future challenges/directions for the sector

In this chapter, we have elaborated on the considerable challenges in health and wellbeing and on the range of opportunities that design for behaviour change can bring to this domain. The chapter has also demonstrated that a variety of theories, methods and tools can be applied. A notable divide in the different approaches is that some interventions target the individual (e.g. in taking responsibility over personal health issues) and that others target the general public to influence social behaviour that promotes improved health (e.g. encouraging people to use stairs instead of escalators). The divide between design for behaviour change targeted at the individual and at the general public has also been shown to be of importance in other domains as was brought forward in earlier chapters of this volume. It is particularly relevant to the health and wellbeing domain since the health challenges we face today are no longer problems influencing a small group of people – they have become important for whole populations. This calls for design to target society at large, focussing on the design of infrastructures and environments in such a way that we create holistically healthy places to live in. At the same time, a focus on approaches that target the individual remains important and may even become increasingly important with new opportunities to offer personalized solutions in healthcare as well as in coaching. Personalization has been put forward as one of the four Ps that change healthcare: this is ICT driven and data driven. However, at the same time, this also calls for designers' expertise in understanding people and involving them in a design process that explicitly incorporates behaviour change methodologies.

Changes in the organization and delivery of healthcare have been substantial over the last decade and they are expected to further change considerably over the coming years through the development and implementation of technology and a drive towards more efficient and lean healthcare systems. These developments call for design and healthcare to seek each other in order to come to solutions that truly empower people in taking responsibility not only for their personal health and self-care, but also in the way health systems are run.

To conclude, we would like to state that design and design for behavior change has much to offer to the domain of health and wellbeing. However, evidence of the efficacy of the approaches put forward in this chapter is still scarce. Future work should focus on creating evidence-based examples, including a focus on large-scale and longitudinal implementation and validation within the specific context the intervention was designed for. Opportunity also lies in unifying the link between healthy lifestyles and management of illness with the provision and design of future healthcare services.

Acknowledgements

We would like to thank the designers of the case studies presented in this chapter: Marleen Offringa, Valerie Mencke and Linda Meekhof. This chapter builds on ongoing work of the authors that has been partly published elsewhere.

References

Ajzen, I., & Fishbein, M. (1980). *Understanding attitudes and predicting social behavior*. London: Prentice-Hall.

Alzheimer's Society. (2014). *Dementia 2014: Opportunity for change*. Retrieved July 25, 2016, from www.alzheimers.org.uk/site/scripts/download_info.php?fileID=2317

Anderson, R. M., & Funnell, M. M. (2005). Patient empowerment: Reflections on the challenge of fostering the adoption of a new paradigm. *Patient Education and Counseling, 57*(2), 153–157.

Blake, H. (2008). Mobile phone technology in chronic disease management. *Nursing Standard, 23*(12), 43–46.

Boex (2016). *Hospital Courtyard seating*. Retrieved July 25, 2016, www.boex.co.uk/project/hospital-outdoor-furniture/

Breedveld, K., & van den Broek, A. (2004). *The demanding society. The social – economical context of psychological fatigue* (in Dutch). The Netherlands Institute of Social Research (SCP).

Cuijpers, P., Smit, F., Oostenbrink, J., de Graaf, R., Ten Have, M., & Beekman, A. (2007). Economic costs of minor depression: a population-based study. *Acta Psychiatrica Scandinavica, 115*(3), 229–236.

Design Council (2014). *10 great examples of active design*. Online report. Retrieved from http://designcouncil.org.uk/news-opinion/10-great-examples-active-design.

Desmet, P., & Pohlmeyer, A. (2013). Positive design: An introduction to design for subjective well-being. *International Journal of Design* [Online], 7(3), 5–19.

Diener, E., & Chan, M. Y. (2011). Happy people live longer subjective well-being contributes to health and longevity. *Applied Psychology-Health and Well Being, 3*(1), 1–43.

Dolan, P., Peasgood, T., & White, M. (2008). Do we really know what makes us happy? A review of the economic literature on the factors associated with subjective well-being. *Journal of Economic Psychology, 29*, 94–122.

Douglas, C. H., & Douglas, M. R. (2005). Patient-centred improvements in health-care built environments: perspectives and design indicators. *Health Expectations, 8*, 264–276.

Driessen, M., & Hooftman, W. (2011). More employed develop burnout symptoms. *CBS Webmagazine*. Retrieved October 25, 2011, from https://cbs.nl/en-gb/news/2011/43/more-employed-develop-burnout-symptoms

Fogg, B.J. (2003). *Persuasive technology: Using computers to change what we think and do*. San Francisco: Morgan Kaufmann.

Folkman, S., & Lazarus, R. S. (1988). The relationship between coping and emotion: Implications for theory and research. *Social Science & Medicine, 26*(3), 309–317.

Folkman, S., & Moskowitz, J. T. (2000). Positive affect and the other side of coping. *American Psychologist, 55*(6), 647.

Gable, S. L., & Haidt, J. (2005). What (and why) is positive psychology? *Review of General Psychology, 9*(2), 103–110.

Gabriel, M., Faulkner, D., & Stirling, C. (2015). *Housing Priorities of People With Dementia: Security, Continuity and Support*. AHURI Final Report No. 242. Melbourne: AHURI.

Hagger, M. S., Anderson, M., Kyriakaki, M., & Darkings, S. (2007). Aspects of identity and their influence on intentional behavior: Comparing effects for three health behaviors. *Personality and Individual Differences, 42*(2), 355–367.

Heywood, F. (2005). Adaptation: Altering the house to restore the home. *Housing Studies, 20*(4), 531–547. doi:10.1080/02673030500114409

Hoogduin, C., Schaap, C., Methorst, G., Peters van Neyenhof, C., & Van de Griendt, J. (2001). Burnout, klinisch beeld en diagnostiek [Burnout: Symptomatology and assessment]. In P C. Hoogduin, W. Schaufeli, C. Schaap, & A. Bakker (Eds.), *Behandelingsstrategie ën bij burnout* (pp. 13–20). Houten: Bohn Stafleu van Loghum.

Howell, R. T., Kern, M. L., & Lyubomirsky, S. (2007). Health benefits: Meta-analytically determining the impact of well-being on objective health outcomes. *Health Psychology Review, 1*, 83–136.

Huber, M., Knottnerus, A. J., Green, L., Horst, H. van der, Jadad, A. R., Kromhout, D. et al. (2011). How should we define health? *BMJ, 343*: d4163.

Kaplan, S. (1995). The restorative benefits of nature: Toward an integrated framework. *Journal of Environmental Psychology, 15*(3), 169–182.

Lamers, S. M. A., Bolier, L., Westerhof, G. J., Smit, F., & Bohlmeijer, E. T. (2012). The impact of emotional well-being on long-term recovery and survival in physical illness: A meta-analysis. *Journal of Behavioral Medicine, 35*(5), 538–547.

Lee, M., Kiesler, S., & Forlizzi, J. (2011). Mining behavioral economics to design persuasive technology for healthy choices. In *CHI '11 Proceedings of the SIGCHI Conference on Human Factors in Computing Systems* (pp. 325–334). New York: ACM.

Leigh, S., & Flatt, S. (2015). App-based psychological interventions: Friend or foe? *Evidence Based Mental Health, 18*(4), 97–99.

Ludden, G. D. S., & Meekhof, L. (2016) Slowing down: Introducing calm persuasive technology to increase wellbeing at work. *OZCHI '16, ACM,* Launceston, Tasmania, 28 November–2 December.

Ludden, G. D. S., & Offringa, M. (2015). Triggers in the environment. Increasing reach of behavior change support systems by connecting to the offline world. *Proceedings of Persuasive Technology,* Chicago, June 4–5.

Ludden, G. D. S., van Rompay, T. J. L., Kelders, S. M., & van Gemert-Pijnen, J. E. W. C. (2015). How to increase reach and adherence of web-based interventions: A design research viewpoint. *Journal of Medical Internet Research, 17*(7): e172.

Lyubomirsky, S. (2008). *The how of happiness: A scientific approach to getting the life you want.* New York: Penguin Press.

Mackrill, J. B., Jennings, P. A., & Cain, R. (2013). Improving the hospital 'soundscape': A framework to measure individual perceptual response to hospital sounds. *Ergonomics, 56,* 1687–1697.

Marquardt, G., Bueter, K., & Motzek, T. (2014). Impact of the design of the built environment on people with dementia: an evidence-based review. *HERD, 8*(1), 127–157.

Marquardt, G., Johnston, D., Black, B. S., Morrison, A., Rosenblatt, A., Lyketsos, C. G., & Samus, Q. M. (2011). A descriptive study of home modifications for people with dementia and barriers to implementation. *Journal of Housing for the Elderly, 25*(3), 258–273.

Mathers, C. D., & Loncar, D. (2006). Projections of global mortality and burden of disease from 2002 to 2030. *Plos Med, 3*(11), e442.

NHS Forest (2014). Retrieved from http://nhsforest.org.

Niedderer, K. (2013). Mindful design as a driver for social behaviour change. In *Proceedings of the IASDR Conference 2013,* Tokyo, Japan.

Niedderer, K., Mackrill, J., Clune, S., Lockton, D., Ludden, G., Morris, A., Cain, R., Gardiner, E., Gutteridge, R., Evans, M., & Hekkert, P. (2014). *Creating sustainable innovation through design for behaviour change: Full report.* Wolverhampton: University of Wolverhampton, Project Partners & AHRC.

Oinas-Kukkonen, H., & Harjumaa, M. (2009). Persuasive systems design: Key issues, process model, and system features. *Communications of the Association for Information Systems, 24*(1), 485–500.

Pohlmeyer, A. E. (2012). Design for happiness. *Interfaces, 92,* 8–11.

Pollock, A., & Fuggle, L. (2013). Designing for dementia: Creating a therapeutic environment. *Nursing & Residential Care, 15*(6), 438–442. Retrieved from http://search.ebscohost.com/login.aspx?direct=true&db=cin20&AN=2012123472&site=ehost-live

Pucher, J., & Buehler, R. (2007). At the frontiers of cycling: Policy innovations in the Netherlands, Denmark, and Germany. *World Transport Policy and Practice,* December 2007.

Seligman, M. E. P. (2011). *Flourish: A visionary new understanding of happiness and well-being.* New York: Free Press.

Siepel, A., van der Zwaag, M., & Ludden, G. D. S. (2015). *Bright light therapy in de thuisomgeving, implicaties voor interactie.* Presented at Supporting Health by Tech Conference VI, The Netherlands. Retrieved from www.utwente.nl/bms/supporting-ehealth/files/Presentaties/presentatie-anika-siepel-supporting-health-by-technology.pdf (full manuscript in English forthcoming).

Steptoe, A., Wardle, J., & Marmot, M. (2005). Positive affect and health-related neuroendocrine, cardiovascular, and inflammatory processes. *PNAS, 102*(18), 6508–6512.

Ulrich, R. (1984). View through a window may influence recovery. *Science, 224*(4647), 224–225.

Ulrich, R. S., Simons, R. F., Losito, B. D., Fiorito, E., Miles, M. A., & Zelson, M. (1991). Stress recovery during exposure to natural and urban environments. *Journal of Environmental Psychology, 11*(3), 201–230.

Ulrich, R. S., Zimring, C., Joseph, A., Quan, X., & Choudhary, R. (2004). *The role of the physical environment in the hospital of the 21st century: A once-in-a-lifetime opportunity.* Concord, CA: The Center for Health Design.

van Dulmen, S., Sluijs, E., van Dijk, L., de Ridder, D., Heerdink, R., & Bensing, J. (2007). Patient adherence to medical treatment: a review of reviews. *BMC Health Serv. Res., 7*, 55. doi:10.1186/1472-6963-7-55.

Visch, V. T., de Wit, M., Dinh, L., vandenBrule, D., Melles, M., & Sonneveld, M. H. (2011). Industrial design meets mental healthcare: designing therapy-enhancing products involving game-elements for mental healthcare – three case studies. *IEEE Proceedings of SEGAH Serious Games and Applications for Health*, Braga, 184–189.

WHO. (2006) *Constitution of the World Health Organization.* Retrieved from www.who.int/governance/eb/who_constitution_en.pdf

Wong-Rieger, D., & Rieger, F. (2013). Health coaching in diabetes: Empowering patients to self-manage. *Canadian Journal of Diabetes, 37*, 41–44.

17 Designing for behavioural safety

Andrew Morris and Graham Hancox

Introduction

Safety in general is defined as "The state of being protected from or guarded against hurt or injury; freedom from danger" (Oxford English Dictionary, 2016) whilst behavioural safety describes a behaviour that is directly related to increasing safety such as wearing a crash or safety helmet or driving in a responsible manner. Safety has become an increasingly essential feature of modern society, particularly as so many accidents which cause injuries are caused by the human operator; for example, the US National Highway Traffic Safety Administration (NHTSA, 2016) reported that 94% of traffic accidents are caused by human error. Given that this applies much more widely, it is recognized that there is an explicit need for safety design in many everyday situations. Irrespective of where and what we design, safety should be an integral part of the design process. We therefore need to understand what constitutes safe design and then adapt everyday procedures – and more importantly the behaviours of those engaging in the processes in response to those procedures – to make safety more instinctive. Design must consider safety over the whole product lifecycle, from inception, to development, implementation, commissioning, operation and maintenance, and if relevant, eventual decommissioning and disposal. The principle of Designing for Safety should also apply across a broad spectrum of different scenarios including occupational safety (particularly in work and industrial environments), healthcare (e.g. hospital environments), transport and, perhaps most importantly, the domestic environment.

In the industrial context, Grinle et al. (2000) noted that there have been two main routes to changing behaviour to a safer level in the workplace: engineering and behavioural interventions. The engineering perspective has also been termed Safety Engineering and involves the fitment of rails, guards and personal protective equipment to reduce the hazards prevalent in the industrial environment. Grinle et al. noted that the main disadvantages of this method include the time, resources and capital required to identify and then mitigate every possible hazardous condition within the environments. This would be particularly problematic for the Small to Medium Enterprises (SMEs) who are unlikely to have the necessary capital to conduct such reviews and interventions. This approach also has the drawback of not expressly developing a safety culture but instead possibly nurturing an over-reliance on safety systems. In turn, this could lead to accidents as a result of unsafe areas which are presumed to be safe, because they have not been identified and mitigated, e.g. through barriers or guards. Finally, any safety design or barrier put in place could potentially be circumvented or mitigated – intentionally or otherwise – thus vastly reducing the effectiveness of such interventions.

Table 17.1 Summary of different theories, concepts and applications of behaviour change

Concept/Theory	Author	Application
Safety Engineering	Grinle et al. (2000)	Rails, guards, protective equipment within the manufacturing environment
Theory of planned behaviour	Ajzen (1985)	Encouraging parents to pack healthy foods into children's lunch-boxes
Health Belief	Hochbaum (1958)	Prediction of health-related behaviours, particularly in regard to the uptake of health services.
Stages of Change	Prochaska and DiClemente (1983)	Prevention of musculoskeletal disorders in the occupational environment
Motivational Interventions	Sigurdsson et al. (2012)	Incentivized interventions for workstation use
Choice Architecture	Thaler and Sunstein (2008)	Washing machine/spin-dryer that cannot be opened until function is complete
Health and Safety by Design	Office of Rail Regulation (ORR) (2016)	Closure of the rail network for safe maintenance operations; safety of construction sites
Design with Intent	Lockton et. al. (2010)	Traffic calming measures to slow vehicle speeds
Mindful Design	Niedderer (2013)	Shared space road design

In the following, the chapter first looks at principles of designing for safety more generally before it focuses specifically on designing for behavioural safety. The discussion is supported by references to underpinning theories and by a number of examples and case studies. Specifically, the numerous concepts and theories that are under discussion here are summarized in Table 17.1, together with the authors and examples of how the theories have been applied in real-world situations.

Design for Safety and design for behavioural safety

The concept of 'Design for Behavioural Safety' can be considered as an approach that encourages safer products, environments and behaviours. It brings together the collective skills of designers and safety professionals who may have differing perspectives – for safety professionals, the prevention of injuries and fatalities may be their main function whilst designers typically are tasked with effectively creating processes, products and facilities.

The concept can be seen to have at least two different approaches.

First, it can refer to responsible professionals within a given situation or an organization to eradicate safety risks through design during any design development process. This means there is an attempt to design out risks at source so that there is actually no need to change people's behaviour and practices. We refer to this approach here as 'Design for Safety'. This approach recognizes that along with a number of other important parameters including purpose, usability, quality and cost, safety should be determined during the design stage.

Historically this hasn't always been the case. An example of how the principle of Design for Safety works can clearly be demonstrated by studying the evolution of vehicle design. In Figure 17.1, which shows a stylish Lotus 7, it can be seen that the vehicle contains many

Figure 17.1 Interior driver environment of Lotus 7

unforgiving surfaces. These include sharp edges on the dash and a thin-rimmed steering wheel with a somewhat prominent feature on the centre of the wheel, each of which could be highly likely to cause injury to the driver in the event of an accident.

When this is compared to modern-day cars such as the one in Figure 17.2, it is evident that injuries are much less likely in the modern design – the steering wheel is designed to be much less hostile in the event of an accident and an airbag is also present within the steering-wheel hub which will offer enhanced protection in an accident scenario.

Such safety features are examples of exactly what Design for Safety aims to achieve; it involves an understanding of the potential hazards that a product introduces and determines a way to minimize potential consequences in the event of an accident or misuse. Therefore, in the earlier example, design engineers and manufactures in the vehicle manufacturing industry are preventing injuries by considering the hazard of the car crashing early in the design process. In many ways, this is similar to the concept of the Choice Architecture approach (Thaler & Sunstein, 2008) in that the safety of the operator is considered in the technological functioning of the product; for example, certain everyday items (washing machine, spin-dryer, microwave etc.) cannot be opened when they are operating in order to prevent injury. Thus the chance of harm is reduced by modifying the architecture or environment of the feature. In other words, this is one end of the behavioural change spectrum that shifts the context.

'Choice Architecture' is therefore a process used to describe the way in which decisions may be influenced by how the choices are presented. This term essentially refers to the

Figure 17.2 Interior driver environment of modern vehicle design

practice of influencing choice by changing the manner in which options are presented to people. For example, this can be done by setting defaults, framing, or adding decoy options. Choice architecture often involves a 'nudge' (as opposed to some other intervention) that alters people's behaviour in a predictable way without forbidding any options or significantly changing their economic incentives (Quigley, 2013). Choice Architecture simply refers to the context in which we choose and make decisions, but this is important because the context itself can influence the way we think and the decisions we make. Thus, where our behaviour *changes* due to some aspect of the choice architecture which surrounds us, we can be said to have been 'nudged'.

In addition to the design process itself, 'Design for Safety' should also be considered an important, if not essential feature of any institutional practice, particularly where there is a previous history of unsafe habits. This might include occupational situations as well as numerous everyday social settings: for example, in the domestic environment to ensure child safety or in healthcare situations where patient safety is paramount. In these contexts, the concept of designing for safety can be considered to include the design of facilities, processes and products in a way that minimizes hazards and risks to the people who will use them.

As an example of patient safety, in 2003, the UK Department of Health acknowledged that the use of design in many safety-critical industries had produced significant improvements in safety, quality and efficiency and recommended that a similar approach was now needed within the healthcare industry. As every year, more than 900 million items are dispensed in hospitals, community pharmacies and, in some doctors' surgeries in England and Wales, it was recognized that potential harm could occur from medicines if patients were not able to easily identify their medicine, or could not work out how to use it safely and effectively and could not readily identify any special precautions required. As the majority of medicines are dispensed for older people or people with long-term medical conditions including mental, sensory and physical disabilities, a re-think of the design on dispensing methodology was undertaken to ensure that important information on the dispensing label was presented as legibly as possible. This led to recommendations for a redesign of the dispensing label so that it could not obscure important information on the commercial medicine pack, including the braille labelling intended for patients with poor vision (National Institute of Health Research, 2007).

The second approach to design for behavioural safety seeks to change people's behaviour from involving in actions that are largely unsafe, to actions which are less likely to be associated with risk of harm. This also includes guiding people in a certain way (i.e. changing their behaviour) to either establish or maintain personal safety indirectly through design. For example, in the early 1990s, Conoco introduced STOP (Safety Training Observation Programme) on a number of their gas production platforms in the Southern North Sea (Fleming & Lardner, 2001). STOP was designed to encourage safety observations and conversations at the worksite, and allowed the identification and correction of unsafe trends in behaviour or working conditions. Training and supervisor-led coaching was used to introduce employees to the five-step STOP "safety observation cycle", which involved the following:

1. **Decide** to make observations;
2. **Stop** or pause during other work, to make time for observations;
3. **Observe** people at work, and working conditions to identify unsafe behaviour or conditions;
4. **Act** on observations, for example speaking to a colleague observed working safely or unsafely, and providing encouragement or taking corrective action, as required;
5. **Report** observations and corrective actions on using a pocket-sized STOP card, which was then handed to a supervisor for review, collation and any further action required.

The remainder of this chapter will focus specifically on the second meaning described above, i.e. on how design can either directly or indirectly lead to behavioural modifications which ultimately affect safety. In other words, it will look at how we should consider designing for behavioural safety as being an important aspect of everyday social and occupational functioning across a range of situations.

Design for behavioural safety

In practice, it is not always easy explicitly to Design for Safety, particularly where risk is uncertain or actions of individuals are unpredictable. Therefore it is useful to try to affect or change behaviour so that essentially people act in a manner that is intrinsically and predictably safe for a given situation or scenario.

Principles and background theories of designing for behavioural safety

There are some general principles to designing for safer behaviour: first, behaviour should be guided so that it operates within the limitations of a particular system so that individuals do not or cannot exceed those limitations. Second, changing behaviour should not be seen as a quick-fix to improving overall safety performance. Behaviour modification strategies should ideally be introduced gradually and should be targeted at specific requirements. Third, interventions that are introduced to secure a more general behaviour change result or are targeted at individuals without taking into account technological, social and environmental influences are unlikely to work. For example, advising motorists to slow down in certain areas for 'safety reasons' is usually insufficient without helping individuals to understand the social (and often catastrophic) consequences of what might happen if they did not.

In order to understand these concepts better, it is worth considering how the principles of designing for behavioural safety fit within theoretical frameworks of behaviour change. Behaviour change has become relatively prevalent in general theories of behaviour, and models are largely based on the socio-psychological literature. Such theories encompass a wide range of psychological, social, societal and contextual factors including emotions, habits and routines. The theories of change support interventions by describing how behaviours develop and change over time. Behavioural models are designed to help us understand behaviour and identify the underlying factors that influence it. Therefore an understanding of both aspects is needed in order to develop effective intervention strategies.

Some early theoretical models of behaviour change have much relevance to modern approaches to designing for behaviour change and they are now discussed with regard to their applicability and relevance to behavioural safety.

First, the theory of planned behaviour (TPB) is perhaps one of the most widely cited and applied behaviour theories and is one of a closely inter-related family of theories which adopt a cognitive approach to explaining behaviour which focusses on individuals' attitudes and beliefs. The TPB (Ajzen, 1985, 1991; Ajzen & Madden, 1986) evolved from the theory of reasoned action (Fishbein & Ajzen, 1975) which proposed that intention to act was the best predictor of behaviour. In the safety domain, the Theory of Planned Behaviour probably has limited applicability overall but is does provide the foundation for subsequent models of behavioural change. For example, the Health Belief Model (HBM – Hochbaum, 1958; Rosenstock, 1966; Janz & Becker, 1984; Sharma & Romas, 2012) is a cognitive model which supposes that behaviour is determined by a number of beliefs about threats to an individual's well-being and the effectiveness and outcomes of particular actions or behaviours. Some constructs of the model feature the concept of self-efficacy (Bandura, 1997) alongside these beliefs about actions. Perceived threat is at the core of the HBM as it is linked to a person's 'readiness' to take action and perceived benefits associated with a behaviour (i.e. likely effectiveness in reducing the threat). This can be weighed against the perceived costs of, and negative consequences that may result from, the behaviour (perceived barriers) – such as the side effects of treatment – to establish the overall extent to which a behaviour is beneficial. As with the Theory of Planned Behaviour model, the applicability of the HBM to safety in the industrial environment is somewhat limited although it could well be applied in other situations where safety is imperative, such as the domestic environment.

The Stages of Change (SoC) model (also referred to as the Trans-theoretical Model) (Prochaska & DiClemente, 1983; Prochaska et al., 1992) is a widely applied cognitive model which sub-divides individuals between five categories that represent different milestones, or 'levels of motivational readiness' (Heimlich & Ardoin, 2008), along a continuum of behaviour change. These stages are (i) pre-contemplation, (ii) contemplation, (iii) preparation, (iv) action and (v) maintenance. First developed in relation to smoking (and now commonly applied to other addictive behaviours), the rationale behind using a staged model is that individuals at the same stage should face similar problems and barriers, and thus can be helped by the same type of intervention (Nisbet & Gick, 2008). Whilst practitioners acknowledge many hundreds of different interventions, the SoC model identifies a key number of 'processes' which are most widely used and investigated.

The three models (TPB, HBM, SoC) just described certainly help to explain how behavioural change occurs although their relevance to designing for behavioural safety could be considered as somewhat tenuous. Nevertheless, they do provide a basis for understanding how human behaviour can be altered and therefore illustrate how it is necessary to consider both behavioural theories and design approaches when developing successful interventions that will encourage safer behaviour. What is required is to understand the link between behaviour and design more comprehensively.

The need for a systemic approach to designing for behavioural safety

In relation to the models earlier described, Anderson (2003) observes an increase in the use of behaviour modification approaches to designing for safety. Such modifications generally involve the observation and assessment of certain behaviours of 'frontline personnel' in an industrial context. The rationale behind design for behavioural safety approaches within industry is that accidents are caused by unsafe behaviours and that by modifying the behaviour, changes in safety will eventuate. Such approaches, whilst loosely based on the behaviourist theories already described could be summarized by the statement 'behaviour that is strongly reinforced will be maintained'. There are reports of some successes with such behaviour modification in a range of industrial and commercial environments as well as in everyday scenarios. These approaches have a number of advantages in addition to reducing incidents, including increased communication about safety, management visibility and employee engagement. Whilst such approaches are not necessarily based on what are now recognized Behaviour Change theories, they do illustrate how strategic behavioural change can effectively improve safety. Using the offshore industry (Fleming & Lardner, 2001) again as an example, Time Out For Safety (TOFS) was another technique developed on BP Amoco's Andrew Platform, which is located in the North Sea. TOFS was designed to encourage all Platform employees to stop any operation if they were unsure about anything or had concerns about safety. It also aimed to encourage employees to take more ownership for their own and others' safety. TOFS was adopted by the entire Andrew Platform six months after platform commissioning and a distinctive feature was its simplicity. The technique provided team members with a mechanism to stop any operation if they were uncertain about anything or had safety concerns. Employees 'called a TOFS' by making a 'T' sign with their hands and this signal was particularly necessary in noisy environments where it could be difficult to hear colleagues. The technique provided a medium to promote this positive behaviour and made it clear that employees were able and in fact expected to stop a job if they felt this was necessary. Supervisors and managers encouraged frontline staff to call a TOFS by reacting positively and leading by example – on occasions, senior management demonstrated their commitment to TOFS by shutting down the platform for a TOFS.

Continuing with the application of designing for behavioural safety theory, it is thought that not only are many accidents caused by human error as stated earlier, but that up to 90% of all accidents are triggered by unsafe behaviours which tend to interact with other negative features that are evident within a particular system. More often than not, the unsafe behaviour maybe the final action that is needed to cause a failure within the system even though there may have been many other components of the system that had been far from perfect for days, weeks or even years (Heinrich, 1959; Reason, 1990). For example, company operational procedures, equipment maintenance and training of staff, to name three aspects, may in some cases all have been deficient for many years prompting an untrained member of staff to eventually perform an unsafe action leading to an accident. Whilst the unsafe action may have ultimately and directly caused the accident, it is easy to see how the other operational deficiencies within the system would have played their part in this action. So there are concerns that traditional design for behavioural safety approaches applied in industrial contexts could focus simply on the operators, as observed by Anderson (2003). Whilst as many as 90% of accidents may be caused by 'human error', company management often see the 'human' in the term human error as referring to the 'operators' whereas the actual problem may in fact lie within the company mind-set. Focussing on individual operators (i) ignores the latent conditions (the operational aspects described above) that may underpin accidents all along; and (ii) implies that accidents can be prevented simply by operators taking more care. As Anderson maintains, for a design for behavioural safety programme to be successful, it must of course identify at-risk behaviours and then observe them with the aim of encouraging safe behaviours and removing unsafe ones. However, as operational and management decisions can often be excluded from design for behavioural safety approaches it is essential that there is a visible management of safety and that there is a high level of trust between management and employees. Otherwise, any management decision to initiate a behavioural approach to encourage safer behaviour may itself be flawed.

Applications of design for behavioural safety: preventing work-related musculoskeletal disorders

There are as yet few studies which directly look into how design leads to behavioural safety changes in the occupational health and safety domain. Furthermore, there are factors which can influence adoption of a particular design and, in turn, influence how effective that design is in promoting safety once it has been produced or implemented. Some application of theoretical models of design for behavioural safety, such as those described in previous sections, are however evident within the research literature.

For example, Whysall et al. (2004) examined a number of strategies designed to reduce the incidence of work-related musculoskeletal disorders (MSD) in a number of organizations. They found that most organizations focused heavily on the physical aspects of work such as force, posture, cycle time, workstation layout and so on. They also found that, although organizations were generally receptive to such advice aimed at reducing the risks which lead to MSD, the effectiveness of the advice in reducing actual numbers of employees suffering from MSD depended on the organizations accepting and implementing the measures recommended, involving changes of both individual and collective behaviour. They used the example of (safer) 'Stages of (Behaviour) Change' theory (Prochaska & DiClemente, 1983; Prochaska et al., 1992 as listed earlier) to explain this by commenting that if behaviour change is to take place in this regard, recipients needed to hold positive attitudes and beliefs relating to the desirable behaviour if efforts to effectively achieve change were to be successful. Another factor identified in the study concerned the lack of post-project follow-up to assess the effectiveness of the MSD reduction strategies. This led to uncertainty as to the extent to which certain interventions were effective.

In an attempt to address the lack of post-project follow-up in their first study (Whysall et al., 2004), two years later Whysall et al. (2006) again utilized the Stages of Change model (Prochaska & DiClemente, 1983, described earlier) for MSD prevention. However, this time, they evaluated the effectiveness of various interventions at a number of stages following the original intervention. There was an initial evaluation at six months' post-intervention and then follow-up research including repeated evaluations at 15 months and at 20 months' post-intervention. The organizational and worker surveys used comprised three sections including the following:

- Demographic characteristics and background information (e.g. size of company, role of respondent, tenure)
- Stage of change assessment
- Attitudes toward reducing MSDs.

The worker survey included additional sections:

- Musculoskeletal discomfort experienced in the previous seven days
- Discomfort rating.

The findings of the study were that targeted organizational interventions that were introduced according to the workers' 'stage of change' indeed resulted in significant reductions in MSD, as opposed to workers who followed standard interventions where no reductions in MSD were found. Within the Stages of Change model, the phases include pre-contemplation (resistance to recognizing or modifying problem behaviour); contemplation (recognition of the problem, thinking about changing, but not ready to act); preparation (intending to change in the next 30 days, and/or having made specific plans to do so); action (having engaged in behaviour change, no longer than six months ago) and maintenance (initiated changes over six months ago, working to consolidate gains made and avoid relapse). Prior to the implementation of the interventions, the majority of workers in the tailored intervention condition were in the pre-contemplation and preparation stages (36% and 41%). At 20 months' post-intervention the majority were in maintenance (33%). The study supported the view that scope exists for improving interventions, at least for MSD, by targeting advice according to the 'Stages of Change' model.

Some of the current literature relating to the theoretical work on avoidance of MSD either through application of the Theory of Planned Behaviour or the Health Belief Model suggests that an improved design alone (for example, a new IT workstation) is not enough to cause behaviour change or affect safety. To counteract this, some effective methods for initiating or helping to develop this change of behaviour have been proposed. One such example is from a recent study by Robertson et al. (2013) amongst workers in two separate groups: (i) those who were trained in safe behaviours for sitting and standing when using workstations and (ii) those who were not. Those who were trained were observed to follow the safety guidelines more often than those who were minimally trained. Furthermore the trained group also reported significantly lower amounts of discomfort and MSD across the 15 days of testing. According to these findings, appropriate design along with training on how to effectively use the design can lead to a behavioural change towards safer working practices.

The study could suggest that training can be at the heart of a behavioural change programme and that design is relatively unimportant. However, other recent research is not in agreement with this finding, instead suggesting that training alone is not sufficient to effectively alter behaviour to be more in line with recognized safe practices. There are suggestions that other methods are further required to bring about the desired change. One such method suggested by Sigurdsson et al. (2012) was the use of Motivational Interventions. Their study involved training workers in how to optimally set up and use their keyboard for safe operation. The participants were separated into two groups: those who received vouchers as incentives if they were observed to be using their keyboard with a negative tilt, as instructed; and those who received no incentive at all. It was found that those who were incentivized applied the best-practice rules when using their keyboard whereas those who were not incentivized made no alterations to its position following the training course. Furthermore, after the discontinuation of incentives, two out of three of the participants continued to use the keyboard in its optimal position. This suggests that incentives may have a lasting effect on safe behaviour even after the incentives have ceased, although this may be rather because it allows people to get into the habit of the correct usage rather than because of any motivation related to the voucher at this stage. This study finds not only that design alone is not enough to change behaviour (most keyboards have the ability of negative tilt but few people use it) but training in a design's proper usage may still not be sufficient to alter individual behaviour. In turn, this would suggest that it is most effective if a design intervention and a behavioural intervention are applied together, while in isolation they are not sufficient to invoke a sustainable change in behaviour.

In a similar vein, Yu et al. (2013) conducted a study to establish whether designing a system which gave feedback on maintaining a safe-seated postural performance could influence the extent to which participants altered their behaviour when seated. A chair was designed which automatically monitored performance with regard to best-practice guidelines and either gave: (i) no feedback; (ii) immediate feedback – whereby a pop-up appeared on their computer informing them of their poor posture or (iii) delayed feedback where feedback on their posture was given by a pop-up at the end of each test session. It was found that both feedback conditions led to improvements in seated posture compared to the no feedback condition. The immediate feedback condition was also found to be more effective in encouraging participants to maintain a safe posture compared to the delayed feedback condition. A similar study by Sigurdsson and Austin (2008) supported these findings and also found lasting effects on maintaining a safe posture even when the level of feedback on performance was reduced. These provide further evidence of the need to support a design intervention with either training or explanation of what is expected when a design intervention is introduced.

All of these studies are important as they suggest that not only is feedback essential for changing behaviour but also that a design which incorporates this feedback can be a particularly effective mechanism to initiating the desired behaviour change and may even lead to prolonged results even when the feedback has been reduced or removed. Furthermore, if the intervention is supported by formal training as well as feedback, then the intervention may yield the most desirable and sustainable results of all approaches.

Applications of design for behavioural safety: risk prevention in the construction industry

Perhaps some of the clearest examples of how design can influence behavioural safety can be found within the construction industry and there are several published studies which examine this in practice. The UK construction industry has attempted to improve the safety of its workers and reduce the number of accidents and deaths within it for many years (Hartley & Cheyne, 2010). Interventions and initiatives have tackled various aspects of risk, ranging through design, elimination, protective equipment and behaviour. However, the construction industry is still dangerous, accounting for typically around 30% of fatal injuries to employees and 10% of reported major/specified injuries. In Hartley and Cheyne's study, a number of visual cues which helped to encourage safe behaviour were identified repeatedly, including housekeeping, pedestrian walkways, safety signs, personal protective equipment (PPE) usage and the behaviour of people already on site. Influences on behaviour were discussed through focus groups involving those working on-site. 'First impressions' were thought to impact on risk-taking behaviour amongst the workers on the construction sites by the workers adopting the best safety practices through these initial observations.

Such findings relating to construction sites have potential implications for the general management of safety within the construction industry. They establish the importance of creating an impression of a high level of safety culture at all times. Based on the increased risk of injury and death within the industry, the Health and Safety Executive (HSE, 2012) described the concept of 'Safe by Design' which involves the integration of hazard identification and risk assessment methods early in the design process to eliminate or minimize the risks of injury throughout the life of the building or structure being designed. This includes construction, use, maintenance and demolition. It encompasses all design including facilities, hardware, systems, equipment, products, tooling, materials, energy, controls, layout and configuration. The 'Safe by Design' approach begins in the conceptual and planning phases with an emphasis on making choices about design, materials used and methods of manufacture or construction to enhance the safety of the finished product. Ultimately, the Safe by Design concept is a clear example of designing for behavioural safety.

Following the HSE's lead, numerous organizations now recognize and actively use the principles of 'Safe by Design' within the working environment. The construction industry in particular is one obvious key stakeholder in this regard but a further clear example of implementation of the general principles of 'Safe by Design' can also be found within the UK's Network Rail (The Rail Engineer, 2012). Within railway operations, closure of the railway network for carrying out work is costly and therefore work carried out in such circumstances normally has strict time constraints. Detailed planning is therefore required to ensure that 'hand-back' of the railway infrastructure can be safely achieved. Under such conditions 'Safe by Design' is critical when assessing all aspects of the work to be undertaken. Safety systems for personnel and materials handling must be considered and incorporated into all work designs and those planning the work must consider whether or not a safe system of work can be established that allows the railway to continue running. If a safe and practicable system cannot be identified, then work may need to be undertaken by shutting down the railway network which is costly and creates poor public relations between the industry and the customer.

Applications of design for behavioural safety: enhancing road safety

Another example of design for behavioural safety was described by Lockton et al. (2010) in their model of 'Design with Intent' (DwI). Within this concept, Lockton et al. propose that certain designs are intended to influence or result in certain user behaviour including crossing the road at designated locations (Figure 17.3). The starting point of the DwI

Figure 17.3 Pedestrian crossing facility

method is the existence of a product, service or environment – a *system* – where users' behaviour is important to its operation, or where it would be strategically desirable to alter the way it is used. The goal of the design process is to modify or redesign the system to achieve this: in other words, to influence the users' behaviour towards a particular 'target behaviour'. Lockton et al. also reviewed examples from a variety of disciplines and, whilst many of them relate to changes to encourage sustainable design, there are some obvious safety-related examples. For example, in road safety, several 'traffic calming' measures (Figure 17.4) built into the road environment can be thought of as 'Design with Intent' since the principle of the design concept is to slow the traffic down (thereby changing driver behaviour towards safety) particularly in a built-up environment. Other road safety measures include pedestrian crossing facilities where the road-users are prevented from crossing the road at undesirable locations through the use of guard-rails and barriers.

The concept of 'Mindfulness' is another example where the ultimate goal is behavioural safety achieved through design interventions, especially in social contexts (Niedderer, 2013). It proposes that the benefit of 'mindful' design is its ability to shift the focus from an external to internal 'locus of control'. The latter enables conscious decision-making and commitment in the individual as an essential basis for attitude change and for lasting behaviour change. To once more use road-user behaviour as an example, the principle of 'shared space' in road design could be conceptualized in terms of 'mindful' design within behavioural safety since it supposes that the road-users will take responsibility for both their own safety and also that of other road-users when using a particular road junction. In 'shared space' environments (Figure 17.5), the control of the road manoeuvre is entirely

Figure 17.4 Traffic calming

Figure 17.5 Shared space road design

determined by the actions of the road-users rather than being controlled by conventional traffic engineering measures such as signage, road-markings and signals. This creates a radical behaviour change forcing the users to proceed with much greater caution within a shared space intersection compared to a conventional intersection as the users are 'mindfully' aware that all other road-users are in a similar 'uncontrolled' situation.

Summary

Overall this review has found that the research area of how design can lead to behaviour change in a safety environment is at this point not a mature research area. There is still a lot that can be explored and that needs to be tested to further aid insight. The current review started by giving an overview of several theories of design for behaviour change which helped to initially establish the foundations on which the research area is built. Current literature shows how design can lead to change in behaviour in the safety domain (Grinle et al., 2000 and Wirth & Sigurdsson, 2008). The findings of the most appropriate studies were then reviewed and illustrated by the studies of Robertson et al. (2013), Hartley and Cheyne (2010), Rail Engineer (2012), Lockton (2010) and Niedderer (2013). Overall it appears that in order to implement effective behavioural changes in the safety domain it takes more than the simple installation of barriers or the implementation of new designs. Instead it involves a more holistic approach involving analyzing what stage an organization or an individual is at, in terms of its readiness for change, effective training in optimal safety practices followed by immediate feedback on performance and positive reinforcement of these practices. This will in turn lead to the most effective adoption of new and ultimately safer methods of thinking and behaving within an organization.

The review of theories, approaches and examples has shown that design for behavioural safety is an evolving landscape of work that utilizes many theories and debates. More 'traditional' theories tend to be distinct and sit within either the individual or contextual spaces. Adding design to these traditional approaches and new domains of use perhaps starts to lead to theories and approaches utilizing the middle ground, which is a more system-based approach where individual and contextual factors are not mutually exclusive.

The review indicates that in the event that a behaviour change in a given situation is desirable or necessary, it is probably not sufficient to try and invoke this through design alone. Rather, the literature suggests that a design intervention supported by feedback is the most effective approach to initiating the desired behaviour change and may even lead to prolonged results even when the feedback has been reduced or removed. Furthermore, in the event that the intervention can be supported by formal training as well as feedback, sustainable and desirable modifications to behaviour can eventuate. In isolation, neither feedback/training nor design are sufficient to invoke a long-lasting change in behaviour.

References

Ajzen, I. (1985). From intentions to actions: A theory of planned behavior. In J. Kuhl & J. Beckman (Eds.), *Action-control: From cognition to behavior* (pp. 11–39). Heidelberg, Germany: Springer.

Ajzen, I. (1991). The theory of planned behavior. *Organizational Behavior and Human Decision Processes*, *50*, 179–211.

Ajzen, I., & Madden, T. J. (1986). Prediction of goal-directed behavior: Attitudes, intentions, and perceived behavioral control. *Journal of Experimental Social Psychology*, *22*, 453–474.

Anderson, M. (2003). Human factors and COMAH: A regulator's perspective. 'Process Safety: Fulfilling Our Responsibilities'. *Conference proceedings, Hazards XVII Symposium*, Institute of Chemical Engineers, pp. 785–792.

Bandura, A. (1997). *Self-efficacy: The exercise of control*. New York: Freeman.

Fishbein, M., & Ajzen, I. (1975). *Belief, attitude, intention, and behavior: An introduction to theory and research*. Reading, MA: Addison-Wesley.

Flemming, M and Lardner, R. (2001). Behaviour Modifications Programme – Establishing Best Practice. Health and Safety Executive Publications, London, UK: Crown copyright 2001.

Grinle, A. C., Dickinson, A. M., & Boettcher, W. (2000). Behavioral safety research in manufacturing settings: A review of the literature. *Journal of Organizational Behavior Management, 20*(1), 29–68.

Hartley, R., & Cheyne, A. (2010). At first sight: Impressions of safety culture on construction sites. In C. Egbu (Ed.), *Proceedings of the 26th Annual ARCOM Conference*, 6–8 September 2010, Leeds, UK, Association of Researchers in Construction Management (pp. 213–222).

Health and Safety Executive. (2012) *Safe by design*. Retrieved from www.hse.gov.uk/construction/cdm/safety-by-design.pdf

Heimlich, J. E., & Ardoin, N. M. (2008). Understanding behavior to understand behavior change: A literature review. *Environmental Education Research, 14*(3), 215–237.

Heinrich, H.W. (1959). Industrial accident prevention: A scientific approach (4th ed.). Chicago: McGraw-Hill. *quoted in* Grimaldi, J.V., & Simonds, R. H. (1973). *Safety management* (p. 211). Homewood, IL: R. D. Irwin.

Hochbaum, G. M. (1958). *Public participation in medical screening programmes – a socio-psychological study*. Public Health Service Publication, No 572, Washington DC: General Publication Office.

Janz, N. K., & Becker, M. H. (1984). The health belief model: A decade later. *Health Education Behavior, 11*(1), 1–47.

Lockton, D., Harrison, D., & Stanton, N. (2010). The Design with Intent Method: A design tool for influencing user behaviour. *Applied Ergonomics, 41*(3), 382–392.

NHTSA. (2016). *NHTSA data shows traffic deaths up 7.7 percent in 2015*. Retrieved May 18, 2017, from https://nhtsa.gov/press-releases/nhtsa-data-shows-traffic-deaths-77-percent-2015

National Institute of Health Research. (2007). *Design for patient safety – A guide to the design of dispensed medicines*. The National Patient Safety Agency, UK. Retrieved 30 October 2016 from http://www.nrls.npsa.nhs.uk/resources/?EntryId45=59829.

Niedderer, K. (2013). Mindful design as a driver for social behaviour change. In *Proceedings of the IASDR Conference 2013*, Tokyo, Japan.

Nisbet, E. K., & Gick, M. L. (2008). Can health psychology help the planet? Applying theory and models of health behaviour to environmental actions. *Canadian Psychology, 49*, 296–303.

OED. (2016). Safety. Oxford English Dictionary Online. Oxford University Press. Online. URL: <http://dictionary.oed.com>.

Office of Rail Regulation. (2016). *Strategy for regulation of health and safety risks – Chapter 12: Health and safety by design*. Retrieved October 29, 2016, from http://orr.gov.uk/__data/assets/pdf_file/0009/21402/2016-03-18-New-Strategic-Chapter-12-Health-and-Safety-by-Design.pdf

Prochaska, J. O., & DiClemente, C. C. (1983). Stages and processes of self-change of smoking: Toward an integrative model of change. *Journal of Consulting and Clinical Psychology, 51*, 390–395.

Prochaska, J. O., DiClemente, C. C., & Norcross, J. C. (1992). In search of how people change: Applications to addictive behavior. *American Psychologist, 47*, 1102–1114.

Quigley, M. (2013). Nudging for health: On public policy and designing choice architecture. *Medical Law Review, 21*(4), 588–621.

Rail Engineer. (2012, June). Retrieved from www.railengineer.uk/2012/06/26/safety-by-design/

Reason, J. (1990). The contribution of latent human failures to the breakdown of complex systems. *Philosophical Transactions of the Royal Society of London. Series B, Biological Sciences, 327*(1241), 475–484. doi:10.1098/rstb.1990.0090

Robertson, M. M., Ciriello, V. M., & Garabet, A. M. (2013). Office ergonomics training and a sit-stand workstation: Effects on musculoskeletal and visual symptoms and performance of office workers. *Applied Ergonomics, 44*(1), 73–85.

Rosenstock, I. M. (1966, July). Why people use the heath service. *Milbank Memorial Fund Quarterly, 44*(3, Suppl), 94–127. PMID: 5967464.

Sharma, M., & Romas, J. (2012). *Theoretical foundations of health education and health promotion.* Sudbury, MA: Jones & Bartlett Learning.

Sigurdsson, S. O., Artnak, M., Needham, M., Wirth, O., & Silverman, K. (2012). Motivating ergonomic computer workstation setup: Sometimes training is not enough. *International Journal of Occupational Safety and Ergonomics-JOSE, 18*(1), 27.

Sigurdsson, S. O., & Austin, J. (2008). Using real-time visual feedback to improve posture at computer workstations. *Journal of Applied Behavior Analysis, 41*(3), 365–375.

Thaler, R., & Sunstein, C. R. (2008). *Nudge: Improving decisions about health, wealth, and happiness.* New Haven, CT: Yale University Press.

Whysall, Z., Haslam, C., & Haslam, R. (2006). A stage of change approach to reducing occupational ill health. *Preventive medicine, 43*(5), 422–428.

Whysall, Z., Haslam, R., & Haslam, C. (2004). Processes, barriers, and outcomes described by ergonomics consultants in preventing work-related musculoskeletal disorders. *Applied Ergonomics, 35*(4), 343–351.

Wirth, O., & Sigurdsson, S. O. (2008). When workplace safety depends on behavior change: Topics for behavioral safety research. *Journal of Safety Research, 39*(6), 589–598.

Yu, E., Moon, K., Oah, S., & Lee, Y. (2013). An evaluation of the effectiveness of an automated observation and feedback system on safe sitting postures. *Journal of Organizational Behavior Management, 33*(2), 104–127.

18 Is 'Nudge' as good as 'We Think' in designing against crime? Contrasting paternalistic and fraternalistic approaches to design for behaviour change

Lorraine Gamman and Adam Thorpe

Design for behaviour change and Design Against Crime

In the UK in 2015, 45% of adults who were sent to prison did not change their law-breaking behaviour and were reconvicted within one year of release (see Prison Reform Trust, 2015 who report that this figure rises to 58% for those adults serving sentences of under 12 months). Whilst the design of prisons and their experience of it may deliver short-term conformity amongst inmates, it fails to deliver long-term transformation of criminal behaviours for almost half of those that experience it. This may not be surprising given the tangle of difficulties facing ex-offenders as returning citizens on release, including addiction, employment, skills, housing, health, debt and relationship issues, all of which may challenge their emotional stability, decision-making and mental health. Thus, 'correction' of criminal behaviours through prison is effective less than half of the time, and alternative approaches are urgently needed – prevention rather than cure.

Design Against Crime (DAC) offers a different approach to crime prevention and behaviour change. Like other forms of health and safety design, DAC seeks to find new ways to modify the environment in which routine 'accidents' (or in this context 'crimes') take place by anticipating and designing against actions before they happen, so that they are prevented. It aims to achieve this by attempting to inhibit, deter or thwart criminal behaviours or, alternatively, to generate new types of behavioural responses that exclude crime. In short, Design Against Crime considers opportunities for use, misuse and abuse of products, environments and services to reduce criminogenic affordances (i.e. those which allow or promote crime) and thus reduce the likelihood of crime.

DAC draws on a number of approaches to modify behaviours and design out crime. Crime Prevention through Environmental Design (CPTED) originates from the writings of Oscar Newman (1972), C. Ray Jeffrey (1971) and Jane Jacobs (1961). Since then CPTED theory and practice has been updated by many authors including Armitage (2013), Knights et al. (2002), Cozens et al. (2005), Kitchen and Schneider(2007), Armitage and Monchuk (2009) and Ekblom (2011) to develop rules and procedures about management of physical space that aim to harden targets, manage or control access, increase surveillance and guardianship, promote maintenance and support social activity in the built environment to reduce crime and anti-social behaviour. DAC's approach also draws on Situational Crime Prevention (SCP) first outlined by Clarke (1983), which has been more successful in developing principles for behaviour change than CPTED. SCP draws on rational choice theory, routine activity theory and crime pattern theory (Clarke & Felson, 1993; Felson, 1994) that consider the offenders' ability to weigh up the risks and rewards of a given situation and the conjunction of key characteristics necessary for crime to occur. In doing so SCP addresses more than design for the built environment and has, led by Clarke (1997), produced rigorous evaluation of its effectiveness. SCP has consequently been applied to reduce many kinds of crimes, including robbery, burglary, shoplifting and vandalism. These principles and how to apply them in specific situational contexts have informed many problem-specific guides to help police, produced by the Centre for Problem-Oriented Policing (2016a). SCP is proven as a systematic approach to crime reduction, linked to the manipulation of the objects and systems of consumer society and their impact on behaviour. It is an approach that has informed crime prevention for almost 35 years. It acknowledges that crime happens and that some objects are 'criminogenic', contributing to the likelihood of criminal outcomes. Following this logic, designing out criminogenic objects reduces opportunities for crime, as explained by Felson and Clarke (1997) and more recently by Clarke and Newman (2013) and Ekblom (2012). Clarke's SCP techniques have grown from 12 in 1992 to 25 today (see Table 18.1, Centre for Problem-Oriented Policing, 2016b) and are fairly self-explanatory. They include overt physical and psychological 'prompts' that increase the effort and risk involved in crime and remove the rewards, provocations and excuses that allow crime and criminals to be effective, thus impacting on criminal behaviours. These techniques have been widely and internationally adopted by police to manage behaviour in order to prevent crime.

More recently, Lockton et al. (2010a) and (2010b) and Tromp et al. (2011) have described four basic principles for design for behaviour change that appear to replicate the principles applied with Clarke's 'situational techniques' (Clarke, 1992) applying a descriptive language, more familiar to design (Table 18.2).

Behaviour change interventions are complex when linked to Design Against Crime: understanding the causality between crime situations, human behaviours and criminal outcomes; hypothesizing how design interventions might disrupt this causality; designing interventions that test the hypothesis besides indicators and methods for measuring their impact; implementing the interventions and methods; collecting relevant data linked to the indicators and reviewing the (typically empirical) data to determine whether the hypothesis was correct. The number of variables and interdependencies in a given crime scenario suggests many different points and strategies for intervention. This complexity is addressed in Paul Ekblom's frameworks, including the *Conjunction of Criminal Opportunity* (2010) (which integrates all the SCP approaches and more). Also, his work with Martin Gill on *crime scripts* (Ekblom & Grill, 2015) that describes a criminal's view of crime processes so as to facilitate identification of the most effective intervention points. These 'conjunctions of opportunity', and the scripts that describe the dynamics and roles of actors within them, must be understood for behaviour change interventions to be appropriately measured and evaluated. This is usually linked to understanding the significance of the criminal behaviours being promoted and the changes to the crime situation 'before' and 'after' an intervention is made, typically measured in relation to crime statistics.

In their work, the Design Against Crime team not only draw upon ideas associated with CPTED and SCP, as outlined, but also engage with design approaches that structure the application of design methods and tools to identify the exact interactions and conditions (people, places, objects, environments) in which crimes occur. For example, the team engages with an extended version of the Design Council's (2005) 'Double Diamond' design process, to review wider questions about the crime problems addressed and how they might be tackled in user-friendly ways. This process moves through eight phases of

Table 18.1 Twenty-five situational crime prevention techniques. This chart started in 1992 with 12 techniques and has grown over the years

Increase the Effort	Increase the Risks	Reduce the Rewards	Reduce Provocations	Remove Excuses
1. Harden targets • Steering column locks and immobilizers • Anti-robbery screens • Tamper-proof packaging	6. Extend guardianship • Take routine precautions: go out in group at night, leave signs of occupancy, carry phone • 'Cocoon' neighbourhood watch	11. Conceal targets • Off-street parking • Gender-neutral phone directories • Unmarked bullion trucks	16. Reduce frustrations and stress • Efficient queues and polite service • Expanded seating • Soothing music/muted lights	21. Set rules • Rental agreements • Harassment codes • Hotel registration
2. Control access to facilities • Entry phones • Electronic card access • Baggage screening	7. Assist natural surveillance • Improved street lighting • Defensible space design • Support whistleblowers	12. Remove targets • Removable car radio • Women's refuges • Pre-paid cards for pay phones	17. Avoid disputes • Separate enclosures for rival soccer fans • Reduce crowding in pubs • Fixed cab fare	22. Post instructions • 'No Parking' • 'Private Property' • 'Extinguish camp fires'
3. Screen exits • Ticket needed for exit • Export documents • Electronic merchandise tags	8. Reduce anonymity • Taxi driver IDs • "How's my driving?" decals • School uniforms	13. Identify property • Property marking • Vehicle licensing and parts marking • Cattle branding	18. Reduce emotional arousal • Controls on violent pornography • Enforce good behaviour on soccer field • Prohibit racial slurs	23. Alert conscience • Roadside speed display boards • Signatures for customs declarations • 'Shoplifting is stealing'
4. Deflect offenders • Street closures • Separate bathrooms for women • Disperse pubs	9. Utilize place managers • CCTV for doubledeck buses • Two clerks for convenience stores • Reward vigilance	14. Disrupt markets • Monitor pawn shops • Controls on classified ads. • License street vendors	19. Neutralize peer pressure • 'Idiots drink and drive' • 'It's OK to say No' • Disperse troublemakers at schools	24. Assist compliance • Easy library checkout • Public lavatories • Litter bins
5. Control tools/weapons • 'Smart' guns • Disabling stolen cell phones • Restrict spray paint sales to juveniles	10. Strengthen formal surveillance • Red light cameras • Burglar alarms • Security guards	15. Deny benefits • Ink merchandize tags • Graffiti cleaning • Speed humps	20. Discourage imitation • Rapid repair of vandalism • V-chips in TVs • Censor details of modus operandi	25. Control drugs and alcohol • Breathalysers in pubs • Server intervention • Alcohol-free events

Source: Centre for Problem Oriented Policing (2016b)

Table 18.2 Four tenets central to design for behaviour change

1.	Lockton et al., 2010b, Tromp et al., 2011 advocate **making [crime] preventative behaviours easier to engage with**.	Clarke, 1992 describes: *assisting compliance with rules.*
2.	Lockton et al., 2010, Tromp et al., 2011 advocate **making an undesired [criminal] behaviour harder to perform – which may inhibit some further behaviour or have concomitant effects, but not always**.	Clarke, 1992 describes: *increasing the effort of criminals.*
3.	Lockton et al., 2010, Tromp et al., 2011 **persuading anti-crime users to adopt or want to perform a particular behaviour [that leads to increased security]**	Clarke's model includes *reducing 'provocations' for criminals* and *'removing excuses'* e.g. alerting conscience. Also, *reducing 'rewards'*
4.	Lockton et al. 2010, Tromp et al., 2011 **trying to decrease users' inclination to perform a particular behaviour (that leads to risk of crime) or an offender's inclination to attempt a crime**	Clarke's model includes *removing 'provocations'* and for both users and criminals. Also, *removing rewards and increasing the risks and the effort for criminals*

design research activity including Scope, Discover, Define, Develop, Deliver, Measure, Evaluate, Scale/Disseminate (Design Against Crime Research Centre, 2010) to accomplish the following:

- Understand the actors involved in the issue being studied, their role and agendas in relation to the issue and the wider system or process in which the issue occurs (*scope*).
- Understand scenarios and stages of the system or crime process to *discover* more about the people, places and interactions involved, applying design research methods and tools to do so.
- Work with the involved actors, drawing on the aforementioned crime frameworks, to make decisions to *define* what the key challenges are, the affordances and interactions that frame their occurrence, the specific objectives of the intervention to be designed and the indicators that will help to understand whether the intervention is effective in meeting these objectives. The *definition* of objectives is informed by understandings about the complexity of crime processes, as are the interventions seeking to disrupt them.
- Objectives are described as either 'ultimate' or 'intermediate'. An 'ultimate objective' might be the reduction of a certain crime type, as indicated by reported crime figures, whilst an 'intermediate objective' might be the reduction of a certain behaviour known to make that crime more likely to happen or succeed. For example, reducing bike theft by increasing secure locking practices or reducing ATM crime by increasing the distance between ATM users and other users of the streetscape. Such approaches are comparable with those found in public health initiatives (House of Lords Behaviour Change Report, 2011). For example, to achieve the ultimate objective of reductions in cases of lung cancer, initiatives might pursue the intermediate objective of reducing the number of smokers.
- Having defined the intervention opportunity and the indicators that will tell if your intervention is effective, the intervention itself and the method of testing it are *developed*. This is often an iterative process of prototyping and qualitative testing with relevant actors (those that might 'use' the intervention, but also those that might variously

interact with or influence it ['misusers', 'abusers', 'influencers'], thereby impacting its effectiveness).

- Having developed an apparently appropriate and effective intervention one might work with stakeholders to implement a 'controlled' trial to *measure* and *evaluate* whether or not the intervention can be evidenced as effective and should therefore be implemented more widely.

When designing for behaviour change, clear identification and articulation of the process, from researching the intervention opportunity to designing the evaluation, ensures that others can build upon, replicate and retest effective practice. The Design Against Crime Research Centre is cautious not to advocate a 'one size fits all' approach, given the significance of contextual and cultural differences. Appreciation of the 'socially situated' nature of crime and design (Suchman, 1987) has lead the team to consider crime problems not just in terms of the behaviours and practices requiring address to reduce crime, but also the relationship between the incidence and impacts of crime and other social behaviours and practices. In short, given that the built environment and public space is experienced by the law-abiding majority, the team seeks to locate DAC as a socially responsive design approach, that combines design *against* what we want *less* of (crime and anti-social behaviours) with design *for* what we want *more* of (pro-social behaviours). This positivist focus of socially responsive DAC focuses on amplification of positive possibilities rather than solely focussing on the prevention of negative outcomes. In doing so it has an affinity with 'appreciative inquiry', outlined by Cooperrider and Srivastva (1987), which suggests that excessive focus on problems or dysfunctions can actually cause them to become worse or fail to become better.

Design Against Crime case studies

The work of the Design Against Crime Research Centre and the iterative and collaborative design process we have developed and applied, has contributed to a national Design Council/Home Office 'Design Out Crime' initiative (Design Council 2005–2010) delivered in response to government targets for crime reduction; it is explained in detail elsewhere (see Thorpe et al., 2010; Gamman & Thorpe, 2011; Thorpe, 2013; Gamman & Thorpe, 2015). The case studies illustrate this approach and explain how collaborative processes contribute to behaviour change, as well as how the outputs from these processes are used.

Bikeoff (2004–2011)

The Bikeoff research initiative was created by the Design Against Crime Research Centre over 10 years ago as a response to cycle theft experienced by staff and students at Central Saint Martins, an art and design college in London. Bikeoff worked with a broad community of individuals and organizations concerned with cycling, crime and design, aiming to activate 'a design revolution' to reduce cycle theft and increase cycle use (Thorpe et al., 2010). Central to the initiative was collaboration between researchers at the Design Against Crime Research Centre and the University College London Jill Dando Institute of Crime Science, supported by research funding from the AHRC/EPSRC Designing for the 21st Century programme.

The initiative produced design guidance, design resources and design exemplars (products, communication strategies, services and environments) targeted at reducing opportunities for bike theft. Specific outputs included a range of anti-theft bike stands, one of which, the CaMden stand (Figure 18.2) is now specified by Transport for London and installed on the streets of London. The CaMden stand design is the result of ethno-graphic research into bike theft perpetrator techniques and extensive observation of bicy-cle parking practices at sites in central London. This knowledge of bicycle theft techniques and cycle parking behaviours informed the design of bike stands that reduce the oppor-tunities for insecure locking practice, particularly the securing of bikes to the stand using only the top tube of the bike frame. Key to the design response was an understanding of which locking behaviours are more secure, and therefore to be facilitated by the design, and which are less secure and therefore to be prevented. There are 180 ways of securing a typical diamond framed two-wheeled bicycle (75% of observed parked bicycles) to a standard n-shaped 'Sheffield' stand, using two locks. These ways of locking can be divided into three groups, namely:

- Good – *both* wheels *and* the frame locked to the stand,
- OK – one wheel *and* the frame locked to the stand, and
- Bad – either one wheel *or* the frame (or neither) locked to the stand.

By observing and recording the locking behaviours of cyclists using the new stand designs e.g. how many locked their bikes to the stand in 'Bad', 'OK' or 'Good' ways (Figure 18.1), we were able to compare these figures with those for cyclists locking to a standard n-shaped 'Sheffield' stand design and establish which of the stands promoted the most secure locking practices.

The CaMden stand design 'nudges' cyclists to lock both the wheel and the frame of their bike to the stand by making it harder for them to lock the crossbar alone (a common insecure bicycle locking practice identified by the research). By encouraging cyclists to lock both the frame and the wheel to the stand, it makes it harder for thieves to steal the bike using common theft techniques. The 'effectiveness' of the CaMden stand, in terms of

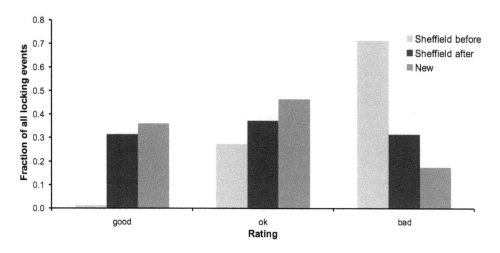

Figure 18.1 Locking practices for Sheffield stands versus the prototype bicycle parking stands as a single group

Figure 18.2 CaMden stand

Source: Design Against Crime Research Centre (2010).

promoting secure locking practice, was tested in control trials evaluated by the Jill Dando
Institute of Crime Science (Thorpe et al., 2012). Cyclists were found to be more likely
to lock securely to the new stand designs – a key intermediate outcome for reducing
opportunities for theft.

Despite the quantitatively substantiated success of the CaMden stand as a design nudge,
what the graph (Figure 18.1) does not explain is the cultural impact of the collaborative process of designing the CaMden stand. Several different secure cycle stand designs
were iteratively developed with the involvement of police, cycle furniture manufacturers,
cyclists and cycling experts and advocates from Transport for London's Cycling Centre
for Excellence and London Cycling Campaign. Whilst these collaborative design activities delivered the 'M' stand, which was evidenced to make a difference to opportunities
for bike theft, the CaMden stand design itself constituted just one of many 'design things',
defined by Binder et al. (2011: 1) as 'socio-material assemblies around issues of concern',

used by the Bikeoff project to promote greater awareness of cycle theft and more secure behaviours amongst cyclists.

The London Bicycle Film Festival, co-produced by Bikeoff for the first time in 2005, features films that celebrate cycling made by cyclists that share their passions and experiences. A common experience was of cycle theft, and consequently many of the films focused on this subject. As part of the festival the Bikeoff initiative used the bike theft–focused film content to support training sessions delivered to police and others concerned with cycle security. We thereby used art and design to introduce the knowledge and experience of cyclists to dutyholders i.e. those paid to address cycle theft prevention. We believe this sort of cultural engagement, plus our co-creation and co-delivery of several national bike crime exhibitions and conferences that identified best practice in reducing bike theft, created new cultural knowledge that was previously absent. In doing so the 'petty crime' of cycle theft was recognized as more significant, informing changes to national policies in street management and policing in addition to market demand for the CaMden stand designs. Geoffrey Crossick and Patriycia Kaszynska, in their 2016 report for the AHRC, recognize such creative cultural interventions as significant in that they 'provide the space in which disruption to established ways of thinking might safely take place' (Crossick & Kaszynska, 2016: 45). Through cultural engagement and collaborative creative practice, we introduced many diverse voices and perspectives to the discussion, that demanded change and influenced design debate. Such activities enabled us to move beyond SCP or nudge techniques, mainly concerned with the **design of choices**, which influence the decisions we make. Nudge theory, associated with Thaler and Sunstein (2008) proposes that the designing of choices should be based on how people actually think and decide (instinctively and rather irrationally), rather than how leaders and authorities traditionally (and often incorrectly) believe people think and decide (i.e. logically and rationally). The design of 'choice architecture', aims to achieve changes in people's behaviours by influencing their choices through design, rather than relying on informed consent and traditional methods of direct instruction, enforcement or punishment. Conversely, participatory design mobilizes a collective approach to informed consent, the articulation of concerns and the review of proposals that might change behaviours to reduce cycle theft. We consider all this socially responsive and collaborative activity and engagement with cycling groups, police and government agencies, as well as designers and design students, and later the Design Council and Home Office, to be our most important design contribution. It helped build informed awareness around the issue of cycle theft, beyond the nudging of the stands users. No wonder the 'M' stand was well-received when launched and despite initial scepticism, participation encouraged many cyclists to carry two locks. This may also be because, for a period, we helped raise the salience of bike theft in key stakeholder minds. We targeted the police in the UK who, certainly influenced by Bikeoff's 'thinking', and changed bike theft to be a 'comparator crime'.[1] Consequently, during this period, bike theft in London diminished whilst cycling increased (Figure 18.3).

The earlier text explains how Bikeoff operated in a collaborative and 'fraternalistic'[2] way to influence cultural values. The project provided a space where knowledge was exchanged, transferred and co-produced and understandings between stakeholders and dutyholders shared. Participatory design methods, including seeking feedback on design prototypes, democratized access and facilitated input to discussions and decisions around cycle security (including design decisions). This helped ensure the designs and communications against bike theft were as contextually appropriate as possible. The involvement of stakeholders in ideation and decision-making processes also engendered ownership

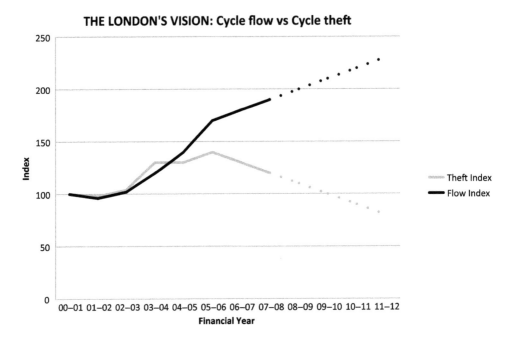

Figure 18.3 Graph by Rose Ades from presentation 'Putting the Brakes on Bike Theft', London Bicycle
        Film Festival, Barbican, 2008

Source: Conference proceedings 'Putting the Brakes on Bike Theft', London Bicycle Film Festival, Barbican (2008).

amongst stakeholders that supported adoption and implementation by them, furthering
the possibility of behaviour change. The contribution of physical prototyping of proposed
solutions to the consideration and resolution of shared problems is understood amongst
design practitioners for whom prototyping has long been a way of exploring possibilities
and supporting decision-making. The appreciation that 'making things makes things happen', and the conception of the prototype object as a site for cultural debate and exchange
is well articulated by design theorists. Bill et al. (2015) state that 'prototypes are not simply
evolving objects, or 'objects-to-be'. The processes by which ideas are refined and tested
through prototyping have much wider social significance' and with Murray et al. (2010:
12) we argue that 'it's through iteration, and trial and error, that coalitions gather strength
(for example, linking users to professionals) and conflicts are resolved (including battles
with entrenched interests)'.

The 'designing coalition' (Manzini, 2015) that the Bikeoff initiative assembled via the
activities described earlier co-produced a new way of understanding and problematizing
bike theft, and gave the issue greater significance amongst stakeholders and dutyholders
in the process.

Considering the behavioural impact of the co-design of the CaMden stand, and the
interactions and iterations that contributed to its creation, what was prototyped was:

(i)   a new way of *using* (the co-articulation amongst stakeholders of a more secure way of
      locking a bike – a new behaviour),

(ii) a new object of *use* (the bike stand that made this new behaviour easier and more intuitive than other, less secure, ways of locking),

(iii) a changed cultural values about bike theft – when we put on *Reinventing the Bike Shed*, the first bike design exhibition in London led by designers, many other designs and expos that weren't commercially focused followed.

Thus, the locking behaviours of cyclists were ultimately influenced in the co-creation of the bike stand as well as in its subsequent use. There was an exchange and a negotiation, by which stakeholders and dutyholders contributed to the definition of what *we think* (Leadbeater & Powell, 2009) is a more secure way to lock a bike (e.g. climate setting) before there was a nudge delivered by the stand design that favours this way of locking.

Whilst the CaMden stand can be considered as a designed nudge, given its effectiveness at changing the behaviour of cyclists through conscious design activity, we think it is a very different kind of nudge design from the conventional understanding of the term which suggests that *Small [design] changes can make a big difference* (Halpern, 2015).

The difference lies in the participatory process by which the desirable outcome of the intervention is co-defined and the strategy for achieving it (the nudge) co-developed. This participatory approach is supported by activities that assemble dutyholders and stakeholders around the issue of concern and foster cultural exchange and debate that, to borrow from Papanek (1995) 'informs' those involved in the process, 'reforms' normative perspectives and values in relation to the issue of concern amongst those involved in the process and their networks and 'gives form' to the co-designed output – the nudge. We consider this participatory approach to be more equitable, more democratic and less paternalistic than other approaches to behaviour change by design.

ATM art mats (2010–2015)

Between 2008 and 2011, the most common ATM crime perpetrator techniques in City of Westminster, London, were 'distraction theft' (between 63% and 77% of reported ATM crime) followed by 'skimmer/reader' or 'trapping' offences (between 4% and 11% – as indicated by the fact that cash was later deducted from the victim's account).[3]

Much has been done through technological intervention to address some of these techniques. Devices are retrofitted to ATMs to incapacitate card 'skimmers', sense when 'card traps' are inserted or to shield ATM users' PINs from prying eyes. However, interventions aimed at 'distraction theft', 'pickpocketing' and 'shoulder surfing' have been limited to the introduction of 'safety zones' around ATMs. These 'safety zones' typically comprise yellow boxes painted on the pavement to define a 'defensible space' (Newman, 1972) that customers can point to when requesting privacy. They work by increasing the distance between ATM users and other users of the streetscape – including those seeking to steal ATM users' cards or cash. This defensible space prevents common theft techniques such as shoulder surfing, dipping and distraction theft, all of which require thieves to be near their target. Whilst these zones have been reported to be effective in reducing crime in the vicinity of ATMs (Holt & Spencer, 2005) there is little enthusiasm amongst banks, businesses, place managers or the public for this solution. This may be because the yellow lines are more commonly associated with instructing vehicles and traffic, rather than people, and many consider their appearance detracts from the appeal of our high streets and signals insecurity. In an attempt to find a more appealing solution for defensible space, the Design Against Crime Research Centre, working with Hammersmith Police,

Figure 18.4 ATM Art Mat

Source: Design Against Crime Research Centre (2010).

trialled ATM Art mats at Royal Bank of Scotland (RBS) cash machines in Hammersmith, London in 2010 (see Figure 18.4). Anecdotal evidence suggested the ATM Art mats were effective in creating a defensible space and that they were well liked by businesses and the public. As part of a multi-channel approach to ATM security, which includes address to technology, environment and behaviour, RBS ATM Fraud Control commissioned a control trial of ATM Art to test its effectiveness in improving customer security and customer experience at ATMs, so as to build a robust evidence base for any future recommendations regarding installation of ATM Art.

Ten NatWest ATM sites within City of Westminster and London Borough of Camden were selected on the basis of being ATM crime hotspots, experiencing the highest levels of reported ATM crime. Of the 10 sites selected, eight were paired according to similarities in the number of reported ATM crimes at the site, transaction volumes and situational site characteristics relating to the ATM itself, its immediate vicinity and the wider environment around the ATM. The remaining two sites, although not suitable for pairing due to unique characteristics, were included in the trial as these experienced the highest levels of reported ATM crime within the study area. Pre-observations (before deployment of the ATM Art) were made between mid-May and mid-July 2012 and data was recorded relating to the behaviours of ATM users and other users of the streetscapes during ATM transactions. At the start of August 2012, four of the paired sites received ATM Art mats along with the two unpaired sites that experienced highest levels of ATM crime. The four sites that did not have ATM Art mats installed acted as control sites to their pairs. After the installation of the ATM Art mats to six of the sites, comparable post-observations were recorded of ATM transactions at all 10 sites. Data relating to the behaviours of ATM users and other users of the streetscape, with and without mats present, were analyzed and compared.

The results demonstrated that the ATM Art Mats significantly increased the distance between the ATM user and other users of the streetscape by, on average, a further 80cm than when no mats were present (Thorpe, 2013). Additionally, the mats were observed to increase the tendency of ATM users to look over their shoulder (a useful defensive behaviour), whilst having no adverse impact on their tendency to cover their PIN (a concern had been that the increase in privacy might result in reductions in PIN covering).

The research evidenced that the ATM Art Mats deliver an effective 'nudge' to streetscape users to 'stand back' when mats are occupied by an ATM user, increasing privacy of ATM users and reducing opportunities for cash, card and PIN theft.

Additionally, a survey into ATM user behaviours, conducted with over 250 ATM users as part of the research, found that nine out of ten ATM users surveyed said that they had, at some time in the past, wanted to request privacy before using an ATM (e.g. by asking another person to step back). However, of those people expressing this desire, only 44% had actually felt able to make such a request. Thus, whilst the 'nudge' is effective in changing the normative behaviours of people around an ATM, granting more privacy to ATM users, more needs to be done to increase the likelihood of the ATM user to request privacy if the 'nudge' of the ATM Art Mat is ignored by other users of the streetscape (as would likely be the case if a criminal were consciously trying to steal from the ATM user).

To address this concern, a collaborative and participatory approach to the creation of the ATM Art Mat artwork was embarked upon. A series of art workshops were conducted in 2014/15 with schoolchildren living near the Camden ATMs where the artworks were to be installed. The students created artworks to be printed onto the Mats and installed at the local ATMs. The workshops started by explaining to students about the issue of ATM crime that the artworks address. The intention is that once installed, the artworks deliver the 'nudge' to users of the streetscape to 'stand back' but also extend the debate amongst local people around why the artworks are there, how they work and the role of the ATM user in protecting his or her own right to privacy. Workshop materials have been produced, along with protocols for implementation, that support bank managers and other stakeholders and dutyholders in implementing ATM Art workshops, and the resulting art mats, as another channel of defence against ATM crime in their local area. This process uses the creation of artworks as a 'thing', a means of public assembly around an issue of concern, to raise awareness for ATM security (and the right to privacy), involving local people to afford greater local ownership of, and pride in, the public realm for 'ATM Artists' and their communities as well as expanding understandings about the cultural significance of instrumental art. At the time of writing, the new ATM Art Mats are awaiting installation.

What is the 'nudge' approach to behaviour change and how is it different to 'we think'

What is 'new' about nudge design is that it often prioritizes psychological prompts aimed at directing choices towards actions with positive social outcomes. For example, changing the defaults on organ donation to 'presumed consent' to save lives, or the messaging on tax forms to create cost savings for government, constitute top down nudges.

Nudge logic holds that through subtle changes to the world around us government can subtly change behaviours so that *we* experience more positive outcomes. These 'nudges' are the result of conscious design decisions that are intended to encourage positive behaviours (Gatsby, 2014). If a nudge is a way of encouraging and guiding behaviour without mandating or instructing, and ideally without the need for heavy financial incentives or sanctions, then clearly its codes and conventions may have a relation to design. Just like the design of roadside signs aimed at guiding traffic to share the road safely are linked to soft emotional prompts, or the design of fruit packaging stored near the till at checkouts are aimed at promoting healthy eating, all these strategies involve psychological cues as well as physical prompts and interaction opportunities.

Strategies that deliver positive behavioural prompts have much in common with Norman's (1988) concept of 'affordance' in design – the idea that the designed appearance of objects communicates a range of action possibilities to their users. Indeed, design has always delivered prompts. What Packard (1957) called 'hidden persuaders' and what Cialdini (2007) calls the 'influence of persuasion', has much in common with what Thaler and Sunstein in their book *Nudge* (2008) redefine as 'choice architecture'.

The UK's Behavioural Insights Team (BIT) – dubbed the 'Nudge Unit' – has used a wide range of measures to successfully 'nudge' citizens towards decisions and behaviours that will improve their lives or safety and save public money. Interestingly, BIT's approach is typically one of promoting positive outcomes rather than denying negative outcomes. It is often concerned with re-designing written materials to promote positive choices by making preferable outcomes easier to achieve than less desirable outcomes; or reminding people of the positive choices their neighbours make already as a way of encouraging others to do the same. Halpern (2015: 158) links this strategy to principles summarized in the mnemonic 'EAST' summarized in Table 18.3, which has much in common with Tables 18.1 and 18.2 featured in section one generated by Clarke's account of SCP and his account of behaviour change.

BIT works for the government and in their 2014–2015 report they state:

> our objectives remain the same: making public services more cost-effective and easier for citizens to use; improving outcomes by introducing a more realistic model of human behaviour to policy; and wherever possible, enabling people to make 'better choices for themselves'.
>
> (Prime Minister's Office et al., 2010 – restated by Halpern, 2015)

Yet success linked to nudges is not about democratizing decision-making and enabling people to make 'better choices for themselves'. Instead, nudges help good social outcomes happen by making choices *for* people about what 'better' looks like, and then discriminating positively for these choices in the design of the interactions. The approach is a 'top-down' one that echoes a managerialist and often cost-saving emphasis currently at the heart of current UK public sector decision-making. Yet there is so far no doubt that such small changes are being designed to mobilize behavioural psychology for the greater good. As Halpern (2015: 121), in his recent book *Inside the Nudge Unit*, observes:

> Behavioural approaches aren't just about invisible nudges that pull in a bit more tax revenue or help deliver some worthy but distant outcome. At their best such interventions are about understanding who we are; about connecting and communicating with each other better; and, frankly, about designing services for human beings.

Despite this positive emphasis, concerns have been raised about the approach as the creation of default settings deliver *presumed consent*, rather than *informed* consent. Consequently

Table 18.3 'EAST' principles

	Headline	Things to think about	Examples
Easy	Make it easy People are much more likely to do something if it's easy and low-hassle	• Simplify • Friction: remove, or add it to inhibit • Defaults: set the easy path as the healthiest, safest option	• Pensions: millions more saving as a result of auto-enrolment • Suicide: reduced when easy routes blocked • University entry: 25% more poor students go when forms pre-filled
Attract	People are drawn to that which catches their attention, and that which is attractive to them	• Personalize: use recipient's name; make relevant • Salience: make key point stand out • Messenger: experts and named individuals beat anonymous or distrusted sources • Lotteries: make incentives more attractive • Emotion: as important as reason	• Tax: 10 times more doctors declared income with salient letter • Giving: 2 times more donations to emergency appeals with story of one child versus statistics of millions affected • Courts: 3 times more likely to pay fines with a personalized text
Social	People are strongly influenced by what others are doing or have done	• Norms: what are others actually doing • Networks: a friend or colleague recommends • Reciprocity and active commitments: promises • Reminders of others: eyes and faces	• Litter: 8 times more likely to drop flyer if others already on the ground • Tax: 16% more likely to pay if informed that most people 'pay on time' • Giving: 7 times more likely to give when learning that a colleague already gave
Timely	Interventions are more effective before habits have formed, or when behaviour has been disrupted for other reasons	• Habit: intervene before they become established • Key moments: when behaviour is disrupted • Priming and anchoring: the power of what just came before • Time inconsistency: discounting of the future	• Development: two-thirds more farmers take up fertilizer offer after harvest when cash-rich • Health: 3 times more workers choose healthy option a week ahead than one day • Tax: 2 times more likely to respond to nudge if late paying previous year

Source: Halpern (2015).

such an approach may be undemocratic or may misuse government budgets, leveraging apathy against democracy. As one senior Minister (quoted by Halpern, 2015: 35) commented the nudge approach is 'not quite cricket is it?'

Many of today's societal challenges are 'wicked' (Rittel & Webber, 1973; Buchanan, 1992; Buchanan & Margolin, 1995) in that they are complex, networked problems with no single origin or owner and that there are multiple, sometimes contradictory, desirable outcomes for the people that experience them. Responses to such wicked challenges benefit from 'open' and collaborative approaches that bring multiple and diverse resources, disciplines and knowledge to bear on a problem. To ensure the engagement of the multiplicity of actors necessary to impact upon these complex, networked problems, the process with which they are required to engage must acknowledge and address the multiple and

Table 18.4 Problem solving and appreciative inquiry

Problem Solving	Appreciative inquiry
Felt need, identification of problem(s)	Appreciating – valuing 'the best of what is'
Analysis of causes	Envisioning what might be
Analysis of possible solutions	Engaging in dialogue about what should be
Action planning (treatment)	Innovating what will be

Source: Cooperrider and Srivastva (1987).

diverse drivers that matter to them, and in that process include a positive focus (in terms of Bikeoff this meant not just *less* bike theft but the promotion of *more* cycling). This positive approach, as mentioned earlier, has been described elsewhere by Whitney and Trosten-Bloom (2010) as 'appreciative inquiry'[4] aimed at delivering change to organizations. This focus moves beyond problem solving and asks positive questions of the potential of a given person, organization or situation in order to realise such positive effects as summarized in Table 18.4.

We can see an element of what is known as 'reframing' involved in appreciative inquiry. Kees Dorst, founder of the Designing Out Crime Research Centre at the University of Technology Sydney that emerged in 2007, has developed and articulated this account of 'reframing' in a clear methodological way (Dorst, 2015). He describes a series of steps supported by a set of design methods and tools that enable groups of actors to identify and articulate their values in order to find new perspectives from which to address previously intractable challenges. Reframing ATM crime as an opportunity for community arts projects is one way of understanding the reframing process.

Further examples include Dorst's own work reframing problems associated with drunkenness and anti-social behaviour linked to the night-time economy of the King's Cross district of Sydney. Instead of persisting in ever-harsher policing of these 'problems' in the existing frame of crime and disorder, Dorst and his team suggested that stakeholders 'reframe' the challenge of policing the area to that of managing a 'festival' and design ways to accommodate or deter the anticipated behaviours, opening the challenge up to more creative and collaborative responses than might be conceivable or achievable through an anti-social/policing lens.

Conclusion

In a time of uncertainty, facing complex societal challenges that demand immediate address, it is no surprise that appreciative inquiry and ideas about 'reframing' should be finding admirers in those interested in organization change, or that the UK government has created a 'nudge' unit to focus on the positive in order to achieve some necessary 'quick wins' and more generally boost compliance with norms. For example, steering publics' decisions in directions that may improve citizens' health and well being (approaches in Wales that opt everyone into organ donation) whilst also delivering cost savings for government are obviously appealing to those looking for solutions. Thaler and Sunstein (2008) were early promoters of such paternalistic strategies in their book *Nudge* that outlined behavioural economics as applied to law. As we have explained, the UK's BIT unit have developed the approach, using psychology to deliver change with sophistication, creativity and with real-world effects that should not be undervalued or underestimated, even if these replace informed consent with manipulation that constitutes presumed consent. Our account of Design Against Crime as *socially responsive design* also seeks urgent address to current complex social challenges, and is similar to appreciative inquiry because it is pro-social in emphasis; but it differs from nudge in that its approach is fundamentally participatory rather than paternalistic. It recognizes that designers cannot ultimately be responsible for the outcomes of the design process and that to be effective and democratic, scenarios require collaboration and compromises between stakeholders – a *fraternal* approach to designing that is *responsive* to the context in which a design activity is situated, and the people with whom a designer is designing, and involved. So whilst we agree with Tromp et al. (2011: 19) that designers can make a difference and 'have to take responsibility as "shapers" of society', we acknowledge limits to the designer's influence and role in a context where economic forces and other political influences and drivers still have significant determination on which designs actually reach the world.

We believe BIT's need to create the right conditions for a 'nudge' to succeed[5] is often positive but undemocratic, whereas the participatory approach the Design Against Crime Research Centre advocates, even when drawing upon SCP, is more inclusive and serves to democratize innovation. We seek to harness the possibility and potential of diverse perspectives and capacities of people, rather than simply using human psychology to manipulate predicted and uniform behavioural responses from an amorphous public. The difference lies in the participatory process by which the desirable outcome of the intervention is co-defined and the strategy for achieving it (the nudge) co-developed.

Putting aside concerns relating to democracy and individual agency, the pragmatist must acknowledge that both strategies work to deliver behaviour change. Nudging is found to be appropriate in situations where *we think* we know the 'right' answer, where the greater good is obvious to all, in scenarios where no intentionality or agency is required, where the greater good will be served by behaviours that are unconsciously redirected. But, nudging does not work to change behaviours at a conscious level. Nor, does nudging work to bring together stakeholders to work out what the 'right answer' or 'greater good' might be in scenarios where contested understandings and competing objectives might limit the possibility of 'one right answer'.

Whilst improved outcomes resulting from unintentional changes to behaviour are welcomed, especially when it saves lives and saves money, there are certain desirable outcomes that necessitate desirable behaviours that require the conscious intention and decision of the involved actors. For example, asking for more privacy at an ATM or championing cycling, cyclists' safety and cyclists' security in our cities. These complex scenarios require open, inclusive and collaborative processes that foster the assembly of publics around issues of concern so that desirable outcomes can be collaboratively defined, and interventions to achieve them collaboratively designed. The kind of democratized climate setting and participatory design that DAC actions and advocates is likely to have an impact on behaviour that is more strategic, more generalized and more durable (i.e. reach beyond the specific effect of a specific momentary change in behaviour – wording on a tax form, say). But, obviously, harder work to accomplish and with a greater chance, with all those actors involved, that the effects may occur in unexpected directions. So, is 'nudge' as good as 'we think' in Design Against Crime through behaviour change? It depends on context. Both 'nudge' and 'we think' offer different opportunities for impact in pursuit of desirable outcomes for citizens, both in the moment and in the future but denial of informed consent and agency of involved actors in the behavioural choices they make is likely to necessitate constant intervention rather than sustained transformation.

Notes

1 A comparator crime is a crime type against which police performance is measured by the Home Office.
2 We use the term *fraternalistic* as an alternative to *paternalistic* – not to denote a gendered account of brotherhood but rather a comradely and co-operative relational interaction) e.g. 'denoting an organisation for people, especially men, that have common interests or beliefs: a network of political clubs and/or fraternal organizations' – http://oxforddictionaries.com/definition/fraternal. Downloaded 1.9.2015.
3 Westminster Police Data regarding the *modus operandi* (MO, or perpetrator technique) used by offenders when committing ATM crime in Westminster (as identified by reading the 'CLASS Method' entry on each of the relevant CRIS records for three years between 2009 and 2011).
4 Appreciative inquiry suggests that excessive focus on problem-solving 'dysfunctions' can actually cause them to become worse or fail to become better. So instead, when all members of an organization are motivated to understand and value the most favourable features of its culture, this is a better method to make rapid improvements.
5 Halpern talks about the need to get right and balance contextual factors before undertaking such interventions such as **A**dministrative support, **P**olitical support, **P**eople, **L**ocation, **E**xperimentation, **S**cholarship (APPLES).

Bibliography

Armitage, R. (2013). *Crime prevention through housing design: Policy and practice*. Crime Prevention and Security Management. Basingstoke: Palgrave Macmillan.
Armitage, R., & Monchuk, L. (2009) Reconciling security with sustainability: The challenge for Eco-homes. *Built Environment, 35*(3), 308–327.
Bill, A., Reay, S. D., & Collier, G. (2015). *Making things happen: Experiments in prototyping from a hospital design tab*. Summer Cumulus Conference, Politicencio Di Milano, June 3–7.
Binder, T., De Michelis, G., Ehn, P., Jacucci, G., Linde, P., & Wagner, I. (2011). *Design things*. Cambridge, MA: MIT Press.
Buchanan, R. (1992). Wicked problems in design thinking. *Design Issues, 8*(2), 5–21.
Buchanan, R., & Margolin, V. (1995). *Discovering design – explorations in design studies*. Chicago: University of Chicago Press.
Centre for Problem-Oriented Policing. (2016a). *Guides*. University at Albany – State University of New York. Retrieved from www.popcenter.org/guides/
Centre for Problem-Oriented Policing. (2016b). *Twenty five techniques of situational prevention*. University at Albany – State University of New York. Retrieved from www.popcenter.org/25techniques/
Cialdini, R. B. (2007). *Influence: The psychology of persuasion*. New York: Collins.
Clarke, R. (1997). Introduction. In R. Clarke (Ed.), *Situational crime prevention: Successful case studies* (pp. 1–44). Guilderland, NY: Harrow and Heston.
Clarke, R. (Ed.). (1992). *Situational crime prevention: Successful case studies*. Albany, NY: Harrow and Heston.
Clarke, R., & Newman, G. (Eds) (2013). *Designing out crime from products and systems*. Crime Prevention Studies 18. Cullompton: Willan.
Clarke, R.V. (1983). Situational crime prevention: Its theoretical basis and practical scope. *Crime and Justice: An Annual Review of Research, 4*, 225–256.
Clarke, R.V., & Felson, M. (1993). *Routine activity and rational choice*. Vol. 5, Advances in Criminology Theory. New Brunswick: Transaction Publishers, Inc.
Cooperrider, D. L., & Srivastva, S. (1987). Appreciative inquiry in organizational life. In R. W. Woodman & W. A. Pasmore (Eds.), *Research in organizational change and development* (Vol. 1, pp. 129–169). Stamford, CT: JAI Press.
Cozens, P. M., Saville, G., & Hillier, D. (2005). Crime prevention through environmental design (CPTED): A review and modern bibliography. *Property Management 23*(5), 328–356.
Crossick, G., & Kaszynska, P. (2016). *Understanding the value of arts and culture*. The AHRC Cultural Value Project Report.

Design Against Crime Research Centre. (2010). *Methodology*. London: University of the Arts. See: www.designagainstcrime.com/methodology-resources/design-methodology. Sections: Why Users & Abusers; Resource Mapping; What's at stake?; List & Description; Why "Open Innovation"; Benefits; References.

Design Council. (2005). *Double diamond design process*. Retrieved from http://webarchive.nationalarchives.gov.uk/20080821115409/designcouncil.org.uk/en/about-design/managingdesign/the-study-of-the-design-process/

Design Council. (2010). *Design out crime*. Retrieved from www.designcouncil.org.uk/resources/case-study/design-out-crime

Dorst, K. (2015). *Frame innovation: Create new thinking by design*. Cambridge, MA: MIT Press.

Ekblom, P. (2010). The conjunction of criminal opportunity theory. In *Encyclopedia of victimology and crime prevention* (pp. 140–146). London, UK: Sage.

Ekblom, P. (2011). New thinking on crime prevention through environmental design. *European Journal on Criminal Policy and Research, 17*(1), 1–6.

Ekblom, P. (Ed.). (2012). *Design against crime: Crime proofing everyday objects*. Crime Prevention Studies 27. Boulder, CO: Lynne Rienner.

Ekblom, P., & Gill, M. (2015). Rewriting the script: Cross-disciplinary exploration and conceptual consolidation of the procedural analysis of crime. *European Journal on Criminal Policy and Research, 22*(2), 319–339.

Felson, M. (1994). *Crime and everyday life: Insight and implications for society*. Thousand Oaks, CA: Pine Forge Press.

Felson N. & Clarke R.V., (1997) Opportunity Makes the Thief: Practical Theory for crime Prevention, Police Research Series Paper 98, Crown Copyright.

Gamman, L., & Thorpe, A. (2011). Design with society: Why socially responsive design is good enough. *CoDesign International Journal of CoCreation in Design and the Arts, 7*(3–4), 217–231.

Gamman, L., & Thorpe, A. (2015). Could design help promote and build empathic processes in prison? Understanding the role of empathy and design in catalysing social change and transformation. In J. Wolfgang (Ed.), *Transformation design* (pp. 83–100). Basel, Switzerland: Birkhäuser/BIRD.

Gatsby, C. (2014, May 6). Social architecture: A new approach to designing social spaces. *Huffington Post*. Retrieved August 1, 2015, from www.huffingtonpost.com/claudia-gatsby/social-architecture-a-new_b_5448130.html

Halpern, D. (2015). *Inside the nudge unit: How small changes can make a big difference*. London: WH Allen.

Holt, T., & Spencer, J. (2005). A little yellow box: The targeting of automatic teller machines as a strategy in reducing street robbery. *Crime Prevention and Community Safety: An International Journal, 7*, 15–28.

House of Lords. (2011). *Behaviour change report*. Science and Technology Select Committee, 2nd Report of Sessions 2010–12. HL Paper 179.

Jacobs, J. (1961). *The death and life of Great American cities*. New York: Random House.

Jeffrey, C. R. (1971). *Crime prevention through environmental design*. Beverly Hills, CA: Sage.

Kitchen, T., & Schneider, R. H. (2007). *Crime prevention and the built environment*. Abingdon, Oxon: Routledge.

Knights, B., Pascoe, T., & Henchley, A. (2002). *Sustainability and crime: Managing and recognising the drivers of crime and security*. Garston, Watford: Building Research Establishment.

Leadbeater, C., & Powell, D. (2009). *We-think*. London: Profile Books.

Lockton, D., Harrison, D. J., & Stanton, N. A. (2010a). *Design with intent: 101 patterns for influencing behaviour through design*. Windsor, UK: Equifine.

Lockton, D., Harrison, D. J., & Stanton, N. A. (2010b). The design with intent method: A design tool for influencing user behaviour. *Applied Ergonomics, 41*(3), 382–392.

Manzini, E. (2015). *Design when everybody designs: An introduction to design for social innovation*. Cambridge, MA: MIT Press.

Murray, R., Caulier-Grice, J., & Mulgan, G. (2010). *The open book of social innovation*. Washington, DC: National Endowment for Science, Technology and the Art.

Newman, O. (1972). *Defensible space: Crime prevention through urban design*. New York: Macmillan.

Norman, D. A. (1988). *The psychology of everyday things*. New York: Basic Books.

Packard, V. (1957). *The hidden persuaders*. New York: D. McKay Co.

Papanek, V. (1995). *The green imperative: Ecology and ethics in design and architecture*. London: Thames and Hudson.

Prime Minister's Office, Deputy Prime Minister's Office and Cabinet Office. (2010). *The Coalition: Our Programme for Government*. London, UK: Crown.

Prison Reform Trust. (2015). *Prison; the facts*. Bromley Briefing, Summer 2015. Retrieved from www.prisonreformtrust.org.uk/Portals/0/Documents/Prison%20the%20facts%20May%202015.pdf

Rittel, H., & Webber, M. (1973). Dilemmas in a general theory of planning. *Policy Sciences, 4*, 155–169.

Suchman, L. A. (1987). *Plans and situated actions: The problem of human-machine communication*. Cambridge: Cambridge University Press.

Thaler, R. H., & Sunstein, C. R. (2008). *Nudge: Improving decisions about health, wealth, and happiness*. New Haven, CT: Yale University Press.

Thorpe, A. (2013). *ATM art evaluation programme*. London: Socially Responsive Design and Innovation Press.

Thorpe, A., Gamman, L., Ekblom, P., Willcocks, M., Sidebottom, A., & Johnson, S. D. (2010). Bike Off 2 – catalysing anti teft bike, bike parking and information design for the 21st century: An open research approach. In T. Inns (Ed.), *Designing for the 21st century. Volume 2: Interdisciplinary methods and findings* (pp. 238–258). Farnham: Gower.

Thorpe, A., Johnson, S. D., & A. Sidebottom. (2012). The impact of seven prototype bicycle parking stands on opportunities for bicycle theft. In P. Ekblom (Ed.), *Designing out crime from products: Towards research-based practice* (pp. 107–130). Crime Prevention Studies, Vol. 26. Monsey, NY: Criminal Justice Press.

Tromp, N., Hekkert, P., & Verbeek, P. (2011). Design for socially responsible behavior: A classification of influence based on intended user experience. *Design Issues, 27*(3), 3–19.

Whitney, D., & Trosten-Bloom, A. (2010). *The power of appreciative inquiry* (2nd ed.). San Francisco: Berrett-Koehler.

19 Design for social behaviour change

Edward Gardiner and Kristina Niedderer

Introduction

It is widely recognized that design in its various forms, including objects, services, interiors, architecture and environments can play an important role in influencing human behaviour (e.g. Lockton & Harrison, 2012, Brown & Wyatt, 2010, Consolvo et al., 2009). Areas of application include environmental sustainability, health, safety and crime prevention. For example, recycling programmes invite people to recycle, cars make people more mobile but walk less or a certain design of bike stand makes it more difficult to steal them.

In addition, it is becoming increasingly apparent that most behavioural solutions are intrinsically linked to social change, because design does not only influence the interaction we have with its products (Norman, 2002: 1, 34; Pearce, 1995: 166) but also 'how human beings relate to other human beings through the mediating influence of products' (Buchanan, 2001: 11). For example, public benches not only offer us to rest in public places but at the same time provide places for social encounter; computers have changed the speed and quality of our social interaction (e.g. more emails, fewer handwritten letters); cars and mobile phones have not only made us more mobile, but they have also changed our social interactions and expectations of connectedness.

These examples illustrate that while design may intend to address one issue, it will also have effects in other areas whether intended or not, and that unintended effects can be variously desirable or undesirable. For example, while cars may have been designed to increase mobility in the first instance, they are also substantially impacting on our social connectedness, on our health and on global sustainability. Similarly, the function of the mobile phone that enables our conversation with the person receiving the call is generally well considered and designed. By contrast, the effect of mobile conversations on people outside the immediate conversation is not generally considered by the design of the phone and leading to often undesirable consequences, e.g. with regard to noise pollution and safety issues.

Although there is an emerging recognition of the social significance and complexity of design in the context of design for sustainability (Lockton et al., 2010, Lockton, 2012; Bhamra et al., 2011), the social potential of design for behaviour change has remained largely ignored and under-researched (Chick, 2012).

Indeed, current design approaches to social behaviour change appear at times 'anti-social' where they are designed to ignore or reinforce existing social behaviours rather than to question and to consider how to utilize or improve them.

The use of mobile phones described is one example of this. Public benches are another: while traditional benches offer versatile uses, modern designs are often restrictive to individual seating use. In extreme cases, seats even face in opposite directions, denying social interaction and reinforcing avoidance behaviour rather than offering to consider the multitude of possible social interactions with people in public places (Niedderer, 2014: 351). Even more extreme are examples of spikes in the cityscape to prevent homeless sleepers resting in certain places (Petty, 2016). In short, current designs regularly reach from ignoring social behaviour to actively disrupting or preventing certain social behaviours, raising attention of the ethical dimension of design.

This chapter reviews the emerging interest in designing for social behaviour change. It starts with an overview of existing approaches to social issues, including social design, social innovation, social entrepreneurship, social interaction design and others, and analyzes them with regard to their position and approach to behaviour change. The discussion further examines the different levels of application of design for social behaviour change, in particular with regard to output, process and intent. It distinguishes different modes and areas of social behaviours and their application. The analysis is underpinned by selected case studies to demonstrate the different areas of the application of design for behaviour change, and its role and benefits for society.

What do we mean by social design?

The recognition of the social dimension of design and its importance for behaviour change has developed for some time, although it has been slow to take hold. Papanek (1984) has offered one of the earliest accounts of social design under the label of 'responsible design' where he considered the environmental and social consequences of design. Two decades later, Margolin has taken up the idea of social design, suggesting a social model of design practice for product design within a process of social service intervention (Margolin & Margolin, 2002: 25, Margolin, 2002). A number of different and divergent perspectives of social design have emerged during this time and since.

In line with these, *social design* can be seen as a broad term that brackets the diverse practices and domains concerned with the role of design in human and humanitarian social engagement (Veiga & Almendra, 2014), comprising anything from tangible objects to virtual services, from organizational design to design for developing countries. It may for example include designing architecture and urban space for social use (e.g. Popov, 2002); social design of virtual worlds, online communities and games (e.g. Kraut et al., 2011; Taylor, 2004, Segura et al., 2013); social design approaches for teaching and in the museum (e.g. Gutiérrez & Vossoughi, 2010; Bitgood, 2011); manufacturing approaches that draw on social networking (Brambilla et al., 2012) and law (e.g. Ritter, 2006: constitution as social design).

This broad understanding and diversity of social design is critically reviewed in two articles: one by Veiga and Almendra (2014) who offer an overview of current social design approaches, and one by Chick (2012), in which she calls for serious research in the area of social innovation in design.

Veiga and Almendra (2014) propose *social design* as an 'umbrella term' for the role of design in the field of socially engaged practices, because it "is the most generally and commonly used term in the discourse of designers" and "it immediately identifies the realm and scope of action of design and it is a holistic and open term" (p. 2). They group current approaches to *social design* into three broad categories: *survival* – addressing humanitarian needs and human rights; *citizenship* – addressing systemic human challenges; and *politics* – relates to the work of institutions and sectors who seek to influence the course of human life (p. 10), and approaches within these three categories include

> Social Design, Design for the Base/Bottom of the Pyramid (BoP), Humanitar-
> ian Design, Design as Development Aid, Socially Responsible Design or Socially
> Responsive Design, Design for Social Good, Design for Social Change, Design for
> Social Impact, Design for Social Innovation, Design for Social Innovation and Sus-
> tainability, Social Economic Environmental Design, Useful Design, Transformation
> Design, Design for Public Good, etcetera.
>
> (Veiga and Almendra, 2014: 2)

Further categories could be added to this already broad list, such as socially conscious design (Simmons, 2011), ethically responsible design (Thackara, 2005), social interaction design (Huang & Deng, 2008), Design with Intent (Lockton et al., 2010), mindful design (Niedderer, 2014), critical design (Dunne & Raby, 2001) and several more.

The diversity of terminology indicates a lack of shared language and discourse (Veiga & Almendra, 2014: 2), which requires some further discussion. For example, social design is also associated with other fields of research and development that share a common social purpose or goal, for example social innovation (TEPSIE, 2012, The Young Foundation, 2012) and social entrepreneurship (Austin et al., 2006). Social innovation is recognized by the European Union (TEPSIE, 2012, The Young Foundation, 2012) and defined as the creation of

> new solutions (products, services, models, markets, processes etc.) that simultane-
> ously meet a social need (more effectively than existing solutions) and lead to new or
> improved capabilities and relationships and better use of assets and resources. In other
> words, social innovations are both good for society and enhance society's capacity to act.
>
> (The Young Foundation, 2012: 18)

They explicitly promote

> the social and public good [. . .] inspired by the desire to meet social needs which can
> be neglected by traditional forms of private market provision and which have often
> been poorly served or unresolved by services organised by the state. Social innovation
> can take place inside or outside of public services.
>
> (Murray et al., 2010: 10)

In other words, social innovation addresses perceived social needs, either through public or private service providers or market forces. These definitions however do not take account of the ownership in this process: generally, the ownership is with those developing social innovation, which may or may not include the stakeholders for whom the intervention is developed in the process. One way to address this is through *social entrepreneurship*, which is closely aligned with social innovation. Social entrepreneurship generally refers to the applications of business expertise and market-based skills to primarily create social value, rather than individual and shareholder wealth (Austin et al., 2006). Social entrepreneur-ship works through and in collaboration with social service provision and social activism. It seeks to enable direct change through enabling individuals on a large scale to change their circumstances (e.g. Martin & Osberg, 2007), often through social initiatives such as those reported by Viravaidya (p. 8) or Hebel (p. 12) in the proceedings of the DRS 2012 conference in Bankok (DRS, 2012).

Chick relates social innovation and entrepreneurship further to design. Building on references to societal transformation and the development of new products, services and programmes, Chick (2012) charts emerging principles of *design for social innovation* to define design's role in achieving social innovation. Chick's approach is a broad appeal to the intention of designing for behaviour change, which she underpins with reference to a variety of process-related approaches to address social problems, such as more generic co-design approaches as well as more specific emerging approaches to design for social behaviour change (e.g. Lockton & Harrison, 2012, Lockton et al., 2010, chapter 6; Tromp et al., 2011, chapter 13).

One of the issues with social design and its sub-categories as proposed by Veiga and Almendra (2014), and the related fields of social innovation and social entrepreneurship is that the term 'social' is used in several different ways. For example, those categories addressing human needs, such as Design for the Base/Bottom of the Pyramid (BoP), Humanitarian Design or Design as Development Aid, are directed towards the individual's wellbeing in terms of nutrition, health, poverty/affluence etc. By contrast, in the context of some of the other categories, such as Socially Responsible Design or Socially Responsive Design, or Design for Social Change, 'social' addresses the social relationship and/or the social interaction that people have to regulate their life in living together.

The difference between social good and social interaction is significant in terms of both design focus and approaches. For the purposes of this chapter, we focus on the notion of the social in the latter sense. Social interaction can be regulated on a legal level such as human rights, through policy or systemic interventions, or it can be guided in a 'bottom-up' approach through people's interaction with design. Humans have constructed an enormously intricate social environment to contend with the challenges of the natural environment and thus are fundamentally motivated to create and maintain relationships with other people. For example, social interaction is important in the maintenance of health and wellbeing and the quality of a person's daily interactions is one of the best predictors of wellbeing (Kahneman, 2011). Design can play an important role in changing behaviour and fostering and supporting inter-relationships that benefit human endeavour, not just in health and wellbeing, but also in other areas such as sustainability, safety or crime prevention.

Both Lockton (2012) and Tromp et al. (2011) have begun to consider the broad range of human behaviours and experiences to understand better the social influences of the design and use of products and product innovations. Tromp et al. (2011) have developed a framework for socially responsible design from the point of the intended user experience, while Lockton (2012: 1) tries to address the problem of user intent. Although focussing mainly on environmental impact, Lockton includes a generally pro-social approach. In contrast to Tromp et al.'s experience-based model, Lockton's model takes a functional approach, which considers motivating (internal constraint) as well as enabling and constraining behaviour (external constraint through design). Complementary to Lockton and Tromp et al.'s approaches is the mindful design approach by Niedderer (2007, 2013, 2014). Rather than on user experience, it focuses on creating responsible social interaction through designing conscious decision-making opportunities. This gives responsibility to the user for his or her decisions in acquiring, using and discarding design objects and services in the widest sense, and the interactions they entail.

These selected examples of approaches indicate that design for social behaviour change can variously address the *intention* (engendering responsibility and change), *process* (how to achieve change) or *outcomes* (e.g. user experience) of social design. We discuss these three categories or stages further in the next section.

Design for social behaviour change

The common thread across the different approaches of social design, and more specifically design for social behaviour change, is the aim to influence human interaction or norms that are in the public interest, defined as leading to improvements in the welfare or wellbeing of the general public (Random House, 2016). Given the importance of these intended outcomes, and the role that design plays in influencing them, it is important to better understand design for social behaviour change and its manifestation in both research and practice.

The outcomes of design for behaviour change and their impact are often the key focus of any intervention. What is important to acknowledge here is that such outcomes are the result of a process and that this process is guided by an intention. Moreover, there is an assumption that the intentions that guide design for behaviour change ought to be in the public interest, although this may not necessarily always be the case. It also raises the question about who decides what is in the public interest, and what happens when individual and public interests collide. This means there is clearly an ethical decision to be made when designing for (social) behaviour change. Although this arguably applies to all design, design for behaviour change aims to reflect on and make explicit this ethical responsibility.

In the following, we discuss design for social behaviour change with regard to these three aspects: the intention, the process, and the outcomes of design for social behaviour change. We discuss how these three different stages of designing can help achieve the outlined social aims. In the further text, we use the term 'social design' as a convenient short form for 'design for social behaviour change'.

Social design as an intention

On a conceptual level, design for social behaviour change can be thought of as the desire or motivation to influence human interaction for some perceived social or other benefit and as such as driven or imbued by social intention. In other words, the intention of social design is the application of design skills and processes to create primarily social value.

To illustrate the ascendance of design, the Design Ladder (Danish Design Centre, 2001) usefully describes the shifting role of design, albeit in a business context. The first step is non-design where design plays a negligible role; the second is design as styling where design relates primarily to style and form; the third is design as process where design is used to improve efficiency; and the fourth and final step is design as innovation where design drives all (business) activities. The use of skills and processes is important in design and may be implicit or explicit. However, design is not only the practice of following these processes, nor will following them automatically make someone a social designer, but it is the conceptual lead that makes design significant and relevant with regard to facilitating social change.

Commonly, designers are asked to design according to a given design brief. While a design brief offers certain criteria for addressing a specific issue at hand, on the other hand it is open to interpretation by the designer. In this context, the intent of the designer can greatly influence the balance between the intent of the client or partner who has provided the brief, the variation in what people who will be affected want and need and what the designer believes is the right approach both in terms of values and in terms of achieving them. Naturally, this can lead to conflict, where design that is intended to benefit a chosen group of people somehow restricting the choice or wellbeing of a different group of people. For example, traffic junctions that make journeys safer for cyclists may slow down journeys for motorists (Bunn et al., 2003). In these instances, a cost-benefit analysis may be undertaken or it may be down to the ethical judgement of the design team and wider management. For example, a utilitarian approach states that the chosen action should be the one that does the greatest good and the least harm for all who are affected (Mill, 1901) – users, customers, employers, residents, shareholders and so forth. However, what constitutes the 'greatest good' and 'least harm' in these cases is open to interpretation. For example, such costs can be assumed to be financial or social, or perhaps concern human dignity. Benefits might be financial or time saving, or the feeling of empowerment on the part of a user or user-group.

This demonstrates that intentions are closely linked to morality and to people's beliefs in the principles that distinguish right from wrong, or good from bad behaviour. Indeed, people may widely differ in their opinions of what is right or wrong, good or bad, based on their philosophy, religion or culture. People's moral principles can both bind them together, and make them blind to other people's interpretations of a better society (Haidt, 2012). While it is still possible for those with opposing views to sincerely want the best for society from their point of view, this constitutes a significant challenge for design for behaviour change. In other words, while social design per se does not make any assertions about the moral principles that underpin or that it should address, when put into the specifics of practice, social design necessarily has to take a position.

What good designers have in common is the desire and intent to improve life for themselves and others by questioning the status quo. In this context, design methods can help designers and other people better understand and respect the principles that other people hold. People everywhere are coming together to take responsibility for championing causes, solving problems or reacting to crises in their community. Many would not describe themselves as designers, entrepreneurs or innovators, or feel comfortable with that terminology, however they share intentions we would associate with social design. As this trend continues, the definition of social design – or a social designer – will begin to blur. The gap between the designer and the user will continue to narrow as people take on both roles, and this might help reduce potential conflicts between the designer's intentions and the wants or needs of users. Allowing people to take an active role in decisions – and designs – that affect society is a key element of democracy. Individuals or organizations that wish to support this type of participatory democracy, for example policy makers or social investors, must provide a supportive environment that gives people the opportunity to work together, develop new skills and abilities, engage in debate and turn their good intentions into action.

Case study 1: design ingenuity driving activism

This case study looks at the blurring between designers and users, and how the role of user as designer can overcome some of the ethical issues.

Activists, generally, are people with the desire to improve society and who are taking action to promote a social, political, environmental or economic change. Normally driven by a personal cause or struggle, the focus is often on how small changes to a service, system or environment can create new opportunities for people to behave or act differently. Taking this aspiration into design, Markussen (2013: 1) defines *design activism* as "design playing a central role in (i) promoting social change, in (ii) raising awareness about values and beliefs or in (iii) questioning the constraints of mass production and consumerism on people's everyday life". Applying his thinking in the context of urban design, he argues for a new framework to understand why and how activism matters, using examples from five categories – walking, dwelling, playing, gardening and recycling – to illustrate his point. For example, in the project "Taking the street", Santiago Cirugeda gives citizens in Seville instructions on how they can transform dumpsters into playful installations to get around local planning legislation, thereby enabling them to take an active role in designing their neighbourhood. The project strengthens the social interactions between local residents, while weakening, or actively resisting, interactions with existing structures of power and bureaucracy. The people become both the designers and the users, and unheard or hidden social behaviours become visible through the transformation of the dumpster.

Case study 2: innovation among communities of refugees

This case study looks at the role of organizations in helping people interact and work together to take an active role in decisions that affect their community.

   People around the world in communities affected by crisis, for example refugee camps, are often able to overcome significant constraints by working together and adapting to their environment to create new enterprises or systems. This type of innovation, driven by affected communities themselves, is known as 'bottom-up innovation' (Betts et al., 2015). When faced with a specific challenge or intention, people adapt to find solutions, drawing on the support and resources available. While activists may be involved, bottom-up innovation does not necessarily involve protest and may be supported by structures of power. For example, the UN High Commissioner for Refugees (UNHCR) support innovation among refugees to challenge humanitarian norms and fill important gaps in goods and services. For example, in the Za'atari camp in Jordan, residents are active in designing their own communications and information networks. One of the publications, *The Road* magazine, aims to "help make good relations in the camp between refugees and the organisations" (Betts et al., 2015: 29). This is just one of many communication systems that refugees and aid agencies have designed to create a flow of information and support interaction between internal and external individuals and organizations in the camp.

Social design as a process

On a strategic level, social design can be thought of as the application of tools, methods and activities for the purpose of influencing human interaction for some perceived social or other benefit. There are now many practical tools and methods to help designers and others engaged in the design process think and act creatively at different stages of the innovation process, loosely covering problem identification, idea generation, implementation and monitoring (Mumford et al., 1991). This design process is not based on a single 'innovative' or 'creative' skill, rather, different skills are important at each stage. Not everybody will be – or needs to be – skilled at every stage. Generically, these tools and methods include, but are not limited to, understanding user experiences, ideation, rapid prototyping and visualization (Mulgan, 2014).

Social design methods more specifically refer to methods that help facilitate the relationship and interaction between designers and the people they are designing with or for in order to understand them and their needs, wants and aspirations better. Cooperating to exchange ideas and expertise enables designers to access people's perspectives, knowledge, skills and abilities to understand a problem or implement an idea. While in the past, creation was largely driven by a designer's expertise and intuition, it is now accepted that this individualistic, passive approach cannot address the complex social issues we face today. Sanders and Stappers (2008) describe the evolution of social design methods from user-centred design, where trained researchers observe largely passive users, to co-design, where users play a more participatory role in idea generation, development and testing. Co-design therefore encompasses the collective creativity of designers and people who are not trained in design. This may happen informally through conversation and networks, or more formally as a part of a structured exercise or paid for service. Cooperation occurs when two or more people observe each other's actions and decide there is enough benefit to invest resources in future interaction. Social design methods facilitate this process, by facilitating communication, observation and empathy with what people really want and need.

Given the growing realization that the people with direct experience of a particular issue or concern are often the people with the best knowledge and experience of that issue, there is an increasing need for design processes that enable more social, creative and collaborative working. As the gap between designers and users continues to narrow, traditional design processes will become less important, and social design methods that focus on inclusivity and interaction between people from different backgrounds will become more relevant. The Social Design Methods Menu by Kimbell and Julier (2012) outlines a range of methods to "understand people's experiences and resources on their own terms" and push for "more effect cross-team and cross organisational working", from describing drivers of change to storyboarding and mapping the service ecology. These methods illustrate the changing design practices described by Sanders and Stappers, and the increasing focus on co-design in which users are active participants in the design process.

Social design processes are changing how people design and who designs. However, the demand for more inclusive, participatory design, in which people are both consumers and designers, must be tempered with the evidence that people are often unaware of their own preferences, don't do what they say and are not good at introspection (Johansson et al., 2006). Traditional market research methods often prompt people to post-rationalize decisions that they are unable to explain. This is why designers couple iterative, collaborative methods with ethnographic and experimental methods, avoiding self-report, to generate a deeper understanding of users. There are many toolkits and activities that aim to help people think and act creatively. For example, the Nesta DIY Toolkit provides practical tools to trigger and support social innovation; the Hyper Island Toolbox is a resource for people who want to work creatively and collaboratively; Service Design Tools curated by Roberta Tassi is an open collection of communication tools used in design processes that deal with complex systems; and the Design with Intent toolkit (Lockton et al., 2010) is a collection of design patterns aimed at socially and environmentally beneficial behaviour change, applicable across product, service, interaction and architectural design.

Case study 3: IDEO design kit

This case looks at how a design team used design methods to interact and strengthen their relationship with people in a town to develop a community-based business.

IDEO.org launched the Field Guide to Human-Centered Design in 2015 (IDEO.org, 2015) as a follow up to their original Human-Centered Design Toolkit launched in 2009. The guide is a set of design methods that people can use within the social sector. One example is the case of Asili, a sustainable, community-owned health, agricultural and water business in the Democratic Republic of Congo (IDEO.org, 2014). The design team first spent time immersing themselves in the context in which they were designing, conducting interviews with the residents of Bukavu to better understand the social dynamics around health. Following interaction with a lot of people in the area, they conducted a two-day workshop with women from the town who were particularly interested in the Asili service. The women took the lead in the design process, fulfilling the roles of designer, prototype and problem-solver, strengthening the relationship between the design team and the community. They then continued to work with the American Refugee Committee (ARC) to devise a sustainable business tailored to meet the realities that people in the DRC face every day, including the business model, staffing structure, launch plan and service components. The ARC took a human-centred approach to implementing the vision for Asili, which continues to build a multi-service offer to the local community.

Case study 4: the Knee High Design Challenge

This case looks at how a diverse range of people were supported in using design methods to develop innovative ideas to improve the health and wellbeing of children under five.

The Knee High Design Challenge is a partnership between the Design Council, Guy's and St Thomas' Charity, and Lambeth and Southwark Councils (Britton & Gardiner, 2015). The programme supported 25 teams of people to develop ideas for raising the health and wellbeing of children under five years old. The approach challenged traditional public health improvement programmes, first by researching and reframing problems that existing approaches to public health had so far failed to address. This involved using methods such as ethnographic research, shadowing and in-depth interviews, stakeholder engagement, community researcher training, a parenting survey and a toolkit for young children to focus down on three design briefs, offering provocations for action in Lambeth and Southwark. An open call was launched, inviting teams to respond to one of the briefs. Through a staged funding process designed to manage the inherent risk of innovation, a select number of teams were given financial and practical support to transform their good ideas into lasting and effective products and services. The support was tailored for each team, ranging from prototyping to experimental design and business planning. The final six teams included the Good Enough Mums Club, delivering theatrical performances and workshops to improve the emotional wellbeing of mothers; Pop up Parks, creating vibrant spaces in urban environments that encourage children and families to spend more time being playful and Kids Connect, informing and inspiring families to make use of the under-fives services in their local area. All the services and products funded through the programme were grounded in current evidence but boldly experimented with different ways to make a lasting difference, in contrast to the uniform approach of many public services. Three of the teams are now working with an external evaluation agency to pilot their ideas (Design Council, 2016).

Design for social behaviour change as an outcome

On a pragmatic level, social design can be thought of as the creation of products, services and spaces that influence human interaction for some perceived social or other benefit.

The cognitive processes that underpin how we make sense of the world are deeply rooted in the body's interaction with the world. Our behaviour is not simply a product of our own intentions and our thoughts. Decisions and actions must be explained in relation to our environment, and the perceptions and emotions it evokes. How the environment is designed, and all the products that are part of it, therefore plays an important role in determining how people interact, experience and process social information, either consciously or subconsciously.

The ability and motivation to form accurate perceptions of our physical and social environment and to react to incoming information is a key to the maintenance of social relationships. As humans, the amount of information we can process is limited (Simon, 1982) and, therefore our behaviour must be understood in terms of how we deal with social and environmental cues in real time (Clark, 1997). People regularly exploit the environment to reduce the pressure on attention and memory, and to hold or manage information in a social context, for example by using address books to store contact information and Facebook to maintain contacts. Such products or environments not only influence how we interact by offering certain aids and channels for communication. How these products and services are designed can also affect cognitive workload, how accurately people perceive social (and other) information, and the speed with which they react to it.

With regard to designing environments, choice architecture has become an important concept. It refers to how the design of the environment determines the way in which choices are presented to people and how this can affect decision-making. Heuristics – simple mental shortcuts that people use to form judgements and make decisions – are effective in many circumstances but can sometimes lead to deviations, or biases, from common normative behaviour (Tversky & Kahneman, 1974). Drawing attention to social norms is a typical example. People often use social norms to guide their behaviour in social situations, not always knowingly. Altering the choice architecture is one way of overcoming such biases. Designing products and services so that relevant norms are more salient can help elicit behaviours that are in line with favourable norms (Cialdini & Goldstein, 2004). For example, people who were given either individual (personal norm) or group feedback (descriptive norm) on the amount of household waste they had recycled both showed significant increases from baseline, and compared to the control group, in the total amount of recycled material over a four-week period (Schultz, 1999), suggesting a relationship between behaviour change and feedback interventions that target personal and social norms.

The intentions of the designer or choice architect greatly influence the outcomes produced in that they affect our decisions in all manner of ways, either implicitly or explicitly. Therefore, it is an ethical imperative to try to influence choices in a way that guides the chooser so that he or she is better off while maintaining freedom of choice (Thaler & Sunstein, 2003). The question 'what constitutes an improvement in wellbeing or welfare', however, leads critics to argue that choice architecture may impose costs, limited choice or a reduction of agency.

Just as the environment in general can be designed to influence perceptions and behaviour, so can specific artefacts in that a product's affordances can be designed in terms of functionality and experience through product semantics and semiotics. For example, cars allow people greater mobility and, by extension, to make or keep contact with people outside of their immediate vicinity. However, products are complex, and may have unintended consequences. For example, cars don't just facilitate mobility, but at the same time increase CO_2 emissions. In another example, increased safety was achieved in the redesign of street crossings in the Netherlands and the UK where the shared space model applied through the design, giving all participants equal status and equal responsibility (see case study 5). These two brief examples show that stimulation or regulation of social interaction can be the main purpose of a design, or it can be the means by which to enable another goal. They also demonstrate that the design of the affordances of products and environments are important, and require all stakeholders to take responsibility as well as a more holistic perspective in the design process. The two case studies below illustrate these two points further.

Case study 5: road safety

This case looks at how redesigning a road to increase road safety can lead to an output that improves the interaction between pedestrians, cyclist and vehicles occupying the same space.

Good design of roads, pavements and junctions is essential for the safety of drivers and pedestrians. The first white line road markings appeared on bends on the London-Folkstone road at Ashford, Kent, in 1914, and there is now a huge array of signs and markings across our streets that aim to change behaviour. The result is often a disagreement between different groups of users over who is being favoured or who is to blame for any resulting problems. Exhibition Road in London attracts over 11 million visitors each year and is the site of many educational institutions, including the V&A, Royal Albert Hall, Natural History Museum and Imperial College London (Transport for London, 2013). The street was redesigned in 2011 with a kerb-free single surface and little street furniture to favour pedestrian use, while allowing flexibility. By reducing the distinction between pavement and road, the idea was to encourage motorists to drive more cautiously, keep within the 20mph limit and pay attention to pedestrians. Exhibition Road was a RIBA award winner in 2012 and is often presented as a triumph for the 'shared space' movement, whereby pedestrians, cyclists and vehicles all occupy the same surface, leading to more responsible and mindful behaviour (cf. Niedderer, Chapter 9).

Case study 6: social media and user behaviour

This case looks at how the modern graphical user interface is changing how people socialize and interact, with potentially both positive and negative outcomes. The modern graphical user interface (GUI) is an excellent example of human centred design principles combined with applied psychology to guide and influence user behaviour. Designing the GUI is an important part of software development, from operating systems to car sat navs and mobile apps, to ensure the visual language is well tailored to the tasks people wish to perform.

The development of social media has allowed people to create and share a vast array of information and user-generated content at the touch of a button. The resulting shifts in human behaviour have led to debates on the positive and negative effects. This is amply evident through cases such as the Facebook news feed experiment, where the absence of positive social norms led to unintended offence because of unacknowledged, conflicting goals (Kramer et al., 2014).

It can be argued that social media has many benefits, including allowing the democratization of the internet, news dissemination and supporting communication during protests and revolutions. On the flip side, it has also been associated with shortening attention spans, narcissistic personality traits and low self-esteem (Forest & Wood, 2012). There are also privacy and trust issues around how much companies are using data on user behaviour to further their commercial aims without user consent.

Discussion and conclusion

This chapter has discussed the role of design for behaviour change within, and its impact on social contexts. It has offered an overview of current understandings of social design in relation to behaviour change to define what we mean by design for social behaviour change (also: social design for behaviour change, or short: social design). This understanding has shown to encompass three stages or characteristics of social design: concept, process and outcome, which have been discussed and illustrated through two short case studies for each. In the remainder of this chapter, we consider the relationship of these three categories or stages, and the role and relationship of designers and stakeholders.

Having discussed the three categories, or stages, of social design, the question is how they relate. Dependent on whether one sees these as stages or categories, the answer will differ. As stages, it seems fairly straight forward: the concept provides the perspective to the approach applied, and the process informs and implements the concept in form of the outcome. This may be in the order concept, process, outcome, but the stages may also be iterative or concurring at times.

As categories, the question changes to asking more specifically about the inter-relationships and whether they can be independent. Social design intentions normally lead to a social output or outcome as intentions drive behaviour. Such outcomes may however be achieved without using social design processes as the boundaries between designers and stakeholders are getting blurred, and many people express these beliefs without calling themselves designers. Such outputs may also be created to serve a different purpose and any social outcome may be unintentional. However, as discussed throughout the chapter, and indeed this book, it seems desirable not to leave such important issues and influences to chance, and therefore it is important for any designers or other stakeholders to take a holistic view that considers the range of aspects influenced by their actions or designs. To implement social design intensions, and achieve social design outcomes, it is not necessarily required to use social design processes. Neither does the use of social design processes necessarily lead to a social output or outcome: People and companies may use the processes for purely commercial aims and have no social intention.

In answer to the earlier-stated question, one might therefore say that social design involves a social intent turning into social outcome, by some kind of process, which may, but doesn't have to, be moderated by social processes. Nevertheless, the use of social processes has the benefit of giving a voice to stakeholders who may have an interest in the outcomes, making design more inclusive and democratic. This is important, because products, services and spaces are often created without understanding how and why people will interact with them, or how it will affect and effect social interactions.

This example demonstrates once more that people may attempt to ignore design, but they cannot ignore the role of design in influencing behaviour and social interactions. People who understand and embrace social design are more likely to create an output that is in the interest of the people they are trying to benefit. People who do not, will not be avoiding social design, but will be inventing their own principles that may be to the detriment of the people they are trying to benefit. Whether or not the social intentions of the designer are in line with the perceived wants or needs of the user depends on individual principles and the processes employed. Ultimately this will be judged by the people concerned, and whether they experience the desired increases in social interaction and wellbeing. The complexity of issues facing society combined with the need to save public money demands new approaches from the ground up. Social design can help anybody with social intentions play a part in designing the future and thus can help place people back at the heart of development.

References

Austin, J., Stevenson, H., & Wei-Skillern, J. (2006) Social and commercial entrepreneurship: same, different, or both? *Entrepreneurship: Theory and Practice Journal*, *30*(1), 1–22.

Betts, A., Bloom, L., & Weaver, N. (2015). *Refugee innovation: Humanitarian innovation that starts with communities*. Oxford: University of Oxford Refugees Study Centre.

Bhamra, T. A., Lilley, D., & Tang, T. (2011). Design for sustainable behaviour: Using products to change consumer behaviour. *The Design Journal*, *14*(4), 427–445.

Bitgood, S. (2011). *Social design in museums: The psychology of visitor studies*. Collected Essays. MuseumsEtc.

Brambilla, M., Fraternali, P., & Vaca, C. (2012). BPMN and design patterns for engineering social BPM solutions. *Business Process Management Workshops*, Volume 99 of the series Lecture Notes in Business Information Processing (pp. 219–230). New York: Springer.

Britton, E., & Gardiner, E. (2015). The knee high design challenge: Taking a different approach to early years. *Perspectives in Public Health*, *135*(3), 122–123.

Brown, T., & J. Wyatt. (2010, Winter). Design thinking for social innovation. *Stanford Social Innovation Review*. Retrieved December 18, 2012, from http://innernorthfoundation.org.au/downloads/design_thinking.pdf

Buchanan, R. (2001). Design research and the new learning. *Design Issues*, *17*(4), 3–23, 11.

Bunn, F., Collier, T., Frost, C., Ker, K., Roberts, I., & Wentz, R. (2003). Traffic calming for the prevention of road traffic injuries: Systematic review and meta-analysis. *Injury Prevention*, *9*(3), 200–204.

Chick, A. (2012). Design for social innovation, Iridescent: Icograda. *Journal of Design Research*, *2*(1), 78–90.

Cialdini, R. B., & Goldstein, N. J. (2004). Social influence: Compliance and conformity. *Annual Review of Psychology*, *55*, 591–621.

Clark, A. (1997). *Being there: Bringing brain, body and world together again*. Cambridge, MA: MIT Press.

Consolvo, S., McDonald, D. W., & Landay, J. A. (2009). *Theory-driven design strategies for technologies that support behaviour change in everyday Life*. CHI 2009: Creative Thought and Self-improvement, ACM Press, Boston, MA.

Danish Design Centre. (2001). *The design ladder: Four steps of design use*. Copenhagen: Danish Design Centre.

Design Council. (2016). *Knee high design challenge*. Retrieved August 16, 2016, from www.designcouncil.org.uk/what-we-do/knee-high-design-challenge

DRS2012. (2012). *Research: Uncertainty, contradiction, value – Design Research Society (DRS) international conference*. Book of Abstracts. Bangkok: DRS and Chulalongkorn University.

Dunne, A., & Raby, F. (2001, August). *Design Noir: The secret life of electronic objects*. Birkhäuser and London: Basel.

Forest, A. L., & Wood, J. V. (2012). When social networking is not working individuals with low self-esteem recognize but do not reap the benefits of self-disclosure on Facebook. *Psychological Science*, *23*(3), 295–302.

Gutiérrez, K. D., & Vossoughi, S. (2010). Lifting off the ground to return Anew: Mediated praxis, transformative learning, and social design experiments. *Journal of Teacher Education*, *61*(1–2), 100–117.

Haidt, J. (2012). *The righteous mind: Why good people are divided by politics and religion*. London: Penguin.

Huang, K. H., & Deng, Y. S. (2008). Social interaction design in cultural context: A case study of a traditional social activity. *International Journal of Design*, *2*(2), 81–96.

IDEO.org. (2014). *Asili*. Retrieved from Design Kit: www.designkit.org/case-studies/6

IDEO.org. (2015). *The field guide to human-centered design*. San Francisco: IDEO.

Johansson, P., Hall, L., Sikstrom, S., Tarning, B., & Lind, A. (2006). How something can be said about telling more than we can know: On choice blindness and introspection. *Consciousness and Cognition*, *15*(4), 673–692.

Kahneman, D. (2011). *Thinking, fast and slow*. London: Palgrave Macmillan.

Kimbell, L., & Julier, J. (2012). *Social design methods menu*. Retrieved November 6, 2016, from www. lucykimbell.com/stuff/Fieldstudio_SocialDesignMethodsMenu.pdf

Kramer, A. D., Guillory, J. E., & Hancock, J. T. (2014). Experimental evidence of massive-scale emotional contagion through social networks. *Proceedings of the National Academy of Sciences, 111*(24), 8788–8790.

Kraut, R. E., Resnick, P., Kiesler, S., Burke, M., Chen, Y., Kittur, N., Konstan, J., Ren, Y., & Riedl, J. (2011). *Building successful online communities: Evidence-based social design*. Cambridge, MA & London, UK: MIT Press.

Lockton, D. (2012, April). *POSIWID and determinism in design for behaviour change*, Working Paper Series. Brunel University. Retrieved December 18, 2012, from http://bura.brunel.ac.uk/handle/2438/6394

Lockton, D., & Harrison, D. (2012). Models of the user: Designers' perspectives on influencing sustainable behaviour. *Journal of Design Research, 10*, 7–27.

Lockton, D., Harrison, D., & Stanton, N. A. (2010). The design with intent method: A design tool for influencing user behaviour. *Applied Ergonomics, 41*(3), 382–392.

Margolin, V. (2002). *The politics of the artificial: Essays on design and design studies*. Chicago & London: The University of Chicago Press.

Margolin, V., & Margolin, S. (2002). A "Social Model" of design: Issues of practice and research. *Design Issues, 18*(4), 24–30.

Markussen, T. (2013). The disruptive aesthetics of design activism: Enacting design between art and politics. *Design Issues, 29*(1), 38–50.

Martin, R. L., & Osberg, S. (2007, Spring). Social entrepreneurship: The case for definition. *Stanford Social Innovation Review*, 27–39.

Mill, J. (1901). *Utilitarianism*. Longmans: Green and Company.

Mulgan, G. (2014). *Design in public and social innovation*. London: Nesta.

Mumford, M. D., Mobley, M. I., Reiter-Palmon, R., Uhlman, C. E., & Doares, L. M. (1991). Process analytic models of creative capacities. *Creativity Research Journal, 4*(2), 91–122.

Murray, R., Caulier-Grice, J., & Mulgan, G. (2010). *The open book of social innovation*. Retrieved May 20, 2017, from https://nesta.org.uk/sites/default/files/the_open_book_of_social_innovation.pdf

Niedderer, K. (2007). Designing mindful interaction: The category of the performative object. *Design Issues, 23*(1), 3–17.

Niedderer, K. (2013). Mindful design as a driver for social behaviour change. In *Proceedings of the IASDR Conference 2013*, Tokyo, Japan.

Niedderer, K. (2014). Mediating mindful social interactions through design. In A. Ie, C. T. Ngnoumen, and E. Langer (Eds.), *The Wiley Blackwell handbook of mindfulness* (Vol. 1, pp. 345–366). Chichester: Wiley.

Norman, D. A. (2002). *The design of everyday things*. New York: Basic Books.

Papanek, V. (1984): *Design for the real world* (2nd ed.). Academy Chicago Publishers.

Pearce, S. M. (1995). *On collecting: An investigation into collecting in the European tradition*. London: Routledge.

Petty, J. (2016). The London spikes controversy: Homelessness, urban securitisation and the question of "hostile architecture". *International Journal for Crime, Justice and Social Democracy, 5*(1), 67–81.

Popov, L. (2002). Architecture as social design: The social nature of design objects and the implications for the profession. *Journal of Design Research, 2*(2).

Random House. (2016). *Dictionary.com*. Retrieved from Public Interest: www.dictionary.com/browse/public-interest

Ritter, G. (2006) *The constitution as social design: Gender and civic membership in the constitutional order*. Stanford, CA: Stanford University Press.

Sanders, E. B.-N., & Stappers, P. J. (2008). Co-creation and the new landscapes of design. *CoDesign, 4*(1), 5–18.

Schultz, P. W. (1999). Changing behavior with normative feedback interventions: A field experiment on curbside recycling. *Basic and Applied Social Psychology, 21*(1), 25–36.

Segura, E. M., Waern, A., Moen, J., & Johansson, C. (2013). *The design space of body games: technological, physical, and social design*. CHI 2013, ACM, April 27–May 2, 2013, Paris, France.

Simmons, C. (2011). *Just design: Socially conscious design for critical causes*. Cincinnati, OH: Krause Publications.

Simon, H. (1982). *Models of bounded rationality*. Cambridge, MA: MIT Press.

Taylor, T. L. (2004). The social design of virtual worlds: Constructing the user and community through code. In M. Consalvo, N. Baym, J. Hunsinger, & K. B. Jensen (Eds), *Internet research annual volume 1: Selected papers from the association of Internet researchers conferences 2000–2002* (pp. 260–268). New York: Peter Lang.

TEPSIE. (2012). *European social innovation research*. Retrieved December 18, 2012, from www.siresearch.eu

Thackara, J. (2005). *In the bubble: Designing in a complex world*. Cambridge, MA & London, UK: MIT Press.

Thaler, R., & Sunstein, C. (2003). Libertarian paternalism. *The American Economic Review, 93*(2), 175–179.

Transport for London. (2013). *Better streets delivered*. London: Transport for London.

Tromp, N., Hekkert, P., & Verbeek, P. P. (2011). Design for socially responsible behaviour: A classification of influence based on intended user experience. *Design Issues, 27*(3), 3–19.

Tversky, A., & Kahneman, D. (1974). Judgment under uncertainty: Heuristics and biases. *Science, 185*(4157), 1124–1131.

Veiga, I., & Almendra, R. (2014). Social design principles and practices. *Proceedings of DRS 2014*, DRS and Umeå Design School, Umeå.

The Young Foundation. (2012). *Social innovation overview: A deliverable of the project: "The theoretical, empirical and policy foundations for building social innovation in Europe"* (TEPSIE), European Commission – 7th Framework Programme. Brussels: European Commission, DG Research.

20 Reflecting on current applications of design for behaviour change

Kristina Niedderer, Stephen Clune and Geke Ludden

This chapter reviews the current engagement with and applications of design for behaviour change approaches reported in the preceding five chapters. The chapter begins with an overview of design for behaviour change models, processes and tools that have been applied within the five domains of sustainability, health and wellbeing, social design, safety and design against crime. The overview shows that several of the models and tools discussed in Part 2 have been applied in the examples of Part 3, or have been used to understand and analyze them. It also highlights several more approaches that have not been explicitly discussed in Part 2. These include co-design, participation and design activism, which are discussed in more detail later in this chapter. These three concepts can be seen as related to what we call an expansion of the design ambition, which shifts attention from the historical focus on products to the broader approach of design thinking (e.g. Brown, 2008).

Indeed, all the authors in Part 3 offer a subtle critique of or warning against applying design for behaviour change strategies as a silver bullet. There is a shared acknowledgement that design must work within the broader societal system that holds everyday practices in place. Part of this discussion is a debate about the ethics of behaviour change, including who decides what should be done for the 'greater good', i.e. for social, ecological and economic sustainability. The chapters offer different ways for addressing such ethical questions, suggesting for example to involve all stakeholders through using participatory processes, or alternatively to avoid deciding for people altogether but rather support them in making their own individual informed choices and to take responsibility for them.

Following the overview and mapping of the examples and underpinning theoretical positions, we discuss three themes that have emerged from the review of the chapters and examples in Part 3 in more detail. These include the expansion of the design ambition, a new awareness of ethical concerns and an expansion in design process thinking that mirrors and supports the first two.

Overview of design for behaviour change approaches applied within the five sectors

In Table 20.1, we provide an overview of the different theories and approaches, which are discussed and applied in the different chapters of Part 3. We have extracted the individual examples, which are grouped by chapter (column of Table 20.1). In the column, we have listed the theory or overriding principle that underpins the example, with the citations in the middle. In this way, the table provides a concise overview of the diverse range of behaviour change theories and design for behaviour change approaches that have been

Table 20.1 Overview table of design for behavioural change examples and application

Theory or overriding principle	Citations	Example
Chapter 15 – Design for Behavioural Change and Sustainability		
Make the 'target' behaviour easier for people to do, undesired behaviour harder.	Lockton et al. (2010), Tromp et al. (2011) and Pucher and Buehler (2007)	Encouraging cycling, and discouraging car use through an extensive range of measures
Understanding individuals conceptualization of energy		Power chord energy feedback device that attempts to reconcile an individuals personal definitions, understanding and conceptualizations of energy, with a feedback mechanisms that is meaningful and works with those understandings
Chapter 16 – Design for Behaviour Change for Health and Wellbeing		
Patient empowerment	Wong-Rieger and Rieger (2013)	Increase treatment efficacy of in home care by utilizing a range of design for behaviour change principles
Environmental design	Pucher and Buehler (2007)	Provision of bike lanes, bridges, priority traffic signals, traffic calmed streets and secure parking to increase levels of cycling to benefit individuals' health
Environmental design		National Health Service (NHS) in the UK is acknowledging this with the project 'NHS Forest'.
Theory of locus of control	Folkman and Lazarus (1988)	Defines the cognitive control of emotion towards environmental stressors
Principles of persuasive technology (triggers, motivation, ability).	Fogg (2003)	Dementia care facilities designed reflect in the design outcomes presented
Behavioural economics/choice architecture	Lee et al. (2011)	Selection of healthy snacks through defaults
Mindful design	Niedderer (2013)	Empowerment of patients by healthcare professionals asking the patient what they have been doing recently to help their health
Design for Healthy Behaviour Framework/ stages of change	Ludden (Chapter 8)	Applied to encourage a reduction of sugary drinks
Theory of reasoned action		Understand the failure of people with dementia and their carers to accept some form of housing adaptation
Prompts and Environmental design		Encouraging people to take a break at work
Chapter 17 Design for Behavioural Safety		
Safety Engineering	Grinle et al. (2000)	Rails, guards, protective equipment within the manufacturing environment
Theory of planned behaviour	Ajzen (1985)	Encouraging parents to pack healthy foods into children's lunch-boxes
Health Belief	Hochbaum (1958)	Prediction of health-related behaviours, particularly in regard to the uptake of health services.

(Continued)

Table 20.1 (Continued)

Theory or overriding principle	Citations	Example
Stages of Change	Prochaska et al. (1992)	Prevention of Musculoskeletal Disorders in the occupational environment
Motivational Interventions	Sigurdsson et al. (2012)	Incentivized interventions for work-station use
Choice Architecture	Thaler and Sunstein (2008)	Washing machine/spin-dryer that cannot be opened until function is complete
Safe by Design	Office of Rail Regulation (ORR) 2016	Closure of the rail network for safe maintenance operations; safety of construction sites
Design with Intent	Lockton et. al. (2010)	Traffic calming measures to slow vehicle speeds
Mindful Design	Niedderer (2013)	Shared space road design
Chapter 18 Design Against Crime		
Crime Prevention through Environmental Design (CPTED)	Oscar Newman (1972), C. Ray Jeffrey (1971) and Jane Jacobs (1961)	25 principles that are applied to reduce many kinds of crimes, including robbery, burglary, shoplifting and vandalism
Situated Crime Prevention (SCP), rational choice theory, routine activity theory, and crime pattern theory	Clarke (1983)	
Increase the effort,	Centre for Problem Oriented Policing (2016)	1. Harden targets, 2. Control access to facilities, 3. Screen exits, 4. Deflect offenders and 5. Control tools/weapons
Increase the risks,	Centre for Problem Oriented Policing (2016)	6. Extend guardianship, 7. Assist natural surveillance, 8. Reduce anonymity, 9. Utilize place managers, and 10. Strengthen formal surveillance
Reduce the rewards,	Centre for Problem Oriented Policing (2016)	11. Conceal targets, 12. Remove targets, 13. Identify property, 14. Disrupt markets and 15. Deny benefits
Reduce provocations,	Centre for Problem Oriented Policing (2016)	16. Reduce frustrations and stress, 17. Avoid disputes, 18. Reduce emotional arousal, 19. Neutralize peer pressure and 20. Discourage imitation
Remove excuses	Centre for Problem Oriented Policing (2016)	21. Set rules, 22. Post instructions, 23. Alert conscience, 24. Assist compliance and 25. Control drugs and alcohol
Double diamond design process, participatory design	UK design council (2005)	Appreciation of the 'socially situated', mobilizes a collective approach to informed consent, the articulation of concerns and the review of proposals that might change behaviours to reduce cycle theft.

Topic	Reference	Description
'Defensible space' (social norms)	Newman (1972)	'Safety zones' typically comprise yellow boxes painted on the pavement to define a 'defensible space', ATM Art mats were effective in creating defensible space and well-liked by businesses and the public
Reframing problems	Dorst, cited in Gammon and Thorpe (Chapter 18)	Looking at 'festival' management techniques as a design to find ways to accommodate or deter the anticipated behaviours, opening the challenge up to more creative and collaborative responses than might be conceivable or achievable through an anti-social/policing lens

Chapter 19 – Design for Social Behavioural Change

Topic	Reference	Description
Design activism	Markussen (2013)	'Taking the street', Santiago Cirugeda gives citizens in Seville instructions on how they can transform dumpsters into playful installations to get around local planning legislation
'Bottom-up innovation'	Betts et al. (2015)	In the Za'atari refuge camp in Jordan, residents are active in designing their own communications and information networks
Co-design	IDEO.org (2015)	Asili, a sustainable, community-owned health, agricultural and water business in the Democratic Republic of Congo, Knee High Design Challenge
Choice architecture and mindfulness	Thaler and Sunstein (2008); Niedderer (Chapter 9)	'Shared space' movement in road design where signage and gutter are removed
Common normative behaviour	Tversky and Kahneman (1974)	Individual (personal norm) and group feedback (descriptive norm) on the amount of household waste they had recycled
	Kramer et al. (2014)	Facebook news feed experiment, where the absence of positive social norms led to unintended offence, because of unacknowledged conflicting goals

applied. The examples range from applying a very specific theory from psychology, such as the Design for Healthy Behaviour Framework that follows the stages of change model, to relatively generic principles, such as making the 'target' behaviour easier for people to do. In this way the table mixes behavioural change approaches and design approaches.

The table also allows identifying more easily the similarities and differences in the approaches and applications between the different domains. For example there are overlapping uses of theory and examples between the domains of sustainability and health, for example, cycling is considered once from the perspective of CO_2 reduction, and once from the perspective of increasing exercise and improving health.

Mindfulness is also used in several domains, included as a theory in the social, health and safety chapters, where an individual's responsibility is required or the adjustment of social norms.

In order to further illustrate the relative positions between the examples and related theories, we have further mapped the content of Table 20.1 against two axes as shown in Figure 20.1. The first axis represents the 'cognition–context' continuum that has been used already for the analysis in Part 2, and that distinguishes whether an intervention is aimed at the individual and cognitive decision-making or at the context determining the behaviour (Chapter 3). The second axis is a separation into product-focused or process-focused interventions. This reflects the heavy emphasis that many authors placed on the process of designing for behavioural change being as important as the outcome (be that a product or service).

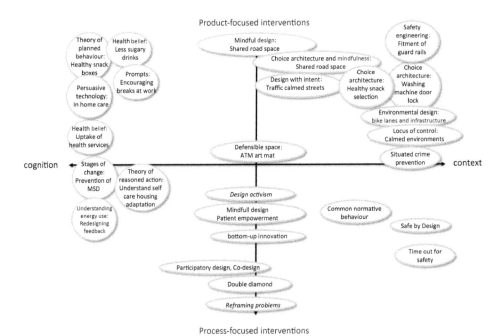

Figure 20.1 Design for behavioural change case examples across the cognition–context and product–process continuum.

Mapping the outcomes of the case study chapters against these two axes reveals several observations. First when attempting to influence behaviour through design for behavioural change in practice, many of the examples once materialized actually alter the context of the designed environment to make it more challenging for a particular behaviour to take place. Figure 20.1 illustrates that context-based solutions appeared more readily than presented previously in Part 2, which was slightly dominated towards cognition-based theories. Second, the figure emphasizes the focus that the authors in Part 3 have placed upon design processes, this is discussed in more detail below, however it is worth mentioning that we have classified the majority of processes as sitting in the middle ground between cognition and context. This may be indicative of the design processes natural tendency to understand people and their environment.

The product/process axis could be extended further to include Niedderer and Gardiner's notion of the designer's intent, which

> can greatly influence the balance between the intent of the client or partner who has provided the brief, the variation in what people who will be affected want and need and what the designer believes is the right approach both in terms of values and in terms of achieving them.
>
> (Niedderer and Gardiner, Chapter 19: 240)

The idea of intent thus could effectively add a third dimension to the diagram, which is the ethical consideration about the benefit of any intervention.

Expansion of the design ambition

As to be expected from any real-world application, all authors of the chapters within Part 3 have offered a discussion in some capacity of the role of design for behaviour change in relation to the broader social and cultural system that we live within. In other words, there is an acknowledgement of the limitation and challenges of encouraging people to act in a particular way via design, especially where these may run counter to established societal structures or norms. In this way, the discourse introduced through the case studies expands the discussion of processes offered in Part 2, adding reflection on the social nature of the design process and its expansion beyond the narrow interpretation of design as physical manifestation of ideas.

Morris and Hancox (Chapter 17) identify that in isolation, neither feedback, training nor design are sufficient to invoke a long-lasting change in behaviour – and that the requirement to foster a culture of safety from the top down is paramount. The example of 'time out for safety' attempts to signal that it is acceptable for any individual in the organization to stop work for safety. Such a strategy will struggle to take hold unless it has the support of all levels of an organization, where time is money, to enable the behaviour to be ingrained and normalized within practice. This is an example of where the socio-environmental context of design for behavioural change is extremely important.

In Chapter 18, for example, Gamman and Thorpe emphasize the role of participation, the voice of stakeholders, and the socially situated nature of the practices that may encourage change, and appear critical. Gardiner and Niedderer (Chapter 19) concur, stating 'the use of social processes has the benefit of giving a voice to stakeholders who may have an interest in the outcomes, making design more inclusive and democratic' (p. 246).

In Chapter 15, Clune and Lockton discuss this expansion of design with respect to the need for a systems perspective in that 'the ambition of designers may need to progress from making product-level improvements, to more systemic innovation' (p. 172). They further cite Brezet (1997) who proposes in the context of sustainability 'that for eco-design to achieve large-scale reductions in resource use, a move is needed from product improvement and redesign to systems innovation' (p. 172). Clune and Lockton suggest transition design as an approach that may address these broader challenges, such as the work of Terry Irwin and the meta-design approach (e.g. Ryan, 2011). In a similar fashion Ludden, Cain, Mackrill and Allen argue in Chapter 16 for design to 'target society at large, focussing on the design of infrastructures and environments in such a way that we create holistically healthy places to live in' (p. 196).

All these examples illustrate that design for behavioural change in application takes place within the broader contextual socio-environment. Therefore, it seems essential that design for behaviour change designers are aware of and take into account the holistic picture, and engage in a systemic approach, so as not to place the cart before the horse.

Design ethics

A principle that also all applications of design for behaviour change engage in is the concept of the 'greater good' – as a solution desirable for the majority or all of the population – and who decides on what the 'greater good' is. For some chapters (fields of application) this may appear easier than for others, however if we look back through history we see that there has always been a progression on what may be acceptable and normative behaviour that would now not be acceptable or vice versa. For example, looking at the domain of safety design, the general public opinion on companies' responsibility for the safekeeping of workers has dramatically changed. In today's world, we would never accept working situations that have been normal a century ago. Another example, in the domain of health and wellbeing, is the change in our understanding on what being healthy means, and on what a healthy lifestyle is. This has changed gradually with an increase of our knowledge on health and how lifestyle is related to certain diseases.

However, it is questionable whether this increase in knowledge will necessarily effect decisions that contribute to the 'greater good'. Take, for example, the increase in knowledge over the last century about how smoking relates to certain diseases. This has certainly led to interventions that are aimed at conscious decision-making (e.g. warnings on packages) as well as to contextual interventions in many countries (non-smoking zone policy for many public places). However, nowhere has this gone as far as deciding that smoking should be banned entirely 'for the greater good'. This indicates that such decisions are not always rational, nor is it necessarily the individual that is not prepared to change. Individual aims and social norms and benefits may collide in various ways: at times an individual may wish to quit (smoking, alcohol, drugs, car usage etc.), but succumb to the social norms and environment which keeps the habit alive; at other times, it may be individuals who resist the public good, succumbing e.g. to their addiction in spite of the dangers of secondary smoking for others or the pressure it might create on the health system. Such situations can be complicated and have multiple causes, and understanding the complex drivers is paramount to any sustainable solutions.

In the context of crime prevention, Gamman and Thorpe (Chapter 18) aptly summarize the ethical dilemma of using explicit design for behavioural change nudge techniques versus more participatory processes. They explain that

> the pragmatist must acknowledge that both strategies work to deliver behaviour change. Nudging is found to be appropriate in situations where *we think* we know the

'right' answer, where the greater good is obvious to all, in scenarios where no intentionality or agency is required, where the greater good will be served by behaviours that are unconsciously redirected. But, nudging does not work to change behaviours at a conscious level. Nor, does nudging work to bring together stakeholders to work out what the 'right answer' or 'greater good' might be in scenarios where contested understandings and competing objectives might limit the possibility of 'one right answer'.

(p. 231)

Expanding design processes

In order to address the challenges of design for behaviour change and to facilitate the changes in design thinking that this requires, it is necessary to consider also the changes in the design process. While Part 2 has focused on models and tools available to design for behaviour change, the case studies in Part 3 have highlighted the broader thought and research processes that underpin design for behaviour change. Part 2 has thus offered an overview over a selection of means, while Part 3 demonstrates how these means can be put to use to facilitate and put into action behaviour change by way of design.

For example, in Part 2, Daae and Boks have outlined a broad range of concepts available to designers in their toolkit, e.g. feedback, persuasion, automation, motivation and restriction which may be utilized to create change. However, the broader design thinking and research process in which the tools are embedded and through which they are applied is critical. Gamman and Thorpe emphasize that good design research has been critical within their case studies on bicycle locking and ATM teller machine redesign. They explain how the application of design for behaviour change strategies (termed nudge strategies in their chapter) utilizes a participatory design research process as well as a broader set of design research methods that aim to understand the contextual situation. Their research process is an extension of the UK Design Council's Double Diamond design process (2005), which follows the eight stages of design research (*Scope, Discover, Define, Develop, Deliver, Measure, Evaluate,* and *Scale/Disseminate*) to investigate the problem context, develop relevant solutions and assess them for suitability and effectivity.

In the context of the social design chapter (Chapter 19), there are three case studies which further communicate how design for behaviour change processes can be applied in a participatory manner: IDEO.org's Field Guide to Human-Centred Design, the Design Council's Knee High Design Challenge and Santiago Cirugeda's guide to guerrilla installations. In the example by IDEO, they had developed mechanisms and processes to enable participants to take the lead in developing their own solutions. The Knee High Design Challenge developed design briefs using ethnographic design research to reframe problems in public health that have proven challenging to address through conventional approaches. These design briefs then formed the basis for an open call for ideas, which was supported by funding and guidance to translate the best ideas into lasting and effective products and services. In the third example, Santiago Cirugeda gave citizens in Seville instructions on how they can transform dumpsters into playful installations to get around local planning legislation.

These three case studies point to the emerging co-design discourses that designers are still grappling with. Even though Sanders and Stappers (2008) have led the way on co-design some time ago, new works in this area such as Manzini's recent work *Design, When Everybody Designs* (2015) and Cruickshank's *Open Design and Innovation: Facilitating*

Creativity in Everyone (2014) indicate that there is still a need for the design community more broadly to adopt co-design principles and practices.

The changing nature of design

Over the last decade or two, designers have significantly expanded the application of what they apply their skills to. The expanding ambitions of design, design's new ethical awareness, and its processes following suit, are a clear and important indicative of the changing nature of design, in particular where the focus is on behaviour change.

The ascendance of design is described in Gardiner and Niedderer (Chapter 19) with reference to the design ladder developed in 2001 by the Danish Design Council (DDC, 2015), which

> usefully describes the shifting role of design, albeit in a business context. The first step is non-design where design plays a negligible role; the second is design as styling where design relates primarily to style and form; the third is design as process where design is used to improve efficiency; and the fourth and final step is design as innovation where design drives all (business) activities.
>
> (p. 239)

One might add a fifth step here where design takes the role of social consciousness, ethical awareness and responsibility. Niedderer and Gardiner identify that – due to this change in the perception of the role of design – the boundaries between designers and stakeholders are becoming blurred, and that many people aspire to the fifth level of design without calling themselves designers.

To aspire to the fifth level of the design ladder requires a substantial reframing of the problem approach. Such reframing is highlighted by Gamman and Thorpe via Dorst's example of rethinking the treatment of anti-social late night behaviour from a policing lens to a lens of exploring how designing 'festival' management techniques may accommodate or deter the anticipated behaviours. This approach was seen to open the policing perspective to the management of expected behaviour up to more creative and collaborative responses than might be conceivable or achievable through an anti-social/policing lens. As Dewey states, a 'problem well put is a problem half solved' (Dewey, 1998: 173). Therefore, in many of the examples in the preceding chapters, reframing the problem is key to reinterpreting any situation at hand and to developing novel approaches and solutions.

A response to this reframing has been the development of novel participatory design processes that acknowledge the social nature of design, the problems it seeks to address and the diverse stakeholders involved. This is summarized aptly by Clune and Lockton (Chapter 15) who state that 'the emergent rise of design thinking, co-design, product-service systems and service design suggests that design's application beyond products is maturing rapidly' (p. 172). Thus, formally, a participatory design approach is now being taught in many design schools around the world and, in a more informal way, the ability for everyone to be a designer is becoming easier through the emergence of digital technology.

References

Ajzen, I. (1985). From intentions to actions: A theory of planned behavior. In J. Kuhl & J. Beckman (Eds.), *Action-control: From cognition to behavior* (pp. 11–39). Heidelberg, Germany: Springer.

Betts, A., Bloom, L., & Weaver, N. (2015). *Refugee innovation: Humanitarian innovation that starts with communities.* Oxford: University of Oxford Refugees Study Centre.

Brezet, H. (1997, January/June). Dynamics in ecoDesign practice. *UNEP Industry and Environment, 20,* 21–24.

Brown, T. (2008, June). Design thinking. *Harvard Business Review.*

Centre for Problem-Oriented Policing. (2016). *Twenty five techniques of situational prevention.* University at Albany – State University of New York. Retrieved October 3, 2016, from www.popcenter.org/25techniques/

Clarke, R. V. (1983). Situational crime prevention: Its theoretical basis and practical scope. *Crime and Justice: An Annual Review of Research, 4,* 225–256.

Cruickshank, L. (2014). *Open design and innovation: Facilitating creativity in everyone.* Oxon: Gower.

DDC. (2015). *The design ladder: Four steps of design use.* Retrieved October 28, 2016, from http://ddc.dk/en/2015/05/the-design-ladder-four-steps-of-design-use/

Dewey, J. (1998). *Ethics, logic, psychology: The essential Dewey, Volume 2 by L. Hickman and T. M. Alexander.* Bloomington: Indiana University Press.

Fogg, B. J. (2003). *Persuasive technology: Using computers to change what we think and do.* San Francisco: Morgan Kaufman.

Folkman, S., & Lazarus, R. S. (1988). The relationship between coping and emotion: Implications for theory and research. *Social Science & Medicine, 26*(3), 309–317.

Grinle, A. C., Dickinson, A. M., & Boettcher, W. (2000). Behavioral safety research in manufacturing settings: A review of the literature. *Journal of Organizational Behavior Management, 20*(1), 29–68.

Hochbaum, G. M. (1958). *Public participation in medical screening programmes – a socio-psychological study.* Public Health Service Publication No 572, Washington DC, General Publication Office.

IDEO. (2015). *The field guide to human-centered design.* San Francisco: IDEO.org.

Jacobs, J. (1961). *The death and life of Great American cities.* New York: Random House.

Jeffrey, C. R. (1971). *Crime prevention through environmental design.* Beverly Hills, CA: Sage.

Kramer, A. D., Guillory, J. E., & Hancock, J. T. (2014). Experimental evidence of massive-scale emotional contagion through social networks. *Proceedings of the National Academy of Sciences, 111*(24), 8788–8790.

Lee, M., Kiesler, S., & Forlizzi, J. (2011). Mining behavioral economics to design persuasive technology for healthy choices. In *CHI '11 Proceedings of the SIGCHI Conference on Human Factors in Computing Systems* (pp. 325–334). New York: ACM.

Lockton, D., Harrison, D., & Stanton, N. A. (2010). The design with intent method: A design tool for influencing user behaviour. *Applied Ergonomics, 41*(3), 382–392.

Manzini, E. (2015). *Design, when everybody designs: An introduction to design for social innovation.* Cambridge, MA: MIT press.

Markussen, T. (2013). The disruptive aesthetics of design activism: Enacting design between art and politics. *Design Issues, 29*(1), 38–50.

Newman, O. (1972). *Defensible space: Crime prevention through urban design.* New York: Palgrave Macmillan.

Niedderer, K. (2013). Mindful design as a driver for social behaviour change. In *Proceedings of the IASDR Conference 2013,* Tokyo, Japan.

Office of Rail Regulation. (2016). *Strategy for regulation of health and safety risks. Chapter 12: Health and safety by design.* Retrieved October 29, 2016, from, http://orr.gov.uk/__data/assets/pdf_file/0009/21402/2016-03-18-New-Strategic-Chapter-12-Health-and-Safety-by-Design.pdf

Prochaska, J. O., DiClemente, C. C., & Norcross, J. C. (1992). In search of how people change: Applications to addictive behavior. *American Psychologist, 47,* 1102–1114.

Pucher, J., & Buehler, R. (2007, December). At the frontiers of cycling: Policy innovations in the Netherlands, Denmark, and Germany. *World Transport Policy and Practice.*

Ryan, C. (2011). Eco-acupuncture: Designing future transitions for urban communities for a resilient low-carbon future. State of Australian Cities Conference, Sydney.

Sanders, E. B.-N., & Stappers, P. J. (2008). Co-creation and the new landscapes of design. *CoDesign, 4*(1), 5–18.

Sigurdsson, S. O., Artnak, M., Needham, M., Wirth, O., & Silverman, K. (2012). Motivating ergonomic computer workstation setup: Sometimes training is not enough. *International Journal of Occupational Safety and Ergonomics, 18*(1), 27–33.

Thaler, R., & Sunstein, C. R. (2008). *Nudge: Improving decisions about health, wealth, and happiness.* New Haven, CT: Yale University Press.

Tromp, N., Hekkert, P., & Verbeek, P. (2011). Design for socially responsible behaviour: A classification of influence based on intended user experience. *Design Issues, 27*(3), 3–19.

Tversky, A., & Kahneman, D. (1974). Judgment under uncertainty: Heuristics and biases. *Science, 185*(4157), 1124–1131.

UK Design Council. (2005). *The design process.* Retrieved March 10, 2012, from www.designcouncil.org. uk/about-design/how-designers-work/the-design-process/

Wong-Rieger, D. & Rieger, F. (2013). Health coaching in diabetes: Empowering patients to self-manage. *Canadian Journal of Diabetes, 37*, 41–44.

Part 4

The current state and future of design for behaviour change

21 Conclusion

Kristina Niedderer, Stephen Clune and Geke Ludden

Together, the three preceding sections contribute to, and expand on, current understandings of how we can (and should) use design for behaviour change models and tools. We can see that the body of work on design for behaviour change is starting to mature and there are many important developments that are worth noting. We therefore use two final chapters of this book to summarize the insights gained, to draw more general conclusions and to discuss the contribution, benefits and limits of the book (this chapter). Further, we will outline future questions and challenges for the sector and provide an overview of the work that is needed to address these (Chapter 22).

Summary

In the introduction to the text, we highlighted that despite design's clear influence on human behaviour, the understanding of how design may lead to desirable behaviour change is still fragmented, with limited frameworks and examples for its effective implementation in professional and public contexts. Therefore, the aims of the *Design for Behaviour Change* volume were twofold:

1. To provide an overview of existing design models that integrate theories from different scientific backgrounds.
2. To offer an overview and practical guidance, through examples and case studies, on the application of design and behaviour change approaches that have been developed for, and used across different sectors within the field.

These aims were addressed by the different parts in the volume. Ultimately, this volume attempts to aid designers and design researchers, design managers, design students and anyone else interested in using design to 'make the world a better place to live in' to find the right approach.

Part 1 of the text has provided a rationale for the approach taken, illustrating design's significant contribution to societal and environmental change, and how the discipline of design has begun to grapple with the task of reorienting the negative elements of this social and environmental change via the emerging discipline of design for behaviour change.

Part 2 of the book has focused on the use of social and behavioural theory in design for behaviour change. The different chapters presented here have shed light on how different frameworks and methodologies in design for behaviour change have originated from different theories from sociology and psychology, and from design itself. Several chapters in

Part 2 not only discuss individual models, but also make some progress towards providing a process for designers of which strategies may be most appropriate for which type of intervention. For example, Daae and Boks's discussion (Chapter 7) considers the distribution of control, and Lilley et al. (Chapter 5) offer the 'axis of influence' in this regard. The summary chapter of Part 2 (Chapter 13) has highlighted the diversity of approaches and their integration of social and behavioural theories, has reviewed how individual models relate to different sides of the agency spectrum and their suitability in different circumstances and situations and it has summarized the development of the specific nature of behavioural design in terms of its focus on situational insights, processes and applications. This review demonstrates that the collection of design for behaviour change approaches and theories presented in Part 2 is significantly more diverse than the dominant individual-focused approaches from behavioural economics or persuasive technology that have historically dominated the literature.

In a complementary approach, Part 3 has outlined the scope of challenges that design for behaviour change in the five key domains of sustainability, health, safety, crime and social design could address, and it has provided an overview of the approaches used in each sector supported by exemplary case studies. More specifically, it has presented an overview of how design for behaviour change models and tools, and underpinning theories stemming from psychology and sociology have been applied in form of design for behaviour change interventions in specific domains. This is illustrated by many examples of how design can be utilized to create positive behavioural change interventions. Design for safety, for example, has had high success in reducing road tolls and improving safety in the workplace.

Throughout Part 3, we have seen that different models and approaches can be situated on different sides of Clark's (2010) context–cognition continuum. That a person's behaviour is a function of his or her own personality or other 'internal' factors (*P*) (related to cognition) and the physical and social environment (*E*) (related to context), therefore $B = f(P, E)$ (Lewin, 1935).

At the same time, many of the authors in Part 3 strongly advocate a holistic view on design for behaviour change that integrates both sides and where there is room for interventions aimed at the individual as well as for interventions that change the broader system in which we live. This holistic view is required to achieve the ambitious changes required for a sustainable and healthy society, such as a 95% reduction in resource and GHG emissions, or addressing obesity in 50% of the adult population, it is critical that there is an engagement with the broader system as a whole while not overly constraining individual choice. These broader interventions could draw increasingly on participatory processes and co-design. Co-design provides a way to include all stakeholders and give them a voice, and so addresses the ethical dilemma of who decides what is desirable change.

The concluding chapter of Part 3 (Chapter 20) has provided an analysis of all the different models, tools and processes that have been introduced throughout the discussion of the different domains and related examples. It has further elaborated on ethical challenges in design for behaviour change thinking as an essential element of applying design to fields that directly change organizations or even our societal system; on the expanding ambition of design to embrace the societal, environmental and ethical challenges as well as the matching development of appropriate processes to address them successfully; and on the changing nature of design that these changes entail.

With respect to the aim of assisting designers, managers and other change practitioners to select an appropriate theory for any particular projects or to address any specific problem, there are no easy 'look-up' tables for what is the best approach in any given situation. This is because of the complexity of the issues and challenges at stake, which include people and environments (in the widest sense) and the negotiations of their interests, affordances and vulnerabilities. Many examples discussed in this book, like the studies on health behaviour, cycling (sustainability) or traffic safety incorporate many parameters and layers of context, social interaction and understanding that have to be negotiated to arrive at a long-term sustainable solution that satisfies the positions and needs of all factors involved. In the absence of any easy look-up tables, this book aims to offer help in understanding and selecting different approaches. Through the overview of the different approaches, their characteristics and individual strengths, and their application in different domains, it becomes clear that each one offers a small but significant contribution in understanding how design may facilitate change. It is this multiplicity of perspectives across all chapters and domains that we hope will assist the reader in shedding light on the area and nature of desired change and help with selecting a suitable approach for any given situation or design problem. Thus we encourage the reader to view the theories presented as different facets of a whole rather than as individual competing approaches. We also hope that this will lead the field ultimately to develop more sophisticated and holistic design interventions for change.

Conclusion: contribution, benefits and limits of the book

Over the last decades, a range of books have emerged that have called designers to action and have given examples of how to design for a better world, thereby broadly defining the role of design in decision-making in society (see e.g. Berman, 2008; van der Zwaag, 2014). However, these books do not generally include specific theories on behaviour change or models and tools to design for behaviour change. Books that do advocate specific ways of creating behavioural change via design usually focus on how specific behaviours can be effectively created through a limited number of dominant strategies. Examples are Fogg's *Persuasive Technology* (2002), Anderson's *Seductive Interaction Design* (2011) and Wendel's *Designing for Behavior Change* (2013). These texts from persuasive technology and behavioural economics have until now dominated the design for behaviour change landscape, yet present only a narrow view of possible ways that design can be utilized to change behaviours and practices. Furthermore, such texts usually focus on one domain, rather than comparing approaches in similar domains to learn from them. This volume has therefore sought to explore the full gamut of possibilities on how design may influence behaviour and change via a broad range of different theories, models and tools as well as across five key domains, and which have been systematically presented and analyzed.

Through its twofold presentation, this book has offered a cross-disciplinary and cross-sectoral overview of the current developments of the field of design for behaviour change. Through offering a kaleidoscope of perspectives, the text seeks to encourage crossing discipline boundaries between the different approaches and application domains to develop a broader picture of the issues at stake. Furthermore, through the positioning, explanation and visual mapping of the diverse approaches, the book also seeks to make design for behaviour change approaches more accessible. It thereby allows readers not only to find a specific model or tool that fits their specific purpose, problem or project, but it also offers a diverse range of views on how change could or should come about. We hope that this will allow readers to make up their own minds on what change they would like to bring about, in what way and for what purpose – matching their unique values.

Finally, comprising a wide and varied range of theories, models and tools, as well as examples and case studies, in five important sectors, of course entails its own limitations: in presenting a variety of approaches and their application in a variety of domains, we had to sacrifice depth of the individual approaches and we could only scratch the surface of the individual domains. In addition, this has restricted us to focussing on a selection of the most recent developments in the field of design for behaviour change. Nevertheless, we hope that the book provides enough reason, detail and references to encourage the readers to explore any of the presented domains and topics further.

References

Anderson, S. P. (2011). *Seductive interaction design: Creating playful, fun, and effective user experiences*. Berkeley, CA: New Riders.

Berman, D. (2008) *Do good design*. Berkeley, CA: New Riders.

Clark, G. L. (2010). Human nature, the environment, and behaviour: Explaining the scope and geographical scale of financial decision-making. *Geografiska Annaler: Series B, Human Geography, 92*(2), 159–173.

Fogg, B. J. (2002). *Persuasive technology: Using computers to change what we think and do*. San Francisco, CA: Morgan Kaufmann.

Lewin, K. (1935). *A dynamic theory of personality – selected papers*. New York and London: McGraw-Hill Book Company, Inc.

van der Zwaag, A. (2014). *Looks good, feels good, is good: How social design changes our world*. Lecturis: Eindhoven.

Wendel, S. (2013). *Designing for behavior change: Applying psychology and behavioral economics*. Sebastopol, CA: O'Reilly.

22 Future prospects

Kristina Niedderer, Stephen Clune and Geke Ludden

Numerous design for behavioural change theories have been presented in this edited text, with supporting case studies illustrating how the models and tools have been applied successfully to lead to positive change. One of the greatest challenges we are facing today is to achieve social and environmental change under a magnitude of scale and time pressures, such as to drastically reduce emissions in a limited time frame. We have argued that design can and has to play a leading role in achieving this challenge and, in this regard, we have synthesized four interrelated themes from the edited text, which we discuss in the following. We believe that these four themes require attention by the field of design for behavioural change in order to progress the aforementioned challenges under the given pressures of scale and time. The four themes are these:

- **Who decides:** who will own and administer required behaviour change interventions and how may they be brought about?
- **Time:** How may we design with longer-term horizons while considering uncertainty and the future?
- **Evidence:** How to strengthen the evidence base via more systematic case studies and evidence based examples of design for behavioural change?
- **Complexity:** How to progress from a focus on singular target behaviours to multiple interrelated practices?

The ethics of who decides: involving multiple perspectives

A question that has been raised in many chapters in this book is where or with whom the responsibility for making changes really lies. We have stated in the introductory chapters that by bringing together these theories, models and tools, we aim to assist designers, design managers and behavioural change practitioners in finding the right approach and tools to assist their specific design for behaviour change problem. Inherent in this aim is the assumption that the tools presented in this book will be used for the 'greater good', i.e. for enhancing environmental and social sustainability, safety, wellbeing and health and reducing crime. This means that it is the application of the tools to these sectors, rather than the tools themselves, which is critical and which needs some thought because these tools could equally be used to the opposite effect (and could be argued are already), that is to sell and consume more at the expense of our social and environmental health and wellbeing. This brings to the fore the ethical dimension of design for behaviour change with the question of what is desirable change and on who decides on this.

If design is involved in devising such large-scale changes, we can make an argument for the ethical responsibility and ethical call to action of designers with regard to the nature of change and who is involved by acknowledging that:

- Design is more than a reflection of society; it is a force that has drastically altered the shape of society;
- Designers therefore should take some responsibility for the current shape of our world; and
- Designers therefore should share the responsibility for solving the major issues that we face as a society with all stakeholders concerned.

If we accept the first statement, which assumes that design is a major factor for change, the second and third statement become a necessary conclusion, which needs further exploration. On the one hand, accepting design's role in change requires the designer and anyone else involved in and facilitating and promoting the (outcomes of) the design process – from the trend forecaster, to the marketing assistant to the chief executive manager of any company. On the other hand, such complex problems have a multiplicity of stakeholders who ought to have a right to have a voice in the shaping of our world. Generally, with serious and large-scale problems such as improvement of sustainability, health, etc., there are many stakeholders involved who all have varying and often contradictory interests. This means that there is a need to negotiate the two roles of the two sides – those who shape the world, and those whose world is shaped, although this is becoming blurred under the recognition that we are all actors and that therefore all of us are responsible for how we have collectively shaped the world.

This brings us back to the deep ethical questions about the role of design, and in particular about what is considered desirable change (what is the 'greater good') and who decides? Who will own and administer the behaviour change (intervention) and to what degree should this change be prescribed or voluntary? It has long been argued that design has a major impact on society, but that as a discipline it is relatively ill equipped to predict or counter any negative impacts of design (e.g. Fry, 1999). Often the responsibility of enacting change has been placed on the individual users, yet there is a recognition that the mitigation and prevention of undesired behaviours can be equally important and may lie with the responsibility of a broader range of stakeholders who share responsibility in designing the environment we live within. Therefore, the careful and long-term consideration of all aspects of design and the problems it is called on to address as well as the recognition and involvement of all relevant stakeholders is a key factor for success.

Long-term thinking: designing with uncertainty and the future

The focus on short-term profits ahead of long-term environmental or social interests is an easy critique within current society. The recommendation that policy makers, strategists and managers promote longer-term thinking beyond immediate financial gain, considering ethical and sustainable benefits (for society and the world as a whole), is critical.

This long-term thinking must take place in an environment that has a high degree of uncertainty. Donald Schön (1971) within his defence of the stable state argued that the only thing for certain is uncertainty and change. This may seem like a get-out-of-goal card to be non-committal to the future. However, the historic trajectories of design (and society) illustrate that society and technologies have always been dynamic, and will continue to be. Fry (1999: 11–12) – acknowledging this uncertainty – takes the position that the future is in part set in place by the present and past and has logic; he explains:

> The future is never empty, never a blank space to be filled with the output of human activity. It is already colonised by what the past and present have sent to it. Without this comprehension of what is finite, what limits reign and what directions are already set in place, we have little knowledge of futures, either those we need to destroy, or those we need to create.

We have duel positions here: that there will be uncertainty in the future, and at the same time that the future is already in part set in motion. This means we have both the opportunity and the obligation to act. The obligation, because we can see today that the current trend of our trajectory is long-term environmental and social destruction. The opportunity, exactly because the future is not yet fully defined: there will be consequences of current pollution and resource use, wars, immigration crises, etc. but there is also the opportunity to shape our future to avert disaster and to create a long-term sustainable world. The environmental and social challenges we face suggest an urgent requirement to take action.

Voros (2001) discusses four classes of developments of the future: those that may be probable, plausible, possible and preferable. One may add that there are also those that may be considered impossible, based on current scientific understanding. Considering these four classes may assist designers to determine where and how to act, in light of the new social, technical and environmental developments that may be influential in the future. For example, the collaborative consumption and sharing movements may place more emphasis on access than to ownership, such as car share or Airbnb (two-out-of-three Airbnb founders were industrial designers), and possibly challenge the dominant model of individual ownership and consumption. Similarly, it is probable that a shifting climate will have an impact, creating new challenges such as additional resource scarcity, species loss, transmission of health and disease and the movement of people from environmental and political conflict.

Such developments represent initiatives for designers to actively identify and respond to for 'desirable' change. If we look back on the text in 50 years, we hope that some of the challenges that are a focus in the text have disappeared, however they will no doubt be replaced by new challenges.

Evidence: qualifying the impact of design for behavioural change

In order to determine the success of any intervention, it is necessary to have a measure, however soft or hard, against which to compare it. The book shows that current approaches to design for behaviour change are still rather eclectic and that it is often hard to draw conclusions on their success. Up to some point, this will always be the case, since full consensus what a successful change would entail is hard to reach. However, assuming a majority consensus, there is still the difficulty that all too often there is a lack of evidence of their implementation. This can have different reasons: it can be difficult to obtain relevant data, and time and money are not available to collect the required evidence; or there may be a fear of litigation or other negative effects for a company if negative evidence is found.

Nevertheless, understanding the results and consequences of any intervention is important. In this regard, in 1935, Lewin (1935) proposed that change occurs at the intersection of the individual and the environment, and, historically, we see that change does and can occur with sustained effort and commitment to both the individual and the environment over time. For example, commuter cycling in Copenhagen increased from 10% in the 1960s to 45% in 2014 (Goodyear, 2012; City of Copenhagen, 2015), and recycling in Belgium increased from 11% in 1991 to 55% in 2014 (OECD, 2016). Attributing causality and responsibility for the impact and consequences of design however still is a major challenge due to a lack of clarity. To further the field, there is therefore a need for more systematic development, evidence-based testing and more systematic and detailed representation of evidence-based examples.

Researchers in the field of design for behaviour change will need to find (new) ways of predicting and measuring the impact of behaviour change. Currently, and the chapters in this volume effectively sum this up, the larger body of work is focused on determining the theory and strategy behind behaviour change. At best, studies consider the short-term impact of an intervention. In the future, the field may need to shift its focus towards developing methodologies and models that consider the long-term impact of behaviour change interventions. A valuable approach could be to develop interventions in collaboration with professional stakeholders and to evaluate them in practice. Ultimately, this should lead to agreed and accessible methods of evaluation, including longitudinal means of evaluation. Only by using these we can start building a library of fully evidence-based case studies and examples of effective behaviour change that are more easily adopted by industry to create sustainable innovations (see also Niedderer et al., 2016).

A library of successful and validated case studies could also instigate convincing recommendations to policy makers, strategists and managers. Evidence of long-term impact of interventions can promote thinking that looks beyond immediate financial gain to ethical and sustainable benefits (for society and the world as a whole) in the longer term. This may enable a more targeted and strategic approach to change under the time and scale pressures, providing confidence for industry to pursue design for behaviour change strategies.

Engaging in complexity and systems thinking: the multi-faceted nature of problems

A characteristic of several of the models and tools presented in this text is that they require the identification of a target behaviour to shift to be effective. However, there is an unlimited number of target behaviours that could potentially be addressed to improve the five themes presented in Part 3. This means that the identification and change of an individual target behaviour may have narrow application and impact. To be more effective, it may be beneficial to move from targeting behaviours in isolation to looking at the multi-faceted nature of problems.

A way to design for behaviour change that has proven to be effective in some cases is to consider both context and individual behaviour and to target multiple behaviours that together determine whether (or not) a change will be realized (holistic approach). Adopting a holistic approach, by targeting both context as well as cognition, seems to be an effective strategy when targeting a complex health issue, such as child obesity, by promoting increased activity and healthier diet at the same time (see also Doak et al., 2006). For example, in 2013, the city of Amsterdam in The Netherlands started a programme (called AAGG) aimed at eliminating the issue of child obesity within the city in the year 2033. The program has adopted a holistic approach that targets parents and children (cognition side) as well as schools, sports societies and community centres (context). Furthermore, multiple factors contributing to the problem of child obesity are targeted: the programme introduced interventions to increase physical activity and to eat a healthier diet at the same time. Furthermore, connections have been suggested that a healthy diet is also a more sustainable one as this generally requires less sugars, fat (meat) and more vegetables. Initial results (Steenkamer & Franssen, 2016) of the programme show that in some areas of Amsterdam child obesity has indeed decreased.

This kind of holistic approach, which is as yet rarely adopted, offers great opportunities for the development and application of design for behaviour change. There is unexplored but promising territory here of combining multiple strategies into one holistic intervention or programme of interventions. This has the potential in many cases to lead to more effective and more sustainable changes than a single intervention that has to overcome multi-faceted problems by itself. As mentioned previously, we therefore hope that the overview and relating of different approaches in this book will encourage readers to consider the application of such holistic strategies by combining multiple contextual and cognitive approaches.

In some of the previous chapters, we have also elaborated on how design is increasingly being applied to non-traditional fields and on how the role of design is changing. Indeed, a number of regional and sometimes national government policies, e.g. in Finland and in Denmark, have given design a central role. A recent example of this development is that the city of Helsinki established a post for a Chief Design Officer. In the job description, it said that the objective of the CDO would be to provide the city with visionary, creative thinking where priority is given to the users. Design professionals were specifically invited to apply, and using design to solve major societal issues in mobility and sustainability was put high on the agenda for the CDO. The Chief Design Officer's role, whether in a company or in a city, therefore is one of the new roles that could put the current and future developments in design for behaviour change to good use. The new knowledge and tools that emerge from the field of design for behaviour change should be added to the repertoire of the designer, and imbedded in design thinking through the academic and professional education systems.

At the heart of successfully addressing future challenges through the effective advance, adoption and application of design for behaviour change will therefore be the acceptance of the challenges and opportunities offered by the four areas discussed in this chapter: in the recognition of the ethical responsibilities of devising change and in the move to the evidence-based development of long-term, complex system thinking. In particular, there has to be recognition that design cannot and must not only be driver for innovation for growth, but for sustainable growth. Only where sustainability is considered in all areas, including social and ecological sustainability, and not just financial growth, can we build a truly sustainable and worthwhile future. We can find first examples of the realization of such future thinking, for example, through the inclusion of a Gross National Happiness (GNH) index alongside the common measure of the Gross Domestic Product (GDP) in Bhutan. A Green index has also been proposed more recently. These movements away from traditional understandings of growth measures as productivity as well as recommendations such as those made in the Stern report (2006) demonstrate that sustainability may not have to be at the expense of growth. They may however necessitate a rethinking and perhaps redefining of what the parameters of growth mean: already the economy has moved from the production of physical goods to the knowledge and digital economies. So perhaps an economy driven by social and ethical values may not be so far fetched.

References

City of Copenhagen. (2015). *Copenhagen city of cyclists the bicycle account 2014.* Retrieved October 31, 2016, from http://kk.sites.itera.dk/apps/kk_pub2/pdf/1382_FvvnTRBSlZ.pdf

Doak, C. M., Visscher, T. L. S., Renders, C. M., & Seidell, J. C. (2006). The prevention of overweight and obesity in children and adolescents: A review of interventions and programmes. *Obesity Reviews, 7,* 111–136.

Fry, T. (1999). *A new design philosophy: An introduction to Defuturing.* Sydney, University of New South Wales.

Goodyear, S. (2012). *Why the streets of Copenhagen and Amsterdam look so different from ours,* Retrieved October 31, 2016, from www.citylab.com/commute/2012/04/why-streets-copenhagen-and-amsterdam-look-so-different-ours/1849/

Lewin, K. (2013 April 16 [1935]). *A dynamic theory of personality – selected papers.* New York and London: McGraw-Hill Book Company, Inc.

Niedderer, K., Mackrill, J., Clune, S., Lockton, D., Ludden, G., Morris, A., Cain, R., Gardiner, E., Gutteridge, R., & Hekkert, P. (2016). Design for behaviour change as a driver for sustainable innovation: Implementation in the private and public sectors. *International Journal of Design, 10*(2), 67–85.

OECD. (2016). Municipal waste, generation and treatment: % material recovery (recycling + composting). *OECD.stat.* Retrieved November 6, 2016, from https://stats.oecd.org/Index.aspx?DataSetCode=MUNW

Schön, D. A. (1971). *Beyond the stable state: Public and private learning in a changed society.* Middlesex: Penguin.

Steenkamer, I., & Franssen, S. (2016). *Outcome monitor AAGG 2016. Gemeente Amsterdam.* Retrieved October 28, 2016, from www.amsterdam.nl/bestuur-organisatie/organisatie/sociaal/onderwijs-jeugd-zorg/amsterdamse-aanpak/programma/ (in Dutch).

Stern, N. H. (2006). *The economics of climate change.* London: HM Treasury.

Voros, J. (2001, December). A primer on futures studies, foresight and the use of scenarios. *Prospect, the Foresight Bulletin No. 6.* Melbourne: Swinburne University of Technology.

Index

above-the-hand category 27, *28*, *29*, 30–2, 35–6
action stage 23, 206
Active by Design initiative 95
activism case study 240–1
adaptive systems 62
affordances: concept overview 26; design for behaviour change 59, 61–2; design-psychological approach on 151
agency divide concept 20–1, 152–4, *153*, *154*
agency-traversing nature of psychological models 151
Ambridge, Alexander *66*, 66–7, *67*
American Refugee Committee (ARC) 243
anti-social late night behaviour 258
application of behavioural models 20
Arduino-based system 178
assembly line process 9
assessment of design impact 12–13
assumptions about people 68
ATM art mats case study 164, 219, 225–7, *226*, 257
attentiveness concept 22
attitudes in behavioural change 60
Australian Food and Grocery Commission (AFGC) 131
Australian Housing and Urban Research Institute 192
automaticity levels 42
autonomy and influence of design 141–4, *142*, *143*
Axis of Influence 54, 75, 153

before-the-eye category 27, *28*, 28–9, *29*, 31–2, 34
Behavioural Insights Team (BIT) 60, 228, 231
behavioural safety design *see* safety-design focus
behavioural sciences 19–20
behavioural targets in DfSB 44–9
behavioural theory 43
Behaviour Change Support System (BCSS) 190

behaviour change tool 77–88
Behaviour Intervention Selection Axis (BISA) tool 49, *50*, 54
behaviour intervention strategy 49–50, *50*
behaviour steering 47, 74–5
behind-the-back category 27, *28*, *29*, 30, 31–2, 35
Bel Geddes, Norman 134–5
Bicycle Institute for Policy Research 174
Bikeoff research initiative 220–5, *221*, *222*, *224*
birdsong prototypes 178
Bright Light Therapy 186
built environment 95–6

CaMden stand design 221–5, *222*
Carbon, Control and Comfort (CCC) 40, 45, 47, 51
carbon dioxide emissions: food concerns 167–8; goods and services, consumption concerns 168–9, **169**; housing and energy 167; increases in 244; introduction to 166–7; reduction in 172, 254; sustainability design and 161, 166–9; transport concerns 168
card-form tools 63
central route persuasion 59
Centre for Problem Oriented Policing 217
Chalmers University of Technology 51
choice architecture 62, 96, 202–3
choice in mindful design 108
Chronic Obstructive Pulmonary Disease (COPD) 162, 184
classification strategies 60–1
Clever Design 75
climate change 161
coaching systems for healthy behaviour 94–5
co-design 242
Coercive principles 75
cognition-based spectrum 21
cognition–context continuum 20–1, 172, *254*
cognition strategies 60–1, 152
cognitive short cutting 42

collective creativity of designers 242
complexity in mindful design 108
Comprehensive Economic and Trade Agreement (CETA) 10
conceptual development 23–4
Conjunction of Criminal Opportunity (Ekblom) 217
consequence intervention 45
constraints on behaviour 59–62
construction industry, risk prevention 209–10
contemplation stage 23, 205–6
content in mindful design 108
context-cognition continuum *see* cognition-context continuum
context strategies 60–1, 255
control dimension 77, 79, *80*
crime pattern theory 216
cross-disciplinary considerations 58–9
Crossick, Geoffrey 223
cultural impact of change 22
cycling case study 172–5, **174**

Danish Design Council (DDC) 258
day-to-day actions/behaviours 155
decision-making: in behavioural change 60; Design for Sustainable Behaviour 44, *45*, 53; introduction to 5, 22; public sector decision-making 228; user actions and 105
Decisive principles 75
delegated morality 26
Delft University of Technology 51, 123
demand-based pricing changes 177
dementia care 191–4, *193*
depression concerns 184
Design, When Everybody Designs (Manzini) 257
design activism 240–1
Design Against Crime (DAC): ATM art mats case study 164, 225–7, *226*; Bikeoff research initiative 220–5, *221, 222, 224*; case studies 220–7; introduction to 163, 216–20, **218, 219**; nudge theory 223, 227–30, **229, 230**; prevention context 256–7; summary of 230–1
Design Against Crime Research Centre 164, 220, 225, 231
Design Council (UK) 187
design for behaviour(al) change: agency divide concept 152–4, *153, 154*; applications for 161–4; behavioural and social sciences 3–4, 19–20; case study *66,* 66–7, *67*; challenges of 12–14; changing nature of 258; classification, context, and cognition 60–1; context-cognition continuum 20–1; contribution of approaches 154–6; cross-disciplinary considerations 58–9; decisions, attitudes, and practices 60; defined 4–5; design pattern format 63–6, *64,* **65**; emergence of 10–12; enabling, motivating, or constraining 59–60; ethics of 256–7; expansion of design ambition 255–6; ideation and

conceptual development 23–4; insight into 22; intrinsic relationship of 9–10; introduction to 3–4, 19, 58, 150, 250; mental models 62–3; models and assumptions 67–9; overview of 5–7, 250–5, **251–3**, *254*; patterns and toolkits 63; process of 22–3, 257–8; psychological approaches to 150–1; sociological approaches to 151–2; summary of 24, 263–6; systems, affordances, constraints, information flows 61–2; uses and contributions for 21–4
Design for Behavioural Safety *see* safety-design focus
Design for Healthy Behaviour Framework 190, 254
Design for Sustainability *see* sustainability design
Design for Sustainable Behaviour (DfSB): behavioural targets 44–9; behaviour steering 47; evaluation of 51–3; feedback interventions *45,* 45–6, *46,* 51; future of 90; Goal Framing theory 43–4, **44**; intervention strategy 49–50, *50*; introduction to 40, 74; persuasive technology 47–9, *48*; strategies of 23; summary of 53–4; user's actions 40–4, *41, 43,* **44**
design for usability 26
designing coalition 224
Designing Out Crime Research Centre 230
Design Ladder (Danish Design Centre) 239
design of choices 223
design pattern format 63–6, *64,* **65**
design-psychological approach on affordances 151
Design with Intent (DwI) toolkit: elements of *64,* 64–6, **65**; patterns and 63–6; road safety 210; social design 242; summary of 67, 75–6
determinism 63
Dimensions of Behaviour Change (DBC): control dimension 77, 79, *80*; direction dimension 77, 83–4, *84*; empathy dimension 77, 84–5, *85*; encouragement dimension 77, 81–2, *82*; exposure dimension 77, 87–8, *88*; importance dimension 77, 85–6, *86*; introduction 74–6, **76**; meaning dimension 77, 82–3, *83*; obtrusiveness dimension 77, 79, *79,* 80; overview 77–88, **78–9**; reflection on 88–90, *89*; summary of 90–1; timing dimension 77, 86–7, *87*
direction dimension 77, 83–4, *84*
disease impact 162
distraction theft 225
distribution of control 75, 153
domestic energy consumption studies 42
Dorst, Kees 230
Double Diamond design 217, 257
Dutch Data Protection Agency 32

ecological interface design 62
Eco-spur 75
Ekblom, Paul 217
embodied technology 34

emotions and mindfulness 108–9
empathy dimension 77, 84–5, *85*
enabling framework 59–60, 99–100
encouragement dimension 77, 81–2, *82*
energy use, understanding 175–80, *177*, *178*, *179*
environmental interventions 95
environment and health and wellbeing 186–7, *188*
ergonomics 11, 58, 156
Erratic Radio (Ernevi) 178
ethics of design 34, 256–7
exposure dimension 77, 87–8, *88*
external locus control 153

feedback interventions *45*, 45–6, *46*, 51
Field Guide to Human-Centered Design 243
Flusser, Vilém 26
Fogg, BJ 26
food concerns 167–8
forgetting to check out 32–4
functional emotional action 109
functionality (functional artefacts) 105–6
futurama exhibition (Bel Geddes) 134–5
futuring *see* ontological designing and futuring

global sustainability 235
Goal Framing theory 43–4, **44**, 151
Good Enough Mums Club 243
goods and services, consumption concerns 168–9, **169**
graphical user interface (GUI) 245

happiness focus 162, 185
Health and Safety Executive (HSE) 210
health and wellbeing: case studies 189–96, *191*, *193*, *195*; dementia 191–4, *193*; design for behaviour change 188–9; environment and 186–7, *188*; future challenges 196; individual support 190–1, *191*; introduction to 184–7, *188*; shifts in care 185–6; work breaks 194–6, *195*
Health Belief Model (HBM) 205
healthcare environments 187
healthy behaviour: built environment 95–6; enabling strategies 99–100; framework for *98*, 98–100, *99*; information campaigns 94; introduction to 93; monitoring/coaching systems 94–5; motivation strategies 100; raising awareness of 98–9; stand-alone objects 96–7; strategies to encourage 93–7; summary of 100–1; termination strategies 100; transtheoretical model of behaviour change 96–8
Heat Me challenge 47–9, *48*
hidden influence on design 144–8, *145*, *146*, *147*
home care 185–6

housing and energy concerns 167
human-car hybrid 129–30
Human-Centered Design 164, 243
human-computer interaction (HCI) 21, 58, 63, 64, 116, 156, 176
human error concerns 207
human-technology relations 31
Hyper Island Toolbox 242

ideation 23–4
IDEO design kit case study 63, 242–3, 257
importance dimension 77, 85–6, *86*
individual decision-making 60
individual support for health and wellbeing 190–1, *191*
influence of design: autonomy and 141–4, *142*, *143*; design of hidden influence 144–8, *145*, *146*, *147*; experience of 139–41; introduction to 138–9; mechanism of 141; medium of 141; origin of 140–1; salience and 141–2, *142*; summary of 147
information campaigns for healthy behaviour 94
information flows 61–2
informed consent 228–9
Inside the Nudge Unit (Halpern) 228
integration of behavioural models 20
Interactive Technology Design and Sustainable Design 123
internal locus control 153
Interpersonal Behaviour theory 151
intervention strategies for problem situations 23

Jacobs, Jane 216
Jeffrey, C. Ray 216
Jeremijenko, Natalie 178
Jill Dando Institute of Crime Science 220

Kaszynska, Patryicia 223
Kids Connect 243
Knee High Design Challenge 164, 243
knock-on effects 10, 132

Lewin's equation 61
libertarian paternalism 139
Liveable Cities project 134
Live Wire (Dangling String) (Jeremijenko) 178
London Bicycle Film Festival 223
London Cycling Campaign 222
Loos, Adolf 11
Low Effort Energy Demand Reduction (LEEDR) 40, 47, 49

maintenance stage 23, 206
management focus 163
MANGO concept 123–4
mass production 9
materializing energy 176

Matthews, Claire 178–9
meaning dimension 77, 82–3, *83*
mental health illness 185
mental reorganization 23–4
mindful design (mindfulness): behaviour change
    through 6, 12; benefit of 211; content, choice,
    and complexity 108; defined 189, 238;
    emotional intelligence and 155; emotions and
    108–9; examples of 111–13; how it works
    107–9; introduction to 12, 104–5, 151, 155;
    reasons for 105–7; summary of 113; three
    stages of 109–11
minimal awareness 143
mobile phone use 235
Model T Ford assembly 9
Molotoch, Harvey 129
monitoring systems for healthy behaviour 94–5
moral frameworks 52
moral objections to technology 138
moral principles of design 240
Morris, William 11
Moses, Robert 26
motivating framework 59–60, 100, 150
musculoskeletal disorders, work-related 207–9

National Health Service (NHS) 186
NatWest ATM sites 226
Nesta DIY Toolkit 242
Newman, Oscar 216
Norman, Donald 11, 26
Norwegian University of Science and
    Technology 51
Nudge (Thaler, Sunstein) 230
nudge theory 223, 227–30, **229, 230**

obesity concerns 13
obtrusiveness dimension 77, 79, *79*, 80
ontological designing and futuring: application
    of future scenarios 134–5; defined 128–30;
    introduction to 128, 152, 154; practical tools
    for 130–4; projecting forward trajectories
    132–3; role of scenarios 133–4; summary of
    135; timelines outlining trajectory of 130–1,
    131; usefulness of 130; viewing as actors 131–2
*Open Design and Innovation: Facilitating Creativity in
    Everyone* (Cruickshank) 257–8
optimal conditions of behaviour 145–8
Ornament and Crime (Loos) 11
OV chip card 32–6, *33*

participatory design methods 223
patient empowerment 186
Pattern Language, A (Alexander) 64
patterns for behaviour change 63
peer pressure 10
personal protective equipment (PPE) usage 210
Persuasive Design Model (PDM) 194
persuasive technology 26, 47–9, *48*, 75

physical coercion 34
point-of-choice prompts 95
Pop up Parks 243
positive psychology concept 185
positive relationships and accomplishment
    (PERMA) 184
Powerchord prototype 178–9, *179*
Power strategies 75
practices-oriented design: as configurations of
    elements 117; disrupting practices 119; as entity
    and performance 117–18; as fundamental unit
    of analysis 117; interpretations of 118–20;
    introduction to 60, 116–18; as reconfiguration
    of elements 118; reconfiguring of 120–5,
    121, 123, 124; reflection on 119–20; situated
    practices, analysis 118; summary of 125; tracing
    in space and time 119; as unit of design 123–5
pre-contemplation stage 23, 205–6
preparation stage 23, 206
presumed consent 228–9
Product Impact Tool: introduction to 26–7;
    model overview 27–31; modes of interaction
    27, *28*; OV chip card 32–6, *33*; repertoire of
    effects 27–31, *28, 29*; responsible innovation
    36–7; theoretical backgrounds 31–2
pro-environmental behaviours 169
prospect theory 60
proto-practices 123
prototyping solutions 224
psychological approaches to behaviour change
    150–1
psychological process of behaviour 144
psychology of products/people 11
Public Health monitors 184
public sector decision-making 228

QR codes 190

Radiator Light concept 45, *46*, 51, 53
rational choice theory 20, 216
readiness-to-hand interactions 21
Reframing Studio project 141
refugee case study 241
repertoire of effects 27–31, *28, 29*
responsible innovation 36–7
RFID technology 32–6, *33*
risk prevention in construction industry 209–10
road induced transport growth 132
road safety 210–13, *211, 212*, 245
Rotter's theory on internal/external locus
    control 153
routine activity theory 216
Royal Bank of Scotland (RBS) 226
rules of the system 61–2

Safe by Design concept 210
safety-design focus: different approaches to
    201–4, *202, 203*; introduction 163, 200–1, **201;**

overview 204–13, *211, 212*; principles and background theories 204–6; risk prevention in construction industry 209–10; road safety 210–13, *211, 212*; summary of 213; systemic approach to 206–7; work-related musculoskeletal disorders 207–9
Safety Engineering 163
safety observation cycle 204
Safety Training Observation Programme (STOP) 204
salience influence of design 141–2, *142*
scenarios, role in ontological designing 133–4
self-care programmes 186
self-determination 164
Service Design Tools 242
Situated Crime Prevention (SCP) 163–4
situated practices, analysis 118
Situational Crime Prevention (SCP) 216, 228, 231
skimmer/reader crime 225
Small to Medium Enterprises (SMEs) 200
smart metering 177
social aspects of decisions 60
social behaviour design: activism case study 240–1; as an intention 239–41; as an outcome 243–5; IDEO design kit case study 242–3; introduction 235–6; Knee High Design Challenge 243; meaning of 236–9; overview of 239; as process 241–3; refugee case study 241; road safety case study 245; social media user behaviour 245; summary of 246–7
Social Design 164, 242
social engineering 9–10
social implication design 58
social interaction with work breaks 194–5
social liberation 100
socially responsive design 231
social media user behaviour 245
social sciences 19–20
social theories of behavioural change 140
social values 112
societal issues 34
sociological approaches to behaviour change 151–2
socio-material assemblies 222–3
sonification 177
Sony Walkman 10
soundscapes 178
stage-matched interventions 97
Stage of Change (SoC) model 97, 205–6
stand-alone objects 96–7
streamlining movement 9
sub-cultural impact of change 22

sugar use and health 190–1
supra-individual aspects of decisions 60
SusLabNWE project 176
sustainability design: carbon dioxide emissions 166–9; case studies 172–80, **174**, *177, 178, 179*; cycling case study 172–5, **174**; energy use, understanding 175–80, *177, 178, 179*; interventions 172; introduction to 164; role of design 169, **170–1**; summary of 180
sustainable behaviour 74
symbolic function 112
systemic structural change 172

technical determinism 35
Termination stage 23, 100
Thakara, John 133
thematization 107
Theory of Interpersonal Behaviour (TIB) 42, 53, 150
theory of planned behaviour (TPB) 205
Theory of Reasoned Action 192
Time Out For Safety (TOFS) 206
timing dimension 77, 86–7, *87*
toolkits for behaviour change 63
to-the-hand category 27, *28, 29*, 30, 31–2, 34
transport concerns 168
Transport for London's Cycling Centre for Excellence 222
transtheoretical model of behaviour change (TTM) 22, 23, 96–8, 151
trapping offenses 225
triggers of behaviour 144–5
Twist Kettle case study *66*, 66–7, *67*

UbiFit garden 94
UK Department of Health 203
UN High Commissioner for Refugees (UNHCR) 241
Urry, John 134
user-centered design 11
user's actions in DfSB 40–4, *41, 43,* **44**
US National Highway Traffic Safety Administration (NHTSA) 200
utopian technology 36

wellbeing focus 162
Where Stuff Comes From (Molotoch) 129
Willis, Anne-Marie 133
work breaks 194–6, *195*
work-related musculoskeletal disorders 207–9
World Health Organization (WHO) 162, 184

Za'atari camp in Jordan 241

For Product Safety Concerns and Information please contact our EU
representative GPSR@taylorandfrancis.com
Taylor & Francis Verlag GmbH, Kaufingerstraße 24, 80331 München, Germany